# Oracle Privacy Security Auditing

***Includes HIPAA Regulatory Compliance***

Second Edition

*Arup Nanda*
*Donald K Burleson*

*Dedication*

*I dedicate this book to my loving parents Asha and Ajay Nanda, for their guidance that shaped me into who I am today.*

*Arup Nanda*

# Oracle Privacy Security Auditing

## *Includes HIPAA Regulatory Compliance*

By Arup Nanda & Donald K. Burleson

Copyright © 2003, 2014 by Rampant TechPress. All rights reserved.

Printed in the United States of America.

Published by Rampant TechPress, Kittrell, North Carolina, USA

Oracle In-Focus Series: Book 47

Series Editor: Don Burleson

Editors: Teri Wade, Don Burleson

Production Editor: Jennifer Kitteson

Cover Design: Janet Burleson

Printing History:

October 2003 for First Edition, October 2014 for Second Edition

Oracle, Oracle7, Oracle8, Oracle8i, Oracle9i, Oracle Database 10*g*, Oracle 10*g*, and Oracle11g and Oracle 12c are trademarks of Oracle Corporation.

Many of the designations used by computer vendors to distinguish their products are claimed as Trademarks. All names known to Rampant TechPress to be trademark names appear in this text as initial caps.

The information provided by the authors of this work is believed to be accurate and reliable, but because of the possibility of human error by our authors and staff, Rampant TechPress cannot guarantee the accuracy or completeness of any information included in this work and is not responsible for any errors, omissions, or inaccurate results obtained from the use of information or scripts in this work.

ISBN: 978-0-9916386-9-7

Library of Congress Control Number:

# Table of Contents

# Using the Online Code Depot

Your purchase of this book provides you with complete access to the online code depot that contains the sample code scripts.

All of the scripts in this book are located at the following URL:

**rampant.cc/audit.htm**

All of the scripts in this book are available in the code depot, ready to load and use on your database.

If you need technical assistance in downloading or accessing the scripts, please contact Rampant TechPress at rtp@rampant.cc.

# Conventions Used in this Book

It is critical for any technical publication to follow rigorous standards and employ consistent punctuation conventions to make the text easy to read.

However, this is not an easy task. Within Oracle there are many types of notation that can confuse a reader. Some Oracle utilities such as STATSPACK and TKPROF are always spelled in CAPITAL letters, while Oracle parameters and procedures have varying naming conventions in the Oracle documentation. It is also important to remember that many Oracle commands are case sensitive, and are always left in their original executable form, and never altered with italics or capitalization.

Hence, all Rampant TechPress books follow these conventions:

**Parameters** - All Oracle parameters will be *lowercase italics*. Exceptions to this rule are parameter arguments that are commonly capitalized (KEEP pool, TKPROF), these will be left in ALL CAPS.

**Variables** – All PL/SQL program variables and arguments will also remain in lowercase italics (*dbms_job, dbms_utility*).

**Tables & dictionary objects** – All data dictionary objects are referenced in lowercase italics (*dba_indexes, v$sql*). This includes all v$ and x$ views (*x$kcbcbh, v$parameter*) and dictionary views (*dba_tables, user_indexes*).

**SQL** – All SQL is formatted for easy use in the code depot, and all SQL is displayed in lowercase. The main SQL terms (select, from, where, group by, order by, having) will always appear on a separate line.

**Programs & Products** – All products and programs that are known to the author are capitalized according to the vendor specifications (IBM, DBXray, etc). All names known by Rampant TechPress to be trademark names appear in this text as initial caps. References to UNIX are always made in uppercase.

# Acknowledgements

First of all, my heartfelt appreciation goes to the only human being who was directly affected by the writing of this book, my wife Anindita. Thank you for tolerating those endless periods where I was literally burning the midnight oil, and depriving you of my company, especially when we were expecting the arrival of our first child. Thank you for walking this path with me and supporting me throughout this process.

I would like to express my sincere appreciation to Donald Burleson, for providing me this opportunity to co-author this book. Don, you put me in charge of designing and let me pen the major portion of the book, even though I did not have a single book to my credit. In other words, you *believed* in me and my potential. From an author of your stature, this gesture is truly touching and I can never thank you enough.

My deepest gratitude to Daniel Lyakovetsky, CIO of IntelliClaim, Inc. of Norwalk, Connecticut, a corporation providing highly scalable and secure claims optimization technology to large health insurance companies and a leader in HIPAA implementations. IntelliClaim offered me an environment where I could experiment with the concepts and techniques of the book in real life – dealing with DBAs, developers, managers, architects, users, and just about anybody who might be connected with an application which demanded security and privacy. The benefit has been mutual - while these techniques catapulted IntelliClaim products to the top of the segment with the impressive security and accountability framework mandated by the HIPAA regulations, the book gained substantial credibility from the real life implementations of the contents.

Many thanks to Robert Vittori, Director of Integration at IntelliClaim, for your incredible support, especially for looking away when I arrived late in the morning at work after a long night of writing this book! And thanks to the hardworking staff at IntelliClaim and its customers for the support I received along the way.

My genuine thanks to Raj Mattamal of Oracle Corporation, for sponsoring me for the Oracle Database 10*g* Beta Program, which opened up the possibilities for exploring the impressive features of the new database, some of which have been described in the book. Raj, thank you for the invitation. I hope I have contributed to your project in a satisfactory manner; you certainly contributed to the cause of this book.

Finally, many thanks to the other members of the Rampant staff for the diligent execution of the project. A special thanks to Jeff Hunter, whose early reviews were exactly what I needed to stay on track.

# Preface

In 1996, the US Congress passed legislation that was considered to be a landmark in protecting the privacy of Americans. The law, the Health Insurance Portability and Accountability Act (HIPAA), was not the first one to make the security and auditability of databases important. It was the first one to make sure corporations take concrete measures to define and enforce their security and accountability measures. Non-compliance was to be penalized heavily with stiff fines and prison terms. The goal was to ensure corporate America took the issue of privacy seriously.

This legislation caused large-scale confusion, similar to what was seen during the year 2000 conversion. While the legal requirements of procedures were interpreted, analyzed, and digested by companies, the part of the law dealing with technology was mainly left in limbo. One of the factors was the fact that the law did not specify the exact technology to be used and left the implementation decisions on the technologists. The technology related to transaction sets was implemented without any major hiccups, but the issues related to privacy and auditing were less understood. The authors, while working on several database projects to make them HIPAA compliant, had no single resource to consult. From this was born the idea of this book. In short, this book is intended to fulfill the needs of the Oracle database professionals with respect to aspects of security and auditing, with specific emphasis on HIPAA compliance.

This book is not about HIPAA regulations in general, nor is it intended to dispense legal advice on compliance issues. The HIPAA law is 75% procedural in how it affects corporations, and 25% technical. Unfortunately, the technical requirements are buried well within the mountains of information found in the HIPAA legislation, the interpretation of various experts, and government and private websites. While planning a compliance strategy, Oracle database and system professionals have little or no resources to inform them of the many requirements. The authors intend for this book to fill that void by becoming a handbook reference for HIPAA compliance issues related to Oracle.

However, security is not just about compliance with HIPAA requirements. Good security and auditing should be integral parts of any good database implementation. This book also covers security and auditing issues related to various other laws and regulations such as the Safe Harbor Act, and the Bailey-Wilmer Act.

This book was written not just with DBAs in mind, but also for Architects, System Designers, Developers, Managers, and just about anybody who is charged with making sure the security and auditing requirements of a database are adequately met.

The first section of the book, particularly the second and third chapters, is written as a primer on security and auditing with advanced topics such as Fine Grained Auditing. The scripts provided should be of immense value. This is not a rewrite of the manuals, but the result of the direct implementation experience of the authors, who pack a whopping forty years experience with Oracle between them.

It is our sincere hope that technology professionals dealing with HIPAA or any other security and auditing requirement will find this book helpful – whether the need is for a primer or help with implementing the complex requirements of sophisticated setups.

## How this Book is Organized

This book is divided into three sections.

Section 1 covers introductions to all the concepts discussed in the book.

Chapter 1 covers the HIPAA regulations, the requirements of the regulations, and the terminology associated with the law.

If you are completely new to Oracle security and auditing, or just want to brush up your understanding, Chapters 2 and 3 are for you. Chapter 2 introduces the various aspects of security in an Oracle context, using an analogy with a real life story to make the understanding easier. Chapter 3 introduces the aspects of auditing in an Oracle database, using the same analogy format.

If you are a seasoned Oracle professional looking for specific tips and tricks in auditing and security, then Sections 2 and 3 are for you. Each of the concepts has been presented with illuminating examples and numerous scripts designed to achieve the objectives. All the scripts can be found on the Rampant TechPress website. The script names have been provided with each script.

# Overview of Oracle Auditing

Foreword

By Donald K. Burleson

## Introduction

This section is a comprehensive overview of database auditing best practices and methods for the IT manager. With the introduction of rigorous Federal laws, the IT manager must plan to fully monitor and audit access to mission-critical and confidential information, all while maintaining a complete and reliable auditing framework.

Managers have realized that the information gleaned from audit trails of database activity can be the company's single largest data resource. They also recognize that their audit trails provide a temporal 'third dimension' of their information, a valuable time-series view of their production systems that contains all-important behavioral aspects of their data access. While there are various approaches to auditing critical database platforms, implementing an enterprise class solution that provides a comprehensive auditing and reporting capability is not an easy task. We'll begin with a summary of the most important concerns of the IT manager and then examine various methods of implementing a successful enterprise auditing solution.

The main points of this whitepaper address the issues of the highest concern for IT management.

## Avoiding business risk and meeting the demands of customers and business partners

While the laws demand a thorough and comprehensive approach to privacy and auditing, the most important reason for protecting your data integrity is your professional reputation. The standards are high, and it is necessary to have a complete top-down auditing and protection solution to work with other businesses. Your partners must cover themselves and they are not likely to have the time, money or patience to audit a complicated home-grown solution. Remember, the driving force is your business need and your customer demands for data integrity and privacy.

## Satisfying the auditors : Implementing best practices including segregation of duties

When considering the Build vs. Buy approach, it should be carefully considered that systems administrators, database administrators and developers cannot have direct access to the auditing solution because exposures result when they have intimate knowledge of the internals of the audit mechanism. Any auditing solution must have the capability of providing for segregation of duties to ensure that these users can be denied access to the resulting audit trail to ensure the integrity of audit reports generated by the system.

## Avoiding civil and criminal penalties

Data asset management practices must address business, operational, legal and compliance needs. Many Federal laws such as the Health Insurance Portability and Accountability Act of 1996 (HIPAA), the Sarbanes Oxley Act (SOX) and the Gramm Leach Bliley Act (GLBA) change the way that databases are secured and audited and some of these federal regulations impose severe criminal penalties for non-compliance and malfeasance with protected data. Non-compliance with these regulations can also expose your company to multi-million dollar civil lawsuits from customers if their private information has been improperly disclosed.

## Choosing the right auditing approach

Many database vendors (e.g., Microsoft, Oracle) offer product-specific utilities to enable auditing, but these audit and trace tools are generally meant to be used only sporadically for investigative and forensic activity. Piecemeal solutions to auditing are difficult to scale, generally impose significant performance impact on the systems, and are very difficult to manage. Approaching auditing and privacy efforts at the application layer leaves direct access to the database unaudited, and results in incomplete coverage and a hodge-podge of in-house and third-party audit logs that are impossible to manage and reconcile.

These are just a few of the IT managers: concerns in this brave new world of security, privacy and regulatory compliance. Your customers and business partners expect you to have a complete privacy auditing solution. Let' s take a closer look at the issues and see how you can protect yourself from common pitfalls and implement a comprehensive and manageable solution.

## Developing a Corporate-wide Auditing Framework

The IT manager must view Auditing as a homogenous system, spanning all applications and database platforms. This is especially important with the new Federal laws that put the onus of maintaining the security and auditing policy on the custodians of the data, the IT management. The Federal laws do not specify or require specific technologies or standards to be followed, and it is your responsibility to decide the best possible approach to assure compliance. However, it is precisely the implementation that requires an exercise of due diligence to select a rigorous security policy.

For any large company, manageability, reliability and scalability are the critical success factors of an auditing solution:

- **Performance** : The solution must have a minimal performance impact with low maintenance and upgrade overhead.
- **Manageable** : The SA, DBA and developer staff cannot be involved in the auditing or have any privileged access rights. The solution must be segregated, unified and platform independent. The solution must be flexible and easy to extend and maintain as IT database requirements change. The system should include centralized ability to configure and deploy across numbers of servers, and regardless of database platform.
- **Provide business value** : The solution must be usable by security and auditing personnel as well as line of business owners with a clear and understandable reporting capability.
- **Complete** : The solution must be complete and comprehensive. Because many applications span database platforms, it should have a unified interface for all databases, regardless of platform. It must be reliable and have an automated and secure mechanism for long-term archival management. Successful companies view their privacy and auditing as a system in-itself, not as a strap-on to existing systems.

## Ensuring a Complete Enterprise Solution

Creating an auditing architecture from diverse data sources and applications is a huge challenge. The IT manager must ensure that every important aspect of privacy, security and auditing are covered and they must do so while ensuring that their solution in easy to manage and scalable. A n effective auditing solution must have these characteristics:

- Reliability and completeness
- Real-time notification of critical events
- Consolidation of audit data streams
- Reporting value and ease of reporting
- Long-term retention of audit trails
- Manageability and scalability

While simple in concept, these requirements are extremely complex and difficult to implement, especially with the huge volumes of data that must be archived. Because auditing is required by both IT best practices and U.S. Federal laws, IT managers typically adopt products designed specifically for this purpose.

## Reliability and Completeness

Many IT shops fail to realize that a haphazard 'sampling' approach to auditing is insufficient. A continuous audit is required and the audit must be archived for long-term access.

This is not an easy task. In cases where you must audit the viewing of confidential data you might need to archive a volume of data greater than the size of the whole database, everyday, 365 days a year. With many shops archiving hundreds of gigabytes of data every day, it becomes critical that all of the archived data be accessible and complete.

For example, HIPAA requirements clearly state that user accesses to the database be recorded and monitored for possible abuse. Remember, this intent is not only to catch hackers but also to document the accesses to medical databases by authorized end-users. In today's litigious society, prudent companies capture the 'who', 'where', 'what', 'when' and 'why' for all access to confidential information. The 'why' aspect is critical because authorized end-users may access confidential information for unsavory purposes.

The data volumes of audit information can be staggering. Larger shops may capture trillions of bytes of auditing information every week, archive and store this data for several years, and have an automated mechanism to easily extract information about any individual in their database.

A comprehensive solution must also have the ability to audit all possible points of entry to the data. It must audit access from the operating system (at the data file level), from the database management layer, the network and from the application layer (Figure 1).

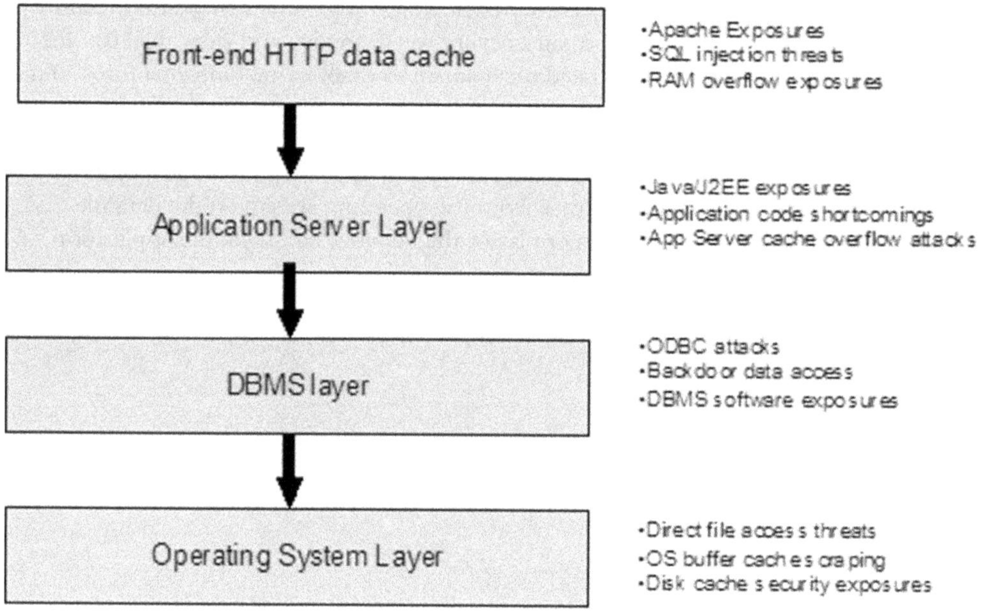


**Figure 1: The multi-layer data exposure issue**

In a typical organization, data access occurs at many levels - - - at the end user presentation layer, at the middle tier, at the application server layer, at the web server layer, at the standalone application screens and finally, at the database level directly. A properly compliant security implementation knows that it is almost impossible to clearly identify and secure all the remote data access points and that proper security and auditing is firmly in-place at the data source. Attempting to audit data from multiple remote layers is suicide, especially when hackers have learned to access information from outside the application layer, accessing the data directly from within the database or accessing the data files directly from the server.

The ability to capture data access at the data source is an absolute requirement for reliable data auditing. While all legitimate data access is done via the application malicious hackers rarely access the system via the application screens. Instead they access the data directly from the files on the operating system or gather the data directly from the database layer. We also see hackers gathering confidential information directly from the web cache layer, using buffer overflow techniques to grab information from outbound HTML pages.

Even at the database layer there are opportunities to bypass the application. Ad-hoc query tools such as SQL*Plus, Crystal Reports and ODBC tools provide backdoors for legitimate users to bypass application layer auditing.

## Consolidation of Audit Data Streams

Very few IT shops have a single database source and it can be a nightmare to try to consolidate auditing archives from heterogeneous database platforms. Each database product manages archives in differing formats and cross-database issues can be impossible to resolve without centralization. Audits from different database products are archived with different character sets, different formats and different organizations (Figure 2).

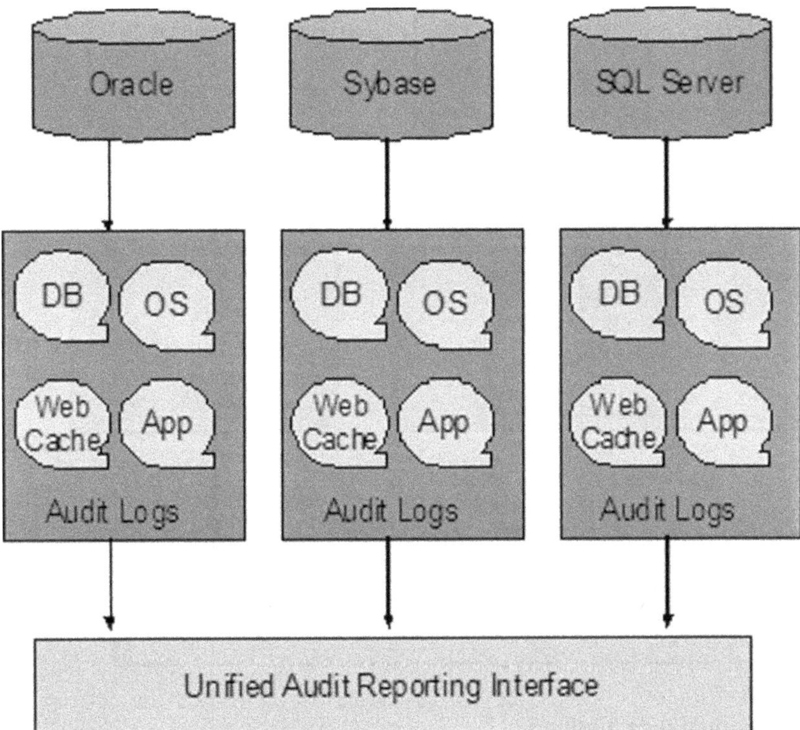


**Figure 2: The problem of auditing diverse data**

Here the problem is consolidating audit information along two dimensions, the multi-layer dimension and the multi-product dimension. The key to success in this type of heterogeneous environment is to simplify the sources for data collection and to collect audit information at the source, the database layer. For those using relational databases such as Oracle, SQL Server and Sybase, using the traditional 'grant' access to authorize end-users allows them to access the data via alternative methods such as ODBC interfaces.

For example, it is nearly impossible to track data viewing at the 'intrusion' levels (i.e. ODBC, Crystal Reports, SQL*Plus) with application-layer auditing tools. Even if we attempt to close backdoors, there is no guarantee that all data access will happen from within the application.

By auditing the data disclosure at the source, we eliminate the need to track access from multiple points and we greatly simplify the data auditing model (Figure 3).

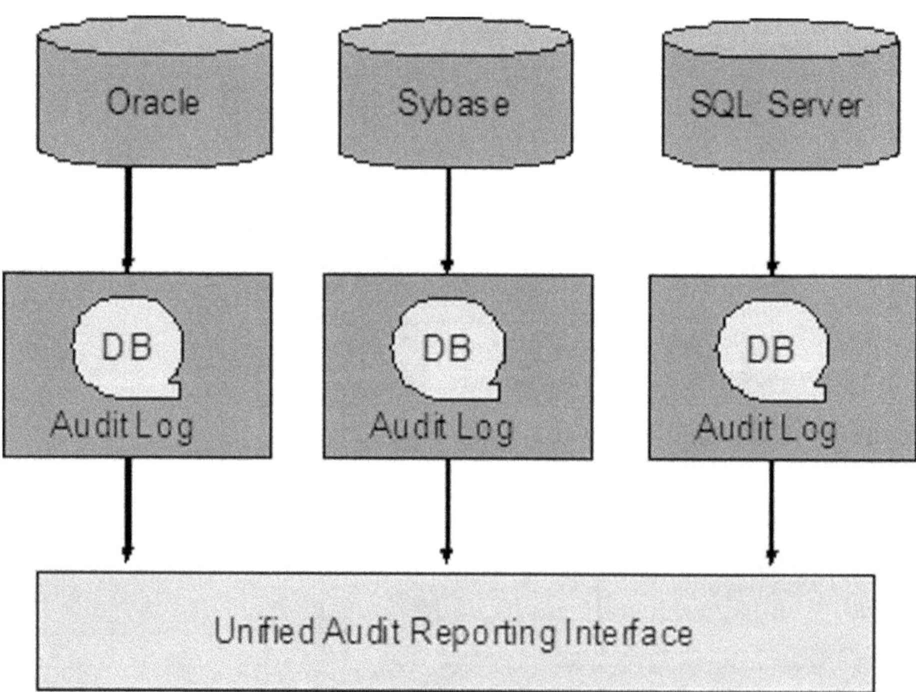


**Figure 3: Cross-product data auditing**

Now that we have ensured that all data access auditing is done at the source of the data, our only remaining issue is dealing with audits from multiple data sources. This is especially problematic for shops with a mix of database architectures such as relational databases (Oracle), object-oriented databases, network databases (CA-IDMS) and hierarchical databases (IMS).

Regardless of the database architecture or specific product, all data audits must capture this information:

- **Who** : A full identification of the person viewing or modifying the data
- **Where** : A log showing the specific application procedure and method used to access the data
- **When** : A reliable date-time-stamp, globalized to Greenwich Mean Time (GMT)
- **What** : A full listing of all data entities that were viewed or modified
- **Why** : Context-based information describing how the data was disclosed

By using a database independent vendor package you can put the audit logs in an identical format and provide a unified audit trail for the all-important reporting interface.

Remember, the audit trail is a database too, and for most shops it is the single largest data repository for the entire company. Just as you purchase a database product that is designed to meet your application needs, many companies choose an auditing solution that is specifically designed for the needs of auditing (Figure 4).

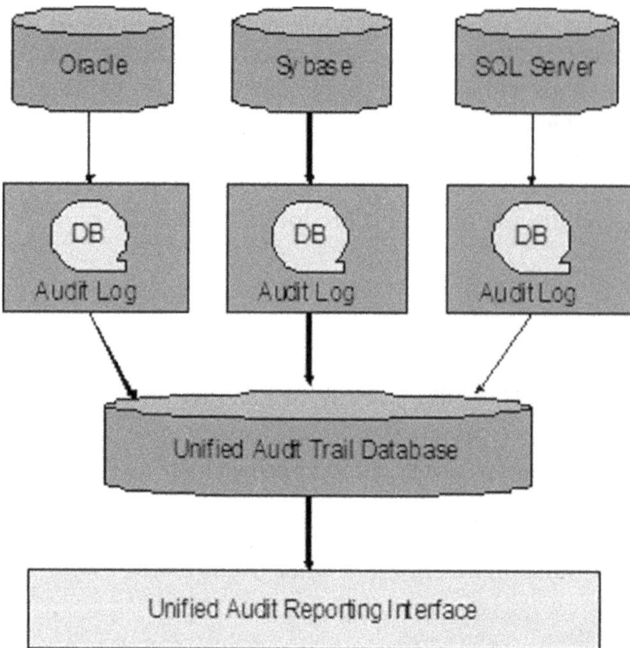


**Figure 4 : A unified database for managing audit information**

Now that we see the high-level architecture of the privacy auditing collection and consolidation mechanism, let's dive deeper and explore how these giant audit databases are managed.

## Minimizing Auditing Performance Overhead

Creating an unobtrusive auditing solution is a primary requirement for many shops. Those companies who have tried to cobble-together auditing using generic database tools often find a huge overhead. For example, Oracle shops are often tempted to use database 'triggers', a generic mechanism that fires an event when a database object is changed. The overhead of using database triggers is significant and can double the resources required to perform database updates, resulting in declining performance and unnecessary hardware stress.

A more reasonable alternative is a passive solution that uses data recovery mechanisms. For example, all relational databases have update logs that are archived and used in cases where disk recovery is required. These logs are the ideal source for auditing changes to the database because they do not add additional processing. We also find that successful enterprise auditing solutions utilize these logs in order to achieve the auditing goal within the absolute minimum overhead.

Now, let's take a look at the characteristics of a successful enterprise data auditing solution.

# Real-time Notification of Critical Events

A comprehensive solution will allow for the ad-hoc definition of alert threshold events and provide a mechanism for real-time notification via e-mail, text mail or pager (Figure 5). Successful companies apply sophisticated filters to the audit trails at data capture time and spot suspicious trends and patterns in data access. Many of these companies report that the system pays for itself in just a few months in cost savings from early-warning fraud detection.

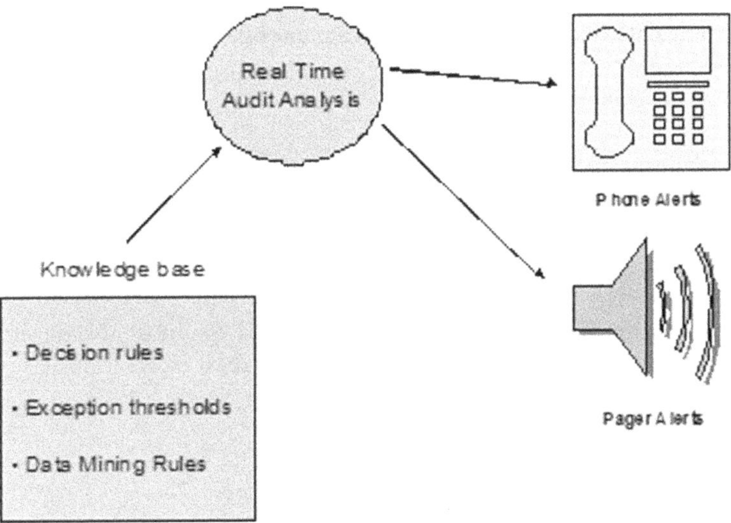


**Figure 5 : Critical real-time exception notification**

## Archiving Issues with Data Audits

Remember, your audit trails will be your single largest data management responsibility, eclipsing your online systems by orders of magnitude. To fully appreciate the data volumes and complexity of privacy auditing, lets take a look at the issues for a typical company. Consider a financial database with 500 end-users and one terabyte of information. Because each end-user is constantly viewing personal financial information as a legitimate part of their job, every week, the audit trail must be able to archive viewing details of over 100 times the size of the original database, in some cases over 300,000,000,000,000 bytes of archived data.

Even though disk become cheaper every year, the expense of archiving trillions of bytes per week on online storage is cost-prohibitive. They are forced to develop a mechanism to archive these vast volumes of data using semi-automated mechanisms. Audit Trail archive processing uses a tertiary storage (tape) jukebox and a tape management system to clearly label the header of every audit tape. The archiving process involves special hardware, complex interfaces and built-in error checking. As each online audit disk requires archiving, an automated process will:

1 : Fetch and label a new tape
2 - Copy the disk onto tape media
3 : Re-process the audit tape:
  a) Check the media for parity errors
  b) Make a copy of the tape for off-site archiving and storage
  c) Apply data mining programs to locate unobtrusive trends and provide real-time alerts
4 : Re-initialize the online disk

This archiving mechanism must be seamless, complete and have built-in redundancy and error checking. When we add-in the additional dimension of data from multiple databases and auditing from multiple access layers, the problem can become unfathomable.

But it gets worse. Archiving the data is just the front-end and you must also develop the ability to allow timely access to the archived data. Let's take a closer look at how this works.

## Long-term Retention of Audit Trails

Long-term data retention is often mandated by business practices and legal requirements and the auditing of data access has imposed a huge burden on many companies. The archival storage of audit trails is often 95% of the company's data, yet it is only accessed 1% of the time (Figure 6).

**Figure 6 : The anomaly of archival data**

This data anomaly also presents challenges due to the temporal nature of the audit capture and the low volume of access. Once lost, the data can never be reclaimed, and the sheer volume of data often means that media verification (duplicitous parity checks) is prohibitive.

Many IT managers have come to realize that their point-in-time production databases only tell a small part of the story and the real value of their database is the temporal dimension. Let's take a look at how establishing a time-series interface allows complete reporting, data mining and fraud detection capabilities.

# Reporting Value with Data Audits

In addition to meeting compliance regulations, many companies discover that they have a valuable data resource in their audit trails. Home-grown solutions often lack an easy-to-use interface and analyzing the valuable hidden information in the audit trails is often impossible. Ad-hoc interfaces are usually non-existent, and it can be extremely difficult to apply data mining techniques to detect unobtrusive patterns of fraud and access violations. What's needed is an enterprise reporting capability that provides the means to derive business value from the audit data.

Any online database is nothing more than a fixed, point-in-time snapshot of the current information. To get the whole picture you must add a temporal dimension to the database, and develop mechanisms to harvest your time-series information (Figure 7). In the following chart capitalization needs to be fixed (lower case 't' in 'To' in headline. Lower case 't' in 'Trends'

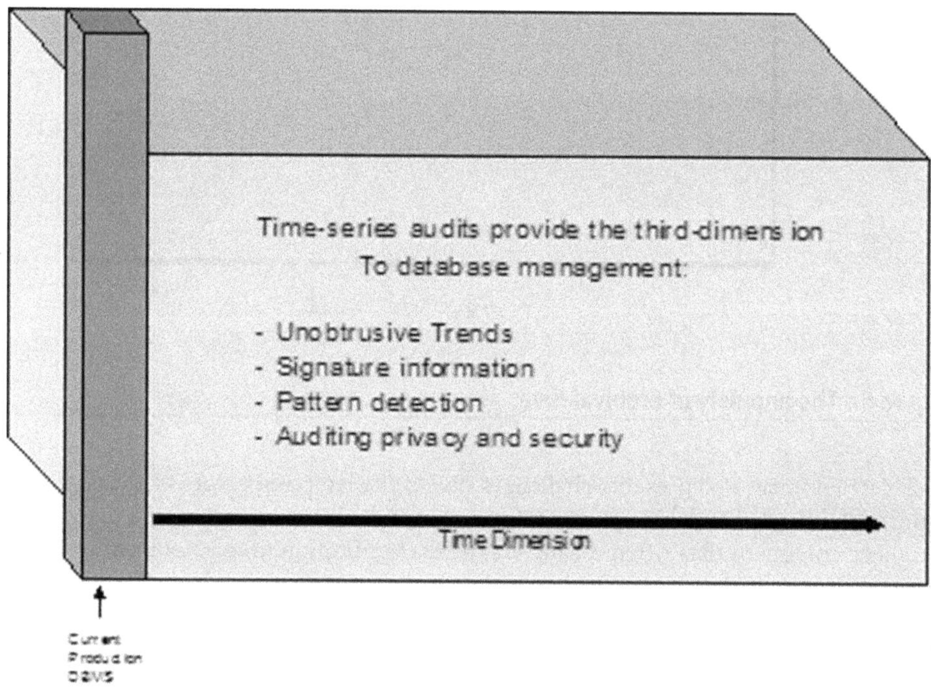


**Figure 7 : Time, the third dimension of Database Management**

Even though disk costs fall 10x every year, online access to petabytes of audit data is prohibitive and this presents special challenges to the IT manager. To confound the issue, simultaneous requests present a unique challenge because of the linear limitations of tertiary storage. To minimize human intervention, the reporting solution must have these characteristics:

- An easy-to-use interface
- A mechanism to audit the audit request
- A complex status-tracking facility

- A notification and delivery mechanism for the completed report
- The ability to access audit information from the application layer, database layer and server layer
- The ability to access audit data from multiple database products

The reporting mechanism must be able to serve the needs of requests from the external community and support your in-house reporting needs. The sheer volume of auditing data makes this reporting unique. Answering this simple query might take hours, require mounting thousands of tapes, and involve reading trillions of bytes of data from multiple databases.

## External Reporting

Your customers and clients may request complete audit trails of access to their confidential information. In financial and medical systems, Federal laws mandate that your company be able to service these requests, providing complete reports in a timely manner.

For example, in a health care database, any patient may request a report showing all users who have viewed their confidential patient information, including who they were, what they viewed, when they viewed the data and why they needed to see their information.

We also have the important business need to have access to the third dimension of your production database. The value of the temporal dimension of the database can be worth millions of dollars and internal reporting capabilities provide a competitive edge to many companies.

## Internal Reporting

Internally, the reporting mechanism must also allow interfaces for in-house reporting, especially in the areas of financial and marketing management. These in-house reporting facilities fall into two general categories:

- **Decision Support** : A mechanism to model 'what if' questions, simulation modeling and hypothesis testing.
- **Data Mining** :Support for multivariate correlation analysis, fraud detection, trend identification and signature analysis.

  As your largest database, your audit trails contain valuable hidden information. Because the audit trails provide a time-series view of your online systems they contain information about the patterns and behavior of the end-users and a time-series view of how the data has changed over time.

Using standard data mining products you can interface with your audit trail database to determine 'typical' processing patterns and quickly identify suspicious patterns of data usage. Data mining products are the result of decades of refinement and are very sophisticated in their ability to spot patterns and trends. The programs are constantly analyzing your audit data, seeking statistically significant data patterns and trends.

The huge benefits of data mining programs are often quite surprising.

- **Savings from Early Warnings** - Financial institutions have discovered the hidden value in their audit trails for proactive fraud detection. By analyzing patterns of known fraud from the audit trails, IT management can apply detection mechanisms to the online system, sending immediate alarms of untypical data access patterns, often preventing the fraud before any financial loss occurs. This technique has saved banks and credit companies millions of dollars, and easily justifies the expense of purchasing an enterprise auditing solution.
- **Optimizing Employee Productivity** - Companies can also use their audit trails to track employee productivity. The audit trails provide an excellent unobtrusive measure of end-user value to the company and this information can be used to spot sub-optimal workers by comparing their data viewing behavior with those of known, productive employees.

Sadly, many companies are unable to reap the benefits of data mining because they do not have a standardized, unified audit trail. This is another major shortcoming of home-grown auditing solutions, but one that can be easily remedied because of the fast pay-back period. Many savvy IT managers will show the projected savings from fraud detection and employee tracking, and get departmental management to pay the cost of buying a unified auditing solution and data mining product.

As we see, the benefits of purchasing a product for auditing are very real and often pay for themselves very quickly. But even without considering the benefits to the company as a whole, in-house auditing solutions carry a host of other exposures and costs. Let's take a closer look at the issues with home-grown auditing.

## Technical Issues with Independent Auditing Solutions

There are many reasons not to use the database vendor-supplied tools for your mission-critical auditing solutions. Yes, they may be free, but the massive overhead and limited scope makes them inappropriate for a company-wide solution.

Many industries are now regulated by Federal laws governing the management, disclosure and security of personal information. HIPAA, SOX and other laws and standards required by government bodies and security organizations make security and privacy mandatory in many situations. Another law in the US, the Gramm-Leach-Bliley Act, mandates financial institutions and their partners to protect non-public personal information by implementing a variety of access and security controls.

It is also a mistake to rely on customized auditing solutions within the application layer. Any code that is written into the application is controlled by your developers and has an innate security exposure. Some of their major shortcomings include:

- Application-side auditing covers only one of many doorways and results in an unmanageable collection of disparate audit logs
- Triggers and traces impose severe performance penalties on the database platform and can be easily altered or disabled by privileged operators
- Database vendor-specific tools (e.g. Oracle LogMiner, Oracle Auditing, and Oracle Fine Grain Auditing) are meant to be used as occasional investigative tools, but were never intended to be a comprehensive solution.

There are also specific traps that catch the unsuspecting IT manager. These traps appear obvious but it is surprising how many of them fail to be detected until the company data is stolen or a lawsuit is filed.

# The Auditing Traps

The common auditing traps are well-known in the IT security field and are taught in almost every business school in the USA. Given the wide knowledge of these exposures it is surprising how often they are disregarded by the IT manager.

- **Cover all layers** - Protecting the application layer is only part of the solution. A comprehensive auditing solution must check for access at the web cache layer (cached HTML data), application server caches, database caches and backdoors, and access violations at the server level.
- **Exclude privileged users** - Another common trap is allowing privileged employees to bypass security and audit mechanisms. Your Systems Administrator and DBA have no business touching your auditing mechanism, and while they may be responsible for the integrity of the data, a third-party must be used to perform all auditing collection, administration and reporting duties. There have been many serious lawsuits where a dishonest DBA entered a database and changed financial data, disclosed confidential information and violated Federal data access regulations.
- **Not knowing how it happened** :Finding a security violation and never being able to determine the cause creates a huge legal liability for any corporation, and this is very common among IT shops that choose to use piecemeal solutions for their privacy and auditing mechanism. In one case, a user was found to be

committing fraud, but without an audit trail of exactly what transpired the organization had no way of understanding the scope of the damage.

- **Non-uniform audit rules** :Another common trap is to apply different rules to auditing of different systems. This is often the result of the limitations of the application code. For example, you may be able to add a complete auditing solution to the system that was developed in-house, but you do not have the same luxury when using an ERP product (SAP. PeopleSoft) because you cannot touch the application code.

With all of these exposures and threats the savvy IT manager must be able to cover themselves from even the most unlikely scenario. Here are some of the common ways that the IT manager ensures that they have a compliant, robust and comprehensive solution.

# Segregation of Auditing Duties

While general security and auditing are passive activities, a comprehensive solution to auditing requires real-time reporting of active attempts to bypass security. Remember, smart shops close all back-door data access (e.g. ODBC) and enforce data access via the application layer. However, we must still create an alert mechanism for all data access attempts at all layers, whether malicious or benign. For example, the Database Administrator (DBA) often needs to view database information as part of their administrative duties, and Federal laws mandate that this data access be tracked just as data access within the application layer.
This issue of 'privilege user' access is a serious security exposure. Because the auditing solution must audit the access of Systems Administrators and DBA's, these employees must not have any control or responsibilities for the auditing mechanism.

This segregation of duties is critical because it is considered malfeasance to give the 'Keys to the Kingdom' to anyone charged with maintaining the servers and databases. In many cases disgruntled employees may view confidential information for personal gain and sometimes create mechanisms to disclose the information if they are terminated from employment (see horror stories later in this paper).

Shops falling under the scope of Federal privacy laws such as HIPPA are required to appoint a full-time employee, independent from the SA and DBA staff to control the auditing. This job role has many names including the Security Privacy Auditing Manager (SPAM), Privacy Access Manager (PAM), Security Privacy Administrator (SPA) and sundry other job titles.

Regardless of the title, the SPA must possess a combination of technical, application and management skills, unique to each organization. For example, large health care companies normally employ a Medical Informatacist as the SPA, usually a highly trained Medical Doctor (MD) with skills in application design, systems architecture, systems administration and database administration. Financial institutions will employ a Certified Public Accountant (CPA) with a strong technical background.

In sum, the auditing collection, consolidation and reporting must be the responsibility of a separate IT entity, solely charged with managing all data privacy audits. Any access outside the application layer, whether malicious or part of routine DBA duties, must set-off alarms for the SPA.

Now, let's change focus and examine how the IT manager can satisfy their due diligence requirements while satisfying their auditing challenges.

## CYA for the IT Manager

The IT manager has a legal and fiduciary responsibility for the corporate data resource. This is a responsibility that should be taken very seriously.

For example, HIPAA laws provides that a leak of information calls for a fine of up to $250,000 per incident and may result in the imprisonment of the executive in charge for a period up to 10 years. The severity of the penalty and the personification of responsibility is enough to make the executives of many organizations take this law and the issue of privacy and information protection very seriously.

As the IT manager you are also required by law (e.g. HIPAA) to provide a clear security policy that can be verifiable and, more importantly, auditable. In the normal course of business in any organization, some personnel will have to access data that is considered sensitive, so prohibiting their use is not feasible. HIPAA does not prohibit that access, but specifies that normal access be recorded as a policy, which should specify who can access what data, and any such access information should be recorded, or in other words, audited.

Even more important, the discovery phase of litigation against home-grown auditing solutions can be devastating. Every line of code is put under a magnifying glass and security experts from around the world will be called-in to judge the lack of quality of your solution. In almost every case the code is found wanting, and the responsible IT manager is held personally accountable for the exposure. Here are some tips from the security experts:

## Don't Underestimate the Bad Guys

Kevin Mitnick, the noted computer felon likes to show how security breeches are commonly the result of employee errors. In his book 'The Art of Deception', Mitnick talks about his techniques to get trusting employees to disclose confidential information and privileged passwords. In one case Mitnick was able to secure a privileged password using the name Lemonjello, and then bragged about the na'e employee who handed-over a system password to someone called 'Lemon Jell-O'. In this case the IT staff was never able to ascertain the root cause of the breech because their mechanism for the dissemination and auditing of secure information was inadequate.

While external fraud remains a serious issue we must also remember that most data access violations happen internally, and most are the result of unintentional access rather than malicious fraud.

- **Don't lose prospective partners** - Whenever you share data with partner companies their due diligence requires them to verify your privacy and security mechanisms. It's far faster and easier to just name a vendor product than it is to make them undertake a multi-week examination of your home-made mechanism. Some Federal regulations also mandate that you have a standardized information exchange interface. For example, HIPAA mandates that the information related to health insurance must be exchanged in a standard, predefined way. For instance, all the information that typically goes to the insurance company from the provider during a claim filing must be in a certain format, defined by the law.
- **Don't get sued by customers** - In today's litigious society, almost every breech of privacy and security is followed by expensive litigation. On the issue of medical records privacy, the situation is even more fluid and prone to severe security lapses. HIPAA addresses this problem by mandating the audit requirements of these records and strictly enforcing the requirements by placing stiff penalties for non-compliance.
- **Don't lose goodwill** - Security and privacy breeches are big news and slack companies are pasted across the headlines anytime a major exposure occurs. This can be crippling to a company's reputation and brand loyalty, especially in the financial services arena when companies are judged by their absolute commitment to financial security.

There are many common misconceptions about privacy and security auditing, even amongst IT management. If you fail to grasp the volume, scope and complexity of an auditing solution you can place your entire company at risk. Let's take a closer look at these common misconceptions.

# Security, Privacy and Auditing Misconceptions

After interviewing dozens of IT managers, a common set of misconceptions arose regarding compliance with Federal regulations for security and privacy. This is not surprising, given that the legalese of the actual laws is almost indecipherable, but the IT manager needs to know about the realities of these important new laws. Some of the most common misconceptions include:

: **Prevention alone is sufficient** :Traditional security measures focused on 'perimeter' security (e.g. firewalls) are an important component of mitigating the risks of inappropriate data access or changes. But with most error and fraud occurring from *within* the organization, it's important to have the ability to understand exactly what is happening to the data . A complete record of data access and change provides this 'detective' capability which augments existing security.

Another important aspect of auditing is recording who was not granted access, not just who was permitted access, depending on the privilege setting. This could be due to a legitimate reason such as a bad password, but it could also be a hacker trying to break in with multiple attempts at guessing the password. It could even be an insider, a disgruntled employee trying to access information he or she is not authorized for. Whatever the reason may be, this kind of activity arouses suspicion and should be investigated.

- **Application access, privilege controls and logging are enough** : This is a very serious misconception because it ignores the other important access areas. As we see, all data access must be audited directly at the data source.
- **Preventing fraud is the only goal** : Many IT managers fail to account for the possibility of human error, which is more prevalent than fraud, in their auditing plan. A comprehensive solution must account for legitimate errors by end-users and IT staff.
- **It is cheaper to build a custom audit mechanism** : This is untrue - and dangerous. While a once-over-lightly solution can be cobbled together quickly, mistakes of omission can cost your company millions of dollars in sanctions. Worse yet, these 'cost effective' solutions almost always cost more in the long run as the IT manager discovers the huge costs associated with reporting, customization and consolidation with other audit trails. Further, most IT organizations cannot afford to develop multiple audit systems to support their

multi-platform environment. We've already discussed that native tools cannot scale to accommodate the needs of a large enterprise.

Now that we have seen the common misconceptions let's examine the importance of auditing data at the data source, the database management layer.

## Auditing Data at the Source

All IT managers know that simple triggers and code extensions can be used to enforce security and privacy at the application layer. The real problem is securing the data source and all intermediate repositories and providing the ability to understand the root cause of the violation.

A 'detective' monitoring approach is used by many successful companies because it allows you to know what actually happened when a breech occurs. Simple auditing based only on preventative measures will not provide this level of insight. Just like a human detective, the detective monitoring approach observes all aspects of data access and keeps complete logs of all database activity. To be fully safe and compliant, you must keep a complete audit trail for the data source and have a complete *who, where, what, and when* record of access and updates.

There are many challenges involved with auditing at the database level. If you want to understand 'how' a violation happens, you must audit all events of interest,. These events include privileged access by IT personnel, the auditing of all changes to the data, auditing all viewing of confidential data, and recording all changes to the database infrastructure, both by DDL and changes to executable database procedures. Let's take a closer look at each auditing requirement.

## Auditing Privilege/Permission and Logon Events

You must have a complete record of the users who have data access including: 'who' is attempting to get it, 'what' they have rights to do with the data, 'why' they are changing the data, and 'when' the data was viewed or changed.

While many databases such as Oracle provide primitive logon triggers for determining logon events, they don't work with many modern ERP products (SAP, Oracle Applications, PeopleSoft) because they use pre-spawned connections to the database. User authentication and access management is done by the application server and the individual users are not exposed to the database.

The 'who' aspect of data auditing can be confounded if you use a tool such as SAP or Oracle applications that pre-spawns anonymous connections to Oracle. The application controls user access and authenticated users are directed into the database under the control of the application (Figure 8).

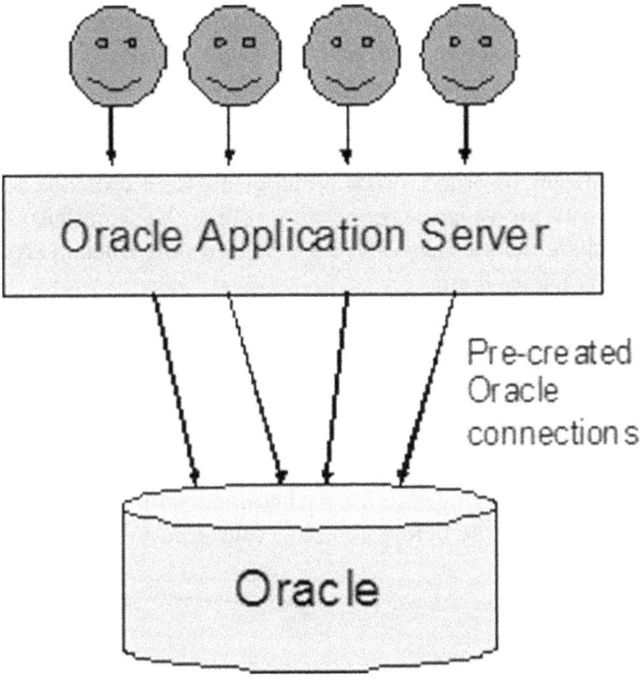


**Figure 8 : External application authentication**

In these types of architectures an end-user has no direct privilege against the data source and the permission to view and access data is granted via the application. Because the application controls all database access, you don't have to be concerned about back-door access with non-application interfaces such as Crystal Reports or ODBC.

However, it is critical to audit the activity of privileged users, including DBAs, who have direct access to the database and can access or modify the application's underlying data.

# Auditing DDL Events

Managing changes to the schema definition of your database is critical. You must have a complete record of all changes to your database system infrastructure and understand the potential security risks associated with each change. This includes knowing that a table has been dropped or permissions have been changed inappropriately.

Many open source solutions such as SCCS are inadequate and many IT managers use third-party products designed specifically to track schema changes, such as Merant PVCS (Serena), Kintana and Oracle Software Configuration Manager.

If the organization has a policy of placing everything in the version control system, the changes made are automatically recorded. But what happens when someone makes an emergency change without using the proper procedure' The setup fails. This is a classic case of a system where the integrity can be guaranteed only when everyone follows the rules and no one bypasses them.

## Auditing DML Events

All auditing solutions must track changes to any of the data items, right-down to the column level. It's not enough to know that a particular financial record was changed; you must also know exactly what has changed in the data content. This includes the access method ('how' it was changed), the before and after values, and the exact time and user ID.

## Auditing SELECT Events

Many Federal regulations mandate that you keep a complete record of access to private and confidential information. For large active databases, it is not uncommon to have daily viewing logs that are larger than the whole database and you must be able to easily run reports against this huge volume of data. For example, the new HIPAA regulations allow any medical patient to request to know who has accessed their data in the past, and this simple query might involve accessing trillions of bytes of audit information. When you have multiple, simultaneous requests for these reports, an improperly designed audit system might become crippled under the weight of the data volume.

## Auditing Execution and Modification of Stored Procedures

Many database shops encapsulate their database access inside code snippets called 'stored procedures'. When using stored procedures an end-user takes-on the privileges required to execute the procedure, but only for the duration of the execution of the procedure. In databases such as Oracle, stored procedures are written in an interpreted procedural language called PL/SQL. As every IT manager should know, any language that is parsed and executed line-by-line is subject to injection attacks. Hence, special audit procedures must be employed for any database that uses stored procedures.

Hardly a week passes without a report of a company suffering major losses due to an information security breach. Let's take a look at the types of exposures faced by companies and see how an enterprise auditing solution can prevent the threats.

# Horror Stories

We need not look far to see the public cases of computer security violations and the liability suffered by the custodian of the data. With millions of dollars at stake, there are many resourceful people waiting for you to make a mistake and expose your confidential information. These attacks on your information take many forms, from malicious hackers, dishonest employees and honest mistakes. Let's look at some specific ways that companies lose control of their information.

## Security Breaches, Hacks (outside-in)

Threats from hackers remain a major concern, especially threats from overseas countries in Eastern Europe and Asia. Some companies report access attempts by automated hacker 'bots' every few minutes as these rogue programs constantly sweep the Internet looking for ports with access vulnerabilities.

These automated bots contain very sophisticated logic and are designed by criminals to identify and exploit weaknesses in online computer systems. Some of the common exploits include:

- **Tipping the user ID** : This is where a telnet or FTP access attempt tells you that you have entered a valid ID, but provided an improper password.
- **No password disabling** : Hacker routines love systems that do not disable a user ID after repeated password attempts and run bots to try hundreds of thousands of password until they gain entry.
- **Man-in-the middle attacks** : Hackers can gain access to computer systems by guessing the IP address of a connected user and sending a TCP/IP packet with that users IP information.
- **Injection threats** : Many database systems have vulnerabilities where access to confidential data can be gained via a SQL injection, a technique where a :1=1:

string is added to a sign-on string. For example, this query might return the :real: password for a user named Jane:

```
userid, password
from
dba_users
where
userid = 'jane'
and
password = 'xxx'
```

- **Buffer Overflow attacks** : In these attacks, the web cache buffer is deliberately overloaded to gain unauthorized entry to the system.

Hacker attempts for web-enabled systems are constant and many companies report thousands of attempts every day. A comprehensive auditing system will record all illegal access attempts and include the time, referrer IP address and all other relevant information. Let's take a look at a real-world case.

## The Extortion Attack Case

In this case a hacker exploited a server vulnerability, siphoned confidential information from the corporate database, and shipped it to a foreign nation that did not honor U.S copyright law. A foreign cohort then extorted the company, proving that they had the data, and threatened to disclose proprietary secrets to a competitor unless they were paid a significant sum of money.

Faced with the loss of their competitive advantage, the company contacted the FBI and was told that there was no reciprocity with the nation and that Interpol would not be able to investigate or arrest the extortionists. Even worse, IT management had not detected the leak, and had no idea how the thieves had accessed their database.

Surprisingly, this is not an uncommon occurrence, and many multi-national companies have accounts for bribery and extortion expenses because they are a legitimate requirement for doing business in some overseas nations. In this case the company quietly paid the extortionist in return for the promise to destroy the data and details about how the data was stolen.

While there are always exposures from the outside world, we must also account for attacks from within our company firewall. In practice, 'inside jobs' are more common than external attacks, and they can often have devastating consequences.

## Internal Fraud (inside jobs)

IT managers report that internal fraud is the most common type of threat and special auditing mechanisms must be used to audit all access by authorized employees. Inside job threats include the following:

- **Root kit attacks** : In a root kit attack, the operating system is compromised. I once fixed a client site with a root kit that had installed a daemon process that was constantly accessing confidential information and e-mailing it to a competitor. This attack went undiscovered for more than a year and virtually all of the company's proprietary information was lost.
- **Fire-me attacks** : Internal IT personnel have been know to write routines that trigger a data extraction on the day when their user ID is removed from the computer system. Because most IT procedures required pulling the user ID before notifying the employee, these hackers will return home to find all of the confidential information waiting for them in their in-box.
- **Trojan horse** : Once an employee gets the internal IP address of another employee, they can map-out phony sign-on screens to their boss and get a privileged password. These attacks are usually easy using tools such as X-Windows that allow screen images to be redirected onto other screens.
- **PC Privacy tools** : Common tools such as PC Anywhere can be used to look-over the shoulder of a co-employee, snooping into their activities and passwords.

Inside jobs are the most difficult to detect, but complete audits will always reveal the 'who' and 'how' aspects of the attack. For example, coded implants can be tracked using your source code control system software that is required by almost all Federal Regulations including SOX and HIPAA.

Here are many documented cases of data disclosure by disgruntled employees, especially 'privileged users' who were given unaudited access privileges. Let's look at some specific real-world horror stories. These are not fictional stories. They actually happened, and they serve as examples of what can happen when a slack IT manager entrusts their access and auditing controls to a Systems Administrator or Database Administrator.

## The Root Kit Case

We received a call from a client who was complaining of performance problems on their Oracle database which was running on a standalone Linux server. The company was in the business of providing credit information to third-party companies to access an individual's probability of financial default.

Upon accessing the server, it was apparent that something was terribly wrong. Even when idle, the database was performing I/O operations and the processors were active, even though Linux did not show any active processes. The Linux 'ps' command failed to reveal any active processes.

After a Linux expert was consulted the real issue was discovered. A disgruntled Systems Administrator had left a time-bomb on the server, to be activated when their user account was removed from the */etc/passwd* file, indicating that they had been fired.

This time-bomb was activated when the System Administrator left the company to 'pursue other opportunities', and the attack was both clever and devastating. The attacker placed a Linux daemon process called 'vacuum' on the Linux server and this process was constantly polling the Oracle database, seeking new information, and e-mailing it to an overseas mailbox.

This attack has disclosed the entire database of confidential information to an unknown party, and the company was held fully responsible because they failed to institute a third-party employee to manage their server security.

The attack was very sophisticated and unobtrusive. The malicious employee had replaced the standard Linux commands with a 'root kit', an attack method readily available on the Internet. In a root Kit attack, the Linux commands are replaced with an alias to disguise the presence of the data stealing mechanism. In this case, the process command 'ps' was replaced with the command ps|grep -i vacuum, such that the process would not appear within Linux.

Sometimes internal fraud occurs when employees are entrusted with data that has value to outside parties. Let's take a look at one such case.

## The Phony College Transcript Case

In this real-world case, a Database Administrator for a major university was caught 'enhancing' college transcripts to allow people to gain acceptance to top professional schools. The DBA had complete control over the database and the auditing mechanism and was charging friends and acquaintances thousands of dollars to add courses and improve existing grades. Because the DBA controlled the audit mechanism she was able to completely erase all traces of the fraudulent changes.

This fraud went undetected for more than five years until a professor discovered the fraud. The professor was asked questions about a former student as part of a pre-employment background check and discovered that the student had never taken his class even though the official university transcript indicated an 'A' for the course.

Ironically, the bulk of the fraudulent transcripts were used to gain entrance to law schools and several of them had graduated and were practicing law. The losses and penalties from this access violation were substantial:

- The Director of Database Systems was fired for malfeasance for allowing the security loophole.
- The university suffered a huge loss of credibility and the accuracy of over 100,000 graduates was tainted, all because of a single privileged violation.
- The perpetrator DBA pled guilty to computer fraud and grand larceny and received 5-10 years in Federal prison.
- The university had to undertake a grade re-verification process that cost more than $600,000 dollars.
- Several practicing attorneys were disbarred, but ironically many of those who had successfully completed their graduate schools were allowed to retain their degrees, even though they entered the schools with falsified transcripts.

Of course, not all privileged disclosures are malicious. Next, let's look at cases where honest mistakes can disclose confidential information to third parties.

## Honest Mistakes

In many cases multi-million dollar losses are the result of human error and bad judgment on the part of the users of the database, and in some cases, the IT staff.

These types of mistakes can take the form of trusting a telephone caller who wants a password (the Kevin Mitnik approach), or a failure to recognize the impact of the disclosure.

There is also an important issue when information is aggregated by the IT department for marketing purposes. The privacy and security laws allow the sharing of summarized information so long as the identity of any individual cannot be ascertained. However, when the summarization includes 'outer bounds' data then it is sometimes easy to violate disclosure laws. For example, a report summary of HIV patients, aggregated by city and profession might reveal the personal identity of the only Taxidermist in Nome, Alaska.

Caution must be taken when sharing summarized and aggregated personal information to remove all results with a limited set of participants so that personal identities are not revealed. Let's take a look at how honest mistakes can cause irreparable harm to your company.

### The Hotel Fiasco Case

In a widely publicized court case from the 1990s, a major hotel chain collected detailed information about their weekday guests' use of their hotels. They employed a data warehouse analyst who created a target marketing campaign, offering special coupons to those guests who frequently used the hotel on weekdays. This targeted mass mailing of weekday-stay coupons were sent to the home addresses of the guests, with disastrous results. More than a dozen people were informed about their spouse's infidelity as a direct result of this coupon campaign and more than six divorces resulted from the company's actions.

While this action was not in violation of the privacy laws per se, the result of the campaign was to disclose private information about embarrassing information to a third party. A more appropriate approach in this case would have been to mail the coupons to the guests work addresses.

These horror stories serve to remind the IT manager that a comprehensive auditing and security system must have controls to audit all telephone disclosures of confidential information, including verifiable information about the recipient of the information.

## Privacy Issues Associated with Data Viewing

The protection of personal privacy is an important aspect of system auditing, and the IT manager must remember that it is their responsibility to ensure that the information is not improperly disclosed to third parties. However, an important legal issue arises when one of your employees accesses private information for non work-related purposes. These purposes might include an employee finding 'dirt' on an ex-friend or previous boss, or using their access to your computer system for extortion or harassment.

In one important appellate case, a woman's job description involved accessing confidential information. As an authorized user, she accessed embarrassing information about her ex-husband and used the information to her benefit in a child custody case. The court ruled that even though the information was obtained with an unsavory motive, the ex-wife was authorized to view the data and the damning confidential evidence was allowed in the case. The ex-husband, outraged at the privacy violation, sued the ex-wife's employer for millions of dollars for allowing his ex-spouse access to his confidential data. In this case, the company needed safeguards to verify 'why' the data was needed. It's not enough to issue a blanket authorization and hope that the privilege is not abused by your employees.

In these cases the IT manager must have a full audit trail but they must also be also be able to show 'why' that employee needed access to the confidential information. To provide this level of detail the IT audit trail must show contextual information about the employees work session and show the flow-of-control within the computer system.

This is another area where a 'detective' approach to audit analysis is valuable. Sophisticated audit control systems allow for specific decision rules to be applied to audit trials and these algorithms are designed to detect unusual patterns of access to private information.

Taken together, these issues make IT privacy security auditing a scary and risky proposition. Let's face it, with something as mission critical and challenging as auditing and IT manager would be insane to attempt to create their own solution. It would be like an IT shop writing a proprietary database management system. Of course, such things are best left to companies who specialize in such matters.

Even more importantly, the IT manager has enough responsibilities without being held accountable for data security software. By acquiring a nationally-known and respected product, the scope of liability for the IT manager drops dramatically and they are only responsible for the proper installation, administration and management of the auditing software.

## Enterprise Data Auditing Solutions

If you accept the conventional wisdom that it is foolhardy to attempt to construct your own auditing solution, the next step is choosing the right product. Small, homogenous shops will be happy to find that there are a small number of database product-centric auditing packages in the marketplace, but large IT shops are perplexed to find that there are very few that provide an Enterprise-wide, unified solution to companies with heterogeneous databases and applications.

- **Comprehensive auditing** : A comprehensive solution captures database activity including DML (including before and after values), DDL (schema and permissions changes), and SELECT statements (who viewed what data, to address privacy concerns).
- **Alerts for early warning :**Alerts on DDL activity of interest can be sent via email or recorded in the event log. This enables early resolution of potential issues *before* they become a big problem (e.g. detecting fraud early to mitigate significant damage.
- **Great management CYA** : Back in the 1970:s when IBM ruled the hardware arena there was a saying in Data Processing that 'Nobody ever got fired for calling IBM'. That principle is alive-and-well with today's Information Systems, and a prudent IT manager has never been fired for choosing a leading vendor tool.
- **Cost savings** : The job of the IT department is to manage the company's data, not to write system management software. Data security and privacy auditing is a complex and dangerous job, and best left to specialized products. The unification of the audit mechanism also opens the door to data mining tools which can rapidly pay for the vendor product.
- **Standardization of audit trail database** : Solutions create and consolidate audit data from multiple database platforms into a uniform audit database. Remember, your audit trail is your largest database and a source of valuable corporate information.
- **Allows for segregation of duties** : A key tenet of auditing principles is 'segregation of duty' ' avoiding the fox watching the hen house. With an enterprise auditing solution you no longer need to bet your business by relying on internal employee honesty. Plus, you are protected by having an audit trail of all employees, including trusted employees.
- **Unobtrusive audit collection mechanism** : Vendor solutions are optimized to use existing logs and they have very little run-time impact on your mission-critical production systems.

- **Unified reporting interface** : Tools offer an intuitive user interface that makes it easy to create, schedule, manage and distribute reports for management or auditors (Figure 8). Reporting enables the audit data to deliver real value to the business by providing insight into how data is being accessed and used.

This section has highlighted the core objectives and issues relating to a successful enterprise-wide security, privacy and auditing solution. The paper articulated the challenges for the IT department which can be summarized in two kinds of business risk categories. First, there is inherent risk in managing corporate data. IT is responsible for the integrity and security of the data which the organization relies on to manage the business. Secondly, the increasing regulatory environment is creating new demands from the executive team and auditors that IT be able to demonstrate exactly who is accessing or changing what data, and how.

We examined the requirements for an enterprise auditing solution, which can be summarized as:

- Comprehensive capture of all database activity
- Enterprise enabled
- Supports multiple database platforms
- Architected for performance
- No 'backdoors' captures activity of privileged users with direct database access
- Alerting for early detection of issues
- Reporting capabilities to derive business value from audit data
- Adheres to auditing and IT best practices, including segregation of duties

Section I

# Overview

| Chapter 1 | Introduction to HIPAA |
| --- | --- |
| Chapter 2 | Introduction to Oracle Security |
| Chapter 3 | Introduction to Oracle Auditing |

# Introduction to HIPAA

CHAPTER

## A Story of John

*AACHOOOO*!! Every autumn, Mr. John Q. Public goes through the same ritual – allergies starting up again, blowing through the umpteenth handkerchief of the day and scaring the family cat in the process, cursing the season, the pollens and the world in general – capped by the never missed "bless you" from Mrs. Public. Leaves change color; so does John's nose and he, for the zillionth time, yearns for that nice dry feeling summer took away with it. Well, it is time for visiting the allergist again, reminds Mrs. Public, in a wry tone. But wait, John's employer changed the insurance carrier, the plan or both, and his regular allergist is no longer in the plan. He selects a new one from the book of providers and pays her a visit.

So far, the story has been quite normal, in fact a little boring; but, here there is a twist - a problem - his records from the old allergist are not transferred by the time of his appointment. When he inquired with his regular allergist about the records, he was told that he couldn't be given those personally, and they would be sent to the new doctor in a few days. Not a problem, the new allergist declares, they would proceed with the visit, wait for the records to arrive, and wait for the insurance paperwork to settle in. She prescribes some medication and off he goes, hoping for a better tomorrow.

Well, the nightmare is just starting to unwind. His condition becomes worse, so severe that he has to be hospitalized. The emergency room doctor diagnoses his condition quickly and asks in a somber voice whether he had changed his medication of late? Through tear-drenched eyes, John asks the doctor grimly, what did he expect him to be – *a PDA*? Was he expected to remember those unpronounceable drug names; especially at times like this? Well, no, the doctor firmly answers. But, according to the doctor, the new allergist prescribed something that may have caused the symptoms to flare up.

What?! John just can't believe it; she seemed so nice and reassuring; how could she have been wrong? Well, the good doctor took *his* rendition of his symptoms and allergy history into account and prescribed something that was completely in line with the history. The critical piece was *his* version of his history, meaning he delivered a record that simply was not accurate and that led to the doctor's wrong diagnosis.

John's trauma doesn't stop at that. His new insurance company declines the claim from the doctor, explaining there are technical irregularities. He is forced to pay the bill himself and then deal with the insurance carrier later. The diagnosis there? *Wrong* data from the doctor's office. It may not have been completely wrong, but it came in a format the insurance carrier's computer system rejected, or worse, might have interpreted incorrectly. John merely scratches his balding head in frustration, tucking at whatever little strands of hair are left.

Fall passes, the leaves bid farewell to the branches as they meet their maker, and for John Q. Public, these problems are a distant memory. He seems to be content. His daughter gets through the medical school program, his son is the class valedictorian, and his wife is elected the chairperson of the local historical society. The plum in the pudding is that things are looking promising on his career front; the grapevine has it that he is next in line for a very senior position in the customer relationship department, a job he has always wanted. Things couldn't be better.

The big day arrives, the eagerly awaited announcement of the name for the top customer relationship manager is finally released, and ... it isn't him! But, why?! He is the most qualified for the position, so why is Willie from across the room the next one to peer through the glass walls of the corner office and not John? He decides to do some digging around; twenty years in the company have forged many contacts through those endless team-building parties. They should come in handy sometime, shouldn't they? And they do.

He learns from clandestine sources that his qualifications are unquestionably superior to Willie's, they fit the job description like a glove. However, his allergies gave his candidature a thumbs-down. Upper management felt that the allergies might interfere with his customer relationships. But, he protests to his source, the allergies were only seasonal and they disappeared within a day or so after proper medication, they weren't life threatening or crippling, so why should they have come between him and his dream job? In a fit of rage, he decides to confront the top management, and his allegations are promptly and vociferously denied.

John pulls out the last of his hairs. He curses the season, the world, his boss, the insurance company, the doctor and … he peers over the cubicle walls at the door that displays a name that should have been his. *Aacchooo*!! He sneezes hard into the handkerchief. Time to go to an allergist again.

## Diagnosis

Let us analyze what went wrong in the story of John Q. Public above. The first problem started with a bad diagnosis of his allergies due to incorrect history information provided by none other than John. Moreover, the wrong information was due to the inability to get access to his information from his old doctor in a timely manner. His information was not, in other words, *portable*.

The second problem was the insurance carrier's rejection of the claim from the provider because it did not come in the proper format. Well, what was the *proper* format? With so many insurance carriers and providers, the definition of proper format varies and the chances of mistakes increase exponentially with each new format. What about a standard format, understood and practiced by all parties? Unfortunately, that does not exist.

The third problem was the leak of information. It's not important to debate whether the use of this information is unfair or not, there is simply no question about its unfairness; rather it is important to ask how the information got out in the first place, and what steps must be taken to stop this leak of sensitive information. In other words, through John's anguished cries of revenge, he essentially asked this question - who accessed this information on his allergy and how can he or she be tracked?

## Here Comes HIPAA

After too many anguished victims let their issues be known, the lawmakers finally noticed. In 1996 the United States Congress addressed these issues head on, and acted to pass a landmark law to eliminate these problems by setting specific mandates in all aspects of the transactions between healthcare companies, providers, and carriers. This law is known as Public Law 104-191, the Kennedy-Kassenbaum Bill, more popularly known as the Health Insurance Portability and Accountability Act (HIPAA), pronounced *hee-paah*. On August 21, 1996, the then President of the United States, Bill Clinton, signed the bill into law, which required US-based healthcare companies to be HIPAA compliant by October 2003.

So what is the law about? In summary, the law has five sections.

- Healthcare Access, Portability, and Renewability
- Preventing Healthcare Fraud & Abuse, Administrative Simplification, Medical Liability Reform
- Tax-Related Health Provisions
- Application and Enforcement of Group Health Requirements

- Revenue Offsets

Most of the law deals with policies and procedures, while approximately one fourth deals with technology. Of these, we are interested in part of the second section, Administrative Simplification, which deals with the solutions for the problems encountered by John Q Public above.

**Patient's Access to Information** In order to eliminate the potential problem and errors due to unavailable records, the law states that patients can access their information any time and in a standard format. This information should be immediately available to the patient and, on request, parties acting on their behalf, such as their new doctors and other healthcare professionals. If the records had been portable in John's case, his new doctor would not have had to ask him for his history and he would not have had to remember all the relevant information. That would have resulted in the proper diagnosis and saved the trip to the emergency room.

**Standardized Information Exchange** HIPAA also mandates that the information related to health insurance must be exchanged in a standard, predefined way. For instance, all the information that typically must go to the insurance company from the provider during a claim filing must be in a certain format, defined by the law. These standard types of transaction records, somewhat reminiscent of the long gone EDI (Electronic Data Interchange) transaction records, are described as numbers. For instance, the initial filing of the claim from the provider to the insurance company is identified as a transaction of type 837. Another type, 835, defines the format for information from the insurance carrier to the provider, typically for payments. The law defines all the record types for the transactions, so that the information exchange is clearly defined as to what to send and what to expect, nothing more and nothing less. In John's story, if the information had been received in that manner, there would have been no miscommunication and the insurance company would not have rejected the record from his doctor.

**Privacy of Information** Finally, HIPAA places a great deal of emphasis on the issue that affects all of us in some form or other – privacy. Medical records are considered private and should be protected, just like any other tangible property, such as money. Prior to the law, the exact nature of the protection and the responsibility of enforcing said protection was not properly defined, and therefore there were many ways for the information to leak out. HIPAA mandates the protection by stressing that the data must be protected strictly and any violation will be severely penalized. For example, a leak of information calls for a fine of up to US $250,000 per incident and may result in the imprisonment of the executive in charge for a period up to 10 years. The severity of the penalty and the personification of responsibility is enough to make the executives of many organizations take this law and the issue of privacy and information protection very seriously.

The law mandates that organizations must establish a clear security policy that can be verifiable and, more importantly, auditable. In the normal course of business in any organization, some personnel will have to access data that is considered sensitive, so prohibiting their use is not feasible. HIPAA does not prohibit that access, but specifies that normal access be recorded as a policy, which should specify who can access what data, and any such access information should be recorded, or in other words, audited.

In the story above, if the requirements of HIPAA were satisfied, the information on John's allergy would not have leaked out without his knowledge and would not have affected his chances of promotion. In every walk of American life, information that is leaked out without authorization affects several related or unrelated incidents. There are real-life cases where the depression related treatment of employees resulted in their dismissal, a clear case of illegal conduct. Instead of battling the unfairness of a system where leaked information might adversely affect people's lives, HIPAA attempts to plug the holes where the leaks occur in the first place.

In summary, HIPAA mandates that the organizations:

- Provide information to patients about their privacy rights and how their information can be used.
- Train employees so that they understand the privacy procedures.
- Designate an individual to be responsible for seeing that the privacy procedures are adopted and followed.
- Perform privacy risk assessment.
- Adopt clear privacy procedures for practice, hospital, or plan.
- Secure patient records containing individually identifiable health information, so that they are not readily available to those who do not need them.

The last three points above involve Information Technology professionals like DBAs, developers, architects, managers, system administrators, and security officials in charge of IT security.

## Enforcement of Security and Audits

Security and auditing simply means plugging any potential holes and recording the fact that an access to the information was made on all allowable access points. In a typical organization, data access occurs at many levels - at the end user presentation layer, at the middle tier, at the application server layer, at the web server layer, at the standalone application screens and finally, sometimes at the database level directly. A proper HIPAA compliant security implementation makes sure all these access points are identified clearly and that proper security and auditing are firmly in place. As any seasoned IT professional would guess, the most sensible way is to seal off all access points except the bare minimum, and to audit access at those points.

The other disturbing trend is the increase of a new type of crime called *identity theft*. The use of the information superhighway, otherwise known as the Internet, and the use of digital vaults to store information about a person, make it easy for thieves to steal information and use that information to assume their identity. In the era of the Internet, the physical presence of a person is no longer required; transactions are carried out over the wires (and sometimes wireless, too) and signatures are replaced by passwords as means of authentication. In this case, the protection of data becomes of paramount importance and building the audit trail of access to information is of prime importance. Enforcing security and implementing auditing of access to data has become the number one priority of organizations around the world, particularly those where the data is the asset, e.g. banks, brokerages, insurance companies, etc.

The important point to observe here is the law simply puts the onus of maintaining the security and auditing policy on the protectors of data, it does not specify or require specific technologies or standards to be followed for the enforcement. This is left for the implementers to decide the best possible approach to assure compliance. However, it is precisely the implementation that requires an exercise of due diligence to select a rigorous security policy.

# Who is covered by HIPAA

Here is a selection of types of organizations covered by HIPAA regulations.

### Healthcare Providers

- Private, Federal and University Hospitals
- Correctional Facilities
- Doctors, Public Clinics
- K-12 School Immunization Programs
- Social Services Programs

### Healthcare Payers

- Federal Payers – Medicare, Medicaid
- Health Insurance Companies

### Other entities that store healthcare information

- Life Insurance Companies
- Employers

As you can see, a vast majority of the US-based companies are affected by HIPAA, meaning the important parts of the law must be understood and implemented by these companies to be compliant.

## But Security is not *just* for HIPAA

Even if your organization is not directly involved with HIPAA requirements, it does not mean that security and auditing are not needed. They are necessities in any organization; HIPAA merely makes it a legal requirement for healthcare companies. There are several other hidden costs of non-secure systems. Increased frequency of litigations, damage to the reputation of the company and subsequent losses in customer base are just some of the unwelcome and unnecessary results of a lax security policy.

In addition to HIPAA, other laws and standards required by government bodies and security organizations make security and privacy mandatory in many situations. Another law in the US, the Gramm-Leach-Bliley Act, mandates financial institutions and their partners to protect non-public personal information by implementing a variety of access and security controls. In the private sector, another standard, the VISA USA Cardholder Information Security Program (CISP), requires that personally identifiable customer data related to credit card transactions be encrypted in the database. In Europe, the Safe Harbor Act specifies that certain information known as Personally Identifiable Information (PII) has to be protected at all costs and the law specifies guidelines that must be followed for compliance. These are all variants of the privacy and security awareness growing around the world.

These laws and standards clearly show the need to have a defined security and audit policy, regardless of the type of business your organization engages in.

## What is This Book About

This book is not intended as a discussion of the general objectives and requirements of HIPAA. Scores of books, articles, presentations, and seminars have deliberated this topic. However, when it comes to implementing those requirements, there is not much available for those who design and manage. A specific case is the applicability of these requirements to Oracle databases and associated systems. This book aims to explore and describe, in clear and unambiguous terms, the various security and auditing features related to Oracle, their relative merits and demerits, and their usage, with examples as applicable to HIPAA. The discussion of these features and options will not only be helpful while designing a HIPAA compliant database system, but any Oracle database where security and auditing are important, which probably means almost all production databases. The examples include financial databases, human resource databases, and even databases for messaging systems that are designed to handle sensitive information. Hopefully, it will serve as a sort of handbook of security and audit features available in Oracle for Database Administrators, Architects, Developers, Managers, Security Managers, and general users of Oracle databases around the world.

The book has been organized according to the requirements placed by the law. The law mandates that organizations evaluate and certify their security plans on the dimensions listed below. The book also follows these dimensions in its narration and examples.

- Authentication
- Authorization
- Confidentiality
- Integrity
- Audits
- Availability

The topic of *Availability* falls under a separate domain for backup, recovery, and high availability, and therefore is beyond the scope of the book. The other parts have been arranged in various sections as follows.

The first act is *Authentication*, which deals with the task of making sure that the user asking to interact with the database is indeed legitimate, and not someone else masquerading as a legitimate user. Essentially, it asks the incoming user connection, "who are you and what proves that you are who you say you are?"

Next comes *Authorization*, which deals with the task of making sure the user asking for a piece of information is allowed to see or change it. If the user wants to see a record of the claim table, this step ensures that the user is authorized to see that information.

Closely tied to the above is *Confidentiality*, which goes a step beyond and ensures that not only is the user authorized to see the records, but is authorized to see all the fields of the record. Certain fields of the record, Social Security Number, for instance, are indicated as very sensitive data, labeled Patient Health Information (PHI) by HIPAA, and require special authorization to view. This step makes sure the user sees this if and only if allowed to see it.

A user may decide to change data after viewing it, but is he or she allowed to do so? This question is posed by the *Integrity* step, which ensures that the user does not deliberately or accidentally modify information without proper authorization.

Finally, HIPAA mandates that all such users who access information must be recorded as having done so – a task called *Auditing*.

The primary focus for Oracle professionals dealing with HIPAA, or security in general, can be broadly divided into two categories – Security (which encompasses Authentication, Authorization, Confidentiality, and Integrity) and Auditing. A section in this book is devoted to each category.

# HIPAA Terminologies as Applied to Data Management

As an IT professional in charge of making your Oracle database security and auditing infrastructure HIPAA compliant, you should be aware of a few terms.

**Protected Health Information (PHI)** – PHI is the information that identifies an individual, such as a Social Security Number. The HIPAA regulations apply whenever PHI is transmitted by electronic media, such as the Internet, tapes, disks, or is stored in any electronic medium described here. Some educational or employment records, even though they contain individually identifiable information, are not covered under PHI.

**Context-Based Access (CBA)** – This is a complex concept to understand. When a user has been given privileges to access certain database resources, the access is known as Attribute Based Access. When the access is further restricted, or completely replaced by other factors not based on the privileges held by the initiator or the target, this is called Context-Based Access. For instance, the time of the day could decide access. A health information database may not be available for regular users between 7 PM to 6 AM to prevent unauthorized access. This type of access is known as Context-Based Access. Other types of CBA are based on the location of the user, where the IP Address of the user's terminal is used to decide which parts of the database he or she is authorized to access, or dependability of the user's authentication process, etc.

**Designated Record Set (DRS)** – HIPAA law covers the health information records of an individual that are maintained by either the individual or by another party, such as a doctor's office on the individual's behalf. Even though a different party holds the information, it's important to know that the information is still owned by the person on which it is based. The information is stored by various entities.

- Health care providers such as doctors and hospitals collect and maintain medical records and billing records.

- Insurance carriers maintain enrollment, payment, claims, case management, and medical management information of the insured.
- Several entities, such as health insurance carriers, life insurers, even some employers (if legally allowed) make decisions affecting the person. This type of information is immediately protected by HIPAA regulation.

**Discretionary Access Control (DAC)** – This is very relevant in database management systems. HIPAA defines DAC as any kind of access control specified for storage containers of information, which could be a file, a database table, or a set of records within a table. This is based on the data. In Oracle, there are some sophisticated options available to provide this DAC, one of them is Virtual Private Database.

**Mandatory Access Control (MAC)** – This also refers to providing privileges to users based on specified objects. However, the difference is in the way this privilege is enforced. In MAC, the privileges are static, not based on content; whereas in DAC, the access is dynamic, based on the data contained within. MAC has been an integral part of Oracle for quite a long time. An example might be appropriate here to explain the concept further. A user may have privilege to only select from a table – this is MAC. However, the user can select only records where the claim amount is less than $1000 – this is DAC. If all the records of the table have claim amounts more than $1000, then the user will not see any row, even though he or she has privilege to select the table.

# In Summary

HIPAA does not prevent information flow; it simply mandates that organizations clearly list where information can be accessed and mandates auditing of the persons who access sensitive information. This is analogous to organizations identifying how many doors they have through which people can come in and go out, recording who comes in and goes out and what they carry through these doors, while sealing off all other possible means to get in or out.

From a database perspective, the logins and sessions are the equivalent of doors. The users are people getting in or out, and the data is equivalent to the things they carry. Auditing enables the recording of the information that was passed or changed, and the audit trails must be protected from malicious use. Finally, all backdoor entries into the database must be identified and protected. HIPAA simply mandates what should already be a part of a best practices list.

# Introduction to Oracle Security

CHAPTER

## What is Security

Before diving into this topic, let's take a moment to define what we mean by the word 'security' and what is expected when something is said to be secure. Security does not mean restricting access, far from it, it may actually allow better access for legitimate users. Compare this concept to a museum with several doors. Security in this context means that the museum authorities have the ability to let a person enter the museum using one of the doors. However, the person can enter the museum only if the authorities allow him or her to do so, *never* without their consent. Being secure means that if the person is denied access, he or she cannot enter in any other way. It also means that there are no hidden or unknown doors, windows, or other access points that an intruder can use to gain entry into the museum. By restricting entry to legitimate museum customers, the museum ensures there are no more than the acceptable number of people inside to comply with the fire code, etc., and in the process, enhances the general experience of ~~museum visitors~~museum visitors.

In this chapter, we will explore the various types of server security from the ground up. With each topic, we will also examine its relevance to meeting HIPAA and other privacy requirements.

## Physical Security

How does the museum protect its displays? The very fact that exhibits are inside the walls of the museum helps prevent thieves and miscreants from getting in and damaging them. The act of isolating the protected from the outside is the first step to securing the building. The same idea can be extended to the protection of computer systems. By placing machines that house the database servers inside protected data centers, and restricting physical access to only a few known personnel who are expected to be near the machines physically, such as system administrators, a great deal of potential threats can be averted. A person with physical access to the machine can simply yank the power cable from the outlet – shutting it down. When an Oracle database server is shutdown in such an abnormal manner, there is generally minimal danger because the database instance will repair itself in a process known as *instance recovery*. But an abnormal server shutdown will rollback all uncommitted transactions.

Some of these uncommitted transactions could be important enough to warrant a shutdown in the process.

This eventuality can be somewhat alleviated by using message queues, Oracle Real Application Clusters (or Oracle Parallel Server), or both. However, the possibility of such an event can be greatly reduced by simply restricting physical access to the machine.

In UNIX based systems, some of the potentially dangerous commands that a person can use to damage the system, such as server shutdown, are limited to the user called *root,* and this user can login only from the console. Someone who can't be physically near the server, then, will not be able to issue these types of commands, and therefore will not be able to harm the server.

HIPAA requirements clearly state that physical security must be enforced with a fixed number of people having access to the server. The correct security practice should include the creation of a list of such personnel, documentation of the reasons for their being near the server, and strict adherence to the guidelines. Human security guards, access cards, or biometric devices like fingerprint readers, or both, should guard the server room. If there are several types of servers with various groups of personnel managing them, then they should be segregated in separate enclosures, and access should be limited to the specific groups.

 First level of security: secure your machines physically. Restrict physical access to them.

## Firewalls

Inside the museum, there are several areas where employees prepare the exhibits for display, for example, unpacking, arranging, assembling and cleaning them, mounting them if necessary, and finally, placing them for public display. Visitors are not allowed to access these areas. Special curators who perform these preparation tasks move freely from one section to the other since they may need tools from another area, or just need to move the exhibits to a pedestal that happens to be in another area.

In this setup, access to these restricted areas can be controlled internally as well, but the access control need not be that stringent. Why? Access is already restricted to museum employees; visitors are not permitted to enter these areas. Therefore, all the people inside are employees, and they can be trusted. Movement from one area to the other is not strictly monitored.

In the systems analogy, a company may have several servers, like web servers, database servers, file servers, print servers, etc. in the company network that outsiders cannot access. Imagine an island in the middle of the ocean accessible only by air. The only place where an outsider can come in is the airport. Therefore, outsiders can be easily monitored when they arrive at the airport, and their activities can be restricted. Inside the island however, the residents can move around freely. In ancient days, cities surrounded themselves with walls as a means of protection from external attack. Moats around castles served the same purpose. These types of structures provide physical barriers between the protected and potential threats.

In the world of networks, the company builds a protective ring around the groups of servers and clients. Inside this wall, the computers can easily communicate with each other, but not with outsiders. Since the outsiders have no access to the machines, they can't pose a threat to them. This hypothetical wall that separates the insiders from the outsiders is known as a *firewall.*

Some companies have a firewall *within* a firewall. Typically, corporate assets such as a database for insurance companies, or marketing data for a consumer products company, are stored inside an inner firewall so that there is another credential required to access them. This increases system security.

Sometimes, a particular type of server may require some access through these firewalls. One example is a web server, which requires access by outsiders, typically customers. How does a company protect the computers inside the firewall and at the same time allow access by customers via the web server?

Opening up holes in the firewall facilitates this type of access. A server can respond to incoming messages only at certain places. If someone whispers near your feet, would you be able to respond? Of course not. But if the whisper occurs near your ears, you would. Your ears can receive and process the signal that is coming from the outsider. Similarly, a computer server can listen only at certain places called *ports*. If a message comes to one of these ports, the computer can receive it (it listens to these ports) and process it. Ports are defined as numbers and are usually well known. For example, a web server listens to a port numbered 80. If a signal comes to port 79, the computer can't respond to the message, because it is not listening to that port. So, by allowing access only to port 80 and nothing else, we can ensure that the outside interaction occurs only at that port. Each port, then, can be configured to process only certain types of information. For example, port 80 will only respond to http-type messages, the type used by web browsers to get data for the display on the browser. Such a request can't do much harm and is therefore allowed. Since that port is not open for any other type of message, and the firewall has no other open ports, the setup is quite safe.

HIPAA regulations do not specify a specific technology to enforce the protection of servers, but since they mandate that the privacy information be preserved in a manner that is consistent with the policy of the company to safeguard data, firewalls are necessary and should be employed. If outsiders need to access the data, the server hosting the database should preferably never be opened up to the firewall. Instead, there should be an application server that interacts with the database, and this application server should be opened to the firewall.

 **Use a firewall to prevent hackers from breaking into the system, while allowing interaction by machines within the corporate network. Open ports on the firewall only when necessary.**

In Chapter 4, we will also discuss how to enforce security at the Operating System level.

## Access Control

Coming back to the museum story, the next logical question is how the authorities decide whom to let into the museum? One method is to maintain a list of people who are allowed to enter. In a computer system or a database, the list of such allowable entrants can and must be maintained. This list is known as an *Access Control List* (ACL). This is the first line of defense in any security setup. ACLs are known by various names and may hold different content in different contexts. In a regular server, the ACL may contain allowable IP addresses. In a database, it can be a list of users.

Remember John Q. Public from Chapter 1? John, after recovering from the nightmare he went through in his allergy episodes, and feeling substantially better since his insurance company is now HIPAA compliant, decides to visit the Metropolitan Museum with his 5 year old son, Jeff. He buys tickets from the museum's website and their names are included in the list of persons allowed to enter. In the computer system's analogy, they were in the ACL for visitors. If the museum were an Oracle database, they would be users.

Commonly, passwords are used to authenticate the users of an Oracle database. Inside the database, the passwords are stored in an encrypted manner. Actually, it's not technically encrypted but *hashed*, making it impossible to read by visual inspection. The password of the user is known only to him or her, not to the DBA. A DBA can change the password, but not know what it is. We will learn more about hashing in the chapter on Encryption.

What are the potential problems with passwords? Unlike a physical key, the password is portable and easy to "steal". All the intruder has to do is learn the password, then use the password to gain access to the database - in many instances without arousing the suspicion of the user whose password has been stolen. For this reason, passwords should be as secure as possible. Ideally, every user should have a unique user ID to access the database, eliminating the practice of a shared user ID among a group of users.

Some passwords are easy to guess – they are as simple as the words *password*, *secret*, *topsecret*, *abc123*, the same as the userID, etc. Sometimes there are logical constructs that can be guessed, e.g. the user's birth date, the names of family members or pets, common words, or a combination of common words and these personal facts. HIPAA requirements mandate that passwords not be easy in order to discourage abuse and enforce security.

The DBA can use Oracle's password function to force users to choose passwords that conform to a certain standard. The details of password management through this function, as well as other password functions such as making passwords expire automatically after a set number of days or after a few unsuccessful attempts, can be enforced through the Oracle password management features. Chapter 4 will discuss the different ways hackers can crack user passwords, how to prevent hacker access, and how to make passwords secure and safe using a password management function. In that section, we will also learn how to make sure password management can be implemented to conform to the HIPAA requirements, and how to implement a password management function.

 **Make passwords as secure and difficult to guess as possible through the password management features of Oracle.**

# Access Entry Points

The museum has two public entrances, East and West Gates. These are the computer equivalents of ports in a server, or listener addresses in a database. They can also be analogous to the applications accessing the database or the server. The museum may have several other entrances, but only these two are available for public access. In a secured system, it is important to have a finite number of access points available for ordinary users and all these access points must be identifiable and known.

In Oracle, the connection to the database from a client system is established through SQL*Net, renamed to Oracle*Net in Oracle8 and Oracle*Net in Oracle 9i and up. The client requests a connection to the database through the listener. Remember the port concept in the servers, discussed above? A port is an entry point where a server listens for incoming connections. The clients connecting to the database send their intention to connect to the specified port on the server where the Oracle listener is listening. Typically, the ports used by the listener are 1521 and 1526. So, any connection coming to these ports where a listener is listening must be an authentic connection for Oracle, otherwise the connection will be refused. So, what is the potential problem with that?

The connection that comes to ports where the listener listens may only be partly authentic, meaning the other part may be malicious and can cause harm. Several known hacker techniques launch an attack on the listener. The best known is the buffer overflow. In Chapter 7, under Oracle Network security, we will cover the details of the threat and how to protect against it.

Another way to enforce security is to accept communication signals only from trusted parties. Friends trust friends. Your database may have to interact only with a handful of servers, typically application servers or web servers, and the IP addresses of these servers are generally known in advance. In Oracle*Net, it is possible to disallow and allow connections coming from specific machines using techniques known as *Node Filtering* or tools such as *Connection Manager*. In Chapter 7, the setup and workings of the Node Filtering and Connection Manager will be described in detail.

 **Identify servers who can be allowed to interact with the database server. Make use of Connection Manager to enforce allowed and disallowed nodes. Use the security features of Oracle Listener to protect against attacks.**

# Authentication

John and Jeff arrive at the East Gate of the museum and the guard checks their names in the Access Control List to verify that they should be allowed to enter. How does the guard know that these two people are indeed the same persons whose names are on the list? He probably asks for some sort of identification, like a driver's license, a passport, a school identity card, or something that is generally considered genuine. John provides his driver's license and Jeff uses his school ID, the guard looks them over, matches their faces to their pictures on the identity documents, and ascertains that they are indeed the same people on the list. In the computer system analogy, this process is known as **Authentication**.

Note the means of authenticating the users. In this example, identity was confirmed through documents, but computer system users could connect through other means -

such as passwords. While withdrawing cash from an ATM machine, you would have to input your Personal Identification Number (PIN), a sort of password. If the security requirements are stricter, the system may ask for a certificate, key or token-based authentication. The certificate must be from a verifiable source, similar to the driver's license being from the Department of Motor Vehicles or its equivalent government body. The guard asked for verifiable identity documentation from the visitor, in computer parlance, he *challenged* the visitor and the visitor passed the license, or *responded* to it. It's a type of authentication known as a *challenge-response* scheme.

What if the guard is a little suspicious of the genuineness of the documents? He could call the Motor Vehicles department to make sure the license is indeed valid. From a systems perspective, that would be similar to certificate verification or verification inside the data dictionary, where the password entered is correct.

In this case, Jeff's school ID is acceptable as an authentication document, but would that be as trusted as a driver's license? Perhaps not. In this case, the subject is a museum and stricter security may not be required. In real life cases, the security levels dictate the assumption of various degrees of authentication. Having a secure system does not mean having the most stringent security setup possible, it simply means the security system should be designed with full knowledge of the risk factors involved.

Other methods of authentication involve using Smart Cards and Biometric Devices. In Chapter 4, we will explore in detail these types of authentication, their problems, and how to work around them.

 **Choose and implement a strong authentication model based on the requirements.**

# Network Security

Before we follow John and Jeff into the museum, let's digress for a moment to mull over something else. The picture on the driver's license resembles the face of the man who presents it. However, it is possible (not likely, but for argument's sake assume it is) that the real John was kidnapped on his way to the museum, and the kidnapper stole his wallet with his license, did a little plastic surgery to look similar and then appeared before the guard. How does the guard know that the person who presents the license is *indeed* the real John and not an imposter? In the systems analogy, the client sends IP packets to the server for the necessary access. The client is genuine; but what if a hacker waylays the packet, steals the access information, and then sends a bogus packet to the server? It is quite possible and it happens. In our story, to prevent such a possibility, the museum security guards might whisk John away through an ultra secured road to the museum right after he buys the tickets, eliminating the chance of a kidnap. In a similar way, clients can establish a secure line of communication between themselves and the server to ensure that the packets are indeed genuine and not tampered.

What about *adhoc* clients, typically clients from *outside* the company? It might not be possible or even desirable to maintain a secured path between the clients and servers. The alternative in that case is the use of *encryption* of the packets. If a hacker waylays these packets, he or she will not be able to decipher the meaning of the information contained within, so stealing it will not be helpful.

**Use Oracle*Net security to achieve security compliance.**

Network security from an Oracle database perspective has been discussed at length in Chapter 7.

# Application Access Control

The Metropolitan Museum is open to the public from 10 AM till 5 PM. The museum staff, however, is supposed to be there from 9 in the morning till 6 in the evening. This is necessary since the staff must prepare some exhibits and fix any problems before the exhibits open and the visitors arrive. Similarly, some work is done after the last visitor leaves. Between 9 and 10 in the morning, only the staff members are allowed to enter the premises, no one else. This is an example of time-based access to the resource. If someone arrives at the museum doors at 7 PM, this would arouse suspicion and that person wouldn't be allowed to enter regardless of whether he or she has a ticket.

Sometimes specialized staffers, like painting restoration specialists, work through the night to prepare the paintings for display. These staffers are allowed to enter the museum after 6 PM, whereas the others are not. In a database system, for instance in a doctor's office which is open from 8 to 5, the database containing patient records is generally accessed between 8 and 6, allowing for an extra hour after the last patient leaves. If an access attempt is made at 10 PM, it is certainly out of the ordinary and may be malicious in nature. The attempt to access, therefore, should not be allowed. Suppose, however, that the office has an accountant who has to access the database to prepare the accounts, and the accountant generally works nights. In this case, the accountant must be allowed to access the database, but not the regular application users. An exception must be made to allow the database access, but since the accountant is required to see the patient's health information, that information should be masked by a view or some other means. A regular application user must be disallowed access any time during non-business hours. Similarly, access should be restricted on holidays and weekends. By restricting access during non-normal hours, the possibility of break-in is significantly reduced.

HIPAA requirements mandate that the applications specify the times of access for the various user groups and enforce that access. As always, the law does not specify the specific technology to be used and leaves it to the DBA to define. In Oracle, we can easily do this by creating a system level *after logon* trigger that does not allow access within the specified time period. Another option is to disable the application user within the time period through a time triggered process such as *cron* in UNIX or *AT* in Windows Operating System.

**If possible, try to limit use of the database to regular times and automatically disallow access using triggers or events.**

# Object Access-Based Security

Now that they are inside the museum, John and Jeff visit various exhibits until they came to a door marked "Museum Repository, Authorized Personnel Only". According to a security guard there, the room contains the most valuable and irreplaceable exhibits the museum sometimes receives as a loan from other museums around the world. Currently it holds the *Koh-I-Noor*, the world famous diamond from ancient India, with an estimated value of several million dollars. The exhibit is being prepared for exhibition and only a select few can be allowed to enter the room. Visitors are not allowed, of course.

So, we come to a setup where the visitors are allowed to enter into the facility (the museum), but not access a *specific* object inside the facility. From a database perspective, this is analogous to allowing users to select all the tables except a few. This is the most rudimentary of the object privileges given in an Oracle database. Several types of accesses, such as select, insert, update, delete, etc. require different types of privileges, and the users are given these privileges selectively, depending on what they need to perform in a specific job. For instance, in the museum case, John and Jeff are mere visitors, so they are not given viewing privileges for the diamond, but the person in charge of preparing the exhibit for the floor, typically the assistant curator, needs access to the room and to the diamond. Therefore, she has been given authority to get inside the room, but not take it out of its mount; in other words, she has only the select privileges on the object, not update, delete privileges, etc.

In Oracle, objects such as tables can be read (SELECTed), DELTEd, UPDATEd, or new rows can be INSERTed. All these privileges can be individually controlled. For instance, the owner of the CLAIMS table granted permission to user JUDY to select and delete from it, insert into it, or update data in it. These privileges can be specified by

```
GRANT SELECT, INSERT, UPDATE, DELETE on CLAIMS to JUDY;
```

However, the user NATHAN has been granted only SELECT privileges, not anything else. That would be enabled by

```
GRANT SELECT ON CLAIMS to NATHAN;
```

There are several other types of possible accesses to the tables. If JUDY has a table whose parent table is CLAIMS, defining the referential integrity constraint requires a different kind of privilege called *REFERENCES*, unlike the ones already defined. Similarly, JUDY may be allowed to modify the structure of the table, and she will need an ALTER privilege to do that. A stored program, such as a stored procedure, package or function, will need an EXECUTE privilege to be granted executable by a user.

If, at any point in time, it is determined that JUDY does not need any DELTE privileges on the CLAIMS table since she does not delete data from that table, the privilege can be revoked from her by using

REVOKE DELETE ON CLAIMS FROM JUDY;

The other privileges granted to Judy remain unaffected.

Granting privileges to an object requires careful analysis and planning. Under no circumstances should a user be granted all the possible privileges on an object. HIPAA requirements clearly mandate that the access privileges of users be documented and enforced. Application developers should specify the exact privilege requirements on the objects, and only those should be granted. This leads to another question – *who has what privilege?* This question falls under auditing for security. In Chapter 4, several scripts have been provided that throw light on the privileges held by users on various objects. The output from these scripts can be reviewed by corporate security for potential holes or just filed away as documentation.

However, doesn't it become tedious to grant specific privileges to all the defined users in the system? Yes, it does. To alleviate the inconvenience, Oracle allows privileges to be granted to *roles*, which can then be granted to users. Roles will be defined later in this chapter.

> 🔔 **Grant users only the privileges necessary for them to perform their role, no more than that. Document the granted privileges and review them from time to time to find potential problems.**

One important aspect to remember in this type of security arrangement is that access is made to the *entire* table. In the above example, JUDY is allowed to see all the rows of the table CLAIMS. If that is not desirable, rows can be selectively displayed with some filtering criteria using views or a more sophisticated setup called Virtual Private Database, explained later.

# Object Masquerading

Inside the museum, there is an exhibit on butterflies of all shapes and sizes mounted on glass plates. A particular butterfly catches John's attention. It is beautiful, but there is something odd about it. A museum tour guide approaches John and Jeff and asks them to read the little story on the mounted display case. The butterfly, according to the card, is not a butterfly at all, it is a *spider* masquerading as one! This way, the other butterflies come near it and get caught in its sticky web.

Camouflage is a trick that has been used since time immortal by all types of living creatures. Some use it for hunting, and some for protection from these hunters. Some, like modern human beings, often use it to make a statement! Whatever the mechanism, the intent is to portray an impression different from the fact, or at least the perception on the surface.

In database systems, methods are sometimes used to masquerade the true meaning of a table or a field of a table. For instance, the table to store credit card numbers of customers is perhaps the most attractive for attackers, so the table may be named *processing_info*, which is logically correct. The table does aid in processing, but the name hides the true meaning of the table from the casual user. A user who has no knowledge of the application but somehow gains access to the data dictionary may try to find tables related to credit card information by using a query similar to this:

```
select table_name
from dba_tables
where table_name like '%CREDIT%'
or table_name like '%CC%';
```

A hacker will not be able to track down the table *processing_info* with this query. Of course, the hacker may know of this trick and may look for columns that look like credit card numbers.

```
select column_name, table_name
from dba_tab_columns
where column_name like '%CREDIT%'
or column_name like '%CC%';
```

To foil the attempts of this relentless attacker, the columns of the table should also be masqueraded without any reference to the words resembling credit card in their names. For instance, the columns for credit card numbers, cardholder's name, and expiration date can be named PROCESSING_DATA1, PROCESSING_DATA2 and PROCESSING_DATA3. The expiration can be a VARCHAR2 field, instead of a DATE type to fool the hacker. It is important to understand that this specific technique is not required by HIPAA or anyone else, but can be used to enhance general security.

 **If possible, name the tables or columns containing sensitive data something counterintuitive, to make it less easy to guess.**

# Encryption

John and Jeff are truly captivated by the exhibit of the spider in the butterfly camouflage. In the process of aiding the little fellow's understanding of the camouflage concept, John pretends to be a spider in a butterfly suit and mockingly pounces on Jeff. The performance is hilarious, causing Jeff and others around them to break into peals of laughter. One of the security guards is watching the fracas. Someone from the control room sees the noisy group on the security camera and calls the guard on the radio, asking the reason for the commotion.

"*Locos!*" replies the guard.

"All right", comes the reply from the control room.

What just happened? Both of these guards know Spanish. The floor security guard replies that there is a bunch of *locos*, or crazy people on the floor, which the guard in the control room comprehends as harmless. The floor guard does not want the group to hear him call them "crazy people", so he uses a different language to convey the message to the intended party.

The important point here is that only the sender and the receiver have the ability to comprehend the message. The message, in other words, is **encrypted**. Of course, anyone who knows Spanish can decipher the words, but that could be an advantage. A message can be quickly spread among a group of people without designating a specific recipient while still protecting the message from others. If the guards decide to have a conversation that is strictly between them, they can invent a different language that is understood only by them, or twist the current language to make it harder for the others to understand. For instance, a simple scheme is to reverse the letters of the words and add a random letter before and after each letter. The sentence "How are you" becomes "awkodhi webrqaz yuvolyc". Drop all the alternate letters of each word starting with the first, and then reverse the order of the letters to get the original text.

Only someone who knows how it was encrypted in the first place can decipher this message. In the case above, what happens if the hacker somehow identifies the table and column names for credit card numbers? A persistent hacker will eventually discover that *processing_info* contains credit card number information. In this case, the information becomes very vulnerable. Can this be protected from theft? In the database, the data could be simply encrypted by some scheme. A user will have to know the decryption routine to decipher the data. A hacker will not be able to interpret the data even if he gains access to it; it will be meaningless.

There are several types of encryption routines, such as DES (Digital Encryption Standard) and DES3 (Triple DES), prescribed by standard's bodies like the National Institute of Standards and Technology (NIST) and the Federal Information Processing Standards (FIPS). These methods provide an adequate amount of protection in most cases. Oracle provides some built-in encryption routines to encrypt and decrypt the data in these formats. All these routines have been implemented using a supplied package *dbms_obfuscation_toolkit.*

There is another type of encryption in Oracle, called hashing or digesting. With this method, the data is converted into some sequence of characters and padded to make it a uniform size. Another variation of hashing in Oracle is the MD5 routine. Hashing and MD5 are described in detail in Chapter 6, under Encryption.

Oracle's implementations of the DES and DES3 encryptions are based on keys. This means that a key is used to encrypt the data. In order to decrypt the encrypted data, the user needs the *same* key. The key and the encrypted data should be stored and retrieved in combination. However, doesn't storing the key itself negate the security of encryption, since the malicious user can retrieve the key *and* the encrypted data, and then decrypt it?

Not necessarily. In chapter 6, we will explore the tips and tricks of storing the key and the encrypted data in such a way that the security is enforced without the insecurity of maintaining the keys along with the data.

> 🔔 **Encrypt sensitive data, such as Patient Health Information and Credit Card numbers, so that even if the data *is* accessed in an unauthorized manner, it will not reveal any meaningful information.**

## Row Level Security

John and Jeff drag on to the next exhibit, which is the re-creation of a city of the Indus valley civilization that flourished over 6000 years ago in India. The exhibit is huge. They enter through the reconstructed ancient archway that led to the city. However, after about one tenth of the exhibit, they are stopped. The exhibit is not included in the admission price of the ticket; it is charged separately. John didn't know that and obviously he didn't have the ticket. The portion of the exhibit they saw was more like a preview, the attendant explains.

Here we witness another very important phenomenon - a visitor accesses a facility (the museum), accesses an object (the ancient Indus Valley city exhibit), but can't access *all* of the contents of the object. In the database world, this is analogous to a user with select privileges over a table who is allowed to see only part of the table's rows, not all, based on certain filtering conditions. For example, First Rate Insurance Company gets a lot of claims from the Top Notch Hospital in the city. To handle those claims, the company has a specific claim analyst, Judy, assigned to handle those claims. Since Judy handles claims coming from Top Notch Hospital only, she should not be allowed to see, update, or even reference the data from other providers. HIPAA requirements clearly state that the users who are not authorized to access certain data should not be allowed to do so. How can that be achieved?

One way to do that is to create another table for Top Notch Hospital claims only, and grant privileges to that table to JUDY. However, it is not feasible to do this for all the providers. The applications have to remember which tables contain data for which providers, and such a system will prove inflexible. A user who has privileges on more than one provider will have to join all these tables to get the data. This, quite simply, is not an acceptable solution.

Oracle has a solution for this problem. It is called **Virtual Private Database (VPD)**, also known as Fine Grained Access Control (FGAC). In this approach, the table can have a *policy* defined on it. A policy can then be assigned to a specific *context*. A user can have a context defined in a session, and the data viewable to the user will be limited to what the policy and the context allow. In the above example, the policy may be defined on the *claims* table to show records related to only the acceptable range of providers for the calling user's application context. When the user JUDY wants to see the claims, she issues the statement

```
select * from CLAIMS;
```

Although she asked to get all the rows (notice: there is no filtering condition), the policy will check the rows and decide whether they are allowed to be accessed or not, and only the allowed ones will be displayed. This works not just for selecting data, but for all types of table access. For JUDY, the table will appear to contain only those rows for which she is authorized. Another user, NATHAN, may have a different context, and therefore may see an entirely different set of rows. Within a single source of data, it is possible to present different information to different users based on the policy and the context, as if the users have their own personal or private database, hence the term Virtual Private Database. This is an excellent tool to meet HIPAA requirements.

The concept of VPD is such a powerful tool in meeting not just HIPAA, but any type of privacy requirements, that it has been discussed in depth in Chapter 6. That chapter will provide enough working examples and scripts to implement quick privacy requirement compliance. We will also explore some of the potential problems, particularly in enforcement of foreign key constraints and how to address them.

Use of VPD also requires that users connect through specific user IDs only. However, most of the third party applications use a single user ID for the database, clearly a violation of good security rules. The users are authenticated by the application. So how does one implement the VPD in such a situation?

In Chapter 6, we will also discover a way to achieve that objective, even if the users are authenticated at the application level.

 **Make use of Virtual Private Database to limit the data accessible to a user.**

# Program Based Security

Touring a museum is hard work, and hard work makes anyone thirsty. John and Jeff stop at the museum cafeteria owned by Jack, a local vendor. When they approach the counter, Jack smiles at them and asks what they want. John wants a sandwich and a soda, Jeff wants a cookie and a soda. They see Jack go over to the soda fountain, fill up the cups, go inside the kitchen to get the sandwich, and come back to them. They pay, thank him, and move along.

After a while, John gets thirsty again, and he stops by a vending machine to get a bottle of soda. He drops some coins and out pops a bottle.

These un-noteworthy events are perhaps the most basic of anyone's life. What do they have to do with security? Let's analyze both situations to see the subtle differences between them. Both involve getting an object (a drink) from a server – the soda dispenser. In the second case, at the vending machine, Jack himself puts the coin in the machine and the machine validates the authorization – the coin – and passes the requested resource. The interaction with the server is *direct.* At the cafeteria, however, the interaction with the server is not direct. John and Jeff can see the server, the soda fountain, but they cannot *approach* it.

They have to enlist the services of another layer, the cafeteria owner, to get the required resource, the soda. In accessing another resource, the sandwich, they can't even see the server because it is hidden behind the kitchen walls. This is done to ensure safety and security of the dispenser. What if the users don't know how to operate the dispenser? They might have broken it. Or there could be vandalism. In the sandwich case, you would never want the users to prepare their own sandwich; they might burn themselves. The owner of the resources - the sandwich and soda - retrieves the resources and passes them on to the users.

Compare that with the services of a database. The database dispenses data in the form of rows, the equivalent of soda, from tables, analogous to the soda dispenser. Usually, the users get the rows directly from the tables by selecting them. However, by doing so, the table's structure, the constraints, the relation of the table to others, the meaning of the rows, etc. have to be known to the users. This creates several problems - the simplest of which is change management. What if a small change occurs in the table structure? All the users, including potential users who have never accessed this table, must be aware of the change, a tedious task. But the bigger problem is security. By publishing the structure of the table, malicious users may have enough ammunition to launch an attack against the table, steal the data, or worse – modify it.

In this model of security, the table is never opened for access by anyone other than the owner. All accesses to the table are handled through stored programs like procedures and packages. For instance, when an application wants to update the *paid_amount* field of the table claims to 1000 for the CLAIM_ID 1234567, the program does not issue

```
UPDATE CLAIMS
SET PAID_AMOUNT = 1000
WHERE CLAIM_ID = 1234567;
```

Rather, it accesses a stored procedure *update_paid_claim*, owned by the owner of the table *claims*. This application user has been given *execute* privileges on this stored procedure.

```
create or replace procedure update_paid_claim (
  p_claim_id IN number,
  p_paid_amount IN number ) is
begin
  update CLAIMS
  set PAID_AMOUNT = p_paid_amount
  where CLAIM_ID = p_claim_id;
end;
```

The process will be quite longer and more robust in real life, but it has been shown in this manner for simplicity. Note how the objective of updating the paid amount field is achieved. The modus operandi is the same in both cases. But in the procedure case, the application does not need to know the structure of the table, the exact name of the paid amount field, etc. This accomplishes three things:

**The table changes are protected from the applications**. The column could be renamed from PAID_AMOUNT to PAID_AMT or CLAIM_PAID_AMOUNT; the applications do not need to know the change. The only change that is required is at one place, the procedure.

**The business logic could be encapsulated**. What if the business decides to use a complicated logic to validate the paid amount, or even make the actual paid amount based on some complex calculation? These changes can be easily handled through the procedure, with the changes being transparent to the users.

**The third, but the most important one is security**. By hiding the table from the applications, we allow the structure of the table to be hidden from most users. Since the users are not given any privilege to update the table data directly, a malicious attacker cannot update the table directly; he or she has to use the procedure. Inside the procedure, we can place many types of checks to ensure that the request is genuine. By retaining a single point of control for the table changes, we can achieve some degree of control on those changes. In most cases, this is desirable to enforce a security policy.

Consider a complex application that needs to update various tables in other databases. One option is to create database links from the application's database to all others, while granting privileges to the calling application to make data changes. The more secure option is to create stored procedures in all the other databases owned by the owner of the respective tables, and granting the execute privilege only to the remote users. The security is somewhat strengthened by this approach.

> **Whenever possible, encapsulate the procedural logic and allow access to the objects through these procedures only.**

## Role-based Security

Let's introduce another character in the story - Sue is a museum tour guide who attends the small group of visitors that includes John and Jeff. When Sue arrives at the museum, she may have gone to a different gate, the employee entrance gate, not one of the two public entrances. In a database, there could be some ports open for the regular users, but one or more ports may be present to allow access by special users, like DBAs and Administrators. These ports should not be advertised to the general population. After the entry into the museum, Sue is handed a special ribbon that pronounces her an Employee.

Once inside the museum, she can pass through a door marked "Employees Only". The security guard at the door looks at her badge and waves her through. Why does the guard not check Sue's name against a list of employees, or an Access Control List? It's because her badge has a special ribbon to indicate that she is an employee. She is authenticated at the employee entrance gate when entering the museum, and once inside there is no need to check for further facility accesses. All that is needed is to ensure that Sue's role inside the museum is not that of visitor, but of employee, as authorized by her employee ribbon.

In Oracle parlance, we can define roles inside a database and assign users to roles. The roles may have privileges assigned to them, so that any user who is assigned the role automatically inherits all the privileges. It's the next step of the ladder in a security setup. Instead of assigning specific privileges to the users so that they can perform what they need, we can define several roles with privileges and assign users to the roles. These roles can be tied very closely to the business functions.

For instance, a role called *claims adjuster* can be created for all the employees who make claims decisions. This role can be given privileges to insert, update, delete, and select on all claims-related tables, but only select against other lookup tables like members and providers. If Jane Doe is a claims adjuster, she can be assigned this role, which will allow her to insert, update, delete, and select all claims tables and only select from the lookup tables. When another employee joins the pool of adjusters, he can also be assigned this role. When Jane moves out of the claims adjustment department to, say, human resources, this role can easily be revoked in one statement, disallowing her access to the tables instantaneously.

> 🔔 **Use roles to assign groups of users the same set of security privileges.**

However, there are several security holes in a role-based authorization model. The details of the role-based model, with working examples and caveats, are explained in Chapter 4 under General Security.

# Profile-Based Security

The staff at Metropolitan Museum pays careful attention to rules, which are enforced strictly to ensure the security and safety of the visitors and the exhibits. One of the rules, unpalatable to some visitors like John's son, forbids running in the museum for fear of hitting one of the exhibits. In other words, younger visitors in particular are restricted on some of their natural movements. However, persons such as security guards and police officers may have to run in order to perform job tasks. What differentiates these free roamers from the visitors with restricted movement?

One factor is the role they perform inside the museum - some are security guards and others are visitors. However, note the difference in the nature of the privilege - it's not about accessing an object like a particular room or exhibit, it's about moving around at a much faster pace, giving orders to other people, and generally behaving in a rather relaxed manner compared to the visitors. So, this is not the same type of privilege we saw earlier, it has more to do with general behavioral disposition.

In the database analogy, this would be similar to a user whose access to specific objects is defined fairly well, while free roaming is rather restricted. Jane and Judy are both Claims Analysts, but Jane is senior and handles a higher volume of claims, as well as the more complicated ones. Due to the nature of their jobs, they are given the same Oracle database role, which provides them identical access privileges to objects like tables, procedures, etc., but since Jane handles more volume and more complicated cases, she perhaps consumes more CPU power to run more complicated queries.

Therefore, Jane should be given more access to the underlying infrastructure, compared to object access privileges. In Oracle, this is known as a **Profile**. A named profile is defined with a specific quota for each of the infrastructural elements, such as the amount of CPU power the user can consume, memory, number of times the user can login, etc. It allows the users to perform their duties as per the requirements.

But how are the profiles related to security in the HIPAA context? Let's see. Profiles are defined with a CREATE PROFILE statement in SQL. A profile can have several parameters that can be individually limited. The parameters important for HIPAA compliance are described below.

**Sessions per User** - This limits the number of sessions or connections to the database a named user can maintain at any point in time. By limiting the number of sessions, the chance that a malicious user may hack his or her way into the database is reduced.

**Connect Time** – This limits the maximum time a user can stay connected to the database. After this limit expires, the sessions are automatically disconnected. If the application is set up in such a way that the legitimate access occurs only during certain time periods – the sessions can be forced to disconnect automatically.

**Idle Time** – This limits the maximum time a session can stay connected without doing anything. Typically, hackers target the inactive sessions to gain access into the database. By reducing the period of time an inactive session stays connected, the probability of that session being a victim of abuse is reduced.

> **Use profiles extensively to restrict multiple logons, unneeded idle times, etc. to achieve the HIPAA mandated security compliance.**

Profiles and how to set them for security will be described in detail in Chapter 4.

# View-Based Security

Another way to hide the implementation of the table structure is to create a view. Oracle views are like portals or windows into the real table data. Perhaps it is better explained through an example. Imagine the user selects the tables through the following query

```
select
   c.claim_id,
   claim_amount,
   p.description as procedure_description
from
   claims c, procedures p
where
   member_id in
   (
      select member_id
      from allowed_members
      where userid = USER
   )
and
   p.proc_code = c.proc_code;
```

This is simply a selection of the columns CLAIM_ID and CLAIM_AMOUNT from the *claims* table, joined with the procedures table to get the description of the procedures. However, the claims the user sees are limited to only those members whose records the user is authorized for. This list of allowable members is maintained in a separate table called *allowed_members*. This query selects data from the claim tables only for those allowable claims. In this way we can ensure that the user does not see the data of those members he or she is not authorized for.

But, we tend to ensure this simply by *assuming* that the user will write a query like the above one. What if the user deliberately, or inadvertently, omits the clause where MEMBER_ID in …? Then he or she will see claims for *all* the members, not just those he or she is authorized for.

To eliminate this problem, the DBA can create a view like:

```
create or replace view
   claim_record
as
select
   c.claim_id,
   claim_amount,
   p.description as procedure_description
from
   claims c, procedures p
where
   member_id in
   (
      select member_id
      from allowed_members
      where userid = USER
   )
and
   p.proc_code = c.proc_code;
```

The user is then granted SELECT privileges on the view *claim_record*, not the *claims* table itself. When the user selects from the *claim_records* view, he or she, in effect, executes the query the view is defined on, and sees all the records he or she is allowed to see. When the user attempts to select from the claims table, he or she gets an error message "Object does not exist." meaning he or she does not have any privileges on the table. However selecting the data from the view succeeds, because he or she does have select access to it.

Let's examine the benefits of the view in this context.

**Object Independence** – Since the user simply has to know the view name, not the underlying tables and how they are defined, what their columns are, etc., the designers have more flexibility in the data architecture.

**Auto Filtering** – Notice how the selection from the view automatically initiates the query and thus filters the records the user is not allowed to see. This filter is based on the table *allowed_members*, but the user selecting from the view does not even have to know the structure of the table or even its existence. This merely adds to the security.

**Object Security** – Since the users are allowed SELECT access to the view, and not the tables themselves, security can be strictly controlled. The users are shown all the columns they need to be shown, but not all the columns. If the columns contain any PHI (patient health information), such as procedure codes or social security numbers, HIPAA specifically prohibits displaying that information to the users who do not need it. Ordinarily, this may demand the creation of separate tables for storage of non-PHI data that other users can access. Using a view, however, allows for control of displayed information.

For instance, take the example of the Procedure Codes that are tightly controlled, such as HIV, with procedure codes 00123, 00124, 00125 and 00126. All other procedure codes can be displayed. The view can be constructed like this:

```
create or replace view
   claim_records
as
select
   c.claim_id, claim_amount,
   decode(c.proc_code,
      '00123','Classified',
      '00124','Classified',
      '00125','Classified',
      '00126','Classified',
      p.description
   ) as procedure_description
from
   claims c, procedures p
where member_id in
   (
         select member_id
      from allowed_members
      where userid = USER
   )
and p.proc_code = c.proc_code;
```

Using a DECODE function, we have ensured that the view displays 'Classified' when the procedure codes are in the banned list. The users will never be able to see the procedure descriptions from the table, because they don't have access to it. By simply creating this view, we have satisfied a huge HIPAA requirement immediately.

**Column Description** – Note how the column PROCEDURE_DESCRIPTION is used after the lengthy clause. When the user selects all the columns from the view, this is displayed as the column name.

**Storage Savings** – A view is not actually stored with its data, unlike a table. It's nothing but a stored query. Therefore as many views as necessary can be created without consuming space.

There is another concept in Oracle called a *Materialized View*, also known as a *Snapshot*. This is not a conventional view because the data from the query is actually stored in the object, or the data from the execution of the query is materialized in the database, and hence the term, materialized view.

This takes care of reading data, but what about *modifying* it? Can we modify a view directly and ensure that only the authorized data is modified, not all the rows of the table? Yes, we can. The above view, known as one of the simple view types, can be inserted, updated, or deleted directly just like a table, and only the rows that would have been retrieved by the table are affected, not all rows. If the view is complex, and the definition of complex views varies based on context, it may not be directly manipulated. In that case, the view can be manipulated using a special type of trigger known as **Instead of Triggers**. These triggers are defined on the view, but instead of acting on that view, they can be directed to act on the underlying table.

**Use of Views can hide specific details of the table row, especially the sensitive data such as Protected Health Information, without creating additional storage needs.**

# Invoker Rights

We previously saw the program level security where the objects are accessed through the programs that are owned by the same schema owner. When an application user invokes the program, the underlying objects are accessed as if accessed by the owner of the procedure. For instance, in the *update_claim_amount* procedure, the schema owner is CLAIM_SCHEMA but the application user is Judy. When Judy calls the procedure *update_claim_amount*, she does not require explicit privileges to update the claim table. Since the procedure and table are owned by CLAIM_SCHEMA, all that is required is for Judy to have execute privileges on the procedure.

Consider another situation: JUDY has a table called *claims* in her own schema. If she calls the procedure, the table *claims* owned by CLAIM_SCHEMA is updated, not hers. This is probably normal in most cases. Let's examine several more situations.

Remember Sue, the museum tour guide? While she is winding up her work at the museum, her manager, Mr. Smith, tells her that one of the fuses in the corridor is blown and there are none in stock. He asks her if she could go over to the drug store and get a fuse. Sue agrees, but there is a problem - her car has no gas, and there is no time to fill the car with gas and get the fuse. "No problem", declares Mr. Smith, "just take my car". Wow! Sue is thrilled because Mr. Smith's car is a sports model she has always wanted to drive.

Let's ponder over a question here. Sue is driving a car owned by Mr. Smith, and he has given her permission to do so. Should she carry her own driver's license?

While we deliberate over the question, she zooms off to the drug store; but in her excitement, she races the car at 80 miles per hour! And within no time, there is a police officer right behind her with flashing lights.

When Sue gets the ticket for speeding, who do you think the ticket should go to - her or Mr. Smith? You might argue - why Mr. Smith? He was not driving, Sue was. Therefore, she should receive the ticket, and she did. What would have happened if she had told the officer that Mr. Smith owns the car, and he should be responsible for the speeding violation? The officer probably would have laughed.

This is an important concept to understand. Although Mr. Smith owns the means of delivery, and he gives Sue permission to operate the means of delivery, Sue carries out the operation and is responsible for actions like speeding. In a database application, a similar question also arises. Security procedures might dictate that all applications in the form of stored procedures and packages be owned by a secure user, and that execute permissions only be granted to the other users who might need them. However, the stored procedure should update the tables only when the application users have privileges to update them.

Perhaps an example will help illustrate the concept better. Take the example of the procedure *update_claim_amount* above, but assume it is owned by another user called PROGOWNER. This user does not own any tables but only the stored procedures. The table *claims* is owned by user CLAIM_SCHEMA. The user JUDY has permission to update the table *claims* but the user PROGOWNER doesn't. So when JUDY calls the procedure *update_claim_amount*, owned by PROGOWNER, who doesn't have the privileges to update the *claims* table, what should happen?

It will fail to update the table. When JUDY executes *update_claim_amount*, the procedure runs with the privileges of the owner of the procedure, i.e. PROGOWNER. Since PROGOWNER does not have any privileges on the *claims* table, the execution will fail. This is desirable.

Oracle8i introduced a new concept called **invoker rights** in execution. In this model, the procedure is created as follows.

```
create or replace procedure update_paid_claim (
  p_claim_id IN number,
  p_paid_amount IN number )
authid current_user
is
begin
  update CLAIMS
  set PAID_AMOUNT = p_paid_amount
  where CLAIM_ID = p_claim_id;
end;
```

The definition of this procedure is identical to the one defined earlier, except for the line "authid current_user." When the procedure is defined this way, a user calling this procedure merely executes the code behind it; the privileges required for the updates come from the calling user. In this case, when JUDY calls the procedure, the privileges given to her are required to update the tables, i.e. JUDY, not PROGOWNER, must have UPDATE privileges on the *claims* table. If JUDY doesn't have the privileges but PROGOWNER does, the procedure execution will fail.

How is this helpful in designing the HIPAA compliant model? This concept alone is one of the single most important rights management setups required for HIPAA. In this case, a user called PROGOWNER, who does not have any other privilege, can own all your code, and all application users must call the stored programs it owns. However, since each user is separately administered in the privilege management framework, the success of the execution of those codes will depend on the calling user's privileges, and this arrangement works perfectly.

In the default model, known as *definer rights*, privileges are required to be granted to the user PROGOWNER, and execute privileges on the procedures are to be granted to all the other users who might potentially need to access these procedures. If the privileges are to be revoked, the execute privilege on the procedure needs to be revoked. If the procedure is a package, all other procedures inside the package would also be inaccessible to the user, and that may not be desirable. The invoker model allows for the modularization of code while at the same time allowing rights to be handled properly.

We will see more examples, caveats, and how to use them in building a complete system in Chapter 4.

> Use the Invoker Rights model of stored programs whenever possible to tie required privileges to the user calling the procedure, allowing a finer granular privilege management.

## Backup and Recovery Security

Finally, HIPAA refers to the security related to the protection of data not from human abuse, but from machine and system failures, too. What if the machine suffers component damage while transactions are being executed? Oracle's transaction processing model ensures that data integrity will be protected, i.e. committed data is recovered and uncommitted data is rolled back. Is that acceptable?

Like most other questions, the answer is obvious – it depends. In particular, it depends on the type of transaction processing that is employed at the organization. In some of the corporations the authors worked in, the transactions – the claims or payments – are fed into a queue-based system such as MQ Series, and data is fed from the queues to the database. If the database fails, and the transaction rolls back, the data is intact in the queue – as if nothing happened. When the database comes back up, the same message in the queue can be processed.

However, if the transactions do not flow through a queue, but happen directly on the database, or the handler does not handle uncommitted transactions this way, there could be cases of lost transactions, a clearly unacceptable situation. The solution in that case is to employ some of the high availability solutions such as Oracle Real Application Clusters (RAC), the next generation of Oracle Parallel Server (OPS), Synchronous Multi-Master Database Replication solutions, or Oracle Data Guard, all of which offer a zero-data-loss setup where the transactions are mined from redo logs and applied to the secondary database.

Sometimes, the recovery requirements are a little relaxed. The last uncommitted transaction may be safe to ignore. Typically, this is the case where the claim information comes in batches and a batch is processed in its entirety, not claim by claim. If the system failure happens during the processing of a batch, the entire batch can be processed again.

However, if the process commits in between, there could be some claims committed inside a batch, creating inconsistency. Some applications, upon encountering a duplicate claim, merely record it as a different "version" of the claim. Since HIPAA requirements mandate that the history of a claim be maintained and that it be auditable, a versioning of some fashion may be feasible and may suffice for the backup protection. But the exact way the error is handled must be recorded.

Next comes another possibility of failure – the physical disks or some parts of them breaking down, a term known as corruption. The HIPAA law requires that data should be backed up in a manner consistent with the application's error handling. Since data is considered a valuable asset, similar to other valuable assets like financial instruments, backup security is a requirement that must be clearly addressed with operational procedures documenting the process of backup and recovery. In subsequent chapters, we will cover this in more detail.

**Backup of healthcare related information is not just a convenience, but also a requirement under HIPAA and other laws. Understand the error handling mechanism of the application and then devise a backup and recovery plan consistent with it. Several options exist in Oracle to make data fault tolerant, like Real Application Clusters, Multi-Master Replication, and Oracle Data Guard.**

## In Summary

This sums up the various types of security features and options the reader should be familiar with, and how they relate to the HIPAA requirements. The exact technical details have been deliberately left out of the discussion so as not to overwhelm the reader who just wants an overview. For a thorough and detailed discussion on each feature, see the appropriate chapters in the remaining sections of this book.

# Introduction to Oracle Auditing

CHAPTER

## What is Auditing

Continuing our story of John and Jeff visiting the museum, they find themselves in an interesting situation. The day after their visit, a newsflash shakes the town. The *Koh-I-Noor* diamond, worth several million dollars, was not found in its place, it has been stolen!

All parties concerned with security spring into action – the security department of the museum, the city police detectives, and even the investigators of the insurance company that insure the museum displays. The first thing they do is check the people who may have entered the room that housed the diamond. But there is a little problem - there is no record of the people who entered the room that day. The only helpful information they can collect is that access to this area of the museum is restricted to museum employees.

Let's analyze the situation for a moment – the museum could not even ascertain who *did* enter the room, let alone who *handled* the diamond. The ability to check who actually handles objects, not just who has the authority, is provided by **auditing**. A good auditing system provides a process of recording the accesses to the objects in a storage system, forming an *audit trail.*

The museum here has a good security system, but not a good auditing system. A good auditing system should meet three very important goals – recording the access of the usage by all users, legitimate or otherwise, protecting the integrity of the audit trail so that no unauthorized person can alter the contents, and using the audit trail to identify the usage later.

In Oracle, like any other database, the importance of auditing is even more pronounced. Databases have storage objects called tables, virtual storage objects such as views, program units such as stored procedures and triggers, etc. When someone accesses the tables, views or executes the stored programs, the fact can be recorded in the audit trail. The audit trail can be an operating system file or a table inside the database. A special and powerful user called SYS owns this table, therefore, regular users cannot manipulate the audit trail.

The museum case merely demonstrates the need to maintain a simple auditing procedure to resolve a rather open-and-shut case. Unfortunately, the lack of this procedure presents enormous obstacles to the investigators. On the issue of medical records privacy, the situation is even more fluid and prone to severe security lapses. HIPAA addresses this problem by mandating the audit requirements of these records and strictly enforcing the requirements by placing stiff penalties for non-compliance.

In Oracle, several types of auditing are available.

- SQL *audit* command (for DMLs)
- Auditing with object triggers (DML)
- Auditing with system-level triggers (DML & DDL)
- Auditing with LogMiner (DML & DDL)
- Fine-grained auditing (select auditing)

In this chapter, we will discuss some of the challenges of HIPAA auditing requirements, auditing options available in Oracle, and how to handle the requirements with what is available. As in the previous chapter, this chapter is written for all types of readers, whether or not they are familiar with Oracle. If you are looking for a specific auditing tool or option, please go to the respective chapter directly. Otherwise, you may want to browse this chapter to connect the HIPAA requirements with the auditing options.

# User Logon Auditing

In the museum theft case, the first act of the investigators is to get the day's visitor records and employee attendance records. Although visitors are not allowed to enter the room, the investigators suspect that the perpetrator(s) might have had a visitor as an accomplice.

In a database, the first thing to check is who entered and when, regardless of the reason. Oracle provides several auditing options to record the fact that a user accessed the database, along with the information on the IP Address of the machine where the connection came from, time of access, the actions performed by the user, the timestamp when the user logged off, the amount of activity the user performed as indicated by number of database blocks read from and written to the database, etc. As you can see, the information captured is venerable and presents a complete picture of the user's activity in the session.

Another important aspect of auditing is recording who was *not* granted access, not just who did come in, depending on the privilege setting. This could be due to a legitimate reason such as a bad password, but it could also be a hacker trying to break in with multiple attempts at guessing the password. It could even be an insider, a disgruntled employee trying to access information he or she is not authorized for. Whatever the reason may be, this kind of activity arouses suspicion and should be investigated. Oracle can audit such attempts, even if they are not successful.

HIPAA requirements clearly state that user accesses to the database be recorded and monitored for possible abuse. Remember, this intent is not just to catch hackers but also to document the accesses to medical databases by legitimate users. In most cases, the very fact that the access is recorded is deterrent enough for malicious activity, much like the presence of a surveillance camera in a parking lot. In Chapter 8, we will explore the details of this type of auditing, with scripts on how to set up and retrieve details to find patterns of abuse and potential threats.

After the auditing system is set up, the resulting report can show the times the users logged on and off, along with other information. An example report is provided below.

```
                           Total
Day        User          Minutes
---------- ---------- -------
02-03-06   APPLSYSPUB          0
           APPS              466
           OPS$ORACLE          7
           PERFSTAT           11

02-03-07   APPLSYSPUB          5
           APPS            1,913
           CUSJAN              1
           JANEDI              5
           OPS$ORACLE          6
           PERFSTAT          134
           SYS                58
```

Similar reports can also be obtained for unsuccessful attempts.

**Enable auditing of access by users, even when the connection attempt is unsuccessful.**

## Object Access Audit

In the theft case, the investigators interview each employee present that day and ask if they entered the room containing the *Koh-I-Noor* diamond. Obviously, this is not the best way to deal with the theft. There is no audit record of the access to the room, so the investigators are trying to piece together the audit records from the security rules – clearly not the correct way to do so.

The museum should have had a specific policy of recording access to the room by posting a security guard who would have checked their badges and recorded them in a register, or by using an automated entry system using keypad access, or by a security camera recording all personnel entering and leaving the room, or perhaps a combination of all of these.

In Oracle, recording object accesses is known as *object auditing*. For example, if the user accesses the table named *claims*, the fact is recorded in the audit trail, along with several other useful pieces of information, like the timestamp of access, IP address of the user's machine, the exact privileges used to access the table, the nature of the access (did the user delete some data, insert some records, update some fields, or simply select some rows), and many others. From this audit trail, a detailed track of the user's activity can be reconstructed. It is different from user auditing, where the fact that the user simply accessed the database is recorded, not the objects he or she accessed.

HIPAA regulations require that object access auditing be enabled and monitored. However, common sense shows that the auditing is not going to be useful for all of the objects, only a few key tables must be audited for unauthorized access. The definition of key tables depends on the data they contain and whether or not the data is sensitive. For instance, the table containing the Protected Health Information (PHI) data such as claims, member, billing information, etc., may be specifically audited.

Auditing can be done on a variety of statements that the user can issue. For instance, the auditing setup can require that a user give a statement to select from a particular table or view, or to execute a particular stored program. Along with the statement, the other information such as timestamp, client machine name, etc., is also recorded. This information alone can satisfy most of the regulations. However, the exact rows that were selected are not recorded. This is done by another feature, called Fine Grained Auditing (FGA).

**Always enable auditing for sensitive tables to identify accesses. This alone satisfies most of the HIPAA requirements.**

# Data Change Auditing

The regular auditing features of Oracle record that the user has updated some rows of a table, but not which particular rows, and more importantly, what the value was before the change. HIPAA compliance requires that the sensitive data be audited for changes, and that means recording the pre-change value as well as the post-change one. Some other security and auditing policies, such as the Safe Harbor Law, may also mandate that.

The usual method of auditing changed data is to use triggers on the tables. A trigger is a piece of code that executes when a certain event associated with that trigger occurs. For instance, a trigger of type After Update Row may be defined on a table. In that trigger, the code may capture the old value before the change, the new value after the change, and insert both values into a table used to capture this type of audit information.

In addition to the old and new data, several other important pieces of information can also be captured and recorded, such as the timestamp, the client machine, etc. In Chapter 9, we will explore how to create these types of triggers with scripts, which can be re-used in a real production environment.

Another way to capture the changes made to the database is from a tool called **LogMiner**. Any change in the Oracle database is written to a special type of file called a *redo log*. When a redo log file is filled up, it is stored as another type of file called an *archived* log file. These files are necessary when the database suffers a failure and the DBA needs to restore the data files up to the point of failure during a recovery.

LogMiner can go through these log files and capture the changes that occurred, along with the user ID, the timestamp, and a host of other information.

LogMiner auditing is explained in detail, along with scripts, in Chapter 9.

 **Use triggers to audit changes to sensitive data. These changes can also be recoded via LogMiner.**

# DDL Auditing

Oracle has two types of SQL statements. The statements that access data in any way, such as SELECT, INSERT, DELETE, and UPDATE etc. belong to a part of the SQL language known as *Data Manipulation Language* (DML). Developers and users accessing the data primarily use this. The other type of statements that define the database and its objects are known as *Data Definition Language* (DDL). The DDLs are used to create tables, views, procedures, etc. They are also used to modify the structure of such objects, e.g. changing the length of a column from 12 digits to 15.

Under HIPAA regulations, any alteration to the structure of the data containers, such as tables and views, should be strictly audited. Therefore, you have to audit these changes and preserve them for future reference. Typically, these audit trails are examined to identify causes of errors or data corruption. For instance, a decrease in length of a number field may not raise an error, indeed, the number may be stored after truncating the first or last few digits. This corruption is not detectable immediately but it may surface later, and an audit trail can come in handy during times of troubleshooting.

The easiest way to achieve this is through the use of some type of version control system software like RCS or SCCS. If the organization has a policy of placing everything in the version control system, the changes made are automatically recorded. But what happens when someone makes an *emergency* change without using the proper procedure? The setup fails. This is a classic case of a system where the integrity can be guaranteed only when everyone follows the rules and no one bypasses them. However, in real life this cannot be guaranteed, and the dependability of the version control system becomes questionable.

To establish a foolproof system to audit these DDL Changes, the best option is to use triggers on these objects to capture changes. An example of such a DDL trigger is given below.

```
create or replace trigger
   DDLTrigger
AFTER DDL ON DATABASE
BEGIN
    insert into
       ddl_log
    (
       user_name,
       ddl_date,
       ddl_type,
       object_type,
       owner,
       object_name
    )
    VALUES
    (
       ora_login_user,
       sysdate,
       ora_sysevent,
       ora_dict_obj_type,
       ora_dict_obj_owner,
       ora_dict_obj_name
    );
END;
```

Whenever a DDL statement is executed, this trigger records the user who issued it, the timestamp of the statement, the type of the DDL (a column was added, a column was dropped, a table was created, etc.), the owner of the object that was created, dropped or modified, and the type of the object (table, view, procedure, etc.).

These triggers, defined and created by the user SYS, will execute when the structure of a table, view, or sequence is changed. Being owned by the special user SYS, which is the equivalent of the *super user* in Oracle, these triggers are protected from unauthorized modification.

Once in place, DDL triggers can provide great reports showing all schema changes for a system. An example is shown below.

```
Date        DDL      Object   Object
of DDL      User     Operatio Type   Name
----------- ------   -------- ------ --------------------
05-21 07:53  MEMBERS ALTER    VIEW   MEMBER_CLAIMS
05-21 09:00  CLAIMS  CREATE   TABLE  CLAIMS
             CLAIMS  CREATE   TABLE  CLAIM_LINES
             CLAIMS  ALTER    TABLE  CLAIM_HEADER
             CLAIMS  ALTER    VIEW   CLAIM_PROVIDERS
```

In Chapter 9, we will discuss in detail how to set up the triggers to capture the changes. These strategies, however, are not part of the general auditing options of the Oracle database, they must be done outside the framework using triggers on the DDL statements.

**Use DDL triggers to capture changes within structures of the database objects. In addition, implement some type of version control system, such as RCS or SCCS, to control the DDL scripts for these objects.**

# Server Error auditing

Although it may not be strictly necessary to audit the errors encountered by the Oracle server, the recording of this information may provide clues on potential threats. Oracle audits errors through an event named *servererror*, which triggers a piece of code. An example will help to clarify.

```
create or replace trigger
   log_errors_trig
after servererror on database
declare
   var_user       varchar2(30);
   var_osuser     varchar2(30);
   var_machine    varchar2(64);
   var_process    varchar2(12);
   var_program    varchar2(64);
begin
```

```
   select
      username,
      osuser,
      machine,
      process,
      program
   into
      var_user,
      var_osuser,
      var_machine,
      var_process,
      var_program
   from
      v$session
   where
      audsid=userenv('sessionid');
   insert into
      servererror_log
   values(
      dbms_standard.server_error(1),
      sysdate,
      var_user,
      var_osuser,
      var_machine,
      var_process,
      var_program);
end;
/
```

After this trigger populates the *servererror_log* table, a complete report on the potential threats, etc. can be obtained. An example of the report is shown below.

```
                                                                  Error
Date      MESSAGE                                                 Count
------- ------------------------------------------------- --------
03-08    ORA-02289: sequence does not exist                       2,421
         ORA-01001: invalid cursor                                  480
         ORA-00054: resource busy and acquire with NOWAIT s         114
         ORA-00942: table or view does not exist                     39
         ORA-00942: table or view does not exist                     10
         ORA-01017: invalid username/password; logon denied           2
         ORA-00920: invalid relational operator                       1
         ORA-01445: cannot select ROWID from a join view wi           1

03-09    ORA-01001: invalid cursor                                   25
         ORA-02289: sequence does not exist                          12
         ORA-00942: table or view does not exist                     11
         ORA-00054: resource busy and acquire with NOWAIT s          10
         ORA-01017: invalid username/password; logon denied           2
```

Note the error encountered: "ORA-02289: sequence does not exist". This simply indicates that a user tried to select a sequence for which they were unauthorized. Most likely it is due to the user mistyping the name of the sequence, but it could be the result of someone trying to access the sequence without knowing the name, potentially a malicious attempt. An analysis of the audit report will help to identify the attacker.

In Chapter 9 on Trigger Auditing, detailed scripts will be provided to accomplish this.

 **Always audit any errors encountered by the Oracle server.**

# Program Source Auditing

Most auditing requirements deal with data changes or structural changes. However, in most cases the data changes occur inside a code segment such as a stored procedure. The audit data indicates that a user executed the procedure - but what if the logic inside the procedure is changed? This is a very common incident. Stored programs can change, either knowingly or unknowingly, and affect data changes, but the changes are difficult to track. Therefore, there is a need to record any changes to these program sources, too.

HIPAA rules mandate that any changes in the execution of code that can potentially change the way data is manipulated be tracked. This means that all the code, including the code outside the database, should be subjected to audit. The code outside the database, such as Java, C, or other code, may not be controlled by the DBA. The code residing within the database, however, can be easily tracked for changes.

An excerpt from an example report is provided below.

```
Date        DDL     Object   Object
of DDL      User    Operatio Type          Name
----------- ------  -------- ------------ ---------------------
05-21 09:00  CLAIMS  CREATE   PACKAGE      CLAIMS.UPDATE_CLAIM
             CLAIMS  CREATE   PACKAGE BODY CLAIMS.UPDATE_CLAIM
             MEMBERS ALTER    PACKAGE BODY MEMBERS.UPDATE_MEMBERS
             MEMBERS ALTER    PACKAGE      MEMBERS.UPDATE_MEMBERS

05-21 09:33  MEMBERS CREATE   PACKAGE      MEMBERS.UPDATE_PROFILE
             MEMBERS CREATE   PACKAGE BODY CLAIMS.UPDATE_ PROFILE
             CLAIMS  ALTER    PACKAGE BODY CLAIMS.UPDATE_CLAIM
             CLAIMS  ALTER    PACKAGE      CLAIMS.UPDATE_CLAIM
```

The regular Oracle auditing features are not useful to track these changes. The same system level triggers as discussed in DDL auditing track these changes. In Chapter 9, we will explore in detail how to set these up and use them to audit the code changes.

**Always use system level triggers to audit changes to the code of stored programs like procedures, packages, functions, type bodies, and even triggers themselves.**

# Grant Auditing

Remember, in the museum, the guards have been given permission to access any room and enter any area at any time. A typical guard may not be assigned keys to get into a specific room; rather just a master key to get into all rooms in the museum. If a guard enters a room using the master key, the action should also be recorded.

In the database, the equivalent of unlimited access to any room is the ability to select data from any table unrestrictedly. In Oracle, this is known as SELECT ANY TABLE privilege. Note the use of the key word ***any***; it simply means the privileged user can select anything from any table, including tables owned by other users and system-owned tables and views. Similar privileges exist for selection from views, snapshots, and sequences, and for a wide range of operations like deletion, update, etc.

What can a user do with the unlimited grants given? Pretty much anything. The privileges granted to the user to control access are irrelevant in this context. Therefore, this type of access must be carefully audited. Oracle provides auditing options to record object accesses only with this privilege. The audit trail can be examined to see what kind of objects the user is accessing. Later, using the information, the user can be given appropriate grants.

It must be said, however, that ideally no user should have this kind of privilege. If a user requests selection from data dictionary tables and views, the role *select_catalog_role* can be granted, which enables him or her to select from the data dictionary views.

> **Always audit the use of the ANY-type system privilege. Better yet, do not grant such a privilege to anyone.**

# Auditing Distributed Databases

Another topic of interest in implementing a secured and auditable database for HIPAA lies in the area of distributed databases. One database is connected to another through a network. A special object called a database link is created that roams the network and can access the other database as if it were locally available.

For instance, a database can be for claims information only, perhaps called *claimsdb*. The other database, named *memberdb*, houses the member-related information. A key table in *memberdb* is *members*, which holds the Social Security Number of the members. An application can connect to the claimsdb database and do its work. What happens when the application needs to read some member data? It can connect to the memberdb database and read from it, but that will create unnecessary complexity. Another way to do this is to use a database link from claimsdb to memberdb, and the user called JUDY can issue a statement like

```
select ssn from members@memberdb;
```

Note the use of an @ sign followed by a name *memberdb*. Actually, the name followed by the @ sign is the name of the database link, not the name of the database. This link is created by

```
create public database link memberdb using 'memberdb';
```

The user Judy must be present in the memberdb database, too. When the select statement is issued, the user temporarily connects to the memberdb database from the claimsdb using this link. Therefore, the user Judy must have privileges to access the member table on the host database. When the select statement is issued, the auditing, if enabled, will record that Judy accesed the members table on memberdb database.

Another way a database link can be defined is

```
create public database link memberdb
connect to claimuser identified by chaigaram
using 'memberdb';
```

Note the use of a userid and password. In this case, when Judy uses

```
select ssn from members@memberdb;
```

she actually connects to the memberdb database using the id CLAIMUSER, not JUDY. Therefore, the audit record indicates that CLAIMUSER, not JUDY accessed the table. This is an important concept to understand.

The general advice is not to use the database links with the username and password embedded, rather use the ones without any username/password combination. The auditing can then be set up more rigorously.

 **Do not use database links with embeded userids. Instead, set links up without userids, so that they will execute under the calling user's security profile and be recorded by the audit.**

## Security for remote data devices

For remote laptop notebook computers that contain classified data (military secret data, confidential corporate data) you should require that the remote devices that will allow mobile processing of government tasks with complete and absolute data security. These devices must have the following characteristics:

- **Oracle Integration** – The devices must have software to synchronize the remote device with the master database. At network connection time the device must push-out all updates from the device, manage possible data collisions, and pull-in any new data in a single transaction.
- **Classified-level Security** – The device must utilize Oracle secure encryption (the *dbms_crypto* package) to protect the data. The device must transport the end-user directly into the APEX application upon biometric confirmation and have all other Windows functions disabled. The device must be useless for any other purpose than using the application.
- **Standard Browser Display** – The device screen must support an HTML complaint browser for APEX display. An additional benefit of a laptop with a larger display is that the applications will not have to be redesigned to render on a small PDA screen.
- **Identity Management** – The devices must support a biometric fingerprint reader as the only supported log-in interface and a built-in camera to record the face of the end-user. One current problem with the finger scanners is that

they will work with a severed finger, allowing access if the end-user is terminated.

- **Camera** – The devices must have a built-in camera to allow the end-user to take photographs of the end-user and capture them into the remote Oracle database.
- **Durability** – The ideal device must be able to withstand harsh treatment and be immune to corrosive salt air, extreme temperatures and extreme humidity. The device must also be able to operate for extended periods in temperatures exceeding 95 degrees Fahrenheit.
- **Theft deterrent** – The devices will contain a permanent engraved message warning potential thieves of the hazards of stealing the device. Something like; *"This is an official government device and unauthorized possession carries a mandatory prison term and a free trip to Gitmo. This device is useless for any function other than its application."*

# Fine Grained Auditing

In regular object-based auditing, the records can show that a user selected from a specific table, along with other helpful information such as timestamp, client machine name, etc. What it does not record is what data the user selected from the table, for instance, when the claim analyst Judy reads the record containing claims for John Q. Public's visit to the allergist, the usual auditing records the fact that Judy selected from the CLAIMS table. However, it does not record which particular record was selected. Since reading is not a *transaction*, the facts are not recorded in Oracle' redo logs, rollback segments or anywhere else. However, HIPAA regulations require that this be audited.

Prior to Oracle 9i, this information was impossible to obtain. In Oracle 9i, there is a very useful feature called **Fine Grained Auditing** (FGA) that can record not only which table was selected, but also what the user was looking for. The information captured is extensive, including the exact SQL statement the user issued, the time of issue, along with most other information that regular audits capture.

All of this audit information is stored in a table named *dba_fga_audit_trail*, which can be queried to find out who selected what. Here is a partial example of such a report:

```
TIMESTAMP     DBUSER OSUSER CLIENT SCHEMA SQL STATEMENT
------------- ------ ------ ------ ------ ------------------------
7/15/03 12:54 JUDY   judy   jdunks CLAIMS select * from claims
                                          where claim_id = 123456
7/15/03 13:05 NATHAN judy   jdunks CLAIMS select * from claims
```

```
                                            where claim_amt > 1200
7/15/03 14:14 JUDY    lane    lwills CLAIMS select * from claims
                                            where paid_amt > 1100
```

Let's analyze the report. The first line indicates the database user JUDY (as shown under the DBUSER column) issued the statement "select * from claims, where the claim_id = 123456" at 12:54 PM on 7/15/03, which triggered the audit record to be generated.

The actual user logged into the client machine named JDUNKS (as indicated by the CLIENT column) under the name JUDY (as indicated by OSUSER column). The select statement retrieved the table under the schema owner CLAIMS (as shown by the SCHEMA column). The schema owner column is important, since the user JUDY may have had a private synonym for CLAIMS defined at that time which might have pointed to a table under another schema owner.

The second line is a little more interesting. The user who issued the query was NATHAN, but the OS User is still JUDY and it is the *same* client machine. What could be the explanation? Could it be possible that Nathan stepped into Judy's office while she was away and issued the query from her PC? Or, is there a simpler explanation – Nathan was near Judy's desk and Judy asked him to issue the query, since she was not authorized to do it herself? Both are possible, and the audit trails provide ample information to help the investigation.

Let's examine the third line. It shows JUDY issued the query, but look at the client name and the OS user – they are LWILLS and LANE, respectively. The OS user ID LANE is not used by Judy and the PC LWILLS is not the PC she uses. So, could it be possible that her database password has been stolen by Lane, who issued this query? Or, is it simply Judy who issued the query from Lane's PC since the latter was not authorized to look at those claims?

Paranoids may propose another theory – it was actually Nathan who stole Judy's database password and ran the query on Lane's PC when she was away! Regardless of what the theories are, all possibilities are to be checked and the information inside the Fine Grained Audit trails provides enough material to aid the privacy breach investigation.

However, it may not be advisable to audit all types of data selection from the table. For instance, if a user selects a total of claims amounts in all claims, the statement may not be relevant for security audits. However, if the selection is the Social Security Number, a component of protected health information, then auditing is necessary.

Another variation of this type is the necessity to audit only when a specific column value is selected, for instance, selecting claims of procedure codes for HIV. Since HIV is a PHI, the action must be audited. However, if the user selects claims of procedure code for the common cold, there is no need to audit anything. This selective recording of access information can be easily set up using FGA.

Since FGA is the best tool a DBA has to immediately implement most of the HIPAA and other privacy requirements, the tool and other aspects will be discussed in detail in Chapter 11.

The biggest challenge to FGA is the need to have identifiable individual users in the database issuing these queries. If several real-life users use the same user ID to access the database, then the database will record all actions as coming from the same user, hiding who actually issued the query. This defeats the purpose and utility of the FGA.

Therefore, to be effective, all real-life users must connect to the database using their individual user IDs, not via a shared user ID. The use of a shared user ID is shunned in the HIPAA regulations anyway, so individual user IDs satisfy both requirements.

This is perhaps easier said than done. An application that needs to be HIPAA-compliant may have originally been developed using the bad practice of assigning a single user ID shared by several real-life users who are authenticated by the application. For instance, a user called JUDY is authenticated by the application, which then connects to the database as user APPUSER. Another user NATHAN then logs in to the application, which connects to the database also as APPUSER. Therefore, for the database, both connections are from the same user – APPUSER, not from different users JUDY and NATHAN. So, the use of FGA is useless here.

In Chapter 11, we will explain a trick to get around this problem using something known as an *application context*.

Another important question is how do we handle data changes in FGA? For example, a column in a table for a particular row may have a value of 15. The user selected that and saw 15. The fact that the user selected the data was recorded. Later the value was changed to 20. When the audit records are examined the fact that the user selected and saw the field will be revealed, but not what the user saw. If a query is made at that time, the result will show 20. Therefore, the important question to answer is *what* the user saw, not what the value is *now*. The security policy may require that, too.

In chapter 11, we will examine this problem and offer a solution using another Oracle feature called *flashback queries*, along with FGA. The chapter will provide complete scripts that can be reused in your environment.

**Use Fine Grained Auditing to identify which SQL statement was issued to view data.**

## Archiving Audit Data

After this unfortunate incident, the museum staff places surveillance cameras in the exhibit handling room, just like the ones in visitor areas. These images are fed to a central monitoring room where they are continuously viewed by security personnel for possible problems. Along with the viewing, the images are also recorded onto tapes attached to the system via a Video Cassette Recorder. When a tape is complete, it is rewound and reused.

What happens when there is a need to examine some recording two days ago? Unfortunately, the tape is overwritten, and the information is lost. In other words, the used auditing information is archived off. To prevent this, the tapes could simply be preserved and a fresh tape used every time.

The size of the data in the audit trail, no matter how it is collected, grows with time. This requires periodic purging so that the size is manageable. However, the old purged data can't just be thrown away in most cases, it might be useful for analysis later. It is archived off before being purged. Typically, the archival is done in some offline storage media like magnetic tape, CD-ROM, or an offsite disk pool such as *Network Attached Storage.*

In Chapter 8, we will discuss the ways to archive and purge the audit data, and provide scripts to setup and display the audit information.

**Set up clear archival and purge routines for the collected auditing data.**

## Auditing Database Log Files

All the audit options described above are based on database objects – be they tables, views, sequences, or any other type. However, another place where audit data can be found is in a set of various log files the Oracle RDBMS and other processes produce.

The Oracle database creates a log file of its activity called *alert log.* Any time a specific database maintenance activity occurs, a record is written into this file. These events include adding a data file, adding or dropping a tablespace, etc. The information in the log file should be preserved to maintain a record of when certain events occur. In subsequent chapters, we will explore the details of this auditing activity.

When the DBA user connects to Oracle without specifying a password, the activity creates a trace file. This type of trace file is very useful in determining who connects as the DBA user and when. In Oracle 9i, it is possible to audit actions by the super user *sys*; so that any action by the DBA can also be recorded.

 **Religiously preserve alert log files of the database instance and back them up.**

# Auditing Network Access

Oracle*Net (also known as SQL*Net or Oracle*Net) creates certain log files during its operation. A prominent one is produced by the listener process, which records the incoming requests for connection, as well as the status, i.e. whether or not those requests are successful. This can be very useful in analyzing database connections.

In subsequent chapters, we will discuss in detail the location, name and content of these files, and how to check them for access and malicious usage. In particular, we will discuss how to audit attempts to break the listener password to mount common attacks, such as buffer overflow.

 **Inspect and preserve network access logs.**

# Auditing Materialized Views

The cafeteria at the museum serves a special type of drink called *Jurassic Whirlwind*, which is a blend of orange soda, limejuice and vanilla ice cream. This is such a hit that the cafeteria staff can't keep up with the demand. To reduce the long lines, they begin preparing the blend in advance and putting it in a self-service vending machine for the customers. The customers have a choice – they can get it from the machine or wait in front of the counter as in the past.

Once, after drinking the concoction from the vending machine, someone got sick. The resulting investigation discovered that the limejuice used in the vending machine was bad. Why wasn't the drink prepared at the counter bad? The answer is simple – the drink from the counter was a freshly prepared one, whereas the vending machine drink was prepared earlier.

In the previous chapter, we discussed a new type of object called a view. We also hinted at another type of object called a *Materialized View* (MV). The MV is not just a query, but the actual data retrieved by the query that is stored in a container similar to a table. This is analogous to the premixed drink in the vending machine, as opposed to the fresh mix from the counter.

The users, instead of executing the complicated and time-consuming query (i.e. waiting in line to get the mix from the counter), select a similar set of data from the MV (i.e. from the vending machine), but with the risk that the data might not be current. Nevertheless, note the important difference – an MV is a query that was executed and the data was saved for later retrieval. When the user queries the MV, he or she sees the data that was retrieved earlier, not at that instant.

Materialized views serve a very important role in Oracle databases. They can offer query rewrite capabilities, where the RDBMS engine *rewrites* a query if it is similar to the definition of the MV. This property of the MV is very useful in data warehouses. Even if not used for query rewrite, MVs can save time by executing the query once and saving the results for future user access, although the data is stale. The MV can be refreshed from time to time.

Because the data is not up to date, the data the user sees depends heavily on the time the MV is created or refreshed. This may sound irrelevant, but consider a situation where the patient record shows that the patient has a common cold. This is not a piece of protected health information and, therefore, the MV is refreshed with this information. Later, the diagnosis is changed to HIV, and this record becomes part of PHI. The subsequent refresh of the MV does not pick the record up. What about some user who accesses the MV between the first and the second refresh – could that user possibly see the patient's record? Yes, he or she could. But, if the user accesses the MV after the second refresh, the patient's record would not be present.

This indicates why it is important to record the time when the refresh is performed – it indicates the nature of the data that was visible to the users at a given time. This type of auditing is not usually set up by DBAs, but it is important to consider recording the refresh times. In subsequent chapters, we will examine the ways to do that along with scripts.

 **Always audit Materialized View refreshes to check the nature of the data at the time of the refresh.**

## Auditing Replication

Along the lines of MV, there is another way data can be transferred for separate manipulation at a different site. The process of maintaining a data image in another database is known as **replication**. For instance, to decrease the load on the production database, the data can be replicated to a different database, and a reporting application can run from there.

The same problem with timing of the refresh comes into play here. The data at the replicated site is not as current as the master site. It is as current as the last time it was refreshed. Therefore, a careful analysis of when it was refreshed must be maintained to identify the nature of the data visible at a certain time.

In subsequent chapters, we will discuss these in detail with scripts to help the user set up the auditing as fast as possible.

 **Replication refreshes must be audited at the time of the refresh.**

## Managing the audit trail

If the audit trail record cannot be written, the audited action will not be executed and errors will be generated. If connections are being audited and the audit trail table (SYS.AUD$) is full, users will not be allowed to log in to the database. The DBA can AS SYSDBA using Server Manager in either GUI or command-line mode to clean out the audit trail.

You should develop an auditing strategy by evaluating the purpose of the auditing and be conservative in the auditing performed. When auditing is being set to investigate possible problems, begin with general auditing and then narrow it down to specific actions. If the purpose of the audit is to provide a record of historical activity, remember to archive (to another table or an export file) and purge data on a regular basis. You can selectively insert records to another table if only a subset needs to be maintained.

Take these recommended steps to truncate the audit trail:

1. Copy any subset of records you may need to keep into a temporary table, or export the entire SYS.AUD$ table.

2. CONNECT INTERNAL.

3. Truncate the SYS.AUD$ table.

4. Insert records from the temporary table back into SYS.AUD$.

To protect the audit trail, AUDIT insert, update, and delete on SYS.AUD$ BY ACCESS (or in whichever user you have created the AUD$ table) so that records cannot be added, changed, or deleted without that action being audited. Even if a user is able to delete records from SYS.AUD$, he or she will not be able to delete the records generated by his or her actions without creating additional audit records. In addition, users should not be granted DELETE ANY TABLE system privilege. Always protect the audit trail (SYS.AUD$).

The maximum size allowed for an audit trail written to the database is determined at the time the database is created. By default, the size reflects the system tablespace default values. The sql.bsq script, which is executed when the database is created, sets the size of the SYS.AUD$ table. It is very important that the audit trail be cleaned up regularly. You should export the data and truncate the SYS.AUD$ table on a regular basis.

If you want to implement processes such as notification when a user logs on, checking of passwords, automated invalidation of passwords, and you don?t have Oracle8 or later, you will want to move the AUD$ table out of the SYS user so that triggers can be created against it. By creating an ON INSERT trigger that monitors for specific event codes in the AUD$ table, you can then use that trigger to implement specific database actions.

Follow these steps to create the AUD$ table in a different user:

1. Turn off auditing.

2. Export the current records in the AUD$ table.

3. Drop the SYS.AUD$ table.

4. Create the new AUD$ table either under SYS in a different tablespace or as a different user.

5. If step 4 created an AUD$ table in a different user, grant all on that AUD$ to SYS user.

6. If step 4 created an AUD$ table in a different user, create a private synonym, AUD$, pointing to that user?s AUD$ table in the SYS user.

# Summary

Let's briefly summarize what we explored in this chapter regarding auditing requirements to satisfy HIPAA, and the options available in Oracle.

- Recording of users' activity inside the database is known as auditing.
- In Oracle, several types of auditing are available to satisfy different requirements.
- The simplest one, AUDIT, is used to record simple auditing events such as a table was selected, a procedure was executed, etc. The timestamp, the user ID, the client machine name, logging off time, etc., are recorded. It does not capture the information on the exact records of the table the user accessed.
- To record the exact rows the user accessed in a table, along with the exact statement issued, a powerful feature called Fine Grained Auditing (FGA) is used. This is available in Oracle 9i and above.
- The changes to the structure of the database objects should be audited, and there is no direct way to do it in Oracle using AUDIT. System triggers, however, can allow such auditing to be implemented.
- The program code inside the database should also be protected by an audit trail. Again, system triggers can allow such auditing to be implemented.
- Some changes inside the database can be tracked using the tool LogMiner. This feature was introduced in Oracle8i and greatly improved in Oracle9i.
- The audit trail grows in size tremendously, affecting performance and creating space shortage. This calls for regular purging of old data and archiving off the purged data for future access.
- Network access should also be audited and the data preserved. The network access is recorded in the log file of the Oracle listener.
- Some database structural changes, such as dropping a tablespace, are also recorded in the log file of the database known as alert log. The information from this file should be preserved as audit data.
- Materialized Views (also known as Snapshots) are refreshed periodically by users, and since they are accessed by users for data, the information regarding the time

of refresh, etc. must be recorded. There is no direct way to do so, but it can be done using scripts provided in this book.

- Replication presents a problem for the auditors in determining what the data value was at a certain time. Therefore, the information regarding the refresh time of the replicated objects should be recorded. Although there is no direct way to do so, this can be accomplished by using the scripts provided in this book.
- Distributed databases pose some problem in identifying which user actually used the link to connect and access objects. The privileges are based on the user that connects to the remote database, not the local database. Similarly, the auditing is also recorded as if it came from the remote user, not local.

# Conclusion

This wraps up our general discussion on Oracle Security and Auditing options and capabilities. The discussion was deliberately kept non-technical and less detailed to give an overview of the process, and let the user connect the requirements to the practice. In the next two sections, we will cover the details of these methods and the tools to accomplish them.

Section II

# Security

# General Oracle Security

CHAPTER

In Chapter 2, we were introduced to the land of Oracle security, but we merely skimmed over the surface. In this section we will explore security options and methods in detail, and how they can be applied to the compliance of HIPAA regulations.

In the sections that follow, we will examine each fundamental area of the Oracle security framework, along with scripts that you can readily use. While browsing these sections, please bear in mind that the focus is on HIPAA regulations. However, since security is also a very common aspect of any database, some generalization is also used.

## Physical Security

As explained earlier, the first level of security should be isolating the physical machine that houses the database, application server, network server, DNS server, etc. from the regular users. This approach is procedural rather than technical, and most security conscious organizations are already employing physical security measures.

Generally, the servers are secured in a room, typically called a server room, or a more esoteric data center (a euphemism carried over from the mainframe era). The room typically has a door that is secured by an electronic key. Either an authentication card, or a numeric keypad on which the user has to punch the correct key combination, or both, can open the door.

The need for this type of security stems from the fact that a person with malicious intent may need access to the machine in order to perform his or her tasks. In UNIX, a shutdown may require physical access to the server console. Of course, this is true only if the server is set up that way, which should be the case. In Windows, a server normally cannot be shutdown without access to the server itself. Sometimes this is not true - servers may have cards already built in that allow the administrator to login and power up/down the server.

Sometimes a perpetrator may decide to wreak havoc by unplugging the power cord from the server, forcing it to reboot. Even if the data center has an Uninterruptible

Power Supply (USP), the cord that powers the server itself is disconnected. Simply barring physical contact with the server can prevent this type of hacking or abuse.

The next question probably comes from this explanation – is this necessary? Let's examine some of the potential cases of server shutdown without proper notice.

When a hacker tries to shutdown a server, several potential threats are possible. For example, if an intruder wants to update some system parameter, or create a user, modify a user, open up a firewall port, or something else, he or she has to access the console and change it. The console may not require a super user (root) password to be entered, and therefore the intruder has a free hand in the abuse. Some system parameter changes can take effect only after a reboot, and the hacker makes sure that it happens.

What else? If the server houses a database, the hacker can gain access to an Oracle account without knowing the password, and simply gain access to the *dba* account (without knowing the password)! After that, he or she can pretty much do anything – add users, drop users, change data – the list is endless!

Even a simple unplanned server shutdown may affect processing in a large way. When a server shuts down, the transactions that are not committed are rolled back (after the server comes back up). In some systems, that may not be acceptable.

For instance, in one system the author worked with, the claim data from the providers arrived in batches. A claim may come twice in normal processing, in which case the second one is called a second version, but the prior one is also stored. If the transaction aborts, the claim may be inserted again, and thus may be erroneously labeled as a second version. In any case, the processing is affected and the system suffers a general outage.

## Biometric Devices

For more stringent security requirements, other types of authentication mechanisms employing biometric devices can be used. Biometric devices were somewhat immature about three years ago. Today, technology enhancements have made these devices quite viable, both financially and technologically.

Technologies such as fingerprint scanners are available now in mass scale at a very attractive price. Typically, the user swipes his or her card, enters a pass code on a numeric keypad, and then places his or her index finger on a scanner. The scanner technology, rather the print matching technology, still has some kinks to be worked out, but the combination of pass code, the swiped identity card, and the scanner provide good accuracy of authentication. The error is mostly on the false negative side, meaning the system might not authenticate a legitimate person, rather than a false positive, where an illegitimate person is authenticated.

The other types of biometric devices becoming increasingly common are retina scanners and voice pattern recognition systems. The retina scanners scan the retina of a person for a pattern. The retina of each human being is different, much like fingerprints. While fingerprints can be tampered with, or give false readings due to smudged fingertips, the retinal scan is quite infallible. Voice pattern matching technology is still in its infancy. A person's voice, no matter how muffled or temporarily altered by cold, has a unique signature pattern that can be detected. This technology identifies that signature and compares against the stored pattern.

## Multiple Server Areas

Sometimes, the organization may have several different departments with different levels of security requirements. For instance, the medical records department, subject to HIPAA, may require higher security than the data warehouse application.

Therefore, the same level of physical protection need not be provided to all the servers and machines. If that is the case, the best thing to do is segregate the servers according to their security needs, and have them in different rooms or enclosures, as described in Figure 4.1 below.

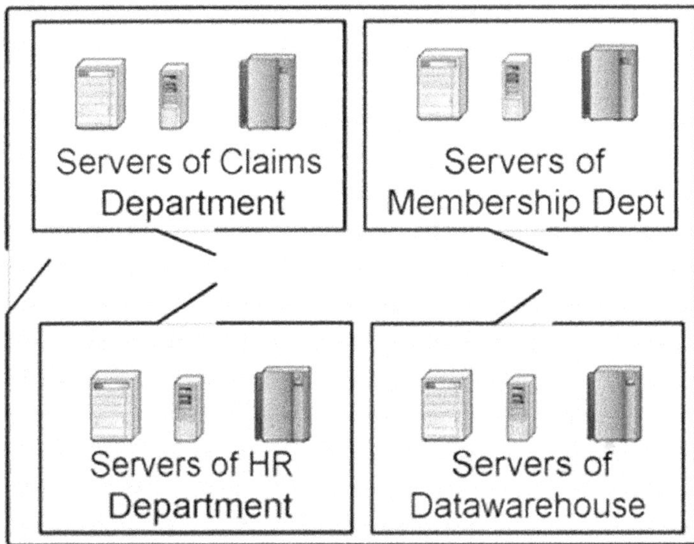


**Figure 4.1** *Security Segregation of Multiple Server Groups*

Each of these should have a specific level of security clearance requirement, and that should be enforced by the keypads on the doors or the other authentication devices described earlier.

HIPAA requirements clearly state that the physical security of the servers be enforced. It does not prescribe the level of isolation of servers based on security, but it does recommend it. Either way, the best approach to security can be implemented by setting aside a non-regular area, secured by some sort of authentication device, which could be as simple as a padlock or as sophisticated as a retina scanner. The use of an automated system is preferred because it also records who went in and came out. This is especially important during investigations.

### Important Points

- Physically isolate servers in a secured enclosure
- Enforce some type of authentication mechanism to allow legitimate users to enter the enclosure
- If needed, separate groups of servers with varying security requirements into separate secured enclosures

## Firewalls

Firewalls offer a logical barrier to external user accesses. Most of the servers inside a company's internal network should not be accessed by outside users. Therefore, they are secured inside a barrier that prevents any kind of access to the machines from outside the company.

However, certain users from outside need access to the servers or clients inside. For instance, when users access an external website, the web server must send the http requested file to the client that requested it. This requires that the firewall open a certain port. Typically, this port is 80, the well-known port for http access. The firewall inspects all traffic passing through this port, and anything other than http traffic is blocked, fearing a potential threat.

In some cases, users may need to send files to and receive files from external entities. These may be done through the ftp protocol. The transfer of these files requires more ports to be opened up, for the ftp traffic. When the port is opened, what is the guarantee that these ports will not be used for attacks by hackers?

There is no guarantee, therefore, the opening of such a port should not be allowed. To facilitate the transfer of files, another method is employed. A server is placed outside the firewall that serves as a recipient and sender machine. The ports on this machine can be opened to external users where the ftp can take place. This external server is then accessed from internal clients, and the file is transferred to them. The special place outside the firewall is known as the *Demilitarized Zone* (DMZ).

Figure 4.2 illustrates the concept of firewalls and DMZ.

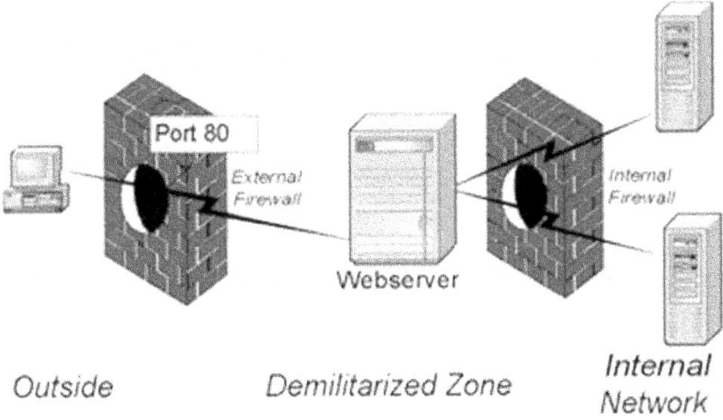


**Figure 4.2** *Firewalls and Demilitarized Zones*

Sometimes, this process is rather complicated, especially in cases where the file transfer is rather regular. In those cases, instead of establishing the server in the DMZ, the external users directly interact with the servers inside the firewall. Instead of using the regular ports for ftp, they use a different port for a different type of ftp, known as *Secure FTP* (sftp or ftps). A similar concept exists for http traffic in a secured manner, known as *secured http* (https).

What if the company's web server interacts with the database server during the normal course of business? Shouldn't the ports of the database be open outside the firewall for these accesses?

Not at all. The architecture should be designed in such a way that the database server never has any ports open to the firewall. All application traffic has to come to the application server, which should then connect to the database server using the port defined by the listener. The only allowable connection to the database server must be from the application server using the listener port (1521, usually; but it can be changed). If the architecture enables the access of this port by the external users and machines, seriously consider changing it. The preferred architecture is shown in Figure 4.3.

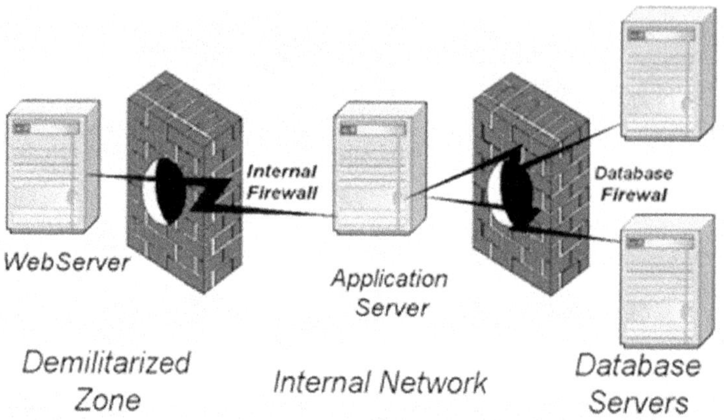


**Figure 4.3:** *Optimal application server, database server interaction*

Some companies utilize more than one firewall – one encompassing all the machines in the network, and the other protecting the most important ones inside this firewall. Examples include a database server, a document server containing important documents, such as claims records, etc.

Generally, the port 80 is used for http traffic. Besides this port, no other ports need be opened to carry out the normal operation of business. If open, they will invite hackers to get in through an unsecured doorway. Therefore, they should be completely closed off.

This type of setup may need some tweaking to allow the application server to connect to the database server. This will be discussed in Chapter 7, under Network Security.

## The Important points

- Always use a firewall.
- If needed, use a firewall around the vulnerable servers like the database server.
- Open only those ports needed for business, no more than that.
- The outside users should never connect from the firewall directly.
- Use a Demilitarized Zone, if convenient.
- Otherwise, use secured ftp and http.

# Operating System Security

The database resides on a server that runs an operating system. The most important task after securing the server behind the firewall is to secure the operating system. The Oracle database runs on the operating system and certain vulnerabilities in the OS will reduce the security of the database to naught. In this section, we will discuss these vulnerabilities and how to protect against them.

Although Oracle software is designed to run on a variety of hardware and operating systems, from DOS all the way to mainframes, most shops use UNIX or one of its variants, such as Solaris, Tru64, HPUX, AIX, Dynix, etc. Therefore, we will focus our attention on the UNIX and clone operating systems only.

## Security in UNIX Environment

In UNIX, the Oracle software is installed under a UNIX user, typically named oracle. The user generally belongs to a group called DBA. The user also belongs to the group OINSTALL.

### File Permissions

The first thing to check in a database server is the file permissions. Before specifying what they should be, let's brush up our knowledge of the permissions in UNIX and how they work. Each file in UNIX can be subject to three operations - reading, writing, and executing. Every file has an owner. The permissions are defined on three sets of users - the owner of the file, the other members belonging to the group to which the file belongs, and finally, the rest of the users of that server. The permissions of a file are represented in UNIX via a set of letters. If the following commands are given

```
ls -l
```

The output will be something like this

```
-rwxr-xr--   1 oracle   dba        24608 Mar  4 03:06 osh
```

The first set of columns containing the letters r, x, and w - denotes the permissions of the file named *osh*. Let's dissect the permissions string to decode what it means.

The letters mean the permission types

- r – read

- w – write
- x – execute

The first character denotes the type of the file. In this case this is a "-", indicating the fact that the file is a regular file. If this were a directory, this column would have shown the letter "d".

The next three characters show the permissions set for the owner of the file. The permissions are set in the format "rwx". If a particular permission is not available to that grantee, then it is denoted by a hyphen, "-". In this case, the letters are "rwx", which means that the owner of the file, the user oracle, has the permission to read, write, and execute it.

The next three characters show the permissions given to the group. In this case, they are "r-x", and it indicates that the members of the group DBA (which is the group of the file) can read and execute the file but cannot write to it.

The last three characters show the permissions given to the rest of the users (sometimes called world permissions). In this example, it shows "r--", which means the users have only read permission on the file, not write and execute.

Another special type of permission exists, called the *Set User ID Bit* (SUID). Let's see how this works. Sometimes the owner of a file needs to operate on other files owned by it, or to modify processes it started. This owner may want to allow other users to perform the same tasks, but not give them special permission for all of these files and processes. Instead, the owner may set a special flag to indicate that the execution of this file by another user should be as if he or she is executing it.

An example is the executable file oracle, which is executed on behalf of the user who is connected to the database. This special flag is called a Set User ID Bit. If this is set, the permissions look like this.

```
-rwsr-s--x  1 oracle  dba  82292320 Mar 17 16:12 oracle
```

Note the letter "s" in the third place on the permissions for both the user and the group, where the letter "x" should have been. For the user permission, this simply indicates that the user executing the file will execute it as per the permissions of the owner of the file, oracle. Similarly, for group permission, the group owner's permissions are set at runtime.

This SUID permission is extremely powerful and should not be granted lightly, in fact, it should be avoided if possible. The Oracle installation itself puts SUID on some files in the bin directory under Oracle Home. Find these files by running the following command

```
ls - l|grep rws
```

Examine these files and determine if the SIOD is necessary as per the following chart. All these files are in the $ORACLE_HOME/bin directory.

| FILE | OWNER | EXPLANATION |
|---|---|---|
| oracle | The Oracle software owner, typically oracle | This is the Oracle executable used by sessions to connect to the database. The SUID should be set. |
| dbsnmp | Root | This is an executable file for the Oracle Intelligent Agent. This is used by the Enterprise Manager as its agent process. If the agent is not utilized, then the suid on this file should be unset. |
| oidldapd | Oracle | This is the executable daemon for the Oracle Internet Directory (OID). If OID is used, then the SUID should be used, otherwise the SUID should be unset. |
| onrsd, namesctl | oracle | These are files used by Oracle Name Server. If Name Server is not used, then these files do not need to have the SUID set. |

**Table 4.1** *Files with SUID turned on*

Other than the files listed above, there should be no other files with the SUID bit set. If any file is found, immediately unset the SUID bit. After examining the above files, if you see that some files do not need to have their SUID bit on, turn them off as well.

Another important fact must be taken into account while examining these files. Most of the above files may have a file named after them, but with the numeral zero. For example, there could be a file called *dbsnmp0*, in addition to *dbsnmp*. When a new version is built, Oracle copies the old file *dbsnmp* to *dbsnmp0*, and recreates the *dbsnmp* file.

This is done to ensure that in case the new file building fails, the old file *dbsnmp0* can be renamed to *dbsnmp* and still be used. The old file *dbsnmp0* still exists with the suid bit on. This could be an important security hole exploited by a potential hacker. Therefore, the suid bit for the 0-suffixed files should be turned off.

The suid is turned off by the following command

```
chmod -s dbsnmp0
```

 **Tip: Turn off the SUID bit on all files except the most needed. The SUID bit should be tuned on for the file *oracle* in *$ORACLE_HOME/bin*. If Intelligent Agent is used, then the SUID should be on for the file *dbsnmp*; if Name Server is used then it should be on for *onrsd*; and if Oracle Internet Directory is used, then it should be turned on for the file *oidldapd*. All other files should have their SUID bits turned off.**

## Removing Permissions from Oracle Executable

In most Oracle installations, the default installation leaves the execute permissions for the *oracle* executable to *x*, i.e. executable by others. However, this creates a severe vulnerability. This allows anyone, including those not even connected with the Oracle database, such as GUEST or NOBODY, to run the program and create log files or at least corrupt some of them. Simply removing the Oracle executable permissions from others as follows can prevent this.

```
chmod o-x $ORACLE_HOME/bin/oracle
```

This will stop anyone other than the DBA group from executing the Oracle executable directly.

Resetting these permissions will result in any non-DBA user not being able to execute Oracle directly, and therefore being unable to connect to Oracle using the *Bequeth* adapter. This is definitely a *desirable* situation. Everyone should preferably connect through the listener, as you will see in Chapter 7, under Network Security. Removing this will force the users to connect using IPC, or even TCP/IP, where a detached process is created for each client process.

Here, the UNIX user NOBODY has tried to login to Oracle when the execute permissions for others have been removed from the Oracle executable.

```
mighty.proligence.com:/usr/users/nobody> sqlplus

SQL*Plus: Release 8.1.7.0.0 - Production on Thu Jul 10 15:20:21 2003

(c) Copyright 2000 Oracle Corporation.  All rights reserved.

Enter user-name: scott/tiger
ERROR:
ORA-12546: TNS:permission denied
```

Note the error: "ORA-12546: TNS:permission denied," meaning the execute on the Oracle executable failed. However, the connection is attempted now using a connect string, i.e. forcing it to go through the regular IPC or TCP/IP process.

```
Enter user-name: scott/tiger@claimdb

Connected to:
Oracle8i Enterprise Edition Release 8.1.7.4.0 - Production
With the Partitioning option
JServer Release 8.1.7.4.0 - Production

SQL>
```

The connection was successful.

 **Remove the execute permissions on Oracle executables from others as a precaution to prevent malicious use.**

## Filesystem Permissions

Oracle uses several filesystems to place a variety of files. We will assume here that the Oracle software owner is *oracle* and the primary group is *oinstall*, with other memberships in the group dba.

The directory where the Oracle software files are stored is called Oracle Home, identified as an environmental variable in UNIX labeled ORACLE_HOME.

Oracle itself recommends files be placed in a format called Oracle Flexible Architecture (OFA). This increases convenience, but at the cost of increased security risk. For that reason, we don't recommend following the OFA for your file placements. Rather we recommend the structure outlined in table 4.2

| FILESYSTEM | DESCRIPTION |
|---|---|

| FILESYSTEM | DESCRIPTION |
|---|---|
| 1 | Oracle Home, where the Oracle software code is stored. It also houses the directories used for background dump destination and core dump destination files. Should be owned by Oracle with permissions rwx for owner, r-x for group and --- (i.e. no permission) for others. |
| 2 | Trace Files are generated in the directory specified by the parameter *user_dump_dest.* This should be placed in a separate directory because sometimes the users might be given permission to read files from here. SQL Trace files are generated here, and any event setting causes files to be written here too. Therefore, this directory should be separate. It should be owned by Oracle, with rwx for owner, r-x for group and others.<br><br>Remember to update the initialization file of the instance to point the parameter *user_dump_dest* to this directory. |
| 3 | The user interaction directory is placed here. The files created using the package *utl_file* are generated in this directory. Since users will frequently read and write files in this directory, this should be separated. The directory should be owned by Oracle with permissions set for read, write and execute for everyone.<br><br>Please note then in Oracle 9i, the *utl_file* package does not need this parameter to be set in *init.ora* to manipulate a file. The DIRECTORY object can be dynamically created and used as the directory. Therefore, the days of this filesystem could be numbered. |

| FILESYSTEM | DESCRIPTION |
|---|---|
| 4 | The rest of the files contain the Oracle required files such as controlfiles, datafiles, redolog files, archived log files, etc. could be placed in a single filesystem or more. The permissions should be similar to the Oracle Home directory. |

**Table 4.2** *Filesystems and their recommended permissions*

We can't stress enough how important it is to set the permissions for Oracle database data files to 640 permission levels, i.e. no read access to others. A hacker could open these files using a hex editor, and try to read the files. It's difficult, but possible. In addition, these files could be copied over to a different server and be replicated.

**Tip: Make sure the *utl_file_dir* parameter in the database is not pointing to "*", i.e. to read and write anywhere Oracle has access to. Change permissions as described in the above table.**

## Other Settings Related to Filesystems

One of the most potentially damaging commands is the ability to create directories with the CREATE DIRECTORY command. A user can create a directory on any filesystem where Oracle has permission to create files. A malicious user can create a directory on some sensitive filesystem and then read or corrupt data on that using BFILE type files. This vulnerability does not seem to be quite understood, otherwise, it would be shut down immediately, and doing so is very easy. All you have to do is to remove the system privilege CREATE DIRECTORY from users.

**No regular user should have the CREATE DIRECTORY system privilege.**

The other problem is setting the parameter *_trace_files_public* in *init.ora* file to TRUE. The parameter is necessary, as some developers may want to create valid trace files such as *sql_trace*, or set events and analyze them in tools such as TKPROF. Ordinarily, these trace files are not readable by the public, therefore, the developers can't get them directly from here. Setting the *init.ora* parameter to TRUE will make them readable by all.

However, setting this to TRUE has serious consequences. The trace files are not only created from user actions such as setting *sql_trace*, but also by the database itself, triggered by setting events, errors or informational messages from other Oracle processes, such as fine grained access control (FGAC), etc.

This information is sensitive and should not be made available to anyone. For instance, a system dump may contain passwords changed in the last few minutes and that is exactly what the malicious user is after. The trace files are not public to prevent exactly these potential threats, and they should never be public. This is a reason why the parameter is an underscore, i.e. hidden one.

 **Do not set the parameter *_trace_files_public* to TRUE in *init.ora*.**

Sometimes hackers employ another tactic to get information. The trace file directories are mounted on another machine, or are shared by another host. This allows the hacker to gain access by simply checking the directory without even logging in to the server.

 **Never mount, share, or export the trace file directories.**

## *utl_file_dir* Wildcarding

The Oracle built-in package *utl_file* needs a special parameter named *utl_file_dir* that points to a directory on the *server*, not the client, where the files can be manipulated via the package. This directory should be such that the OS user ORACLE would be able to manipulate (read and write) files there. Instead of specifying a directory, a wild card character "*" can be entered that will allow manipulation of files in any directory. The wild card parameter is specified in the initialization file as

```
utl_file_dir = *
```

DBAs sometimes, mainly due to a lack of clear requirements, set this to * so that the developers can easily read and write files anywhere they want. Since changing this parameter needs a database recycle, the normal temptation is to set this wildcard. Nothing can potentially cause as much damage as this setting. Remember, the parameter signifies the directory that the Oracle software owner user can manipulate. This will allow a user to open up any file readable and writable by Oracle – including the datafiles! Even legitimate users without any malicious intent could inadvertently damage the files this way.

Therefore, never set the parameter to the lazy setting of *; always use a specific directory name, and that directory should not be one where the Oracle database sensitive files are present.

**Never set the initialization parameter *utl_file_dir* to "*".**

## SYS User Protection

The equivalent of a super user inside the Oracle database is SYS, who can perform any activity such as startup, shutdown, creating users, etc. Naturally, this user account must be protected very carefully, otherwise, a malicious person with the knowledge of this account can shutdown the entire database. However, under certain configurations, the password of the user need not be entered to login as SYS. If the UNIX user's group is DBA, the user can login as SYS using the following command

```
sqlplus "/ as sysdba"
```

Voila! The user is connected as sys without even knowing the password! Note how dangerous it is to leave the passwords of people who login to UNIX under group DBA unsecured. Therefore, be very careful in assigning UNIX users to the DBA group. Typically, you would create two groups

- dba
- oinstall

There should be separate users for the Oracle software installation and the Oracle account owner. In addition, you should also create separate users to manage the database, such as startup, shutdown, etc. These should not be controlled from the software owner or other Oracle users. Besides these users, the DBA group privileges should never be granted to anyone.

**Tip: The Oracle user should have the installed software only, nothing else; the other tasks, like starting up, shutting down, etc. should be performed by the individual dba user.**

## Showing the Process

When a user enters into sqlplus, the most likely way is issuing

```
sqlplus scott/tiger
```

Assuming, of course, that the user is SCOTT and the password is TIGER. However, if on another terminal, a user enters the following command

```
ps -aef|grep sqlplus
```

He will see this

```
sqlplus scott/tiger
```

The password of SCOTT is revealed. Clearly, this is a security hole. The users must be instructed never to use the password directly on the command line.

Either the following command should be used

```
sqlplus SCOTT
```

Oracle should prompt for a password which would then be entered,

Or

```
sqlplus /nolog
SQL> connect SCOTT/TIGER
```

Some other ways to connect from a program include

```
sqlplus /nolog << EOF
connect SCOTT/TIGER
… your sql statements go here
EOF
```

Similar warnings exist for other Oracle utilities such as export, import, SQL loader, and RMAN. Some programs written in Pro*C or Java may need the parameter to be passed in the command line. These also expose the password, and should be strictly prohibited. The programs or utilities will prompt for passwords if not supplied, and the password may be fed from a file via redirection (using the "<" character).

Sometimes we have found it useful to store the password in some secured file owned by the software owner, and readable only by the owner. Although it is not absolutely secure by any means, it's nevertheless a deterrent to theft.

Sometimes DBAs, the very people in charge of security, also make mistakes that expose the password. A common example is using the TKPROF tool. The DBA might give a command like this

```
tkprof tracefile.trc tkout.out explain=sys/changed
```

Note the use of the sys password for the explain clause. Although the explain clause needs a password, it can be given later during the prompt. In any case, unless the sys owned objects are explained, the user sys should never be used to explain the plan. Rather the application user should be used to explain the plan.

## Some Tips for Password Management

We need to have a solution to securely pass the password to the program to make it automated. Here are a few ways.

One option is to create an environmental variable, say, USERPASS passed to script as

```
sqlplus -s judy/$USERPASS @report
```

This is still vulnerable to attack via the /usr/ucb/ps command. The problem with environmental variables is they are visible to all users on the system, without the user having to hack into the environment. Executing

```
/usr/ucb/ps uxgaeww
```

shows all the environmental variables and the values used by all the users currently logged in to the system, including root's. The /usr/ucb/ps call is present for compatibility with BSD.

This variable may be set in a file that could be hidden. It's simple but not very secure. Another option is to create a file of passwords named *.passlist*. Note the period at the beginning. This makes the file invisible in a routine examination. This file has a permission set as 600, i.e. no privileges to anyone other than the owner. Here are the contents of the file

```
judy 5ucc355
nathan fr33w!113y
```

and so on. As you see, it has the usernames and passwords of all users. Next we will create a shell script to use this file named *.retrieve_password.sh*. Note the period at the beginning of the file. It makes it invisible in a regular *ls –l* command, too. Here is how the script looks.

```
fgrep $1 $HOME/.passlist | cut -d " " -f2
```

When the user issues sqlplus, he or she would issue

```
.retrieve_password.sh | sqlplus -s judy @report
```

The program will retrieve the password and feed it to the sqlplus executable. An execution of *ps –aef* on the UNIX prompt will not show the password.

**Tip: Make sure that no one types any kind of password in the command line. If passwords need to be passed from the command line, use a secured file to store the password and then use redirection to feed it to the program.**

## User Access Control

Once the machine is physically secured and the firewalls are protected, the next security vulnerability comes in the area of database access. The users need access to the database to perform their job functions.

When users wish to connect, the database makes sure that they are indeed authorized to access, a process known as *Authentication*. This can occur in several ways – the users could be defined as users in the database and then authenticated, or they may have been authenticated elsewhere and their credentials are passed on to the database as valid.

There are two ways the database authenticates users:

- By password
- By OS authentication

Let us discuss how they are different.

### By Password

A user is created in the database with a password as in the following SQL command.

```
create user judy
identified by judypass;
```

This creates a user in the database, specifically in the data dictionary table **USER$** owned by the user SYS. When the user wishes to connect to the database, he or she can do that with the user ID and the password as defined. The method of connection will vary from tool to tool. For instance in SQL*Plus, the user would connect as

```
connect judy/judypass
```

This is the most common use of authentication.

## By Operating System

Oracle provides another method to connect users using the authentication provided by the operating system, known as *ops$* accounts. In this case, the following parameters in the initialization file control the authentication process.

```
NAME                                 TYPE        VALUE
------------------------------------ ----------- -----
os_authent_prefix                    string      OPS$
remote_os_authent                    boolean     TRUE
os_roles                             boolean     TRUE
remote_os_roles                      boolean     TRUE
```

Note the use of *ops$* as the value of the operating system prefix. The user is created as

```
Create user ops$judy
Identified externally;
```

In this case, the user JUDY exists in the operating system and is authenticated there using a password, token card, or some other means. Oracle does *not* authenticate Judy, as indicated by the use of externally identified keywords. When Judy decides to connect, she issues

```
connect /
```

Note there is no password. Oracle assumes that the OS has properly authenticated Judy, so there is no need to authenticate further to access the database.

This is reminiscent of the old days, where the world was much more secure and servers were still islands unconnected by the internet. Hackers typically needed to get to the physical network to do the damage. The advent of the internet changed the rule. A hacker halfway around the world can launch an attack while sipping coffee in his basement. The intent of user access control is to place as many barriers to unauthorized access as possible.

It is probably unnecessary to show how dangerous the above practice is. If a malicious user ever gets into the operating system, getting into the database is easy. Of course, the security aspects of the underlying OS make the call – if it is substantially secure, then this type of authentication can be trusted. Otherwise, getting into the database is less of a challenge for a hacker.

Therefore, the OS Authorized accounts should be used with extreme caution. The usual rule of thumb is granting just enough privileges to the account to do the job, no more than that. Moreover, powerful accounts with sweeping privileges, such as DBA, alter system, etc. should never be able to be identified externally.

There are two types of authentication used externally – one is done on the same server, and the other is done outside the server. There are different levels of security requirements for each, so they will be discussed separately.

## Local OS Authentication

Many people aren't aware of the feature in the user creation process that can lead to security challenges. This is better explained through an example. Suppose the *os_authent_prefix* is *ops$* and a user is created as

```
create user OPS$SCOTT identified by TIGER;
```

This will create a user named OPS$SCOTT as a regular user. However, the use of OPS$ in the name makes it externally identifiable too. The OS user SCOTT can login as

```
sqlplus ops$scott/tiger
```

Or

```
sqlplus /
```

Note that the account can be accessed either way. Sometimes it may be desirable, but mostly it will add to confusion and create security holes. You should preferably have users who are authenticated by either the database or the OS, not both. However, there is no way to prevent the user OPS$SCOTT from logging in without supplying a password.

To alleviate the confusion, never use the IDENTIFIED BY *password* clause when the intention is to use an externally identified account. When the identification has to be done in the database, don't use the *ops$* in the name.

 **If the *os_authent_prefix* is "" (Null), then the OS Authenticated accounts cannot log in using the password. For instance, if the parameter is null, and a user SCOTT is defined as identified externally, then SCOTT has to login with "sqlplus /". If the user is created as "identified by tiger", then it's not an OS authenticated user, it's a regular user who must supply a password to login. This explains why Oracle recommends setting the parameter to null.**

If you must use OS Authorized accounts, make sure only the OS authorizes them, i.e. they can't login using a password. This setup will at least allow you to pursue security infrastructures where the OS authentication can be rigorously implemented. This can be accomplished by setting *os_authent_prefix* to "" (null).

## Remote OS Authentication

The above discussion was for users defined in the same server where the database resides. What about users in a separate server or a client machine that connects to the database server? This is controlled by the parameter *remote_os_authent.* If set to TRUE, remote users can connect to the database without supplying a password. This is shown in figure 4.4.

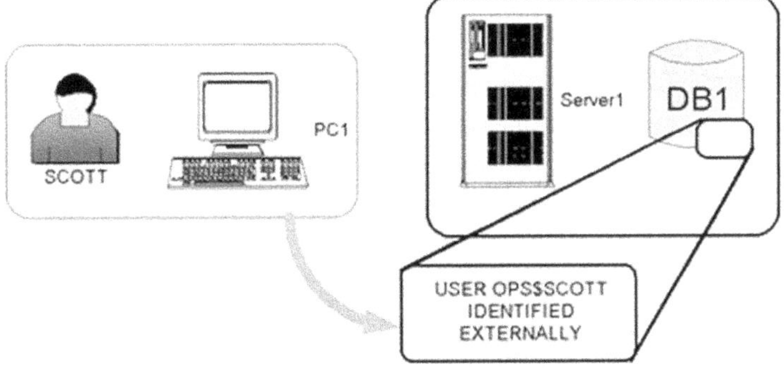


**Figure 4.4** *Remote User Authentication*

The database `DB1` is on a server named `Server1` and the client machine is `PC1`. The user SCOTT is a PC user, not the user in the server Server1. However, when the user connects to the database

```
sqlplus /@db1
```

the connection is accepted if the *remote_os_authent* parameter is TRUE, otherwise it is rejected.

Note the potential security hole the parameter may open up. A user authenticated in some operating system, which could be as inherently insecure as a PC, can login to a database. Therefore, the practice of allowing such users should be very carefully examined, and perhaps be completely disallowed.

One circumstance where it may be allowed is a setup in which the clients and servers are isolated from the rest of the network, and the clients are somehow secured well enough to be trusted. However, for most purposes this parameter should be set to FALSE.

To disable this feature, place the following lines in the initialization file, or change the lines to the following if they already exist and bounce the database.

```
os_authent_prefix = ""
remote_os_authent = FALSE
```

## Windows Domain Authorization

A somewhat secure way to authenticate users is to use Windows domain names as a part of the username. This is, however, applicable only to Windows server-based databases.

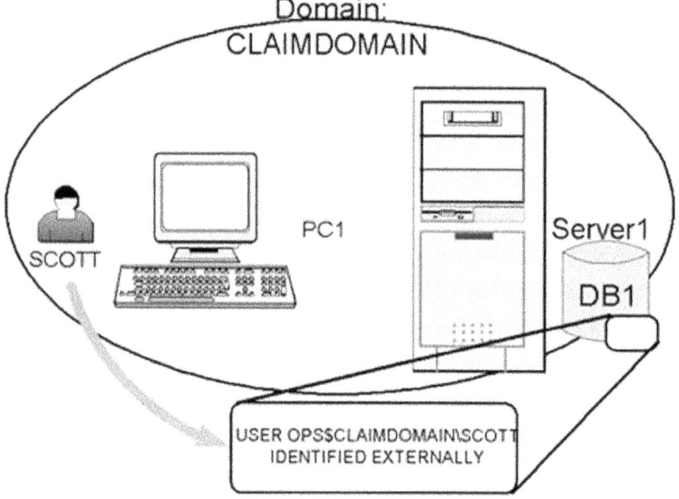


**Figure 4.5** *Domain Authorization as a part of Authentication*

Typically, the Windows servers are authenticated by the domain in a setup where all the computers, including the database server, are members of a domain. To join the domain, the user must supply the domain user's password, not the local user's.

For instance, in Figure 4.5, we have a server Server1 and a client machine PC1, both running Windows 2000, that are part of a domain CLAIMDOMAIN. The machine PC1, as well as the domain, could authenticate the user SCOTT. When the user logs in to the domain, the username is shown to the database as OPS$CLAIMDOMAIN\SCOTT, not just OPS$SCOTT. Note how the domain name is part of the user's name in the database. The user can be created as such.

```
create user "OPS$CLAIMDOMAIN\SCOTT"
identified externally;
```

Note the username is in uppercase. When the user SCOTT does not log on to the domain but rather logs on to the local PC, his domain will be PC1 (the name of the computer), so the username presented to the database will be OPS$PC1\SCOTT, not OPS$CLAIMDOMAIN\SCOTT. The database will reject the connection request.

This parameter is controlled by a value in the registry – *osauth_prefix_domain* under the key HKEY_LOCAL_MACHINE\SOFTWARE\ORACLE. If this is set to TRUE, which is the default for Oracle 8i and above, the domain information must be part of the username. Of course, if due to some reason this should not be enforced, the value can be made FALSE.

How does this help? If a rogue user creates a user called SCOTT in his PC and tries to connect to the server, the server will not accept the connection request. The rogue user must log on to the network domain, but that will be another hurdle to overcome. If remote authentications must be allowed, the security can be strengthened using this technique. However, if possible, try to disallow remote authentication altogether.

## OS Group Management

The other set of parameters pertain to group management. In the past, to facilitate the management of roles in the database, the DBA could use some help from the OS in setting the necessary privileges. Based on the group the user belonged to, his or her role inside the database was set properly. This was added as a convenience, but it increased the chances of hacking into the database, and these parameters should therefore also be set to false.

```
os_roles = FALSE
remote_os_roles = FALSE
```

- **Always set *os_authent_prefix* to a null value ""**
- **Always give the least amount of privileges to an account externally identified.**
- **Never name a user with *ops$* as the starting letters where the authentication method is database.**
- **Do not let remote users connect to the database without the password. Always set *remote_os_authent* to FALSE**

# Oracle Created Accounts

After Oracle is installed and a database is created, several users are created that may not necessarily be required by the application. In Oracle 9i, at least they are prompted to have a non-default password and most of them are locked. But in Oracle 8i and prior versions they are not. These accounts, such as the user DBSNMP, may have sweeping privileges and provide a back-door security hole. These must be identified and shutdown.

First, find out the users and their status in the database.

```
select username, account_status
from dba_users
/

SYS                    OPEN
SYSTEM                 OPEN
DBSNMP                 OPEN
XDB                    OPEN
OUTLN                  OPEN
SCOTT                  OPEN
OEM_ANANDA             OPEN
OPS$ARUP               OPEN
QS_OS                  EXPIRED & LOCKED
QS_CBADM               EXPIRED & LOCKED
QS_ADM                 EXPIRED & LOCKED
ODM_MTR                EXPIRED & LOCKED
ANONYMOUS              EXPIRED & LOCKED
WMSYS                  EXPIRED & LOCKED
RMAN                   OPEN
PERFSTAT               OPEN
OPS$ANANDA             OPEN
CTXSYS                 EXPIRED & LOCKED
MDSYS                  EXPIRED & LOCKED
ORDPLUGINS             EXPIRED & LOCKED
ORDSYS                 EXPIRED & LOCKED
WKSYS                  EXPIRED & LOCKED
ODM                    EXPIRED & LOCKED
WKPROXY                EXPIRED & LOCKED
QS_CB                  EXPIRED & LOCKED
QS_CS                  EXPIRED & LOCKED
HR                     EXPIRED & LOCKED
OE                     EXPIRED & LOCKED
PM                     EXPIRED & LOCKED
SH                     EXPIRED & LOCKED
QS                     EXPIRED & LOCKED
QS_WS                  EXPIRED & LOCKED
QS_ES                  EXPIRED & LOCKED
ARUP1                  OPEN
PCOLLINS               OPEN
HOLYCROSS              OPEN
CLAIM_SCHEMA           OPEN
NATHAN                 OPEN
JUDY                   OPEN
```

```
ANANDA                  OPEN
```

Note the accounts that are in OPEN status. Are they necessary? If you can't drop them, just expire their passwords and lock their accounts

```
alter user scott expire password account lock
/
```

The accounts that should draw some attention are discussed below.

**OUTLN** – This is used for stored outlines and is necessary, you can't drop it. However, if you don't use the stored outline functionality, the best option is to lock it and expire its password.

**PERFSTAT** – Generally used for STATSPACK as the report collection user. The default password is typically the same, PERFSTAT. It should be changed to something else.

**SCOTT** – This is the demo user with the password TIGER. Although the privileges granted to this user are very little, there is no reason this account should be present in a production database. This user should be dropped.

**DBSNMP** – This account is used by *Oracle Intelligent Agent* and the password defaults to *dbsnmp*, the same as the username, a huge security hole. This is important in securing any database and needs a separate discussion as explained below.

**TRACESVR** – This user is required for Oracle Trace, which is generally not used in many organizations. In Oracle 9i, it is supported, but Oracle10g may not have it. The default password of this user is TRACE, and should be changed.

## Securing the DBSNMP User

Let's see the privileges granted to DBSNMP.

```
select
    privilege
from
    dba_sys_privs
   where
       grantee = 'DBSNMP'
union all
select
    granted_role privilege
from
    dba_role_privs
where
    grantee = 'DBSNMP'
union all
select
    privilege||' on '||owner||'.'||table_name privilege
```

```
from
    dba_tab_privs
where
    grantee = 'DBSNMP'
/

PRIVILEGE
-------------------------------------------
SELECT ANY DICTIONARY
CONNECT
```

Selecting the privileges of the role CONNECT, we find:

```
CREATE VIEW
CREATE TABLE
ALTER SESSION
CREATE CLUSTER
CREATE SESSION
CREATE SYNONYM
CREATE SEQUENCE
CREATE DATABASE LINK
```

Observe how the DBSNMP user can select from any data dictionary view, create objects like table and view, or can alter session to enable trace. In essence, this is a powerful account. The select privilege from the data dictionary itself will let the user know all about the database – the users, tables, views, packages, procedures, and everything else. This account should be as secured as possible.

However, if you change the password of this user, the Oracle Intelligent Agent will cease to work. To make it work, you need to update the intelligent agent configuration file *snmp_rw.ora* under $ORACLE_HOME/network/admin. Add a line as the following

```
snmp_connect.SERVICE1.password = 5urf43v3r
```

where 5urf43v3r is the password of the user SNMP. But doesn't the presence of a password in the file make it less secure?

In Oracle 9i, after the IA connects for the first time, it will read the password and encrypt it in the file. In Oracle 8i, however, the file *snmp_rw.ora* must be secured using file permissions such as 600.

It might make sense to completely drop the user DBSNMP. This username is used in default, but is not necessary. Any other name can be used. For example, you could create a user ANU that performs this function.

This is a twist on the security by obscurity philosophy, a hacker will look for a user named DBSNMP, not ANU. Therefore, changing the user ID that the agent uses makes perfect sense. If the user ID is changed, the same should be reflected in the parameter file *snmp_rw.ora* as:

```
snmp_connect.SERVICE1.name = ANU
```

## In Summary

Here are the steps to secure the DBSNMP user.

1. Stop the agent. From the UNIX prompt as user oracle, issue:

   ```
   $ lsnrctl dbsnmp_stop (in Oracle8i and below)
   $ agentctl stop (in Oracle9i and above)
   ```

2. Remove all the jobs and events for this database.
3. Decide on a password and a username, if desired. Create the user and grant proper privileges.
4. Edit the file $ORACLE_HOME/network/admin/snmp_rw.ora to include the following lines:

   ```
   snmp_connect.SERVICE1.password = 5urf43v3r
   snmp_connect.SERVICE1.name = ANU
   ```

   The second line is needed only if the username is changed, too.

5. Change the permissions on the file *snmp_rw.ora* to 600.
6. Restart the agents. From the UNIX prompt issue:

   ```
   $ lsnrctl dbsnmp_start (in Oracle8i and below)
   $ agentctl start (in Oracle9i and above)
   ```

7. If a different user has been used, the user DBSNMP can be dropped.

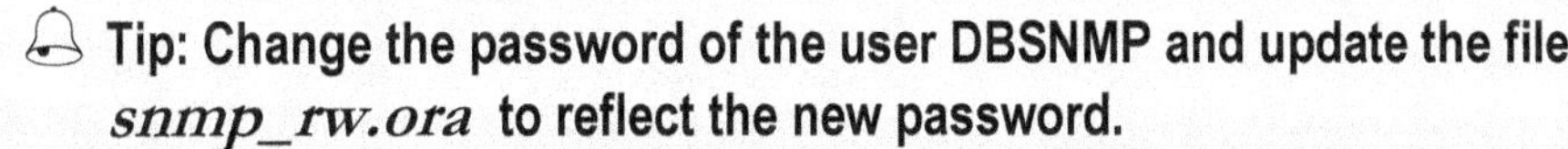

**Tip: Change the password of the user DBSNMP and update the file *snmp_rw.ora* to reflect the new password.**

# Oracle Password Management

After we establish that all the users connecting to the database must be users with passwords, the next important question is how we can make sure that the password authentication can be enforced in an acceptable manner.

As we discussed in Section I, passwords are like keys to a house, just as a malicious person can break into your house if he or she can get the key, a hacker can enter into the database if he or she learns the password. It's even worse since the password theft may not be noticed by the user. Therefore, management of passwords becomes a key security issue.

HIPAA regulations clearly mandate that password management policies be established in order to ensure that they are safe. So, what are the potential threats in the management of passwords?

Passwords can be learned by the hacker in several ways. Typically, the blame lies with the lax attitude of the authorized user. Some users write their password on some sort of paper – be it their diary or a yellow sticky note affixed to the monitor. All the thief has to do is go to the monitor and physically get it.

What are the other ways? The thief may be able to guess the password. Some users make up a password that is easy to remember – names of their spouses, children, pets, parents, maiden names, or numbers like Social Security Numbers, the date of birth, house numbers, telephone numbers, or a combination of all these. In that case, it becomes easier to guess a password. Compare the user JUDY's password, "fred1211" as opposed to "Pr3tt1f@c3".

The first one is based on her husband's name (Fred) and his birthday, December 11th (1211). If a thief knows her even a little socially, he will be able to guess the password. The second one, based on a pet name her husband bequeathed to her (*prettyface*), is contorted to become a list of characters, numbers and symbols that are easy to remember but difficult to guess.

What if someone learns her password? It has to be changed immediately. In fact, it is a good policy to change it frequently so that even if someone has the persistence to go through all the combinations and eventually figure out the password, it might have changed in the meantime.

What if someone persistently tries to guess the password? It is normal for Judy to forget her password occasionally, so a failed login attempt with an invalid password may not be a sign of an attempted forced entry. However, a large number of failed attempts do indicate attacks. The best approach at that time is to lock the account, or disable it from any further access.

## Profile Enforced Password Management

A password management policy can be established and this system can be built into the database so that all passwords are set according to the policy. In Oracle, this policy is enforced by a concept called a **profile**.

A profile can be created by the CREATE PROFILE command, and this profile can be attached to the policies of established password management. The parameters passed to the profile and their descriptions are explained in Table 4.3.

| PARAMETER | DESCRIPTION |
|---|---|
| FAILED_LOGIN_ATTEMPTS | The number of failed attempts made to login to the account before the account is locked out. In our example, we set it to 3, i.e. after 3 failed attempts to logon, the account is locked. |
| PASSWORD_LIFE_TIME | The password must be changed frequently to discourage guessing. This parameter indicates the number of days a password can be used before it becomes invalid automatically. In our example, we set it to 30. |
| PASSWORD_REUSE_TIME | Some users cheat the system by using the same password used earlier. This parameter makes sure that the same password cannot be used within a designated number of days. In this example, we set it to 90. |

| PARAMETER | DESCRIPTION |
|---|---|
| PASSWORD_REUSE_MAX | To discourage the use of the same password by the users, a certain number of characters specified by this parameter must be changed before the password can be changed again. Please note, both password reuse time and max cannot be used at the same time, only one should be set. In this example, since the time is set, max is not set. |
| PASSWORD_VERIFY_FUNCTION | A function to verify that the password conforms to the security standards. This is described in detail later. |
| PASSWORD_LOCK_TIME | After an account is locked out, this much time must pass before it is unlocked. In our example, we have the DBA reset the password immediately after the investigation; however, to prevent the hacker from somehow tricking the system to reset it, we can set this to 30 minutes. |
| PASSWORD_GRACE_TIME | When a password is expired, the user must change his password; however, a grace period may be given during which the connection is allowed with the old password, but a warning is issued. In this example, we will set the grace period to 5 days. |

**Table 4.3** *Password Features in Profile*

Based on the above, we can establish a policy for the management of passwords and easily construct a profile that enforces this policy. Following is the SQL statement that can be used to create the policy.

**create_policy.sql**

```
CREATE PROFILE senior_claim_analyst LIMIT
   FAILED_LOGIN_ATTEMPTS 3
   PASSWORD_LIFE_TIME 30
   PASSWORD_REUSE_TIME 60
   PASSWORD_REUSE_MAX UNLIMITED
   PASSWORD_LOCK_TIME 1/2/24
   PASSWORD_GRACE_TIME 5
```

Note the use of the password features we decided to use in our example. Now we can assign this policy to a specific user.

```
alter user judy
    profile senior_claim_analyst
/
```

In the same manner, we can easily set up profiles for junior and middle level claim analysts, and assign them to the appropriate users based on their roles. Why did we set up different profiles for different levels of analysts? Shouldn't it be same for all users? In theory, the profile should indeed be the same for all analysts. However, some of the resource limits are different for different types of claim analysts, and therefore the profiles are different.

Simply by creating a profile and attaching it to a user, or a set of users, you achieved the first requirement in secure password management, a very important HIPAA requirement. For the sake of other types of security, you shouldn't stop here, you should categorize all the users and create profiles for each group. Nevertheless, for HIPAA this should be enough.

**Achieve immediate compliance of the law by creating and documenting the password features of the user profiles.**

## Password Management Function

The HIPAA requirements, as well as good security management practices, demand that the hacker be discouraged as much as possible from guessing the password. This prevents the kind of attacks called brute force. In this approach, the hacker employs a dictionary of words which can be potentially used in the password, makes up combinations of them, creates users with that password and then matches the hashed version of the password with the target user's password, also hashed.

To discourage this, the password should not be too easy to guess. Some of the most commonly used passwords are words like "secret", "password", "topsecret", even "abc123". These are too obvious and should never be allowed in a password. Similar examples include the username itself; you would never want the user JUDY to have a password JUDY, would you?

Oracle provides a way to verify that the password chosen by the user satisfies your norm. First, you have to define what is or is not a good password. Some of the rules could be:

- Should not be the same as the username.
- Should not be one of "secret", "topsecret", "abc123", "password", "oracle", "database" or a variant of those words, such as "secret7".
- Should have at least one number, one character and one special character (e.g. w!nst0n is a good password, easy to remember as "Winston", but with the variants of characters as numbers, it is difficult to guess).
- Should be at least 6 characters (the longer passwords are difficult to crack by automated programs, since they have more permutations to go through).
- Should not be close to the old password. In this case, we specify that any three characters of the old password should not be used in the new one.

With these restrictions in mind, we will create a password complexity enforcement function as follows.

### password_check.sql

```
create or replace function password_check
   (p_username varchar2,
   p_new_password varchar2,
   p_old_password varchar2)
return boolean is
   i              number;
   j              number;
   scanlen        number;
   l_differ       number;
   numpresent     boolean := false;
   alphapresent   boolean := false;
   scpresent    boolean := false;
   sclist       varchar2(25)  :=
```

```
'abcdefghijklmnopqrstuvwxyzABCDEFGHIJKLMNOPQRSTUVWXYZ';


begin
-- check 1: is password same as the username
if p_new_password = p_username then
   raise_application_error(-20001,
         'password cannot be the same as the userid');
end if;

-- check 2: is the password in the list of banned words
-- or a variant.
if (
   upper(p_new_password) like  '%SECRET%'
   or upper(p_new_password) like  '%PASSWORD%'
   or upper(p_new_password) like  '%DATABASE%'
   or upper(p_new_password) like  '%ORACLE%'
   or upper(p_new_password) like '%ABC%123%'
) then
   raise_application_error(-20002,
      'password too simple');
end if;

-- check 3: is the length of the password >= 6
if length(p_new_password) < 6 then
   raise_application_error(-20003,
       'password should be at least 6 characters long');
end if;

-- check 4: does the password contain at least one
-- letter, one digit and one special character.
scanlen := length(p_new_password);
-- Is number present?
for i in 1..scanlen loop
   if substr(p_new_password,i,1) in
           ('0','1','2','3','4','5',
              '6','7','8','9')  then
       numpresent := true;
       exit;
   end if;
end loop;
--
if numpresent = false then
  raise_application_error(-20004,
     'password should contain at least one digit, one character and one
special char');
end if;
--
-- Is character present?
for i in 1..length(alphalist) loop
  for j in 1..scanlen loop
    if substr(p_new_password, j, 1) =
       substr(alphalist, i, 1) then
       alphapresent := true;
        exit;
    end if;
```

```
if alphapresent = false then
  raise_application_error(-20004,
     'password should contain at least one digit, one character and one
special char');
end if;

--. Is a special character present?

for i in 1..length(sclist) loop
    for j in 1..scanlen loop
        if substr(p_new_password,j,1) =
            substr(sclist,i,1) then
                scpresent := true;
                exit;
        end if;
    end loop;
end loop;

if scpresent = false then
     raise_application_error(-20004,
     'password should contain at least one digit, one character and one
special char');
end if;


-- check 5: does the password differ from the
-- previous password by at least 3 letters
l_differ :=
   length(p_old_password) - length(p_new_password);
if abs(l_differ) < 3 then
    if l_differ < 0 then
        scanlen := length(p_new_password);
    else
        scanlen := length(p_old_password);
    end if;
    l_differ := abs(l_differ);
    for i in 1..scanlen loop
        if substr(p_new_password,i,1) !=
             substr(p_old_password,i,1) then
                  l_differ := l_differ + 1;
        end if;
    end loop;
    if l_differ < 3 then
         raise_application_error(-20005,
            'password should differ by at least 3 characters');
    end if;
end if;
    return(true);
end;
```

This function should be created under the user sys. Let's dissect this function a little. Most of the code is self-explanatory with the help of the inline comments. It accepts the username, the old and the new passwords, checks the conditions, and returns

TRUE or FALSE depending on the password checked against the compliance. This format cannot be changed.

Once this password check function is created, it is enforced by assigning it to a profile. Remember the profile we created earlier, SENIOR_CLAIM_ANALYST? This profile will have this password checker function.

```
alter profile senior_claim_analyst limit
    password_verify_function password_check;
```

When Judy changes her password to 43v3r

```
SQL> password
Changing password for JUDY
Old password:
New password:
Retype new password:
ERROR:
ORA-28003: password verification for the specified password failed
ORA-20003: Password should be at least 6 characters long
Password unchanged
SQL>
```

the function does not allow her to change it to something less than six characters.

All users assigned to the profile of SENIOR_CLAIM_ANALYST will have their passwords enforced against the password check function. This achieves another measure of compliance with security requirements. The password function ensures that the complexity of the password makes it difficult for the hacker to guess it. In the same manner, this password check function can be assigned to all of the defined profiles.

If you don't want a password management function for a certain profile, you can turn it off by

```
alter profile senior_claim_analyst limit
    password_verify_function NULL;
```

**Tip: Use the password check function and assign it to the profiles to enforce the policy of passwords being difficult to guess.**

## Grant execute security

Under the grant execute model, and individual needs nothing more than connect privileges to attach to the Oracle database. Once attached, execution privileges on any given stored procedure, package, or function can be directly granted to each end user. At runtime, the end-user is able to execute the STORE procedure, taking on the privileges of the owner of the STORE procedure.

As we know, one shortcoming of traditional role-based security is that end users can bypass their application screens, and access their Oracle databases through SQL*Plus or iSQL. One benefit of the grant execute model is that you ensure that your end users are only able to use their privileges within the scope of your predefined PL/SQL or Java code. In many cases, the grant execute security method provides tighter control access security because it controls not only those database entities that a person is able to see, but what they're able to do with those entities.

The grant execute security model fits in very nicely with the logic consolidation trend over the decade. By moving all of the business logic into the database management system, it can be tightly coupled to the database and at the same time have the benefit of additional security.

The Oracle database is now the repository not only for the data itself, but for all of the SQL and stored procedures and functions that transform the data. By consolidating both the data and procedures in the central repository, the Oracle security manager has much tighter control over the entire database enterprise.

There are many compelling benefits to putting all Oracle SQL inside stored procedures, including:

- **Better performance** — Stored procedures load once into the shared pool and remain there unless they become paged out. The stored procedures can be bundled into packages, which can then be pinned inside the Oracle SGA for super-fast performance. At the PL/SQL level, the stored procedures can be compiled into C executable code where they run very fast compared to external business logic.

- **Coupling of data with behavior** — Developers can use Oracle member methods to couple Oracle tables with the behaviors that are directly associated with each table. This coupling provides modular, object-oriented code.

- **Improved security** — By coupling PL/SQL member methods and stored procedures with grant execute access, the manager gains complete access control, both over the data that is accessed and how the data is transformed.
- **Isolation of code** — Since all SQL is moved out of the external programs and into stored procedures, the application programs become nothing more than calls to generic stored procedures. As such, the database layer becomes independent from the application layer.

The grant execute security can give much tighter control over security than data-specific security. The DBA can authorize the application owners with the proper privileges to perform their functions, and all of the end-users will not have any explicit GRANTS against the database. Instead, they are granted EXECUTE on the procedure, and the only way that the user will be able to access the data is though the procedure.

Remember, the owner of the procedure governs the access rights to the data. There is no need to create huge GRANT scripts for each any every end-user, and there is no possibility of end users doing an "end-run" and accessing the tables from within other packages.

The grant execute access method has its greatest benefit in the coupling of data access security and procedural security. When an individual end-user is granted execute privileges against a store procedure or package, the end user may use those packages only within the context of the application itself. This has the side benefit of enforcing not only table-level security, but column-level security. Inside the PL/SQL package, we can specify individual WHERE predicates based on the user ID and very tightly control their access to virtually any distinct data item within our Oracle database.

The confounding problem with procedures and packages is that their security is managed in an entirely different fashion from other GRANT statements. When a user is given execution privileges on a package, they will be operating under the security domain of the owner of the procedure, and not their defined security domain. In other words, a user who does not have privileges to update employee rows can get this privilege by being authorized to use a procedure that updates employees. From the DBA's perspective, their database security audits cannot easily reveal this update capability.

## Object Privileges

Our discussion now turns to the traditional security model used by databases, file systems, and operating systems of all types – limiting access to a specific object for a specific type. These accesses can be given to almost all types of objects in Oracle – tables, views, sequences, and much more.

In this section, we will discuss what these privileges are and how they should be enforced. We will also discover the data dictionary views that show the current level of allocation of privileges, and how they can be reported so that potential holes can be unearthed.

Here is an example of the SELECT privilege given on the CLAIMS table to user JUDY. This is executed by the schema owner of the table CLAIMS.

```
grant select on claims to judy;
```

Certain privileges only matter for specific types of objects. For example, a procedure can have an execute privilege, a table can't. Similarly, a table may have a select privilege, a procedure can't. Here is a list of privileges that can be assigned to a user.

| PRIVILEGE | DESCRIPTION |
|---|---|
| ALTER | Allows the grantee to modify the structure as in ALTER TABLE. This is valid only for tables and sequences. No other user can alter any other object types owned by other users. |
| DELETE | Allows grantee to delete records in that object. This is valid only for tables, views and materialized views. Note that the DELETE privilege makes sense only when the materialized view is updateable. |
| EXECUTE | Allows the grantee to execute some stored code. Naturally, it's applicable to only the code in the database such as procedure, function, package, library, methods inside user-defined types, user defined operators and index types. |

| PRIVILEGE | DESCRIPTION |
|---|---|
| DEBUG | This allows the grantee to run a debugging session on the object where the object is code. However, the privilege applies to TABLEs and VIEWs too, since the DEBUG privilege allows debugging of triggers defined on the tables and views. In addition, the privilege allows debugging on methods inside user-defined types. |
| FLASHBACK | Oracle 9i introduced a new concept called flashback query where the user can see the value of an updated object as of some time in the past. This privilege allows the grantee to enable flashback on the object. Can be granted on tables, views and materialized views only. |
| INDEX | This allows the grantee to create an index on some other user's table. This should not be granted. Ideally, the owner of the table should own all indexes; there is no advantage to indexes owned by JUDY on tables owned by CLAIM_SCHEMA. |
| INSERT | Allows the grantee to insert records into the object. Since inserts can be specific to only some objects, they can be granted on tables, views and materialized views. |
| ON COMMIT REFRESH | In real time data warehouse or OLTP environments where the materialized view (a.k.a. snapshot) has to be refreshed as soon as the source table row is updated, the MV must be created with the ON COMMIT REFRESH clause. This privilege allows the grantee to create an MV in that manner. |
| QUERY REWRITE | In data warehouse environments, the MVs could be pre-created as the queries the users might execute, and when users actually run those queries, Oracle merely retrieves the data from the pre-created MVs, increasing performance. This process is called query rewriting. This privilege allows the grantee's session to rewrite the query to select from the MV. |

| PRIVILEGE | DESCRIPTION |
|---|---|
| READ | This applies only to the database objects of type directory. This privilege allows the grantee to read from that directory. |
| REFERENCES | While defining foreign key constraints, the child tables must select from the parent table to validate data. However, that is not the same as selecting data from the parent table and for security reasons, the selection from the parent table may be restricted. This privilege resolves that problem. The grantee can create FK constraints on this granted table without needing a SELECT privilege. For instance, CLAIM_SCHEMA owns the table CLAIMS, which has a FK relationship to table MEMBERS owned by MEMBER_SCHEMA. The MEMBER_SCHEMA can issue GRANT REFERENCES ON MEMBERS; This will allow the user CLAIM_SCHEMA to define a FK on CLAIMS pointing to MEMBERS. |
| SELECT | Allows the grantee to select from the object. This can be granted on tables, views, sequences, and materialized views only. |
| UNDER | Oracle 9i introduced a new concept called *subview*, which can be defined under a view. Similarly, a user-defined type can be defined under another type. This privilege allows the grantee to create subviews and subtypes. |
| UPDATE | Allows the grantee to update the object. Naturally, it applies to the objects that can be updated which are tables, views and materialized views. |
| WRITE | Oracle 9i introduced a new type of table called an External Table, which is actually a flat file residing on the filesystem that can be read as a table. While reading the external table, Oracle needs to write a log file and a bad file to a directory. This privilege on a directory allows the grantee to invoke an external table whose bad file and log file can be written to that directory. |

**Table 4.4** *Common Object Grants*

One of the more important things to assess in HIPAA compliance or any other security and privacy law is who has what privilege on which object. The data dictionary view *dba_tab_privs* holds this information. Note the name with the inference to TAB, or tables, actually, the view contains privilege information on all types of objects – tables, views, procedures, packages, etc., not just tables. Here is a brief explanation of the view and its columns.

| COLUMN NAME | DESCRIPTION |
|---|---|
| GRANTEE | The user or role the privilege is granted to. |
| OWNER | The owner of the object on which the privilege is granted. |
| TABLE_NAME | The name of the table or other object on which the privilege is granted. Please note that the name of the column is misleading – it's not just tables. (see note above) |
| GRANTOR | The user who granted the privilege. It may not be the same as the owner of the object. Described later. |
| PRIVILEGE | The exact privilege granted, e.g. SELECT or UPDATE, etc. |
| GRANTABLE | If this privilege is grantable by the grantee, discussed later. |

**Table 4.5** *Columns in dba_tab_privs*

In the view *dba_tab_privs*, the column name TABLE_NAME is a misnomer, it contains all types of objects.

A role is described later in this chapter. For the moment, please consider users and roles as the same, an entity to which the privilege is granted.

Another important concept to understand is the grants with GRANT OPTION. In this case, the owner of the original object grants the privilege on the object first with the special clause called GRANT OPTION. This enables the grantee to grant it further to the other users. If the grantee indeed does so, then the grantor column is different from the schema owner in *dba_tab_privs*.

To illustrate this concept, let's assume the user SYS grants execute privilege on the package *dbms_session* to JUDY. SYS also grants execute privileges with the GRANT OPTION on package *dbms_lock* to JUDY.

```
SQL> connect sys/53cr3t
SQL> grant execute on dbms_session to judy;
SQL> grant execute on dbms_lock to judy with grant option;
```

If the data dictionary view is now queried for privileges granted to JUDY as follows

```
select
   owner,
   table_name,
   grantor,
   privilege,
   grantable
from
   dba_tab_privs
where
   grantee = 'JUDY'
/
```

The output will be like this:

```
OWNER      TABLE_NAME      GRANTOR    PRIVILEGE      GRA
---------- --------------- ---------- -------------- ---
SYS        DBMS_SESSION    SYS        EXECUTE        NO
SYS        DBMS_LOCK       SYS        EXECUTE        YES
```

Note for the column GRANTABLE, the value is YES for one, where the GRANT OPTION was used and for the other the value is NO.

Since JUDY has the privilege with the GRANT OPTION, she can grant this to NATHAN.

```
SQL> connect judy/5ucc355
SQL> grant execute on sys.dbms_lock to nathan;
```

Now selecting the privileges for NATHAN:

```
select
   owner,
   table_name,
   grantor,
   privilege,
   grantable
from
   dba_tab_privs
where
   grantee = 'NATHAN'
```

```
/

OWNER      TABLE_NAME      GRANTOR    PRIVILEGE      GRA
---------- --------------- ---------- -------------- ---
SYS        DBMS_LOCK       JUDY       EXECUTE        NO
```

Note the GRANTOR of the privilege; it's not SYS, the owner of the package. Instead, the GRANTOR is the user who actually granted it, JUDY.

For good security, you should never have privileges granted with the GRANT OPTION. All the privileges should be given directly by the schema owner and controlled from there. The GRANT OPTION just creates numerous permutations for the grants to be given, and is a management nightmare.

The following script shows whether you have any granted privileges with the grant option.

```
select
   owner,
   table_name,
   grantor,
   privilege
from
   dba_tab_privs
where
   grantable = 'YES'
and
   owner not in ('SYS','SYSTEM')
/
```

If there are any such privileges, immediately revoke them and re-grant them without the grant option. The following script shows privileges where the original owner did not grant the privileges.

```
select
   owner,
   table_name,
   grantor,
   privilege
from
   dba_tab_privs
where
   owner != grantor
and
   owner not in ('SYS','SYSTEM')
/
```

There shouldn't be any such privileges. If you find some, revoke them and re-grant from the schema owner.

**Tip: The privileges on the objects should be given directly by the owner of the object and without the GRANT option. Check to see if these conditions are met. If necessary, correct them.**

Finally, it's time to gather information on who has what privileges. This report satisfies the HIPAA requirement that the capabilities (or privileges) should be documented.

### show_obj_grants.sql

```
select
   grantee,
   owner,
   table_name,
   grantor,
   privilege,
   grantable
from
   dba_tab_privs
where
   grantee not in ('SYS','SYSTEM')
order
   by 1,2,3,4
```

A sample output is given below:

```
GRANTEE  OWNER TABLE_NAME    GRANTOR    PRIVILEGE GRA
------- ------ ------------- ---------- --------- ---
ANANDA   SYS    DBMS_LOCK       JUDY     EXECUTE   NO
ANANDA   SYS    LOGMNR_DICT     SYS      READ      YES
ANANDA   SYS    LOGMNR_DICT     SYS      WRITE     YES
ANANDA   SYS    MYDIR           SYS      READ      YES
ANANDA   SYS    MYDIR           SYS      WRITE     YES
```

This report can be run periodically and filed away for documentation. The above example is intentionally shown with unsecured privileges granted to user ANANDA - can you spot them?

**Tip: Run the script periodically and file the output for later review. This simple act will satisfy the requirements of many security policies.**

Finally, there is an ALL privilege, which simply grants all the privileges to the grantee in one shot. This is granted as

```
grant all on CLAIMS to JUDY;
```

Judy can now do anything – modify the structure, create a trigger, even drop the table. Naturally, this creates a huge security hole and should never be granted to any user.

In the chapter for auditing grants security, we will cover this in more detail.

## Column Privileges

A lesser-known feature of Oracle is the ability to grant privileges on individual columns, rather than complete tables. For instance, the user CLAIM_SCHEMA can grant privileges to JUDY so that she can update only the PAID_AMOUNT field of the table CLAIMS, nothing else. The CLAIM_SCHEMA can issue:

```
grant update (paid_amount) on claims to judy;
```

If the user JUDY updates any other column as:

```
update
   claim_schema.claim
set
   claim_amount = 10000
where
   claim_id = 1234
/
```

The output comes back as:

```
update claim_schema.claim
                    *
ERROR at line 1:
ORA-01031: insufficient privileges
```

She gets an insufficient privileges error. To find out the column privileges granted, you could query the data dictionary view *dba_col_privs* as follows:

### find_col_privs.sql

```
select
    owner,
    table_name,
    column_name,
    grantor,
    privilege,
    grantable
 from
```

```
grantee = 'JUDY'
```

The output may look like this:

```
OWNER        TABLE_ COLUMN_NAME GRAN  PRIVILEGE  GRA
------------ ------ ----------- ----  ---------- ---
CLAIM_SCHEMA CLAIMS PAID_AMOUNT JUDY  INSERT     NO
CLAIM_SCHEMA CLAIMS PAID_AMOUNT JUDY  UPDATE     NO
```

Note the column COLUMN_NAME. It indicates which column has been granted the privilege to the grantee. Just like the above discussion on object privileges, the privileges can be granted with GRANT OPTION. If someone other than the owner grants it, the GRANTOR column will be different.

In addition to the UPDATE privileges, the column level privileges can be set on INSERT and REFERENCES statements. If set on INSERT, the grantee can insert some value into those columns only; all other columns will be merely defaulted or left with null values. Setting this on REFERENCES limits the grantee's ability to create foreign key constraints against those columns only.

**For HIPAA requirements, one of the key things is to protect the Protected Health Information (PHI). This can be easily met by protecting the PHI columns on the tables with the INSERT and UPDATE column privileges, as described.**

# System Privileges

The preceding section talked about the privileges required for the regular users to access certain specific objects in some specific manner, e.g. the user JUDY can SELECT from table MEMBERS, but not UPDATE it. However, they can do that only when they have privileges to get into the database in the first place. Similarly, the user can create a table, but we can control which tablespace she can create the table on, etc.

These types of privileges, which are not tied to any specific objects, are known as system privileges. Oracle has several system privileges, as described in the Administrators Manual of the Oracle documentation. We will not repeat the information. In this section we will discuss only a few of the system privileges related to the security of the database as defined in table 4.6.

| PRIVILEGES | DESCRIPTION |
|---|---|
| CREATE SESSION | This allows a user to connect to the database, but that is all this privilege can do. It does not allow creation of any objects, nor does it allow the reading of data. All users who need a connection to the database need this privilege. |
| ALTER SESSION | Typically, this privilege is not necessary in regular operation. Users can issue session altering statements such as ALTER SESSION SET NLS_DATE_FORMAT without needing this privilege. Therefore, this is not necessary. The only time it is needed is when the session has to write something on the server side filesystem, such as in ALTER SESSION SET SQL_TRACE = TRUE statement. |
| RESTRICTED SESSION | When a database is started in restricted mode, typically to conduct some maintenance operations, regular users are not allowed to connect. However some non-DBA users can be allowed to connect during this restricted session status; and this system privilege allows that. Suppose a report program uses an id called REPUSER that has only SELECT privileges on the tables, not any modification privileges. This user can be allowed to connect during the time when some maintenance is going on since the user does not modify anything. However, issue this privilege if and only if you determine that the user does not do something that is consistent with the maintenance activities. |
| CREATE DATABASE LINK | This allows the user to create database links. Typically, you would give these privileges very selectively, only to those users who might create private database links to other databases. However, good security models suggest that PUBLIC database links be created by the SYS user instead, without password, whenever possible. |

| PRIVILEGES | DESCRIPTION |
|---|---|
| CREATE TABLE, CREATE INDEX, CREATE SEQUENCE, CREATE VIEW, CREATE SNAPSHOT, etc. | Create Table privilege, as the name suggests, allows the user to create a table. However, it does not allow the creation in a tablespace where the user does not have a quota. We will discuss more about quotas later. In the meantime, this privilege should be granted only to the users who will have schema objects. Typically, in an application, a specific user or a group of users own the table, and all other users are given access to them. Only the former, never the latter, should be given these privileges. |
| CREATE ANY TABLE, CREATE ANY VIEW, etc. | Note the keyword ANY before the object type. This allows the user to create an object of that type in any schema, not just his or her schema. For example, if JUDY is given this privilege like:<br>Grant create any table to JUDY;<br>Judy can now create a table like<br>Create table NATHAN.CLAIMS (..);<br>Note the table was created as owned by Nathan, not Judy. This is a very powerful privilege; Judy can even create objects owned by the SYSTEM user! Needless to say, *never* grant this privilege to anyone. |
| UNLIMITED TABLESPACE | This privilege allows the user to create objects without any boundaries in any tablespace, including the SYSTEM tablespace. This should not be given to any user. |
| SELECT ANY TABLE | This privilege allows the user to select from any table/view owned by any user, including the data dictionary tables and views. Obviously, this creates several security holes as the user can see data that could be sensitive. Therefore, this privilege should not be given out without a proper analysis. In most cases, this privilege is never required and should not be given. If a user truly has to select from other users' tables, say, for reporting, then explicit grants should be given to the user on those objects. |

| PRIVILEGES | DESCRIPTION |
|---|---|
| SELECT ANY DICTIONARY | This privilege, new in Oracle 9i, allows the user to select any data dictionary table. This may not be necessary in any normal case. Suppose you want to create a user for a performance-monitoring tool you installed. This tool will have to query all the data dictionary views such as v$sysstat to get the performance metrics. Earlier, the SELECT ANY TABLE privilege was needed, but not anymore. The SELECT ANY DICTIONARY privilege allows the user to select any dictionary table and at the same time protect sensitive database tables. |

**Table 4.6** *Important System Privileges*

The system privileges are granted by the following command.

```
GRANT CREATE TABLE TO JUDY;
```

The privileges can be retracted using:

```
REVOKE CREATE TABLE TO JUDY;
```

## Quotas

When a user has the CREATE TABLE privilege, the user can't just create the table in any tablespace. He or she must have explicit privileges to create any type of stored object in a tablespace. This privilege is not given in a regular privilege granting statement, rather through a separate ALTER USER command as follows.

```
ALTER USER JUDY QUOTA 10K ON USER_DATA;
```

This will allow Judy to create only 10 Kilobytes of stored data, such as tables and materialized views, inside tablespace *user_data*. Although this command is designed for storage management in Oracle, it offers powerful solutions for security. By limiting how much storage the user can create in a tablespace, the user is not allowed to take over available space in a tablespace and cause failure in other applications. If a user should have unrestricted space, the word 10K should be replaced by UNLIMITED as in:

```
ALTER USER JUDY QUOTA UNLIMITED ON USER_DATA;
```

However, if the user has the UNLIMITED TABLESPACE system privilege, he or she can create tables in any tablespace, including the SYSTEM tablespace! Surely, that is not desirable. You should not grant this system privilege to any user. The following script shows the quota of each user in each tablespace.

### find_ts_quota.sql

```
select
   username,
   tablespace_name,
   bytes,
   max_bytes
from
   dba_ts_quotas
where
   username not in ('SYS','SYSTEM')
order
   by username,
   tablespace_name
```

A sample output is as follows:

```
USERNAME   TABLESPACE      BYTES  MAX_BYTES
---------- ---------- ---------- ----------
ANANDA     XDB                 0      12288
HR         EXAMPLE       1638400         -1
JUDY       XDB             65536     102400
```

The output is only partial and needs some explanation. The first line shows that the user ANANDA has been allowed only 12288 bytes on the tablespace XDB, as indicated by the MAX_BYTES column. Out of that, the user has not used any space, as indicated by the BYTES column. The user HR has UNLIMITED quota on tablespace EXAMPLE as shown by the value of "-1" in the MAX_BYTES column.

**As a rule of thumb, you should never grant any regular user sweeping privileges like SELECT ANY TABLE, CREATE ANY TABLE, etc. If a user needs access to another user's tables, then he or she should be given specific grants on those objects only.**

Here is a complete list of system privileges that can be granted.

| | |
|---|---|
| ADMINISTER DATABASE TRIGGER | CREATE TYPE |
| | CREATE USER |
| ADMINISTER RESOURCE | CREATE VIEW |

MANAGER
ADMINISTER SECURITY
ALTER ANY CLUSTER
ALTER ANY DIMENSION
ALTER ANY EVALUATION CONTEXT
ALTER ANY INDEX
ALTER ANY INDEXTYPE
ALTER ANY LIBRARY
ALTER ANY OPERATOR
ALTER ANY OUTLINE
ALTER ANY PROCEDURE
ALTER ANY ROLE
ALTER ANY RULE
ALTER ANY RULE SET
ALTER ANY SECURITY PROFILE
ALTER ANY SEQUENCE
ALTER ANY SNAPSHOT
ALTER ANY TABLE
ALTER ANY TRIGGER
ALTER ANY TYPE
ALTER DATABASE
ALTER PROFILE
ALTER RESOURCE COST
ALTER ROLLBACK SEGMENT
ALTER SESSION
ALTER SYSTEM
ALTER TABLESPACE
ALTER USER
ANALYZE ANY
AUDIT ANY
AUDIT SYSTEM
BACKUP ANY TABLE
BECOME USER
COMMENT ANY TABLE
CREATE ANY CLUSTER
CREATE ANY CONTEXT
DEBUG ANY PROCEDURE
DEBUG CONNECT ANY
DEBUG CONNECT SESSION
DEBUG CONNECT USER
DELETE ANY TABLE
DEQUEUE ANY QUEUE
DROP ANY CLUSTER
DROP ANY CONTEXT
DROP ANY DIMENSION
DROP ANY DIRECTORY
DROP ANY EVALUATION CONTEXT
DROP ANY INDEX
DROP ANY INDEXTYPE
DROP ANY LIBRARY
DROP ANY OPERATOR
DROP ANY OUTLINE
DROP ANY PROCEDURE
DROP ANY ROLE
DROP ANY RULE
DROP ANY RULE SET
DROP ANY SECURITY PROFILE
DROP ANY SEQUENCE
DROP ANY SNAPSHOT
DROP ANY SYNONYM
DROP ANY TABLE
DROP ANY TRIGGER
DROP ANY TYPE
DROP ANY VIEW
DROP PROFILE
DROP PUBLIC DATABASE LINK
DROP PUBLIC SYNONYM
DROP ROLLBACK SEGMENT
DROP TABLESPACE
DROP USER
ENQUEUE ANY QUEUE
EXECUTE ANY EVALUATION CONTEXT

CREATE ANY DIMENSION
CREATE ANY DIRECTORY
CREATE ANY EVALUATION CONTEXT
CREATE ANY INDEX
CREATE ANY INDEXTYPE
CREATE ANY LIBRARY
CREATE ANY OPERATOR
CREATE ANY OUTLINE
CREATE ANY PROCEDURE
CREATE ANY RULE
CREATE ANY RULE SET
CREATE ANY SECURITY PROFILE
CREATE ANY SEQUENCE
CREATE ANY SNAPSHOT
CREATE ANY SYNONYM
CREATE ANY TABLE
CREATE ANY TRIGGER
CREATE ANY TYPE
CREATE ANY VIEW
CREATE CLUSTER
CREATE DATABASE LINK
CREATE DIMENSION
CREATE EVALUATION CONTEXT
CREATE INDEXTYPE
CREATE LIBRARY
CREATE OPERATOR
CREATE PROCEDURE
CREATE PROFILE
CREATE PUBLIC DATABASE LINK
CREATE PUBLIC SYNONYM
CREATE ROLE
CREATE ROLLBACK SEGMENT
CREATE RULE
CREATE RULE SET
EXECUTE ANY INDEXTYPE
EXECUTE ANY LIBRARY
EXECUTE ANY OPERATOR
EXECUTE ANY PROCEDURE
EXECUTE ANY RULE
EXECUTE ANY RULE SET
EXECUTE ANY TYPE
EXEMPT ACCESS POLICY
FLASHBACK ANY TABLE
FORCE ANY TRANSACTION
FORCE TRANSACTION
GLOBAL QUERY REWRITE
GRANT ANY OBJECT PRIVILEGE
GRANT ANY PRIVILEGE
GRANT ANY ROLE
INSERT ANY TABLE
LOCK ANY TABLE
MANAGE ANY QUEUE
MANAGE TABLESPACE
ON COMMIT REFRESH
QUERY REWRITE
READUP
READUP DBHIGH
RESTRICTED SESSION
RESUMABLE
SELECT ANY DICTIONARY
SELECT ANY SEQUENCE
SELECT ANY TABLE
SYSDBA
SYSOPER
UNDER ANY TABLE
UNDER ANY TYPE
UNDER ANY VIEW
UNLIMITED TABLESPACE
UPDATE ANY TABLE
WRITEDOWN
WRITEDOWN DBLOW

| | |
|---|---|
| CREATE SECURITY PROFILE | WRITEUP |
| CREATE SEQUENCE | WRITEUP DBHIGH |
| CREATE SESSION | |
| CREATE SNAPSHOT | |
| CREATE SYNONYM | |
| CREATE TABLE | |
| CREATE TABLESPACE | |
| CREATE TRIGGER | |

**Table 4.7** *List of System Privileges*

With so many privileges, shouldn't you keep track of who has what privileges? The following query selects that information from the dictionary for the user JUDY.

```
select
    privilege,
    admin_option
from
    dba_sys_privs
where
    grantee = 'JUDY';
```

The output will be similar to:

```
PRIVILEGE                                ADM
---------------------------------------- ---
CREATE VIEW                              NO
CREATE TABLE                             NO
CREATE SESSION                           NO
CREATE SEQUENCE                          NO
SELECT ANY TABLE                         NO
```

The column ADMIN_OPTION will be discussed later. For now, see how the grants are given. JUDY is a regular claim analyst who uses the application. So why does she need CREATE privileges such as VIEW, TABLE, etc.? Worse, why does she have SELECT ANY TABLE privilege? These questions should be asked and answered. The unnecessary privileges should be immediately revoked.

> **Tip: If the application user needs the CREATE TABLE privilege to create temporary tables, as in the case of reporting, etc., suggest using alternative methods, such as PL/SQL tables, instead.**

## A Note on ALTER SESSION privilege

This particular privilege needs special mention since it defies logic in some cases. Granting this privilege will merely allow the user to do operations that file I/O on the server, for example, setting *sql_trace*, or setting events. Otherwise, this privilege has no effect. A user without this privilege can still do all of the following:

```
ALTER SESSION SET NLS_DATE_FORMAT …
ALTER SESSION SET SORT_AREA_SIZE …
ALTER SESSION SET OPTIMIZER_MODE …
```

As you can see, this is one of the many idiosyncrasies of the Oracle server. Contrary to what you may expect, the ALTER SESSION system privilege does not affect these potentially dangerous commands. It only affects the ability to set *sql_trace* or events.

This can be partially prevented by the use of Product User Profiles in SQL*Plus, described later in this chapter. However, that will simply prevent only commands entered from SQL*Plus. Any other tool will bypass the security scheme. Moreover, only the ALTER command can be blocked in the product profile table. This means any ALTER, including ALTER TABLE, ALTER VIEW, etc. will be blocked too. This may not be desirable.

There is no workaround for this problem. You are advised to watch out for this specific vulnerability just in case it may resolve some potential or materialized problems in your environment.

**The ALTER SESSION privilege only controls the setting of *sql_trace* and events; all other session altering commands are always available to the user, regardless of this system privilege.**

## Identify Users with Sweeping Privileges

Some privileges are so powerful that they can do many things a normal user is not supposed to do, but they are not generally considered harmful and are ignored in a security audit. One example is CREATE ANY TABLE. These privileges should be immediately revoked. Here is a script to find out who may have these sweeping privileges.

### find_sweeping_privs.sql

```
    grantee,
    privilege,
    admin_option
from
    dba_sys_privs
where
    privilege not in
(
   'ALTER SESSION',
   'QUERY REWRITE',
   'CREATE DIMENSION',
   'CREATE INDEXTYPE',
   'CREATE LIBRARY',
   'CREATE OPERATOR',
   'CREATE PROCEDURE',
   'CREATE SEQUENCE',
   'CREATE SESSION',
   'CREATE SNAPSHOT',
   'CREATE SYNONYM',
   'CREATE TABLE',
   'CREATE TRIGGER',
   'CREATE TYPE',
   'CREATE USER',
   'CREATE VIEW'
)
and
    grantee not in
       ('SYS','SYSTEM','WKSYS','XDB',
        'MDSYS','ORDPLUGINS','ODM')
    /* Place all the user names you want to exclude */
order by
    grantee,
    privilege
```

The output will tell you which of the users have these sweeping privileges, and they should be reviewed.

## Identify Non-Schema Owners with Schema Privileges

After identifying and rooting out these unwanted privileges, the next step is to find out which of these users have the privileges needed by a schema owner. For instance, CREATE TABLE should be given to the users who own the tables, not to all.

find_schema_privs.sql

```
select
    grantee,
    privilege,
    admin_option
from
    dba_sys_privs
where
    privilege in
(
   'CREATE DIMENSION',
   'CREATE INDEXTYPE',
   'CREATE LIBRARY',
   'CREATE OPERATOR',
   'CREATE PROCEDURE',
   'CREATE SEQUENCE',
   'CREATE SESSION',
   'CREATE SNAPSHOT',
   'CREATE SYNONYM',
   'CREATE TABLE',
   'CREATE TRIGGER',
   'CREATE TYPE',
   'CREATE USER',
   'CREATE VIEW'
)
and
    grantee not in
       ('SYS','SYSTEM','WKSYS','XDB',
        'MDSYS','ORDPLUGINS','ODM')
    /* Place all the user names you want to exclude */
order by
    grantee,
    privilege
```

Note the use of some objectionable privileges. Analyze them and revoke them if needed. You will see some regular users with unneeded privileges.

**Never give any sweeping authorities to any user. Analyze the current privileges granted and adjust them if need be.**

# Grants with Admin Option

In the previous section, we selected a column called ADMIN_OPTION, but we did not elaborate on that. A privilege can be granted to a user, who in turn can grant it to another user, provided the first user received the grant with a special option, called ADMIN OPTION.

For instance, SYS can grant CREATE TABLE to JUDY with this option as follows

```
SQL> grant create table to judy with admin option;
```

Then Judy can grant the same privilege to Nathan.

```
SQL> connect judy/5ucc3ss
SQL> grant create table to nathan;

Grant succeeded.

SQL> grant create view to nanthan;

grant create view to scott

*
ERROR at line 1:
ORA-01031: insufficient privileges
```

Note how the grant CREATE TABLE was successful, but not the create view. JUDY was granted the create table with grant option, but there was no grant option for the create view as the following query shows.

```
Select
   privilege, admin_option
from
   dba_sys_privs
where
   grantee = 'JUDY'
/
```

The output comes back as:

```
PRIVILEGE                                ADM
---------------------------------------- ---
CREATE VIEW                              NO
CREATE TABLE                             YES
CREATE SESSION                           NO
CREATE SEQUENCE                          NO
SELECT ANY TABLE                         NO
```

Note the ADMIN_OPTION field for CREATE TABLE has the value YES, but not for the record with CREATE VIEW.

You should not have any user with any kind of admin options. If the applications create tables dynamically, the user creating them can grant it without needing the ADMIN OPTION. Therefore, there is no need for this option to be present. The following query will determine the privileges granted with this option.

### users_with_sys_grant_admin_option.sql

```
select
     grantee,
     privilege
from
     dba_sys_privs
where
     admin_option = 'YES'
and
     grantee not in ('SYS','DBA','SYSTEM')
```

Review each line from this output and see if the grant is needed. Otherwise, revoke the grant and grant again without the admin option.

## With Grant Option

Another type of grants exists – WITH GRANT OPTION, and it is used in case of object privileges. For instance, CLAIM_SCHEMA grants select on tables *claims* and *claim_headers* as follows.

```
grant select on claims to judy with grant option;
grant select on claim_headers to judy;
```

Note the grant to one is with the option and the other is not. Now JUDY wants to grant these privileges to NATHAN.

```
SQL> grant select on claim_schema.claims to nathan;

Grant succeeded.

SQL> grant select on claim_schema.claim_headers to nathan;
                     *
ERROR at line 1:
ORA-01031: insufficient privileges
```

The grant on *claim_headers* fails, since Judy never received the grants with the grant option. She doesn't have any privilege to assign anything on that table to another user.

In a typical database, you probably would never have a need to have these grants with grant option. The grants with this option are hard to manage and follow. In a secured environment, these types of grants should not be given. The following script identifies these grants.

### users_with_obj_grant_admin_option.sql

```
select
    grantee,
    privilege,
    owner,
    table_name
from
    dba_tab_privs
where
    grantable = 'YES'
and
    grantee not in ('SYS','DBA','SYSTEM')
```

Note all these items and revoke grants from them.

> **Tip: Do not give any grants with the ADMIN or GRANT OPTION.**

# Security through Roles

Managing users and their privileges on a one-on-one basis makes administration a little bit of a challenge. Therefore, Oracle introduces another concept called ROLE. A role can be assigned a set of privileges, such as SELECT on a particular table, UPDATE on another, etc. If this role is assigned to a user, then the user inherits all the privileges of the role. An example might make this easier to understand.

In our example used throughout the book, JUDY is the senior claim analyst who has some privileges to do her job. After a while, NATHAN is promoted to the senior analyst position. Now, he must be given all the privileges pursuant to the position. However, instead of executing these statements to grant the privileges to him, a role can be created instead, called SENIOR_CLAIM_ANALYST. This role can be given all the privileges the position requires, and then this role can be granted to the users JUDY and NATHAN, or anyone else who joins as a senior analyst.

A role is created as:

```
create role senior_claim_analyst;
```

Privileges are granted as in the case of a user:

```
grant select, insert, update, delete on claims to senior_claim_analyst;
grant select, insert, update, delete on claim_header to
senior_claim_analyst;
```

```
grant select, insert, update, delete on claim_line to senior_claim_analyst;
...and so on
```

After the privileges are granted, the role can then be granted to the users:

```
grant senior_claim_analyst to judy, nathan;
```

Now Judy and Nathan inherit all the privileges defined on the role. A user who has the grant role system privilege can grant the role to the users. A role can be given just like a privilege, think of it as a basket of privileges. A role can be granted to another role, too.

The next question in managing the environment is to find out how many roles have been defined and what privileges they have been assigned. This shows how many roles have been defined in the database.

```
select
   role
from
   dba_roles;
```

## Default Role

Users can have one or more roles granted to them, passing several types of privileges in the process. However, not all the roles are enabled when a user creates a session. Only the roles defined as default are enabled. For instance, NATHAN has been granted both the roles as follows

```
grant junior_claim_analyst,
    senior_claim_analyst to nathan;
```

Selecting this from the dictionary we see:

```
Select
   *
from
   dba_role_privs
where
   grantee = 'NATHAN';
```

The output comes back as:

```
GRANTEE        GRANTED_ROLE                 ADM DEF
-------------- ---------------------------- --- ---
NATHAN         JUNIOR_CLAIM_ANALYST          NO YES
NATHAN         SENIOR_CLAIM_ANALYST          NO YES
```

Note how the default role shows YES for both the roles. This is because NATHAN has not been granted any *specific* default role, so *all* roles granted to him are default, by default (no pun intended!).

Next, we specify the default role for NATHAN as JUNIOR_CLAIM_ANALYST as follows.

```
alter user nathan default role junior_claim_analyst;

select
   *
from
   dba_role_privs
where
   grantee = 'NATHAN';
```

The output comes back as:

```
GRANTEE        GRANTED_ROLE                 ADM DEF
-------------- ------------------------- --- ---
NATHAN         JUNIOR_CLAIM_ANALYST          NO YES
NATHAN         SENIOR_CLAIM_ANALYST          NO NO
```

Note how the role SENIOR_CLAIM_ANALYST is no longer default for NATHAN.

When Nathan needs to do some work that requires the privileges of the SENIOR_CLAIM_ANALYST role, he can issue a statement

```
SET ROLE SENIOR_CLAIM_ANALYST;
```

This leads to a rather complicated affair where the roles are granted but not enabled. To verify which roles have been enabled in a session, the view *session_roles* may be queried. In the following example query, NATHAN can see which roles are enabled when he is connected:

```
select *
   from session_roles;
```

This shows the current role that is enabled:

```
ROLE
------------------------------
JUNIOR_CLAIM_ANALYST
```

Nathan's currently enabled role is JUNIOR_CLAIM_ANALYST. When he enables another role and selects from the same view:

```
SET ROLE
   SENIOR_CLAIM_ANALYST, JUNIOR_CLAIM_ANALYST;

SELECT *
   FROM SESSION_ROLES;
```

The result comes back as:

```
ROLE
------------------------------
SENIOR_CLAIM_ANALYST
JUNIOR_CLAIM_ANALYST
```

See that the role SENIOR_CLAIM_ANALYST is now enabled.

In addition to using the SET ROLE command, the Oracle-supplied utility SET_ROLE in the package *dbms_session* can also be used. Here is how it is used:

```
dbms_session.set_role ('SENIOR_CLAIM_ANALYST');
```

This is especially useful in situations where the roles have to be set inside a procedure, or be called by a client program other than SQL*Plus.

> **Important: Unless a default role is explicitly defined for a user, all roles granted to the user are default and enabled. Therefore, have one default role for the user and explicitly enable the other roles by SET ROLE in the application.**

## Reporting Privileges on Roles

The following query shows the privileges granted to users and other roles.

### role_privs.sql

```
select
    grantee           role_name,
    privilege         privilege,
    admin_option      admin_grantable
from
    dba_sys_privs
where
    grantee in
    (
        select
```

```
            dba_roles
    )
UNION ALL
select
    grantee             role_name,
    privilege           privilege,
    grantable           admin_grantable
from
    dba_tab_privs
where
    grantee in
    (
        select
            role
        from
            dba_roles
    )
```

The view *dba_role_privs* shows the roles granted to users and other roles. The following query determines the roles granted to different users and other roles.

```
break on grantee skip 1
select
    grantee,
    granted_role,
    admin_option,
    default_role
from
    dba_role_privs
where
    grantee not in ('SYS','SYSTEM')
order by
    1,2
/
```

Here is a sample output:

```
GRANTEE              GRANTED_ROLE                   ADM DEF
-------------------- ------------------------------ --- ---
DBA                  DELETE_CATALOG_ROLE            YES YES
                     EXECUTE_CATALOG_ROLE           YES YES
                     EXP_FULL_DATABASE              NO  YES
                     GATHER_SYSTEM_STATISTICS       NO  YES
                     IMP_FULL_DATABASE              NO  YES
                     JAVA_ADMIN                     NO  YES
                     JAVA_DEPLOY                    NO  YES
                     PLUSTRACE                      YES YES
                     SELECT_CATALOG_ROLE            YES YES

DBSNMP               CONNECT                        NO  YES

DPAUL                DWREADER                       NO  YES

DSHERMAN             DWREADER                       NO  YES
```

```
DWOWNER              PLUSTRACE                              NO   YES

EXECUTE_CATALOG_ROLE HS_ADMIN_ROLE                          NO   YES

EXP_FULL_DATABASE    EXECUTE_CATALOG_ROLE                   NO   YES
                     SELECT_CATALOG_ROLE                    NO   YES

IMP_FULL_DATABASE    EXECUTE_CATALOG_ROLE                   NO   YES
                     SELECT_CATALOG_ROLE                    NO   YES

JAVASYSPRIV          JAVAUSERPRIV                           NO   YES

LOGSTDBY_ADMINISTRAT CONNECT                                NO   YES
OR
                     RESOURCE                               NO   YES
```

Note the grantee column lists other roles too.

For the sake of simplicity, remember only three views:

- *dba_sys_privs* - For system privileges granted to various users and roles.
- *dba_tab_privs* – For object privileges and roles granted to users and roles.
- *dba_role_privs* – For roles granted to users and other roles.

In all these views, the GRANTEE is the user or role that received the privilege and the GRANTOR is the user who granted it. The OWNER column indicates the owner of the object that was granted.

## Oracle Built-In Roles

Oracle provides several roles that are built into the database. Some of them are DBA, RESOURCE, and CONNECT. Most DBAs use them to make their tasks easier and simpler, but each of them is a security nightmare.

Let's examine RESOURCE. This is generally given to schema owners. Did you know that it has UNLIMITED TABLESPACE system privilege, making it able to create any table anywhere in the database – including the SYSTEM tablespace? Obviously, this is not what you want. You would want to restrict the tablespaces to specific users only.

Similarly the role CONNECT, by default, has the CREATE TABLE/SEQUENCE/SYNONYM and a few more options. The name CONNECT somehow conveys the impression of the ability to connect only, not anything else. As you can see, however, the ability is much more than that. Another privilege, ALTER

SESSION system privilege, allows the grantee to issue *sql_trace* = TRUE in their session. This can have far reaching consequences.

Therefore, it is not prudent to use built-in roles. Rather, identify the privileges users will need, put them in the appropriate roles which you have created, and use them to control authorization.

 **If possible, try not to use the Oracle built-in roles like RESOURCE and CONNECT. Create your own roles.**

# Object Masquerading

We briefly discussed this topic in the introduction. Although this is not used much, object masquerading can be a very effective tool to discourage malicious users from getting what they want.

Think of an example – if a burglar breaks into your house to rob the family safe, would he or she look inside the laundry closet? Probably not. The thief will look for a box-like object that may appear similar to the thief's image of the safe. If the safe was designed to look like, say, a dirty clothes hamper, with some actual dirty underwear on the top, the thief would probably never be able to guess that, and thus the safe will be indeed exactly that - safe. (Now everybody knows where the safe is in my house! However, I assure you, there is nothing of value inside, just a few *stones* my wife collects!)

A similar concept can be applied to database objects, too. A hacker will look for a table named *credit_card* or something similar. If the credit card numbers are stored in a table named *process_data*, the hacker will most likely ignore it. However, all the legitimate users will know exactly where to find the data. This technique not only applies to table names, but to column names as well, e.g. the credit card numbers are represented by a column name PROC_DATA_VALUE, or something similar.

This technique of hiding an object behind a meaningless name is adapted from the concept of camouflage in everyday life. Although it may be a little complex to use, in a small development group this can easily be implemented. The added advantage of this object masquerading as a form of security is that it protects against the prying eyes of internal employees who have no authorization to look into the database, but are not necessarily hackers.

HIPAA rules specify that the database be accessible only by authorized users. All users without any authorization to the database, whether they are benign, like a curious internal employee, or a jumpy teenage hacker trying to prove his coming of age to his girlfriend, or malignant hackers trying to steal credit card and health information with the intent to profit from it, should find access to the database very difficult. Object masquerading will help to prevent disclosure of protected information to these types of intruders.

> **If possible, use a misleading name for tables and columns containing sensitive data to fool intruders. This follows the principle of "Security by Obscurity"!**

# Profile-Based Security

We discussed the use of profiles in the password section. However, in addition to the password enforcement functions, profiles can be used to enforce the HIPAA security requirements very effectively. The law says that you have to make adequate arrangements to ensure that malicious persons do not abuse connections to the database.

The following parameters can be controlled by profile.

***sessions_per_user*** – Hackers typically break into the database using a username, not by stealing the SYS password. Internal employees also break into the database using a user id they already know. In the case of lax users, the password may be stolen and the hackers may use their password.

What if we limit the number of sessions a user can have active at any point in time? We know beforehand how many sessions a specific user needs. Typically, a senior claim analyst uses a session to do his or her work, and perhaps opens up another to answer a question from a junior analyst. A maximum of two sessions, then, is adequate for a senior analyst, but only one is adequate for a junior analyst. Profiles are used to limit the number of concurrent sessions for a specific username. This parameter specifies that limit.

***connect_time*** – The other technique that hackers employ is using the database session of other legitimate users after their regular work. However, if there is a limit on the maximum amount of time a user session can stay connected to the database, the sessions are automatically disconnected.

HIPAA rules do not mandate this, but they do recommend using some sort of mechanism to limit the time so that a malicious intruder has fewer resources. This parameter in the profile enforces that limit. Expressed in seconds, it limits the maximum time a user can stay connected to the database. After this limit expires, the sessions are automatically disconnected.

In this case, let's assume the senior claim analyst connects at 8 in the morning, goes to lunch at 12 noon, comes back at 1 and works till 5. Therefore, she works for only 4 hours at a stretch. Given another hour for some extra work, 5 hours should be the maximum time for the senior claim analyst to work, and that should be the limit. Expressed in seconds, it is 5 times 60 times 60, i.e. 180000.

***idle_time*** – Hackers typically wait for a legitimate user to be connected but idle. Then they hijack the session to carry out their task. Idle time while connected is one of the most dangerous periods for handling security. This parameter limits the maximum time a session can stay connected without doing anything. By reducing the period of time an inactive session stays connected, the probability of that session being a victim of abuse is reduced.

The profile also has other parameters, but only these are relevant for security.

Based on our decision, we can create the profile to enforce it. Since we already have the profile, we will merely update it with the new parameters.

```
alter profile senior_claim_analyst limit
    Connect_time       180000
    Sessions_per_user  2
    Idle_time          1800
/
```

Voila! You have immediately achieved a very important requirement of HIPAA, to limit user activity to discourage the malicious intruder.

We have seen three separate discussions on profile-based security – the password function, the password management guidelines, and the database usage. Let's put them together to see a complete profile definition.

### create_policy.sql

```
CREATE PROFILE SENIOR_CLAIM_ANALYST LIMIT
   FAILED_LOGIN_ATTEMPTS     3
   PASSWORD_LIFE_TIME        30
   PASSWORD_REUSE_TIME       60
   PASSWORD_REUSE_MAX        UNLIMITED
   PASSWORD_LOCK_TIME        1/2/24
   PASSWORD_GRACE_TIME       5
   PASSWORD_VERIFY_FUNCTION  PASSWORD_CHECK
   CONNECT_TIME              180000
   SESSIONS_PER_USER         2
   IDLE_TIME                 1800
```

If the profile is already created, you can add or change the parameters by using the ALTER PROFILE command. In the same manner, identify and classify all your users to several profiles and assign resource limits to each profile.

 **Use Profiles to enforce connection limits to the database.**

# View-Based Security

In the first section, we saw the use of views to enforce privacy. This is perhaps the easiest way to enforce privacy as required by HIPAA. The law states that sensitive information such as member records, treatment records, and other protected health information remain protected. This information should not be made visible to the users who are authorized to see all the tables except these sensitive fields.

Assume we have a table CLAIMS described as follows:

```
CLAIM_ID                    NUMBER
SSN                         CHAR(9)
MEMBER_ID                   NUMBER
PROVIDER_ID                 NUMBER
CLAIM_AMOUNT                NUMBER(10)
PAID_AMOUNT                 NUMBER(10)
STATUS                      CHAR(1)
```

The intent is to somehow shroud the SSN (the Social Security Number) from the other users. This can be done by:

```
create view
    vw_claims_no_ssn
as
select
    claim_id,
    'XXXXXXXXX' as SSN,
    member_id,
    provider_id,
    claim_amount,
    paid_amount,
    status
from
    claims
/
```

Selecting from the *claims* table directly gives us this output.

```
SQL> select * from claims;

  CLAIM_ID SSN        MEMBER PROVIDER_ CLAIM_AMOU PAID_ S
---------- --------- ------ --------- ----------- ----- -
```

```
        1 123456789  12345  1234567   1200        1100 P
        2 234567891  12345  1234567   1800        1700 P
        2 234567891  12345  2345671   1400        1300 P

SQL> select * from vw_claims_no_ssn;

  CLAIM_ID SSN        MEMBER PROVIDER_ CLAIM_AMOU PAID_ S
---------- --------- ------ --------- ---------- ----- -
         1 XXXXXXXXX  12345  1234567   1200        1100 P
         2 XXXXXXXXX  12345  1234567   1800        1700 P
         2 XXXXXXXXX  12345  2345671   1400        1300 P
```

Note how the SSN field is masked by the Xs, effectively blocking them from being seen. If a user needs to see the member and other information, but the SSN cannot be disclosed, this view can be provided to them so that they can freely select anything but the protected health information.

Let's look at a little more complex requirement. A provider, i.e. a doctor or a hospital, will want to see the SSN number of his or her own patients for billing purposes, and it should be allowed. This can be achieved by somehow linking the provider's tables with their user names. Since we have a table called providers, the usernames can be stored in a column. This is how the provider table looks.

```
PROVIDER_ID                NUMBER
PROVIDER_NAME              VARCHAR2(200)              )
PROVIDER_USERNAME          VARCHAR2(30)

Let's look at the data stored inside the table providers.

PROVIDER_ID PROVIDER_NAME        PROVIDER_U
----------- -------------------- ----------
    1234567 HOLY CROSS HOSPITAL  HOLYCROSS
    2345671 DR. PHIL COLLINS     PCOLLINS
```

The values in PROVIDER_USERNAME are actually users inside the database.

Now comes the time to construct the view. This can be done as in the script below.

```
create view vw_claims_provider
as
    select * from claims
    where provider_id in (
        select provider_id
        from providers
        where provider_username = user
    )
/
```

Note how the user is authenticated using the function USER that returns the current user. By getting the PROVIDER_ID from the table or that user, we can get the claims for that provider. We used the IN operation, not equality, since a provider username may have listings for more than one provider, as in the case of a billing company working for several doctors.

The owner of this view is CLAIM_SCHEMA, the same user who owns the *claims* table. The users for the providers, as mentioned in the PROVIDER_USERNAME column of the *providers* table, are given SELECT privileges on this view, nothing else. These users are *not* granted SELECT on the table *claims* itself.

When user HOLYCROSS logs in and selects from this view

```
select
    claim_id,
    SSN,
    claim_amount,
    status
from
    claim_schema.vw_claims_provider
/
```

The output is:

```
  CLAIM_ID SSN         CLAIM_AMOUNT S
---------- --------- ------------ -
         1 123456789         1200 P
         2 234567891         1800 P
```

Note, only the claims with the PROVIDER_ID = 1234567 come back, not the one with 2345671. Why? Because that is how the view is defined – to automatically filter the rows the user is not authorized to see.

In a later chapter, we will explore another concept called Virtual Private Database, or Fine Grained Access Control, that provides even more functionality without the use of views or complex definitions.

Combining the column masking and the view filtering, we can provide the important functionality HIPAA requires. The law says that users should not accidentally see the data they are not supposed to see.

For instance, a senior claim analyst like JUDY should be able to see all claims, but junior analysts like NATHAN should see only the claims below $2000, according to the policies of the company. Nathan can be granted select privileges on a view that filters the claim amounts automatically. Similarly, creating a view to mask the sensitive data also satisfies the requirement.

 **Action Plan: Identify the different visibility requirements for various users and construct views for each group. Revoke privileges from the base tables and grant on these views.**

# Program-Based Security

Program-Based Security was introduced in Section I, and will now be explored in detail. Essentially, it means that the users should not access the tables directly to do any type of manipulation. Rather, they should call stored programs like stored procedures, functions, and packages to accomplish this task.

For instance, the user JUDY, when approving a claim, probably issues a statement like this:

```
update
    claims
set
    paid_amount = 1200,
    status = 'P'
where
    claim_id = 1
/
```

Instead, the functionality should be encapsulated in a program, such as a stored procedure, like the following

```
create or replace procedure pay_claim
(
    p_claim_id    IN number,
    p_paid_amount IN number

) is
begin
    update
        claims
    set
         paid_amount = p_paid_amount,
         status      = 'P'
    where
         claim_id    = p_claim_id;
end;
/
```

The user JUDY calls the procedure in this way:

```
execute pay_claim ( 1, 1200)
```

In this case, JUDY does not own the stored procedure. The user CLAIM_SCHEMA owns it and it grants the execute privilege to JUDY. Judy does not have any privileges on the table *claims*, either. Therefore, the update claims statement would not be possible.

This does the same thing as the above piece of code. So, what else did we achieve here?

**The table changes are protected from the applications**. Typically, the development group goes through a Rapid Prototype Development cycle where the columns are probably renamed or are enhanced. The column could be renamed from PAID_AMOUNT to PAID_AMT or CLAIM_PAID_AMOUNT - the applications do not need to know the change. Even the table name could be changed. The only change that is required is at one place, the procedure.

**The business logic could be encapsulated**. What if the business decides to use complicated logic to validate the paid amount, or even make the actual paid amount based on some complex calculation? These changes can be easily handled through the procedure, with the changes being transparent to the users. In the example above, the status was automatically changed to 'P' by the program, not by the user. If, at some point in the future, the code for processed is changed from P to, say, R, the users don't have to know about it. The program logic is the only place it has to be changed.

**The third, but the most important one is security**. By making the table hidden from the applications, we keep the structure of the table hidden from most users. Since the users are not given any privilege to update the table data directly, a malicious attacker cannot update the table directly, he or she has to use the procedure. Inside the procedure, we can place various types of checks to ensure that the calling of the procedure is genuine. By retaining a single point of control for the table changes, we achieve some degree of control on the changes. In most cases, this is desirable to enforce a security policy.

This is one model of security for the data. However, we will unearth some potential problems and issues with this approach later.

This approach is very useful in the case of procedures that are frequently called to validate something or do something repeatedly. For instance, a procedure can be constructed to authenticate users of an application, not the database. A typical approach is to create a table to hold the user ids and passwords. The application connects using a generic id, reads the table for the password of the user, and matches it with the one supplied by the user.

However, the system is fraught with large security holes. Anyone can select the password table and read the password of another user. It's not acceptable in the security model we propose. Here is another approach.

## Application Password Management

A table may contain the user IDs and passwords in the following manner.

```
USERID          VARCHAR2(10)
USERPASS        VARCHAR2(30)
```

Selecting from this table:

```
select * from app_users;
```

We see:

```
USERID     USERPASS
---------- ------------------------------
APPUSER1   ╝♫sÆfíµ☺
APPUSER2   ¼FK-╟=▼
```

Note how the password has been encrypted. Encryption is discussed in Chapter 4, for now, assume the password is encrypted in some way. However, every encryption system needs some key to encrypt and decrypt, and this key is literally the path to discover the password. Therefore, the key must be protected at all costs. How do we achieve the task of authenticating these application users?

One option is for the application to issue a statement like:

```
select userpass from app_users where userid = 'APPUSER1';
```

Then decrypt the value, match it against the password supplied by the user, and allow the application to proceed if they match. However, this scheme assumes that the application user knows how to decrypt the password. This can create a security lapse, and should be covered as thoroughly as possible. The use of a password verifier function is helpful in this situation.

We will create a function that accepts the user ID and password values, and examines them against the data stored in the database. It will return YES if they match or NO if they don't. This procedure uses an Oracle supplied function named *dbms_obfuscation_toolkit*, that is described in detail in the chapter on Encryption.

Using a function to check passwords also prevents a very common but serious form of attack known as SQL Injection Attack. This is described later in this chapter.

### is_password_correct.sql

```
create or replace function is_password_correct
(
    p_userid    IN varchar2,
    p_password  IN varchar2
)
return varchar2
is
    v_userpass     varchar2(2000);
    v_password     varchar2(2000);
    errm           varchar2(2000);
    v_key          varchar2(2000) :=
        'adfwff2dwcc3299fmc0cecc0fc';
begin
    -- First get the encrypted password from the table
    select userpass
    into   v_userpass
    from   app_users
    where  userid = p_userid;
    -- Decrypt the string to get the password
    -- Note the key used.
    dbms_obfuscation_toolkit.DES3Decrypt (
        input_string     => v_userpass,
        key_string       => v_key,
        decrypted_string => v_password,
        which            => 1);
     -- Compare the passwords
     v_password := rtrim(v_password);
     -- compare the passwords
     if (v_password = p_password)
     then
         return 'YES';
     else
         return 'NO';
     end if;
exception
    when OTHERS then
        errm := SQLERRM;
        raise_application_error (-20001,errm);
end;
```

Note the use of the function. It does not actually return the value of the user's password. Rather it returns YES if the password supplied by the user is correct and NO if it isn't. This is analogous to the challenge-response type of authentication, where the challenge is merely answered with a *yes* or *no* response. The application user never needs to know the decrypted value of the password.

Some user who is not normally involved in the process of the application owns this function. The authors recommend using a user id called SECUSER, who owns all the security related objects. In this case, the user SECUSER owns this function and grants execute privileges to APPUSER1 and APPUSER2 (or more, if necessary).

When the application user APPUSER1 needs to authenticate himself or herself, he or she calls the function in the following manner

```
if (
    secuser.is_password_correct (
        'APPUSER1','app1') = 'YES'
) then
    -- user is authenticated
else
    -- user is not authenticated
end if;
```

The user *never* knows the value of the password string inside. All he or she knows is that the password is app1 and the function responds with a YES or NO answer. Even if the user APPUSER1 selects from the table APP_USERS (which will not happen, since he or she does not have the privilege, but assume the privilege was granted by mistake), he or she will not know the password of APPUSER2. It will be encrypted, and the user does not know the key to decryption.

The other part of the puzzle is how to encrypt the passwords and store them in the table. We will achieve that using the following function

### get_app_password.sql

```
create or replace function get_app_password
(
    p_password  IN varchar2
)
return varchar2
is
    v_password      varchar2(2000);
    v_userpass      varchar2(2000);
    errm            varchar2(2000);
    v_passlen       integer;
    v_extra         integer;
```

```
        'adfwff2dwcc3299fmc0ceccOfc';
begin
    -- The input to the encryption routine needs to be
    -- multiples of 8 bytes. So we will pad it if it
    -- is not so.
    v_passlen := length (p_password);
    if (v_passlen < 8)
    then
        v_padlen := 8;
    else
        v_extra := mod(v_passlen, 8);
        if (v_extra = 0)
        then
            v_padlen := v_passlen;
        else
            v_padlen := v_passlen - v_extra + 8;
        end if;
    end if;
    v_password := rpad(p_password,v_padlen);
    -- Encrypt the the password
    dbms_obfuscation_toolkit.DES3Encrypt (
        input_string     => v_password,
        key_string       => v_key,
        encrypted_string => v_userpass,
        which            => 1);
    return v_userpass;
exception
    when OTHERS then
        errm := SQLERRM;
        raise_application_error (-20001,errm);
end;
```

Note the very important concept, the key, which is the same in the Encryption and Decryption procedures. If the key is different, the password is never retrieved.

This function returns the encrypted value, which can then be stored in the database table by this user. For example, when a third user called APPUSER3 is created with password app3, the user SECUSER can call:

```
insert
    into app_users
values
    (
        'APPUSER3', get_app_password('app3')
    )
/
```

When the time comes to update the password of the user APPUSER1, the following approach may be used:

```
update
    app_users
set
    userpass = get_app_password ('newpass1')
/
```

Another way is to create a procedure that accepts the user ID and password, and then inserts into the table directly. That way, the user who executes the procedure does not even know which table contains the passwords.

Note an important concept here – the user executing the procedure is not aware of the table behind the authentication or the authentication keys. This offers tremendous security advantages and a flexible password management framework for application users.

HIPAA requires that all users, whether they connect through the database or the application, should be securely authenticated. Until now, there was no proper way of authenticating the application users who were not database users. Using these password management utilities, this requirement can be easily fulfilled.

 **Action Item: Identify if there are some applications that use authentication via passwords stored in tables. Change the method to the secured method described here.**

# Definer and Invoker Rights

In the program-based security model, we discussed a way the internal tables and other objects can be hidden from the view of the user who calls the procedure. Let's revisit that quickly.

User CLAIM_SCHEMA owns the table CLAIMS and the procedure *pay_claim()*. The user JUDY, a senior claim analyst, decides on the claim and when the time comes to pay, executes the procedure. Judy has no privileges on the CLAIMS table, just the execute privilege on the procedure. Since the procedure is owned by CLAIM_SCHEMA, that user's privileges, rather than July's, are used while updating the table. This is the simplest authorization scheme in programs, and is known as the **definers rights** model.

So, what is the problem with this model? The problem occurs in situations where the program is too generic and is not tied to a specific user and its schema objects. In the *pay_claim()* procedure, we have determined that the procedure updates only objects owned by the user CLAIM_SCHEMA, who owns both the procedure and the object. However, if the procedure were so generic that it is callable by any user to update his or her own tables, or tables owned by others they have privileges on, then authorization is almost nonexistent. In other words, the program merely becomes a code execution piece, not an encapsulation device to be the sole operator of the objects. The users have individual grants to the objects underneath, and use the program merely as code to execute steps. This is known as the **Invoker Rights** Model because the privileges of the invoker, not the definer of the programs, prevail.

Let's explore this through an example. The *pay_claim()* procedure was defined earlier. The user JUDY tries to select from the table CLAIMS, as follows, and gets an error.

```
SQL> select * from claim_schema.claims;
select * from claim_schema.claims
                           *
ERROR at line 1:
ORA-00942: table or view does not exist
```

This is expected, since Judy does not have select privileges on the table. Nor does she have any other privileges – update, insert, or delete. Therefore, she can't see the table.

However, she executes the procedure that updates the claims table.

```
SQL> exec claim_schema.pay_claim(1,1000);

PL/SQL procedure successfully completed.
```

Why does this procedure go through without any error? The answer is simple. The procedure `pay_claim()` is owned by claim schema, which also owns the table claims. Therefore, when Judy executes the procedure, she is actually using the privileges the procedure owner has been granted, *not the ones she has been granted.* The procedure owner, CLAIM_SCHEMA, has the privileges to update its own table, *claims*, and thus Judy's execution is successful.

Now let's try the Invoker Rights model. The same procedure is declared using this model.

### pay_claim_invoker.sql

```
create or replace procedure pay_claim_invoker
(
    p_claim_id     IN number,
    p_paid_amount  IN number
)
authid current_user /* Important */
is
begin
    update
        claims
    set
         paid_amount = p_paid_amount,
         status      = 'P'
    where
         claim_id    = p_claim_id;
end;
```

Note that this is identical to the procedure *pay_claim()*, with the exception of the use of the clause *authid current_user* in the code. This makes it an invoker rights procedure. Let's see what happens when JUDY calls this procedure.

```
SQL> exec claim_schema.pay_claim_invoker(1,1000);
BEGIN claim_schema.pay_claim_invoker(1,1000); END;

*
ERROR at line 1:
ORA-00942: table or view does not exist
ORA-06512: at "CLAIM_SCHEMA.PAY_CLAIM_INVOKER", line 10
ORA-06512: at line 1
```

What happened? Shouldn't Judy be successful in updating the claims table just like the earlier case? No. Since the procedure is defined as Invoker Rights model, the privileges enjoyed by Judy (the invoker) are used, not those of the owner of the procedure. Judy has no update privilege on the table *claims*, and therefore the code inside the procedure couldn't perform the desired task.

However, if JUDY had a table named *claims*, then the code would have referenced her table instead of the table owned by the owner of the procedure. After creating the table *claims* in her schema, she executes the procedure again.

```
SQL> exec claim_schema.pay_claim_invoker(1,1000);

PL/SQL procedure successfully completed.
```

Why was it successful? It was because the code acted on her own table.

Let's analyze this information:

- JUDY owns table *claims*
- CLAIM_SCHEMA owns table *claims*
- CLAIM_SCHEMA owns procedure *pay_claim_invoker()* defined as invoker rights.
- CLAIM_SCHEMA owns procedure *pay_claim_definer()* defined as definer rights.
- CLAIM_SCHEMA grants execute on both these procedures to JUDY. JUDY has no other privilege.
- Both the procedures have identical logic. Inside, an UPDATE CLAIMS statement exists.
- When JUDY executes the procedure *pay_claim_definer()*, the *claims* table owned by CLAIM_SCHEMA is updated.

- When she executes the procedure *pay_claim_invoker()*, the *claims* table, which she owns, is updated.

This information is explained by Figure 4.6.

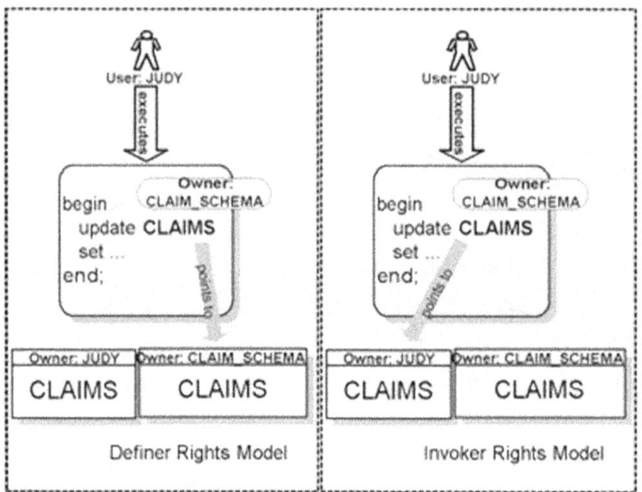


**Figure 4.6** *Comparison of Definer and Invoker Rights. Note how the behavior of the same procedure changes in updating the table claims when created in different manners.*

This is an important concept to understand and apply in a security model. The invoker rights model allows the creation of several generic functions that are then executed by other users using their own thoughtfully designed privileges. This leads to a reduction in the number of stored programs and increases overall security.

 **In Definer Model, the privileges of the owner of the code are used. In Invoker Model, the privileges of the calling user are used.**

# SQL Injection attacks

This is a technique used by hackers to gain access to data for which they are not authorized. We will explain the concept of SQL Injection, how it is done, and how it can be prevented.

One of the biggest problems DBAs face from developers is the passing of a SQL string to the database. Most developers, coming from a client tool background such as Visual Basic, Java, PowerBuilder, etc., are comfortable in passing a string of characters that makes up a query to the database.

For instance, an Active Server Page (ASP) program might use this program to validate the user trying to log into the database. Don't worry about the exact syntax of this program, it not important. The idea is to explain the concept of SQL Injection, not ASP programming.

```
DIM userName, password, query
DIM conn, rs
userName = Request.Form("userName")
password = Request.Form("password")
set conn = server.createObject("ADODB.Connection")
set rs = server.createObject("ADODB.Recordset")

query = "select * from app_users where userid ='" & userName & "' and
userPass='" & password & "'"

conn.Open "Provider=SQLOLEDB; Data Source=CLAIMDB" rs.activeConnection =
conn
rs.open query

if not rs.eof then
    response.write "Welcome to Claims Database"
else
    response.write "Invalid Userid or Password"
end if
```

Essentially, the user supplies a user ID and password, then the program validates them against the database by selecting from the *app_users* table. We came across the *app_users* table earlier in the *Application Password Management* section.

The important part of this script is the line:

```
query = "select * from app_users where userid ='" & userName & "' and
userPass='" & password & "'"
```

This query is a pass-through query, i.e. it is passed as it is to the database for execution. The variables username and password are taken from the user's input to the form. If the user enters

```
UserId   : JUDY
Password: 5ucc355
```

The variable `query` now becomes:

```
select * from app_users where userid ='JUDY' and userpass = '5ucc355'
```

This is passed on to the server and since JUDY exists and her password matches, the program gets a response back, and then it executes successfully and logs in the user.

But, if a hacker enters these values for the same prompts:

```
UserId      : JUDY
Password: somepass' or '1' = '1
```

The variable query now becomes:

```
select * from app_users where userid ='JUDY' and userpass = 'somepass' or
'1' = '1'
```

Executing this query in the database, the output is:

```
USERID     USERPASS
---------- ------------------------------
JUDY       5uc355
NATHAN     5urf43v3r
```

The application received some records and concluded that the user JUDY has a password SOMEPASS! The hacker got through without knowing the password. Worse, if the program displays some of the output on the screen, all the users and their passwords will be displayed

This technique is known as SQL Injection, named after the addition of the extra characters 'somepass' or '1' = '1' after the password. The technique has many variants based on the technology used, but the concept is still the same – placement of a query that will always return true, e.g. "OR 1=1".

Another form of SQL Injection is done through the programming practice utilized. Some developers use dynamic SQL to construct the query, instead of using bind variables. For example, consider a procedure that returns *claim_details* of all claims of a member, the parameter passed is the Social Security Number. The developer may write a query like this in PL/SQL:

```
l_query := 'select claim_id, claim_amount from claims where SSN = '||l_ssn;
```

This is then executed by an EXECUTE IMMEDIATE or an elaborate OPEN - FETCH - CLOSE process. The proper SSN is passed to the program. What will happen if, at the prompt for SSN, the user passes the following?

```
'123456789' union all select claim_id, claim_amount from claims
```

The value of the *l_query* variable is transformed to:

```
select claim_id, claim_amount from claims where SSN = '123456789' union all
select claim_id, claim_amount from claims
```

Note what happens now, the user will get all the claims, not just of the SSN 123456789. This is another variant of SQL Injection.

## How to Prevent SQL Injection Attacks

**Bind Variables** - The first one is rather simple – do not use dynamic SQL. If possible, use a construct like:

```
select field1, field2, field3
into :1, :2, :3
from table
where ….
```

and then pass parameters to it. This way, the hacker can't inject an extra string after the predicate of the query.

**Special Characters** - Filter out the special characters, such as quotation marks.

**No Pass-through Queries** - Do not pass the SQL as a pass-through, rather, use bind variables. Using concatenation (such as "&" in Visual Basic and "=+" in JavaScript) may be convenient, but allows hackers to inject.

**No Sweeping Privileges** - Carefully review the privileges granted to the users. Remove sweeping privileges such as ANY. Utilize the principle of least privileges – if a users does not need a privilege, don't grant it. Without required privilege, the hacker can't see much data.

**Invoker Rights Model** - Using the Invoker Rights model in procedures and functions makes sure the calling user's privileges are used, reducing the chances of the hacker getting into a user with large privileges.

**Datatype** - Use proper datatypes for the parameters. If the parameter is numeric, define a numeric value for it. Some developers tend to declare everything as character, because it makes coding easier, but this invites hackers.

**DBSNMP Password** - Change the default passwords for the DBSNMP user, a user with sweeping privileges such as SELECT ANY DICTIONARY. Better yet, use a different username for the Oracle Intelligent Agent user, following the technique described earlier in this chapter under DBSNMP User Security.

**Function for Password Management** - In the application password management, use a function described in the appropriate section to authenticate users, do not select directly from a table.

**Encryption** - Finally, encrypt the sensitive data. Even if the hacker gets through via SQL Injection, he or she will not be able to see anything of value.

> 🔔 **You should review the chances of SQL Injection and take steps to prevent an attack. As we saw earlier, the technique is rather easy and often results from bad coding practice and poor privilege management.**

# SQL*Plus Security

The last frontiers of security, often neglected, lie in the domain of SQL*Plus, the ubiquitous tool used by DBAs and developers alike to interact with the database. Securing SQL*Plus is easy, the specific parts of SQL*Plus can be easily controlled using built in facilities. In this section, we will describe each of the security facets of the tool, and how to configure them to achieve compliance.

## Product User Profile

This is a facility provided by Oracle itself to limit the abilities of its own tools to some extent. If you have used SQL*Plus for a while, you know that there are ways to produce reports using this tool, and in some cases these reports have become the mainstream reports of the organization. A typical script is invoked by, in the case of UNIX, in this manner.

```
sqlplus -s userid/password @report.sql
```

*report.sql* is the actual script run by the session. It may contain a SPOOL command that places the output in an output file, and then with an EXIT command, it exits the SQL*Plus environment.

What if the user, while the report is running, presses Control-C and breaks the report generation, i.e. the execution of the query? The SQL*Plus prompt comes up, aborting the query:

```
SQL>
```

The user can do anything here. Even though you may have forbidden the user from invoking SQL*Plus, this technique circumvents that. The SQL*Plus security feature called Product User Profiles protects against such a misuse.

The central object behind this security model is a table called *sqlplus_product_profile*, owned by the user SYSTEM, not SYS.

This table should have already been created in the database creation process. If it does not exist, you can create it by running the script *pupbld.sql* in $ORACLE_HOME/sqlplus/admin directory as user SYSTEM. Note: this must be run as SYSTEM, not SYS.

To prevent user JUDY from entering a HOST command at the SQL*Plus prompt, you would insert a record into this table.

```
insert
    into sqlplus_product_profile
    (product, userid, attribute, char_value)
values
    ('SQL*Plus','JUDY','HOST','DISABLED')
/
```

After this is inserted, every SQL*Plus session of JUDY is scanned for a HOST command. If she issues that command, she gets an error as shown below.

```
SQL> host
SP2-0544: invalid command: host
SQL>
```

Note the error SP2-0544, an *SQL*Plus* error, not an Oracle error, which starts with ORA. For JUDY, the host command is gone, as if it never existed before. For other users, the host command works fine. This is how the security is controlled at the execution level.

Now let's examine the table *sqlplus_product_profile* in detail.

| COLUMN | DESCRIPTION |
|---|---|
| PRODUCT | The name of the Oracle product, uses "SQL*Plus" as the only value. This table was designed for all types of products such as Forms and Reports, but only SQL*Plus stuck around. |
| USERID | The username you want to restrict. |
| ATTRIBUTE | The command you want to restrict, e.g. HOST. |
| CHAR_VALUE | Should contain the value DISABLED for the products that should be disabled for the user. |

**Table 4.9** *Relevant Columns of sqlplus_product_profile Table*

Other columns are neither relevant nor used by the present setup.

How can you restrict the host command for all users? Just enter a % sign for the USERID column. This will not, however, prevent SYS and SYSTEM from using HOST.

Now, let's see what commands can be restricted by this facility.

| SQL*PLUS COMMAND | DESCRIPTION |
|---|---|
| COPY | Disables the COPY command in SQL*Plus |
| EDIT | Disables the user from entering the edit command to edit a script or the current SQL |
| EXECUTE | Disables the execute command, i.e. execution of procedures, packages, pl/sql blocks, etc. |
| EXIT | The user is disallowed to enter EXIT command |
| GET | GET is used to get a script to the SQL*Plus environment but not execute it. This disallows that command. |
| HOST | This command takes the user to the prompt of the host operating system, such as the shell in UNIX or the command prompt in Windows. Disabling this command also disables the shortcuts defined for that. For instance, the exclamation mark "!" is a shortcut for HOST in UNIX, and that is disabled too. |
| PASSWORD | This command is used by the user to change his or her own password without the ALTER USER command. |
| QUIT | Same as exit. |
| RUN | This disables running of an SQL script. This also disables the shortcuts '@" and "@@" used to run the scripts. |
| SAVE | This disallows saving the current SQL to a file. |
| SET | All SET commands as in SET PROMPT, SET ROLE, etc, are disabled. |
| SPOOL | Disallows saving the output to a file. |
| START | START is used to get an SQL script file and execute it. This disables that command. |

**Table 4.10** *SQL*Plus commands that can be restricted by Product Profile Security*

In addition, product profile security can also be used to disable SQL commands, not just SQL*Plus. Here are the SQL commands disabled by the facility.

| | |
|---|---|
| ALTER | ANALYZE |
| AUDIT | CONNECT |
| CREATE | DELETE |
| DROP | GRANT |
| INSERT | LOCK |
| NOAUDIT | RENAME |
| REVOKE | SELECT |
| SET CONSTRAINTS | SET ROLE |
| SET TRANSACTION | TRUNCATE |
| UPDATE | |

**Table 4.11** *SQL Commands Restricted*

Please note the important difference between this and system privileges. This facility merely disables the command in SQL*Plus. The user can execute the command in any other tool. To prevent the user from doing SELECT against a specific table in any tool, revoke the grant.

The following PL/SQL commands can also be restricted

- BEGIN – This disables a user from entering BEGIN as the first line of SQL*Plus. The user can enter EXECUTE to execute a pl/sql block, and it must be disabled separately.
- DECLARE – This disallows the user from entering DECLARE as the first line of a statement. By disallowing BEGIN, DECLARE, and EXECUTE, the user can be disallowed from running any kind of Pl/SQL in a SQL*Plus environment.

## Controlling Roles

The same facility can also be used to control which role is enabled at the prompt. Suppose the user Judy has three roles: SENIOR_CLAIM_ANALYST, which allows her to modify the tables; SENIOR_CLAIM_READER, which lets her only read these tables; and MEMBER_READER, which lets her read the members related tables.

Typically, we want to enable her reader's role only. Her analyst role should be enabled by the application, and we don't want her to issue a SET ROLE to do this. If we let her use SET ROLE, then she can set the analyst role as well. To prevent that, we will insert the records into the *sqlplus_product_profile* table as follows.

```
insert
    into sqlplus_product_profile
    (product, userid, attribute, char_value)
values
    ('SQL*Plus','JUDY','ROLES','SENIOR_CLAIM_ANALYST')
/
```

Note how we specified the roles we want to disable in the CHAR_VALUE column. When JUDY logs in to SQL*Plus, the following command will automatically be executed for her.

```
SET ROLE ALL EXCEPT SENIOR_CLAIM_ANALYST
/
```

This, in addition to disabling the SET command in the *sqlplus_product_profile*, will ensure that JUDY is not able to login to SQL*Plus and enable for herself some role we don't want her to use.

## SQL*Plus Restrictions

These are also some lesser-known features of SQL*Plus. In most of the articles and recommendations that come from Security experts, one thing stands out – remove the SQL*Plus executable, generally named `sqlplus` in UNIX or *sqlplus.exe* in Windows.

This advice has some merit. It prevents the hacker from using a tool that is used by the DBA in administration. However, can we really remove it? If this is removed, how does the DBA connect to the database to do maintenance?

The solution for that is to administer a server remotely, say from Oracle Enterprise Manager. Nevertheless, this needs remote authentication using a password file, not necessarily a better security practice. Therefore, the dilemma is to choose between leaving a powerful tool like *sqlplus* on the server, and making security slightly weaker by enabling remote authentication.

How about a middle ground - what if we restrict the ability of the `sqlplus` executable? That should work. Oracle provides a way to achieve this by using command line options to restrict the ability of the `sqlplus` executable.

In this way, we will rename the `sqlplus` executable to `sqlpluss` (for *secured* sqlplus). Then we will create a shell script (or batch script for Windows) called `sqlplus`, which will look like this:

```
sqlpluss -RESTRICT 1
```

Note the use of the command line parameter *restrict* with a value 1. We will then make this shell script executable by all, just like the old *sqlplus* executable. The execute privileges of the renamed one, *sqlpluss*, is limited to the DBA group only.

When someone other than a DBA goes to SQL*Plus and then issues:

```
SQL> host
SP2-0738: Restricted command "host" not available
```

Note the messages, HOST command is *not* available. This has the same effect as the *sqlplus_product_profile* described earlier. No user, even SYS, will be allowed to execute the HOST command. The use of *restrict* 1 as a command line parameter does the trick.

What is the difference between this and the profile table method used earlier? As you can see, the profile method needs a connection to the database first to check the table. The use of the *restrict* option does not need a connection. The `sqlplus` executable itself is aware of the limitation and is more secure.

In addition to HOST, the value 1 after the parameter *restrict* also disables the EDIT command. Let's see the use of the other parameter values.

A value of 2 disables the commands HOST, EDIT, SAVE, SPOOL, and STORE

In Addition to the commands disabled by a value of 2, a value of 3 disables the commands GET, START, and RUN (along with @ and @@).

Please note that only these commands will be restricted, not the others such as EXECUTE, BEGIN, SET ROLE, etc. Therefore, this is not as comprehensive as the profile table approach.

Let's see a practical example of this option.

In one of your scripts, you run a pretty lengthy report called *report.sql*, called from a shell script as:

```
sqlplus -s scott/tiger @report
```

While the *report.sql* is running, the user could press Control and C and come to the SQL*Plus prompt. From there, he or she could issue all the commands like SAVE, START, HOST, etc. If you use the following instead:

```
sqlplus -s -restrict 3 scott/tiger @report
```

Pressing Control-C will terminate the run and the SQL*Plus prompt will appear, but, when the user enters any of the commands, SQL*Plus will generate an error. The only command the user can execute is EXIT to get out of the prompt.

## Logon Only Once

One method used by hackers to break into the database is to guess passwords, and then try to login to *sqlplus*. When the user ID/password combination is wrong, the database displays the message:

```
ORA-01017: invalid username/password; logon denied
Enter user-name:
```

It errors out, but the username prompt remains. After three failed attempts, the return goes into the OS prompt. Until then, the username prompt remains. In a good security practice, say in the case of batch files, we may not want that. We may want the OS prompt to appear as soon as the first error is reported.

Oracle 9i introduced a new option, LOGON, to stop connection attempts after the first failure. For instance, in the above case, you would issue:

```
sqlplus -s -LOGON scott/tiger
```

or

```
sqlplus -s -L scott/tiger
```

If the connection fails, regardless of the reason, the control returns to the operating system immediately after reporting the error, the username prompt is not displayed.

This is also very useful in writing a script to automate the checking of a database's availability. A common approach is to have a shell script with:

```
sqlplus -s scott/tiger@service1.mycompany.com
```

If the connection does not succeed for some reason, because either the listener is down or the database is down, or because the user ID and password combination is wrong, the script does not return to the operating system prompt. In an automated script, it hangs, making the script useless. Using the –LOGON option can make the script useful.

# Final Checklist

To help you in implementing these policies, here is a checklist that summarizes the concepts and tips presented in this chapter.

- The server machines are physically secure, with access restricted to those who have to have physical contact with the machines. If multiple server machines serve different departments with varying security requirements, they are placed in different enclosures.
- Firewalls for the servers exist and the database server is not directly accessible from the firewall.
- Demilitarized Zones exist.
- UNIX file permissions for key Oracle executables are acceptable as per Table 4.1.
- Oracle executable has the execute permissions removed for others.
- UNIX filesystem permissions are as per the acceptable security standard as shown in Table 4.2.
- The trace directories are not mounted or shared with any other host.
- The *init.ora* parameter *utl_file_dir* is not set to "*", but some specific directory, and that directory does not contain any sensitive files.
- The *init.ora* parameter *_trace_files_public* is not set at all, or is set to FALSE.
- The SYS user is protected against any unauthorized access from the OS user belonging to the group DBA or OINSTALL.
- Any UNIX process does not display the passwords. If a password must be used, it is protected by a password supplying script so that the *ps –aef* command dos not show the password.
- A user is authenticated either by password or by the OS, never both.
- The remote operating system authentication is turned off.
- The operating system authenticated users are kept to the minimum and they have the least privileges.
- The parameter *os_authent_prefix* is set to "" (null).
- The domain authentication (in Windows) is TRUE (default).
- Remote user group management is false.
- Oracle created accounts such as HR are dropped or expired, if not used.

- The password of the DBNSMP user is not the default, DBSNMP. The Oracle Intelligent Agent parameter files are updated accordingly.
- A password management function exists and is enforced by a profile.
- No user has sweeping system privileges. Run the script *find_sweeping_privs.sql.*
- No user has CREATE DIRECTORY privilege.
- No non-schema user has schema creation privileges. Run the script *find_schema_privs.sql.*
- No user has more than required space quota on any tablespace. Run the script *find_ts_quota.sql.*
- The users have only those grants required by the application, not more. Run the script *show_obj_grant.sql.*
- No user has grants with ADMIN option. Run the scripts *users_with_sys_grant_admin_option.sql* and *users_with_obj_grant_admin_option.sql.*
- Roles have adequate privileges, not more. Run script *role_privs.sql.*
- Profile is set to disconnect users after a certain time and idle time.
- A view-based security exists for critical data that should be shown only based on the user who logs in.
- Critical functionalities in an application are encapsulated via stored programs.
- If an application is used to authenticate the user, the authentication is not simply a check on the table where the usernames and passwords are stored. Rather, it should be a robust system where the password can't be guessed via rogue processes such as SQL Injection. The application password management setup described in this chapter may be used as a guideline.
- The programs are created with the Invoker rights model so that the privileges can be checked at the run-time.
- Adequate measures have been taken to protect against SQL Injection attacks.
- SQL*Plus is secured using Product Profiles.
- Restrictions have been placed in `sqlplus` for some commands such as HOST, which can be potentially vulnerable in the hands of malicious users.

## Summary

In this chapter, we explored the various types of security features built into Oracle that can be used to enforce the HIPAA requirements. We also saw some classic hacker attack techniques, such as SQL Injection, and how to prevent them. In enhancing the available features, we explored the use of an application user password management system using encryption and safety from SQL injection.

In subsequent chapters, we will dig deeper into the topics that are powerful and offer immediate HIPAA compliance needs such as Encryption, Virtual Private Database, and Network Security.

# Virtual Private Database

CHAPTER 

## Introduction

Almost all claim management systems have a similar setup – a set of tables for managing members, another for providers, yet another for claims, and finally a set of supporting tables, such as counties, states, and all other sundry data. When a call comes for extra security, the usual reaction is to segregate data into separate tables, schemas, and sometimes into separate databases, the ultimate holy grail of security.

Let's consider the setup of insurance company databases, which HIPAA is most relevant to, in order to better understand things.

Providers are health care providers such as doctors, hospitals, doctor groups (or medical groups), or any other service providers, such as a laboratory doing analysis. A company enters into a contract with an insurer to provide health insurance to its employees. The representatives of the customer company and the insurer discuss and draw up a contract that specifies the amount of coverage, the co-payment amount and all such small details. This is called a plan. Of course, a company may have more than one plan with the insurer, and employees may choose from a variety of plans.

Members are the insured persons and their dependents who are insured in the same plan. When a member obtains a service from the provider, the provider does not bill the customer. Instead, the provider sends the bill, in accordance with the terms and conditions of the contract, to the insurance company. This is called submitting a claim.

Upon receiving the claim, the company assigns it to a claim analyst, who examines the claim for any abnormality and error. If everything is correct, the claim is approved and the payment is sent to the provider. In some cases, primarily when there is a mis-interpretation of the contractual obligations, the insurance company may decide to pay less than the claimed amount. This amount is called paid amount.

One of the primary objectives of HIPAA is to streamline the flow of information between various entities via the use of standardized files. For instance, the record format that is sent from the provider to the insurance company is known as a transaction of type 837. Another type, 835, records the transaction that flows with the payment from the company to the provider. Discussion of these transactions is related to standardization, not security, and is beyond the scope of this book. The concept is presented briefly here to help the reader better understand the law.

Typically, junior claim analysts are assigned claims coming from a single plan. After working on several claims from the same plan, the analysts become familiar with the exact details of the contract and are therefore better equipped to make decisions on that plan.

Senior analysts are assigned claims from more than one plan. In addition, the senior analysts may be assigned claims based on claim amounts, procedures performed, or both. For instance, junior analysts may handle claims of less than $2,000, while senior analysts handle any claim for more than that amount. Similarly, some companies may handle sensitive procedures, such as an HIV test, through a senior analyst regardless of the dollar amount.

The extra level of security required by HIPAA adds visibility restrictions on the database. If a person is not authorized to work with certain information, he or she should not be aware of the *existence* of that data, let alone be able to view or modify it. This is the basic tenet of the HIPAA regulation.

In any other privacy regulations, such as the Gramm-Leach-Bliley Act and the Safe Harbor Act, the same principle applies. Only authorized users are supposed to even see the data, not just operate on it. For instance, if the user NATHAN is supposed to handle claims only from the provider 1234567, then he should see only the data from that provider in all tables he is able to access. This is illustrated in Figure 5.1.

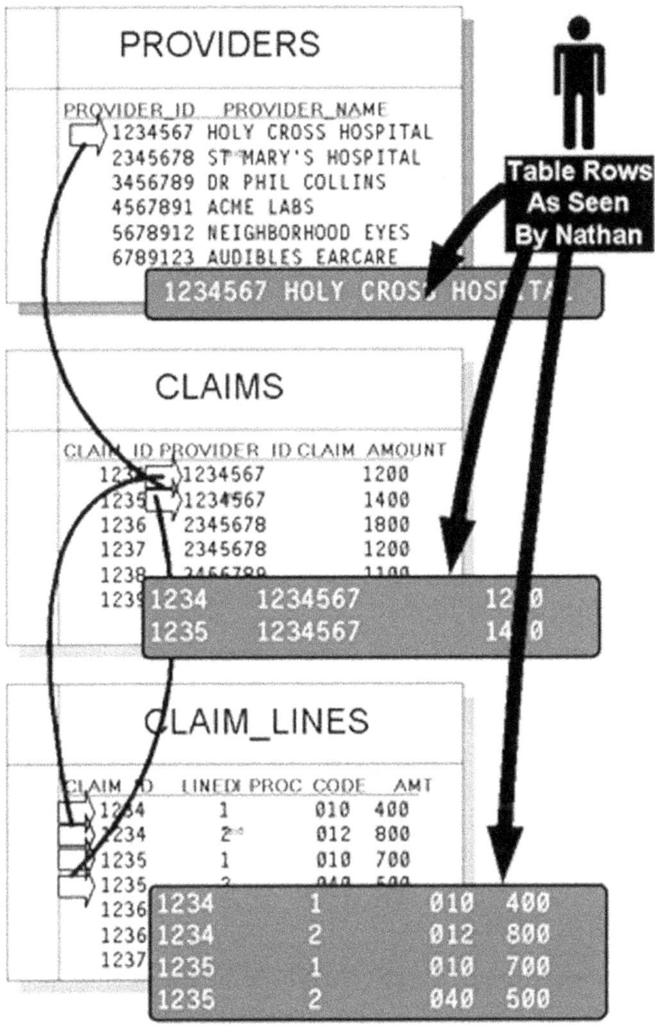


**Figure 5.1** *Selective Viewing of Tables By A User*

Here, the table PROVIDERS contains all the providers the company deals with, but when the user NATHAN queries the table, he should see only the row for PROVIDER_ID 1234567, nothing else. Similarly, if he queries the table *claims*, only claims related to that provider should be visible. It should appear to Nathan that the database contains data about provider 1234567 only, no one else.

Another junior analyst, CLARA, handles providers 2345678 and 3456789. So, for Clara, the database should appear as if it contains only the data related to those provider ids, no others.

How do we achieve this? One way is to create views that offer a filtering condition applied to tables, eliminating all but the authorized rows. The users are given privileges on the view, not on the base table. This works fine for selects, but if the views are complicated, they need additional work for inserts, updates, and deletes. Besides, the proliferation of views complicates the data model.

Another option is to create separate tables in such a way that each user has a copy of the table for which he or she is authorized. The separation of data is the most appealing to security and privacy advocates, but is rather extreme and certainly not practical.

Judy, who is a senior analyst, should be able to see all the providers and their claims. So when she accesses the table, the view should be a union of all such segregated tables. This causes an extra burden on the system, and most of the queries are going to perform badly, due to inefficient joins for the UNION ALL operation.

## How do we resolve the problem?

The solution is to somehow create several virtual tables from the original table so that each user sees only that virtual table for which he or she is authorized. For instance, in the above figure, each of these accessible views is created as a virtual table for each user. When the user NATHAN issues a statement:

```
select * from claims;
```

The rows corresponding to the provider 1234567, for which the user is authorized, come back, nothing else. Note, the user did not specify a where clause. The query was intercepted and was rewritten automatically by the RDBMS as:

```
select * from claims where provider_id = 1234567;
```

No action was required from the user. Similarly, when the user CLARA issues a statement:

```
update claims
set paid_amount = claim_amount - 100;
```

It is rewritten as:

```
update claims
```

```
set paid_amount = claim_amount - 100
where provider_id in (2345678, 3456789);
```

Note how the query was automatically rewritten from the query supplied by the user. The user does not control it, the RDBMS does. The information is presented to the user in such a way that the user does not even see anything for which he or she is not authorized.

This is analogous to a virtual set of tables for each named user, and therefore a virtual database. This setup is known as **Virtual Private Database**, since it offers a private view of the database to the users based on some filtering criteria.

In this chapter, we will discuss how to set it up and how to use it to enforce security and privacy requirements of HIPAA and other laws. We will also discuss how to use it in non-standard environments, as in cases where a named user is not defined.

## Policy

The VPD uses a filtering mechanism to filter out rows that do not match the required authorization of the user. This filter can be either dynamic or static. Static filters are not that useful, but can be used in some cases to exclude a set list of provider ids.

However, in real life the filter is going to be different and dynamic. User Nathan may be promoted or relocated to a different group, and thus he no longer handles provider 1234567, but the providers 4567891 and 5678912. This change in business should be immediately reflected in the view, and should not require a recreation of the view. Therefore, a dynamic filter is necessary. This filter is enforced by the RDBMS using a concept called a *policy*.

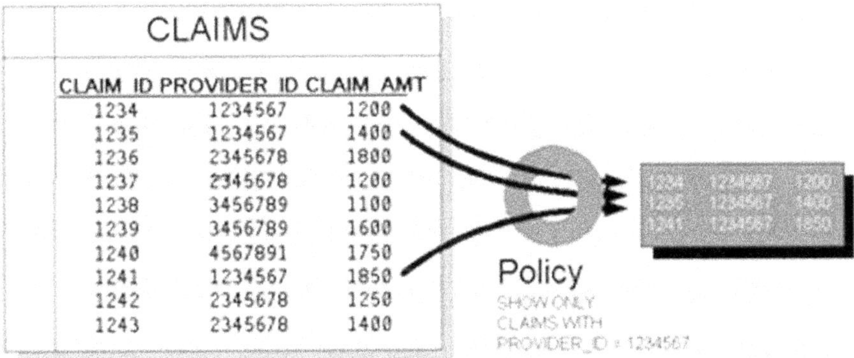


**Figure 5.2** *Policy Applied to a Table in VPD*

Refer to Fig 5.2 for an explanation of the policy. Here the table CLAIMS is subjected to a policy that restricts the tables to those rows that satisfy the restriction. The restriction is controlled by a function such as the following.

```
create or replace function get_auth_providers
(
    p_schema_name    in varchar2,
    p_object_name    in varchar2
)
return varchar2
is
    l_ret        varchar2(2000);
begin
    -- if the user calling it is the same as the owner,
    -- we want to return all rows, so a where condition
    -- of 1=1 will always return TRUE.
    if p_schema_name = user
    then
        l_ret := '1=1';
    else -- if the user is different from the owner
        for prov_rec in
        (
            select provider_id
            from provider_view_policy
            where username = user
        ) loop
            l_ret := l_ret||','||prov_rec.provider_id;
        end loop;
        l_ret := ltrim(l_ret,',');
        l_ret := 'PROVIDER_ID IN ('||l_ret ||')';
    end if;
    return l_ret;
end;
/
```

This function returns the list of providers the current user is authorized to see. Let's see how it dynamically changes the output.

```
Connect NATHAN/*
Select
    get_auth_providers ('CLAIM_SCHEMA', 'CLAIMS')
From
    dual;
```

The output is:

```
PROVIDER_ID IN (1234567)
```

But when CLARA logins and executes the same query:

```
Connect CLARA/*
Select
```

```
    get_auth_providers ('CLAIM_SCHEMA', 'CLAIMS')
From
    dual;
```

The output is:

```
PROVIDER_ID IN (3456789,2345678)
```

Note how the output changed. The output returns the list of providers for which the logged in user is authorized.

What do we do with this function? We will apply it as a limit to the rows retrieved from a table. In other words, we will set it up as a *security policy* for the table CLAIMS. The following does this:

```
begin
dbms_rls.add_policy (
    object_schema     => 'CLAIM_SCHEMA',
    object_name      => 'CLAIMS',
    policy_name       => 'CLAIM_VIEW_POLICY',
    function_schema   => 'CLAIM_SCHEMA',
    policy_function   => 'GET_AUTH_PROVIDERS',
    statement_types   =>
        'INSERT, UPDATE, DELETE, SELECT',
    update_check      => TRUE,
    enable            => TRUE,
    static_policy     => FALSE
);
end;
/
```

For the time being, let's not ponder the explanation or the meaning of these parameters, they will be explained in detail later. We have added a policy to the table *claims* owned by CLAIM_SCHEMA. This policy will append the output of the function *get_auth_providers* to any query of SELECT, INSERT, UPDATE, or DELETE on *claims*.

When user NATHAN logs on and issues a query to select from the table as follows:

```
connect nathan/*
select * from claims
/
```

The output comes as:

```
C SSN       MEMBER_I PROVIDER_I CLAIM_AM PAID_AMOUNT S
- --------- -------- ---------- -------- ----------- -
1 123456789    12345    1234567     1200        1000 P
2 234567891    12345    1234567     1800        1700 P
```

Note, only the claims from provider 1234567 are displayed. The select statement was on the table CLAIMS, not a view that had the filtering condition, and the user did not apply a filter using a where clause. Oracle RDBMS automatically applied a where clause to the query to limit the output.

Remember, when NATHAN executed the function *get_auth_providers()* earlier, he got the output as:

```
PROVIDER_ID IN (1234567)
```

This string was applied automatically as a where clause to all the queries NATHAN submitted to the *claims* table. So the query:

```
select * from claims;
```

Was transformed to:

```
select * from
    (select * from claims)
where PROVIDER_ID IN (1234567);
```

Note how the filtering condition was automatically placed. When Clara issues the same statement:

```
connect CLARA/*
select * from claims;

C SSN        MEMBER_   PROVIDER_ CLAIM_AM PAID_AMOUNT S
- ---------- --------- --------- -------- ----------- - -
3 234567891    12345     2345678     1400        1300 P
4 345678912    23456     3456789     2000        1900 P
5 345678912    23456     3456789     2500        2400 P
```

She gets the claims for which she is authorized, not the others. The filtering condition was again applied automatically.

This filtering applies to updates and deletes as well. Say the user Nathan issues a statement:

```
update
    claims
set
    paid_amount = 1200;

2 rows updated.
```

Note, only the 2 rows to which Nathan has privileges are updated, not all 5. What if he tries to update a row that exists but for which he does not have authorization? The table has a claim of CLAIM_ID 3, but since the provider of the claim is 2345678, a provider Nathan does not have permission to see, the claim shouldn't be visible to him.

```
update
    claims
set
    paid_amount = 1200
where
     claim_id = 3;

0 rows updated.
```

Note how the rows weren't even reported as present. It is as if the rows are never there, as far as Nathan is concerned.

Finally, the issue of inserts comes up. When Nathan tries to insert a record with a provider id for which he is not authorized (e.g. 2345678), he gets an error.

```
insert into
    claims
values (
    6,
    '123456789',
    34567891,
    2345678,
    1200,
    1100,
    'P'
);
                         *
ERROR at line 1:
ORA-28115: policy with check option violation
```

Note the new type of error, *ORA-28115: policy with check option violation,* used to indicate this type of error.

By now, you should have a great deal of appreciation for the value of this tool. You didn't create a view or a trigger. You have defined a rule for viewing (implemented through a function), and the filtering condition is applied automatically to any query the users issue against the table.

## The Package *dbms_rls*

With this example in place, let's explore the main implementing package *dbms_rls*, and in particular the procedure *add_policy*. It takes the following parameters.

| PARAMETER | DESCRIPTION |
| --- | --- |

| PARAMETER | DESCRIPTION |
|---|---|
| OBJECT_SCHEMA | The owner of the object against which this policy is applied. If specified as NULL, the current user or the current schema (if defined) is used. |
| OBJECT_NAME | This specifies the name of the object, i.e. the table or view, or a synonym on which this policy is defined. |
| POLICY_NAME | Name of the policy |
| FUNCTION_SCHEMA | The name of the user who owns the function used as a policy enforcer, e.g. the function *get_auth_providers().* |
| POLICY_FUNCTION | The name of the function used to enforce the policy security. |
| STATEMENT_TYPES | A policy can be restricted to apply for a certain statement only, e.g. SELECT. This may be useful when different types of policies are defined for different actions, such as one for SELECT, one for DELETE, etc. The possible values are SELECT, INDERT, UPDATE, DELETE. The value can also contain a combination of these, separated by comma, e.g. 'SELECT, UPDATE'. The default value is all of the statement types. |
| UPDATE_CHECK | In the example given above, we have made the policy to apply even to the new value put by the update statement. The default is FALSE, i.e. the policy does not check for the value replaced by the update statement. It takes Boolean values TRUE or FALSE. |
| ENABLE | Specifies whether the policy is enabled or not. It takes Boolean value and the default is TRUE. |

| PARAMETER | DESCRIPTION |
|---|---|
| STATIC_POLICY | In the example given above, we have seen that policy function returns a where clause that may be different based on who invokes it. This makes the function dynamic. If the policy function was such that the where condition would be the same regardless of who accesses it, then this value should be TRUE. The default is FALSE, and that is the case in almost all cases of use. |

**Table 5.3** *Parameters for dbms_rls_add_policy*

This is a rather simple usage of this great tool. In real life, however, you would probably face a great deal of complexity in defining the security policy. For instance, the access policy of claims could be defined differently for different types of access. Nathan can view the records of providers 1234567, 2345678 and 3456789, but can create a claim record for provider 1234567 only, and update those for providers 1234567 and 2345678, and delete no records.

Another rule may specify that access be restricted based on the claim amount, in addition to the list of authorized providers. Nathan may access claims of $1,500 or less, Judy may access $5,000 or less, and so on and so forth. Keeping this requirement in mind, we created a new table called *claim_provider_policy* to record the permissions as follows.

```
USERNAME                    VARCHAR2(20)
ACCESS_TYPE                 VARCHAR2(10)
PROVIDER_ID                 NUMBER
```

The records were inserted as follows for NATHAN.

```
USERNAME             ACCESS_TYP PROVIDER_ID
-------------------- ---------- -----------
NATHAN               SELECT         1234567
NATHAN               SELECT         2345678
NATHAN               SELECT         3456789
NATHAN               INSERT         1234567
NATHAN               UPDATE         1234567
NATHAN               UPDATE         2345678
```

Similar records may be created for other users, such as Judy and Clara. For the value enforcement, we can have another table called *claim_value_policy* defined as:

```
USERNAME                     VARCHAR2(20)
MAX_CLAIM_AMOUNT             NUMBER
```

The typical records may be similar to the following:

```
USERNAME             MAX_CLAIM_AMOUNT
-------------------- ----------------
JUDY                             5000
NATHAN                           1500
CLARA                            2500
```

Now the function to enforce the policy will need to change, too. Since we have separate enforcements for each type of access, we will have to have different functions. Here is a function for SELECT policy.

```
create or replace function select_auth_claims
(
    p_schema_name    in varchar2,
    p_object_name    in varchar2
)
return varchar2
is
    l_ret        varchar2(2000);
begin
    if p_schema_name = user
    then
        l_ret := '1=1';
    else -- if the user is different from the owner
        for prov_rec in
        (
            select provider_id
            from claim_provider_policy
            where username = user
            and access_type = 'SELECT'
        ) loop
            l_ret := l_ret||','||prov_rec.provider_id;
        end loop;
        l_ret := ltrim(l_ret,',');
        l_ret := 'PROVIDER_ID IN ('||l_ret ||')';
    end if;
    return l_ret;
end;
/
```

Similarly, the INSERT policy is defined as follows:

```
create or replace function insert_auth_claims
(
    p_schema_name    in varchar2,
    p_object_name    in varchar2
)
```

```
return varchar2
is
    l_ret        varchar2(2000);
begin
    if p_schema_name = user
    then
        l_ret := '1=1';
    else -- if the user is different from the owner
        for prov_rec in
        (
            select provider_id
            from claim_provider_policy
            where username = user
            and access_type = 'INSERT'
        ) loop
            l_ret := l_ret||','||prov_rec.provider_id;
        end loop;
        l_ret := ltrim(l_ret,',');
        l_ret := 'PROVIDER_ID IN ('||l_ret ||')';
    end if;
    return l_ret;
end;
/
```

The update function is defined as:

```
create or replace function update_auth_claims
(
    p_schema_name    in varchar2,
    p_object_name    in varchar2
)
return varchar2
is
    l_ret        varchar2(2000);
begin
    if p_schema_name = user
    then
        l_ret := '1=1';
    else -- if the user is different from the owner
        for prov_rec in
        (
            select provider_id
            from claim_provider_policy
            where username = user
            and access_type = 'UPDATE'
        ) loop
            l_ret := l_ret||','||prov_rec.provider_id;
        end loop;
        l_ret := ltrim(l_ret,',');
        l_ret := 'PROVIDER_ID IN ('||l_ret ||')';
    end if;
    return l_ret;
end;
/
```

Finally, we will create a function to check the maximum claim amount for the claims.

```
create or replace function check_claim_value_policy
(
    p_schema_name    in varchar2,
    p_object_name    in varchar2
)
return varchar2
is
    l_ret         varchar2(2000);
    l_max_claim_amount number;
begin
    l_ret := NULL;
    if p_schema_name = user
    then
        l_ret := '1=1';
    else -- if the user is different from the owner
         begin
            select max_claim_amount
            into l_max_claim_amount
            from claim_value_policy
            where username = user;
            l_ret := 'CLAIM_AMOUNT <= '||
                l_max_claim_amount;
        exception
            when NO_DATA_FOUND then
                l_ret := NULL;
            when OTHERS then
                raise;
        end;
    end if;
    return l_ret;
end;
/
```

These functions can be as complicated as you wish them to be. The objective is to find a filtering predicate to be applied to the queries on the table.

Now we have to define three different policies on the table.

```
begin
dbms_rls.add_policy (
    object_schema    => 'CLAIM_SCHEMA',
    object_name      => 'CLAIMS',
    policy_name      => 'CLAIM_SELECT_POLICY',
    function_schema  => 'CLAIM_SCHEMA',
    policy_function  => 'SELECT_AUTH_CLAIMS',
    statement_types  => 'SELECT'
);
end;
/
```

For the INSERT statements:

```
begin
dbms_rls.add_policy (
```

```
    object_schema    => 'CLAIM_SCHEMA',
    object_name      => 'CLAIMS',
    policy_name      => 'CLAIM_INSERT_POLICY',
    function_schema  => 'CLAIM_SCHEMA',
    policy_function  => 'INSERT_AUTH_CLAIMS',
    statement_types  => 'INSERT',
    update_check     => TRUE
);
end;
/
```

For the UPDATE statements:

```
begin
dbms_rls.add_policy (
    object_schema    => 'CLAIM_SCHEMA',
    object_name     => 'CLAIMS',
    policy_name      => 'CLAIM_UPDATE_POLICY',
    function_schema  => 'CLAIM_SCHEMA',
    policy_function  => 'UPDATE_AUTH_CLAIMS',
    statement_types  => 'UPDATE',
    update_check     => TRUE
);
end;
/
```

For the claim value check:

```
begin
dbms_rls.add_policy (
    object_schema    => 'CLAIM_SCHEMA',
    object_name      => 'CLAIMS',
    policy_name      => 'CLAIM_VALUE_POLICY',
    function_schema  => 'CLAIM_SCHEMA',
    policy_function  => 'CHECK_CLAIM_VALUE_POLICY',
    statement_types  =>
        'SELECT, INSERT, DELETE, UPDATE',
    update_check     => TRUE
);
end;
/
```

Note how we have defined several policies on a single table. During a select query, two policies are applied – *claim_value_policy* and *select_auth_claims*. During execution, the predicates retuned by both queries are applied to the table. If NATHAN issues a query:

```
select * from claims
```

It is rewritten to:

```
select * from
(select * from claims)
where
```

```
(
    provider_id in (1234567,2345678,3456789)
    AND
    claim_amount <= 1500
)
```

**Important: When more than one policy is defined on a table, the output of all the policies are AND'd to arrive at the final where clause.**

After the policies are defined, it's now time to test the setup.

```
connect nathan/*

select * from claim_schema.claims;

C SSN        MEMBER_ID PROVIDER_ID  Amou PAID_AMOUNT S
-- --------- ---------- ----------- ----- ----------- -
1 123456789      12345     1234567  1200        1200 P
3 234567891      12345     2345678  1400        1300 P
```

See how both the policies *claim_value_policy* and *select_auth_claims* have been applied to the table, and the filtering predicates from both the policies have been applied to the query? The same effect occurs when UPDATE and INSERT occur on the table, too.

# Security of the Policy

We have defined a policy and enforced it using a function, but is the function itself secured? The cornerstones of this security mechanism are:

- The tables that define the policy
- The functions that enforce them
- The policies themselves

These items must be secured. In our example, we have used the CLAIM_SCHEMA user as the owner of both the tables and the functions. This need not be the case. We could have a separate owner called SECUSER that can own these objects. There is no need to grant any kind of privilege to anyone on these tables and functions. Since SYS creates these policies, there is no way another user can alter them. You could also give the SECUSER execute privilege on *dbms_rls*, if desired.

This makes the policy tamper-proof and secure. You can use policies to enforce all types of security in all types of access methods.

It is important to understand that the user SYS is exempt from being subjected to any type of security policy. This is required. Otherwise, if you define a policy incorrectly by mistake, sys can never do anything.

If you decide to have some special users not be subjected to the policies defined on the objects, they can be exempted as in the following

```
GRANT EXEMPT ACCESS POLICY TO SECUSER;
```

This system privilege will make sure the user SECUSER will not be subjected to any type of access policies. Being a powerful one, this privilege should be granted with extreme care.

## Types of Policies

In Oracle 9i and earlier, the VPD policies were of only one type. In Oracle 10g and beyond there are three different types of VPD policies.

- Dynamic
- Context Sensitive
- Static

*Dynamic* policies are equivalent to the older Oracle 9i style policies. When a policy is defined as dynamic, the policy function is executed every time the table is accessed, even though all things may be the same. While this ensures that the policy picks up the exact variable every time, the repeated execution of the policy function quickly becomes expensive from the performance point of view.

To alleviate this problem, a new type of policy, known as *Context Sensitive*, executes only when the application context changes between the executions, not at every call. This substantially reduces the calls to the policy function. However, if the policy function must be evaluated every time, whether or not the context changes, this type of policy cannot be used.

The perfect example of context sensitive policy is the case where the output of the policy function is a determinant of the current time. To get the current time, the function must execute and therefore the policy cannot be declared as context sensitive.

In some cases, the context sensitive policy is also an overkill, particularly in cases where the policy function merely returns a value regardless of the time of the day or even when the context changes. An example can make this easier to understand. In a typical Application Service Provider (ASP) model, the hosting company might have just one database. The users are assigned application contexts when they login which are used by the VPD policy to build the predicate as in the following:

```
return sys_context('app_ctx', 'l_user_id');
```

In this case, the VPD policy appends the following to the queries:

```
where user_id = sys_context('app_ctx', 'l_user_id');
```

The logon trigger sets the attribute *l_user_id* in the context *app_ctx* when the user logs into the database. Note, here the part of the predicate to the left of the equality sign, i.e. *user_id* is fixed. The right side is fairly static; it only changes when the user disconnects and reconnects; but then it becomes a different session. Hence the change is not really a change, but another invocation of the policy function.

This type of policy, where the function executes only once, not re-executed every time or at every context change, is known as a *Static* policy. Since the policy function is not executed more than once per session, these types of policies are extremely fast.

The policy type is indicated while defining the policy. Taking the example of the code segment provided in Chapter 5, Virtual Private Database, to add the policy to the table:

```
begin
dbms_rls.add_policy (
    object_schema    => 'CLAIM_SCHEMA',
    object_name      => 'CLAIMS',
    policy_name      => 'CLAIM_VIEW_POLICY',
    function_schema  => 'CLAIM_SCHEMA',
    policy_function  => 'GET_AUTH_PROVIDERS',
    statement_types  =>
        'INSERT, UPDATE, DELETE, SELECT',
    update_check     => TRUE,
    enable           => TRUE,
    static_policy    => FALSE
);
end;
/
```

The new parameter *policy_type* indicates the type of policy. The above code can be written as:

```
begin
dbms_rls.add_policy (
    object_schema    => 'CLAIM_SCHEMA',
    object_name      => 'CLAIMS',
    policy_name      => 'CLAIM_VIEW_POLICY',
    function_schema  => 'CLAIM_SCHEMA',
```

```
    policy_function   => 'GET_AUTH_PROVIDERS',
    statement_types   =>
        'INSERT, UPDATE, DELETE, SELECT',
    update_check      => TRUE,
    enable            => TRUE,
    policy_type       => dbms_rls.dynamic
);
end;
/
```

Here, it is assumed that the policy is dynamic, which is the default type. Also note that the parameter *static_policy* is no longer present as a valid parameter.

The behavior of this policy will be exactly the same as the Oracle 9i policy type; where the policy function will be executed for each call to the table.

Setting the values of the parameter *policy_type* to *context_sensitive* and *static*, respectively, indicates the context sensitive and static policies.

## Shared and Non-Shared Policies

The policy types are further subdivided by the way they are added to a group of objects. While defining policies to a group of objects, often it becomes necessary to define the same policy function on all of them. For instance, in our example database, the tables CLAIMS and CLAIM_LINES may have restrictions based on the column CLAIM_ID, i.e. both the tables have been applied predicate

```
where claim_id in (<list of claim ids>)
```

Since the predicate applied is the same, we can define the same policy on both the tables and their values are determined from the predicate function. If this is possible, then we can define the policy as a *shared* one, i.e. shared between multiple objects. Shared policies can be defined for both Static and Context Sensitive ones. They are defined by setting the parameter *policy_type* to either *shared_static* or *shared_context_sensitive*. The following code segment creates a shared context sensitive policy.

```
begin
dbms_rls.add_policy (
    object_schema     => 'CLAIM_SCHEMA',
    object_name       => 'CLAIMS',
    policy_name       => 'CLAIM_VIEW_POLICY',
    function_schema   => 'CLAIM_SCHEMA',
    policy_function   => 'GET_AUTH_PROVIDERS',
    statement_types   =>
        'INSERT, UPDATE, DELETE, SELECT',
    update_check      => TRUE,
    enable            => TRUE,
```

```
    policy_type       =>
            dbms_rls.shared_context_sensitive
);
end;
/
```

Since dynamic policies, by definition, are always executed, there is no equivalent shared dynamic policy. In summary, there are five new types of policy types in Oracle 10g.

- dynamic
- shared_context_sensitive
- context_sensitive
- shared_static
- static

## Relevant Columns

Remember, in Oracle 9i and below, if a policy has been defined on a table, the policy is always applied, regardless of which columns are accessed. Sometimes it may be necessary to relax the policy depending upon the type of data accessed. For instance, when a user selects Social Security Numbers (SSN) from the *claims* table, it should be restricted to only the authorized claims, not all. However, if a user finds out how many rows are there in the *claims* table, the restriction may be relaxed to report the count on all rows, without restriction. In Oracle 9i and below this is not possible; either the policy is not applied or if applied then the policy predicate is applied for each query.

Oracle 10g and beyond allows selective restriction on the rows, based on which columns are accessed in the query, quite similar to the audit columns in Fine Grained Auditing. The relevant columns are indicated in the *add_policy* procedure by a new parameter *sec_relevant_cols*. In our earlier example, if we wanted to apply the predicate only to the columns SSN and CLAIM_AMOUNT, then we would have defined the policy as

```
begin
dbms_rls.add_policy (
    object_schema      => 'CLAIM_SCHEMA',
    object_name        => 'CLAIMS',
    policy_name        => 'CLAIM_VIEW_POLICY',
    function_schema    => 'CLAIM_SCHEMA',
    policy_function    => 'GET_AUTH_PROVIDERS',
    statement_types    =>
        'INSERT, UPDATE, DELETE, SELECT',
    update_check      => TRUE,
```

```
    enable            => TRUE,
    policy_type       => dbms_rls.dynamic,
    sec_relevant_cols => 'SSN, CLAIM_AMOUNT'
);
end;
/
```

Note the relevant columns are defined inside single quotes separated by commas.

## Examples

Imagine the user making several queries on the table. Here are the various situations and the effect on the policy being applied and the rows returned.

- select * from claims;

  **Restricted**. Only the authorized rows are returned.
  The query selected all the columns, including the relevant columns SSN and CLAIM_AMOUNT; hence the restrictions were applied.

- select count(*) from claims;

  **Not Restricted**. The actual count of the records in the table is returned. Since the user did not specifically select any of the relevant columns, the restrictions were not placed.

- select claim_id from claims;

  **Not Restricted**. Since the query has no reference to SSN or CLAIM_AMOUNT, which are the relevant columns, all the records will be returned.

- select claim_id from claims where SSN = '123456789';

  **Restricted**. Although the query did not specify the columns SSN or CLAIM_AMOUNT, the predicate has the SSN column; hence the restrictions are placed.

# Administration

Next comes the question of administration of these policies. These are done through the package *dbms_rls*, an example of which we saw earlier. The main data dictionary view to see the information on policies is *dba_policies*. In this section, we will describe each of these important concepts.

## *dba_policies*

This data dictionary view contains information on all the policies defined in the database. The columns are described below.

| COLUMN | DESCRIPTION |
|---|---|
| OBJECT_OWNER | The schema owner who owns the object on which the policy is defined. |
| OBJECT_NAME | The name of the object |
| POLICY_GROUP | The policy group this policy belongs to; policy groups are explained in detail later. |
| POLICY_NAME | Name of the policy |
| PF_OWNER | The owner of the function used to enforce security of the policy. |
| PACKAGE | Sometimes a package used to enforce the policy. This shows the name of the package if that is the case. |
| FUNCTION | The name of the function that is used to enforce security. |
| SEL | Indicates whether the policy applies to select statements. A value of YES indicates that, otherwise NO. |
| INS | Same explanation as above, but for inserts. |
| UPD | Same explanation as above, but for updates. |
| DEL | Same explanation as above, but for deletes. |
| CHK_OPTION | If the policy has been defined with an update check that will make sure the new value also conforms to the policy after the change. A value of YES indicates that, otherwise NO. |
| ENABLE | Indicates whether the policy is enabled. A value of YES indicates that, otherwise NO. |
| STATIC_POLICY | Indicates whether the policy is static, i.e. the function returns the same value regardless of the user who calls it. |

**Table 5.4** *Columns of dba_policies*

There are similar views, *user_policies*, which show information on policies defined on the objects owned by the user. Another view, *all_policies*, shows information on all the policies to which the user has access.

# Policy Maintenance

## Dropping

Earlier we discussed how to add a policy using the *dbms_rls.add_policy* packaged function. The parameters of the function have been given in table 5.3. To drop a policy, use the function *drop_policy* in the same package. For example, to drop the policy *select_claim_policy*, you would use:

```
begin
    dbms_rls.drop_policy (
        object_schema => 'CLAIM_SCHEMA',
        object_name   => 'CLAIMS',
        policy_name   => 'SELECT_CLAIM_POLICY'
end;
```

This drops the policy. Since there is no procedure to modify a policy, the only way to modify it is to drop, then create the policy again.

## Enabling/Disabling

The policies can be defined but be disabled. To disable a policy, the procedure *enable_policy* of the package *dbms_rls* is used. For instance, to disable the policy *select_claim_policy*, you would issue:

```
begin
    dbms_rls.enable_policy (
        object_schema => 'CLAIM_SCHEMA',
        object_name   => 'CLAIMS',
        policy_name   => 'SELECT_CLAIM_POLICY',
        enable        => FALSE
end;
```

To enable the same,

```
begin
    dbms_rls.enable_policy (
        object_schema => 'CLAIM_SCHEMA',
        object_name   => 'CLAIMS',
        policy_name   => 'SELECT_CLAIM_POLICY',
        enable        => TRUE
end;
```

## Refreshing

When a statement is executed for the first time, it is parsed and stored in a shared pool of the instance. When a policy that may affect this statement is created, the statement must be reparsed for the policy to be applied. To ensure this happens, the procedure *refresh_policy* is used.

```
begin
    dbms_rls.refresh_policy (
        object_schema => 'CLAIM_SCHEMA',
        object_name   => 'CLAIMS',
        policy_name   => 'SELECT_CLAIM_POLICY'
end;
```

# Policy Groups

While going through the example given earlier, you might have noticed that in a real life system, you will soon have a number of policies defined on an object. The larger the number, the worse the setup becomes from an administrative point-of-view. To ease the management of so many policies, there is another concept called a *policy group*, which may contain one or more policies. This group can be enabled or disabled, added, refreshed or dropped as a whole.

In the example we discussed earlier, we could define a policy group called CLAIM_ACCESS_POLICY_GROUP as follows.

```
begin
    dbms_rls.create_policy_group (
        object_schema => 'CLAIM_SCHEMA',
        object_name => 'CLAIMS',
        policy_group => 'CLAIM_ACCESS_POLICY_GROUP'
    );
end;
```

Next, we will have to add the policies to this group.

```
begin
dbms_rls.add_grouped_policy (
    object_schema     => 'CLAIM_SCHEMA',
    object_name       => 'CLAIMS',
    policy_group      => 'CLAIM_ACCESS_POLICY_GROUP',
    policy_name       => 'CLAIM_SELECT_POLICY',
    function_schema   => 'CLAIM_SCHEMA',
    policy_function   => 'SELECT_AUTH_CLAIMS',
    statement_types   => 'SELECT'
);

dbms_rls.add_grouped_policy (
    object_schema     => 'CLAIM_SCHEMA',
```

```
    object_name      => 'CLAIMS',
    policy_group     => 'CLAIM_ACCESS_POLICY_GROUP',
    policy_name      => 'CLAIM_INSERT_POLICY',
    function_schema  => 'CLAIM_SCHEMA',
    policy_function  => 'INSERT_AUTH_CLAIMS',
    statement_types  => 'INSERT',
    update_check     => TRUE
);

dbms_rls.add_grouped_policy (
    object_schema    => 'CLAIM_SCHEMA',
    object_name     => 'CLAIMS',
    policy_group     => 'CLAIM_ACCESS_POLICY_GROUP',
    policy_name      => 'CLAIM_UPDATE_POLICY',
    function_schema  => 'CLAIM_SCHEMA',
    policy_function  => 'UPDATE_AUTH_CLAIMS',
    statement_types  => 'UPDATE',
    update_check     => TRUE
);
end;
/
```

Note how the procedure *add_grouped_policy* is almost identical to the *add_policy* procedure, without the parameter *policy_group*.

Now this group can be refreshed and dropped without affecting the underlying policies. Even though the policies are grouped, they can be individually enabled or disabled using the *enable_grouped_policy* procedure.

The data dictionary view *dba_policy_groups* shows information on policy groups. It has three columns:

```
OBJECT_OWNER
OBJECT_NAME
POLICY_GROUP
```

The column names are self-explanatory. The column POLICY_GROUP in *dba_policies* view identifies the individual policies inside a group.

# Application Context

## SYS Context

Remember, in the function defined to enforce the SELECT statement policy, we used a construct as follows:

```
where username = user
```

Here, USER is a function that returns the user who is currently logged in. For instance, you can determine the current user by:

```
Select user from dual;

USER
------
NATHAN
```

The same can also be returned by the following function:

```
select sys_context('USERENV','SESSION_USER') from dual;

SYS_CONTEXT('USERENV','SESSION_USER')
----------------------------------------------
NATHAN
```

The built-in function *sys_context* is a function that reads a certain part of the memory called *Context*, which can be defined by the user. The context can hold values that are set for a session and can be referenced throughout the session. A different session may hold a different value of the variable inside a context. This is very close to global variables in programming languages.

In the case of the function *sys_context*, there are two distinct parts:

**Namespace** – It defines a set of variables in the context. Inside each set, the names must be unique. In this case, the namespace is USERENV. The user can create his or her individual namespace, as we will explore later.

**Attribute** – This is a variable inside the defined Namespace. An attribute has a value assigned to it. In this case, the attribute is SESSION_USER. The value is NATHAN, since he is the one who logged in.

USERENV is a special type of namespace, used by the RDBMS kernel to store important information, such as the user logged in, the IP address, etc. A complete list of the attributes is found in the Oracle SQL Reference Manual.

## User Defined Context

Just as there is a system defined namespace context, the user can also define a context to hold application data. This is done through the SQL statement CREATE CONTEXT. As we saw earlier, the context has a set of variables called attributes. The primary purpose of the context is to hold these variables in memory and provide them to whoever wants them. These variables are set by the procedure *set_context* in the package *dbms_session*.

Let's define a context for our application called *claim_app_ctx*. In this context, we will define an attribute called ANALYST_ROLE and assign a value 'senior' to it. This is done by:

```
begin
    dbms_session.set_context(
        namespace => 'claim_app_ctx',
        attribute => 'analyst_role',
        value => 'senior'
    )
end;
```

Note, executing the above SQL will return an error, the reason for which we will see in a moment. But that is expected, contexts are not set this way.

Next, we will define a procedure to set the various attributes of the context as follows:

```
create procedure set_claim_app_ctx
(
    p_attribute_name in varchar2,
    p_attribute_value in varchar2
) is
begin
    dbms_session.set_context(
       'claim_app_ctx',
        p_attribute_name,
        p_attribute_value);
end;
/
```

The procedure will be created, but if it is executed, an error will be returned.

```
execute set_claim_app_ctx ('Ns2','Val2')
BEGIN set_claim_app_ctx ('Ns2','Val2'); END;
*
ERROR at line 1:
ORA-01031: insufficient privileges
ORA-06512: at "SYS.DBMS_SESSION", line 78
ORA-06512: at "CLAIM_SCHEMA.SET_CLAIM_APP_CTX", line 7
ORA-06512: at line 1
```

This is a very important concept that will be explored later. Next, we will create the context:

```
create context claim_app_ctx
using set_claim_app_ctx
/
```

Note the use of *set_claim_app_ctx* clause, which is the procedure we created earlier to set the context. *Now* the procedure *set_claim_app_ctx* can be executed.

```
execute set_claim_app_ctx ('Ns2','Val2')

PL/SQL procedure successfully completed.
```

It successfully executed this time, but failed earlier. What happened differently this time?

This procedure was supposed to set some attributes of some context. Without the context being in place, the procedure wouldn't have set anything, and thus it was forbidden. This feature is an important safety attribute of using procedures to set contexts. If the user decides to set the context outside the procedure:

```
begin
    dbms_session.set_context(
        namespace => 'claim_app_ctx',
        attribute => 'analyst_role',
        value => 'senior'
    )
end;
```

He or she will receive an error.

```
ERROR at line 1:
ORA-01031: insufficient privileges
ORA-06512: at "SYS.DBMS_SESSION", line 78
ORA-06512: at "ANANDA.SET_CLAIM_APP_CTX", line 7
ORA-06512: at line 1
```

The user cannot execute the procedure to set the context, nor can he or she set the context directly. This makes this procedure a *trusted* one – meaning that only the procedure can set the context. Thus, the procedure and the context are tightly coupled with one another.

 **Trusted Procedures are procedures that can set a context. The user cannot directly invoke the *dbms_session* package to set the context. Since only a procedure can do that, securing the procedure itself is enough to prevent anyone from setting any context. Also, by forcing users to use a procedure to set a context, we can also satisfy other tasks – such as setting roles – inside the procedure.**

## Managing Contexts

The next question is how to check which contexts have been defined and assigned in a session. The context attributes can be set by the following SQL.

```
exec claim_schema.set_claim_app_ctx ('ATTR1','VAL1')
exec claim_schema.set_claim_app_ctx ('ATTR2','VAL2')
```

After setting them, let's see if they work properly.

```
select * from session_context
/

NAMESPACE           ATTRIBUTE VALUE
------------------ --------- -----
CLAIM_APP_CTX       ATTR1     Val1
CLAIM_APP_CTX       ATTR2     Val2
```

This shows the context defined *claim_app_ctx* and the attributes defined in that context, as well as the value of each.

Note the use of a view called *session_context.* This holds the information on all contexts and their attributes for the current session. Another way the value of the attribute can be retrieved is:

```
select
    sys_context('CLAIM_APP_CTX','ATTR1')
from
    dual
/

SYS_CONTEXT('CLAIM_APP_CTX','ATTR1')
------------------------------------
Val1
```

This construct is the same as the *sys_context* we saw earlier. In this case, we simply used our own context namespace, *claim_app_ctx*, instead of USERENV, which is a special namespace set by the RDBMS directly.

So far, we have discussed how to set, read, and secure a context, but one thing that is missing from this discussion is how we can effectively use the context to resolve problems or attain some advanced functionality. That topic is explained in the next section.

# Application User Management

Ideally, the users connecting to the database must be named users in the database, with no two persons sharing the same user ID. VPD requires that type of setup, otherwise, there is no way the policy manager will know who the user is and which policy to apply.

However, this is easier said than done. Most shops have a well rooted, established application user authentication system, and they will not be amenable to the idea of jettisoning that in favor of creating a large number of database users. These apps typically connect to Oracle using a shared user id and password, and check against a table containing the named application users and their passwords if the they are correct. If, for example, the application users are stored in the table *app_users* and the application connects using an application user ID "judy" with password "success1," and the Oracle user ID is "appuser" and the password is "everyoneknows," then the algorithm is probably similar to the following:

```
Connect to oracle using appuser/everyoneknows
Select count(*) from app_users where app_userid = 'JUDY' and app_password =
'SUCCESS1'
If (rows returned) then
    Display "Login Successful"
Else
   Display "Wrong UserId and Password. Try Again"
End if
```

## Problems

**SQL Injection Attacks** - This scheme is fraught with problems and security holes. One of the major security holes is the potential threat of a SQL Injection attack described in Chapter 4. This setup just invites hackers to use SQL Injection.

**Users Connecting Outside** - The other problem is how to prevent the users from connecting outside the application. For instance, the password of Oracle database user APPUSER becomes well known and can be abused. Someone can easily connect through SQL*Plus as APPUSER and do the data manipulation, bypassing the application security. Since the application was not even involved, the user could not be authenticated.

**Unlimited Privileges** - The user APPUSER must have all the privileges to perform the work. Even if the application user has limited roles, the real user in the database is APPUSER. APPUSER has powerful privileges to do damage because the user privileges for APPUSER are the sum of all required privileges of all application users. Since we rely on the application to limit the privileges, a user connecting outside will not be subjected to such restriction.

**Unable to use VPD** - Since the application user is simply a connection authenticator, the VPD cannot be used to enforce privacy requirements. Rather, the application must ensure that users do not go beyond the boundaries they have been allocated – a task easier said than done.

# Solution

## Authentication

Let's handle the problems one by one. For the authentication mechanism, we will do away with the selection from the table of users. Rather, we will establish an application user validation function, described in detail in Chapter 4. It's not repeated here, but the salient points are highlighted below. The script for the function is also available in the online code depot as *is_password_correct.sql*.

The authentication is performed by a function *is_password_correct* owned by user SECUSER. It accepts two parameters – the application user id and the application password, and returns just a word - YES or NO - depending on whether the user ID and password combination is correct. SECUSER owns the table *app_users* and no one has any kind of privileges on it. Only APPUSER has the execute privilege on the function. So, the above algorithm for authenticating users will change to:

```
Connect to oracle using appuser/everyoneknows
Resp := is_password_correct ('JUDY', 'SUCCESS1')
If (Resp = 'YES') then
    Display "Login Successful"
Else
   Display "Wrong UserId and Password. Try Again"
End if
```

Note the precautions taken to protect against a SQL Injection attack. If the hacker injects extra characters after the password or user fields, the statement will fail. The deliberate avoidance of dynamic PL/SQL inside the function ensures that. This way, the hacker can't just use a string that always evaluates to true and get in.

Second, the table *app_users* is not accessible to anyone, except the users with SELECT ANY TABLE privilege. So there is no danger of someone getting into the table and learning the passwords.

Third, the password field in the table *app_users* is *encrypted.* Even if someone gets in using the stealth SELECT ANY TABLE privilege, the password values will not mean anything.

Merely by using a function to authenticate application users, we have achieved a great deal more security than we had earlier. The use of a function returning YES or NO is critical in designing authentication methods, and should always be followed.

## Application Context

So far, we have merely protected the application user authentication mechanism. This still does not prevent someone from going in as APPUSER and making changes. How do we protect against that? This section deals with that protection.

Adequate protection from a variety of actions is possible by using a database *role*. A role can have several privileges associated with it. Multiple roles can be defined in the database corresponding to multiple privilege requirements. These roles could be turned on or off to assign or revoke privileges.

For instance, we could have roles called JUNIOR_CLAIM_VIEWER, JUNIOR_CLAIM_ANALYST, and CLAIM_SUPERVISOR. The viewer role is supposed to only select from the claims table; the analyst role has full privileges to select, insert, and update claims, but not delete them; and, the supervisor role can do any operation on the claims, including delete.

```
create role junior_claim_viewer
/
create role junior_claim_analyst
/
create role claim_supervisor
/
grant select on claim_schema.claims to junior_claim_viewer
/
grant junior_claim_viewer  to junior_claim_analyst
/
grant insert, update on claim_schema.claims to junior_claim_analyst
/
grant junior_claim_analyst to claim_supervisor
/
grant delete on claim_schema.claims to junior_claim_analyst
/
```

Now, we have to grant these roles to the user **appuser**.

```
grant create session, junior_claim_analyst, junior_claim_viewer,
claim_supervisor to appuser
/
```

One of the problems of assigning roles is that the assigned role becomes the *default* role of the user. This means all the privileges assigned to these roles are immediately available to the user. Since we want to control access depending on the application user, we can't let that happen. Therefore, we will set the default role of the user to no role.

```
alter user appuser default role none
/
```

This will set the default role of the user to nothing. When we want to set the role to JUNIOR_CLAIM_VIEWER, we will issue:

```
set role junior_claim_viewer
/
```

To make sure the role was activated,

```
select * from session_roles
/

SESSION_ROLES
------------------------------
JUNIOR_CLAIM_VIEWER
```

When we want to switch it back to none of the roles,

```
set role none
/
```

In this way, we can control the access to the objects. But, how do we enforce that method?

This is done by the application context. Remember from our previous discussion that the contexts are sort of global variables that can be set and read within sessions. We can create our own context called *claim_app_ctx*, and one of the attributes can be the application user id named *app_user_id*. The other attribute can be the role the user is supposed to have based on the access, named `app_user_role`.

The application user is different from the database user. Let's say our application user is MARK with a password "funny4life." This user must be registered in the table *app_users*.

```
insert into app_users values ('MARK',get_app_password('FUNNY4LIFE'))
/
```

The function *get_app_password* returns an encrypted password that is stored in the table *app_users*.

The application connects to the database as APPUSER. While doing so, it sets the context attributes *app_user_id* and *app_user_role*. This *app_user_id* can be used by a policy instead of the session user, unlike the example we saw earlier. Similarly, the *app_user_role* can be set to determine which role is defined. In order to determine which application user has which role, we have to modify the table *app_users*, adding a column called *app_role*. The table now looks like the following.

```
USERID     USERPASS                  USER_ROLE
---------- ---------------------- --------------------
MARK       I¡àV█≈☺ü                JUNIOR_CLAIM_ANALYST
ANTHONY    H‼@╩ù▄♂ÿ=▲!·▄óg¥        SENIOR_CLAIM_ANALYST
ANNIE      ╟┌§─√^₧» ─↨)S<♂─        CLAIM_SUPERVISOR
```

This indicates that when the application user MARK logs in, although the database user is APPUSER, the *app_user_id* attribute in the context should be set to MARK and the *app_user_role* attribute should be set to JUNIOR_CLAIM_ANALYST. The active database role of the user should also be JUNIOR_CLAIM_ANALYST.

To set the role, we can define a procedure called *set_user_role* as follows, under the schema SECUSER.

```
create or replace procedure set_user_role
(
    p_app_role  in varchar2
)
authid current_user
is
begin
    dbms_session.set_role (p_app_role);
end set_user_role;
/
```

Perhaps you are wondering why we have to define a procedure for something as simple as setting a role. The question is legitimate and will be explained in further discussion.

The application then calls the appropriate procedures to set the context attributes as well as the active role.

```
connect appuser/***

begin
    secuser.set_claim_app_ctx
        ('app_user_role', 'JUNIOR_CLAIM_VIEWER' );
    secuser.set_claim_app_ctx
        ('app_user_id','MARK');
end;
/

PL/SQL procedure successfully completed.

exec set_user_role ('JUNIOR_CLAIM_VIEWER')

PL/SQL procedure successfully completed.

SQL> select * from session_context;

NAMESPACE           ATTRIBUTE     VALUE
```

```
------------------ ------------ --------------------
CLAIM_APP_CTX      APP_USER_ID   MARK
CLAIM_APP_CTX      APP_USER_ROLE JUNIOR_CLAIM_VIEWER

SQL> select * from session_roles;

ROLE
------------------------------
JUNIOR_CLAIM_VIEWER
```

As you can see the database user is APPUSER, the *app_user_id* is set to MARK, the *app_user_role* is set to JUNIOR_CLAIM_VIEWER, and the active role is JUNIOR_CLAIM_VIEWER.

At this time, the user decides to select from the table claims and tries to delete from it.

```
SQL> select * from claim_schema.claims;

C SSN        MEMBER_ID PROVIDER_ID CLAIM_AMOUNT PAID_AMOUNT S
- --------- ---------- ----------- ------------ ----------- -
1 123456789      12345     1234567         1200        1200 P
2 234567891      12345     1234567         1800        1200 P
3 234567891      12345     2345678         1400        1300 P
4 345678912      23456     3456789         2000        1900 P
5 345678912      23456     3456789         2500        2400 P
```

The select was successful since the role JUNIOR_CLAIM_VIEWER does have SELECT privileges on the table *claims*. Note, however, that all the claim records were returned. At this time, we don't have a policy set on the table, so there was no filtering condition.

```
SQL> delete claim_schema.claims;
delete claim_schema.claims
                    *
ERROR at line 1:
ORA-01031: insufficient privileges
```

The role JUNIOR_CLAIM_VIEWER does not have DELETE privileges on the table *claims*; therefore, the delete operation failed, citing insufficient privileges. This is exactly what we want, to enable a specific role based on the application user id.

The scheme is good so far, with only one major glitch. The whole setup depends on the user calling the key procedures, *set_user_role* and *set_claim_app_ctx*. However, the user can set the role any way he or she wants, such as

```
SQL> set role claim_supervisor
/

Role set.
```

Now, the use is a *claim supervisor*! Obviously, this is not as secure as we thought.

## Procedure Authenticated Roles

This is where the procedure *set_user_role* comes in. The previous roles were defined without any *authorization*, i.e. anyone can set them, as long they have been granted the roles. We have to define the roles in a different way.

```
create role junior_claim_viewer identified using secuser.set_user_role
/
create role junior_claim_analyst identified using secuser.set_user_role;
/
create role claim_supervisor identified using secuser.set_user_role
/
```

Note: the roles have been created with the clause *identified using*. The procedure *set_user_role* has been used to authenticate the roles. After these roles were granted to user APPUSER, APPUSER tried to activate a role:

```
SQL> set role JUNIOR_CLAIM_ANALYST;
set role JUNIOR_CLAIM_ANALYST
*
ERROR at line 1:
ORA-28201: Not enough privileges to enable application role
'JUNIOR_CLAIM_ANALYST'
```

The role JUNIOR_CLAIM_ANALYST can't be enabled directly, it must be activated by the accompanying procedure *set_user_role*, which makes it a **trusted** procedure.

```
SQL> exec set_user_role ('JUNIOR_CLAIM_VIEWER')

PL/SQL procedure successfully completed.
```

Note how the role can now be set. This is a very important feature to understand. The roles defined through a procedure are not activated by a regular SET command, but by a *trusted* procedure. The secured user should own this trusted procedure, with execute privileges granted to the other users.

 **A trusted procedure for a role is one that can be used to set that particular role, and the role can't be set by any means other than calling the procedure.**

So far, we have seen that the context and the roles can be defined in such a way that they can be set only by trusted procedures. This powerful feature makes it the foundation of any security policy governing shared user ids.

Since these procedures are called to set the context, they can be called by the function that authenticates the user's password, *is_password_correct*. This function is called every time an application user is authenticated, so it is a perfect place to call these role and context setting procedures. Inside the function, we have to make small modifications as follows.

- We need to select the *user_role* from the *app_users* table in addition to the password.
- We have to then call the context setting procedures to set the context for the *app_user_id* and *app_user_role*
- Finally, we have to call the procedure to set the role.

The final step is not possible. It is not valid to call a procedure that sets a role inside a procedure or function owned by another user. When the *is_password_correct()* function is invoked, the function runs in the context of the user SECUSER, which is the owner. Even if the set role command inside that were successful, when the context changes to APPUSER, the user who called it, the roles would be unset, since that would create a new session. Therefore, we can't use the *set_user_role()* procedure inside the password checking function.

This calls for a change in strategy. We have to define a new procedure that must be called by the user after the login to set the roles. But, obviously, we should not let the calling user pass a parameter to this new procedure, otherwise, he or she will pass the parameter as whatever role he or she decides to activate. Rather, we will activate the role for which the user has been authorized in the *app_user* table. This role is already available to us – in the context *claim_app_ctx*, under attribute *app_user_role.*

Out new role-setting procedure looks like this.

```
create or replace procedure set_user_role
authid current_user
is
    l_user_role   varchar2(2000);
begin
    select sys_context('claim_app_ctx','app_user_role')
    into l_user_role
    from dual;
    dbms_session.set_role (l_user_role);
end set_user_role;
/
```

Note: we removed the parameter to be passed. Inside the code, we selected the context attribute *app_user_role* and used that to enable the role.

The following two lines are placed in the function *is_password_correct()*:

```
set_claim_app_ctx ('app_user_id', p_userid);
set_claim_app_ctx ('app_user_role', v_user_role);
```

The variable *p_userid* is a parameter passed to the function. Selecting the APP_ROLE column from the *app_users* table populates the other variable, *v_user_role.*

After the change, we need to test it make sure it works.

```
connect appuser/****
select is_password_correct ('MARK','FUNNY4EVER')
from dual
/

IS_PASSWORD_CORRECT('MARK','FUNNY4EVER')
---------------------------------
YES
```

The user is authenticated. Let's see the context attributes set by the function.

```
select * from session_context;

NAMESPACE        ATTRIBUTE     VALUE
---------------- ------------- -----------------------
CLAIM_APP_CTX    APP_USER_ROLE   JUNIOR_CLAIM_ANALYST
CLAIM_APP_CTX    APP_USER_ID     MARK
```

As we expected, the context attributes *app_user_role* and *app_user_id* are set to JUNIOR_CLAIM_ANALYST and MARK respectively. What about the role that is active now?

```
select * from session_roles
/

no rows selected
```

This is also as we expected. The default role should be none and no role is active now. We set the role by calling the procedure:

```
execute set_user_role

PL/SQL procedure successfully completed.

select * from session_roles
/

ROLE
------------------------------
JUNIOR_CLAIM_ANALYST
```

The role is now properly set. The user APPUSER can't call the procedure *set_user_role* now to change the active role. He or she can't change the context, can't change the role, and can't modify any of the authorized attributes already defined. In effect, we have made an ironclad security system using the shared user model.

## Client Identifier

Oracle 9i introduces another concept called *Client Identifier*. The default System *Context* is expanded to include another attribute called client identifier that can be passed on to other tools like auditing, and will appear in Session Details. This is set using:

```
exec dbms_session.set_identifier('<identifier_name>')
```

In this example, we want to pass on the application user id as the client identifier. So, we will call:

```
dbms_session.set_identifier('MARK')
```

However, since this identifies the user who we want to show as the user who actually made the changes, we can't let him or her enter this information, it may be abused. Therefore the call to set this value must be made inside the function *is_password_correct()*.

```
dbms_session.set_identifier(p_userid);
```

If the user APPUSER tries to set it himself,

```
SQL> execute dbms_session.set_identifier('ANTHONY')
BEGIN Dbms_session.set_identifier('ANTHONY'); END;
      *
ERROR at line 1:
ORA-06550: line 1, column 7:
PLS-00201: identifier 'DBMS_SESSION' must be declared
ORA-06550: line 1, column 7:
PL/SQL: Statement ignored
```

He does not have privileges to execute *dbms_session* directly, so there is no way he can set it up.

The current setting of this attribute can be seen by:

```
select sys_context('USERENV','CLIENT_IDENTIFIER')
from dual
/
```

## The Introduction of VPD

So far, we have talked about the security for object accesses and other system privileges that are decided through roles. However, another cornerstone of our security policy is the Virtual Private Database (VPD), and that has not been taken into account in this setup. The present definition of policy functions will not be able to cater to the VPD requirements. In the present policy function, we determine the list of providers this user is allowed to see using the following query.

```
select provider_id
from claim_provider_policy
where username = user
and access_type = …
```

Note the use of the built-in function `user` above, which returns the current, logged in *database* user. However, in this setup, the logged in user is always APPUSER, so this policy function is useless for enforcing the VPD. We have to change the strategy of the function enforcing the policy.

In the table *claim_provider_policy*, the username column should contain the name of the application user, not the database user.

In the functions used to enforce the policy, the above query segment must be changed to:

```
select provider_id
from claim_provider_policy
where username = sys_context('claim_app_ctx','app_user_id')
and access_type = …
```

Since the construct "sys_context('claim_app_ctx','app_user_id')" returns the value of the attribute *app_user_id*, which is already set by the function *is_password_correct*, the VPD can work.

Sometimes we may also want to use regular database users to login and perform the work. For instance, JUDY, who is also a database user, can select from these tables. Because Judy is a database user, she has not been created as an application user. Therefore, when she tries to see something, her records will not be found in the *app_users* table and therefore the VPD will not display anything to her.

To resolve this issue, we can modify the construct we set earlier to the following.

```
select provider_id
from claim_provider_policy
where username in (
    sys_context('claim_app_ctx','app_user_id')
```

```
    OR
    user
)
and access_type = …
```

Note how we have checked against both the database users and the application users.

Now we have a complete secured system where the application can authenticate passwords and the virtual private database can be applied.

## Putting It All Together

To understand the concept better, let's start from the very beginning and follow the steps logically to arrive at the expected result.

1. Create the Oracle user that will be used to connect initially. Let's say this user is called APPUSER.

```
connect sys/* as sysdba
create user appuser
identified by every1knows
/
grant create session to appuser
/
```

2. Create the secured user that will hold the security on related objects.

```
create user secuser
identified by no1knows
/
grant
    create table,
    create session,
    create procedure,
    create any context
to secuser
/
```

3. Create the role setting function that will act as the trusted function of the roles.

```
connect secuser/no1knows
create or replace procedure set_user_role
authid current_user
is
    l_user_role   varchar2(2000);
begin
    select sys_context('claim_app_ctx','app_user_role')
    into l_user_role
    from dual;
    dbms_session.set_role (l_user_role);
end set_user_role;
/
```

4. Grant the needed privilege and create the synonym for this procedure.

```
connect sys/**** as sysdba
create public synonym set_user_role
for secuser.set_user_role
/
grant execute on secuser.set_user_role to public
/
```

5. Create the needed roles.

```
Connect sys/* as sysdba
create role junior_claim_viewer
    identified using secuser.set_user_role
/
create role junior_claim_analyst
     identified using secuser.set_user_role;
/
create role claim_supervisor
     identified using secuser.set_user_role
/
```

6. Grant appropriate privileges to these roles.

```
grant select on claim_schema.claims
to junior_claim_viewer
/
grant junior_claim_viewer
to junior_claim_analyst
/
grant insert, update on claim_schema.claims
to junior_claim_analyst
/
grant junior_claim_analyst
to claim_supervisor
/
grant delete on claim_schema.claims
to junior_claim_analyst
/
```

7. Since the database user APPUSER will be used to operate on the tables, grant these roles to it.

```
grant
    create session,
    junior_claim_analyst,
    junior_claim_viewer,
    claim_supervisor
to
   appuser
/
```

8. Since we don't want to give any privilege to APPUSER initially, make the default role NONE.

```
alter user appuser default role none
/
```

9. Now we will create the all-important *context.* Before we do that, we have to create its trusted function.

```
connect secuser/no1knows
create procedure set_claim_app_ctx
(
    p_attribute_name in varchar2,
    p_attribute_value in varchar2
) is
begin
    dbms_session.set_context(
       'claim_app_ctx',
        p_attribute_name,
        p_attribute_value);
end;
/
```

10. Then create the context.

```
create context claim_app_ctx
using set_claim_app_ctx
/
```

11. Create the table that holds the application users, their passwords and their roles.

```
connect secuser/no1knows
create table app_users
(
    userid    varchar2(20),
    userpass   varchar2(30),
    user_role  varchar2(20),
       primary key (userid)
)
/
```

12. Next, we create the function that will encrypt the password.

**get_app_password.sql**

```
create or replace function get_app_password
(
    p_password  IN varchar2
)
return varchar2
is
    v_password      varchar2(2000);
    v_userpass      varchar2(2000);
    errm            varchar2(2000);
    v_passlen       integer;
    v_extra         integer;
    v_padlen        integer;
    v_key           varchar2(2000) :=
        'adfwff2dwcc3299fmc0cecc0fc';
begin
    -- The input to the encryption routine needs to be
    -- multiples of 8 bytes. So we will pad it if it
    -- is not so.
    v_passlen := length (p_password);
    if (v_passlen < 8)
```

```
    else
        v_extra := mod(v_passlen, 8);
        if (v_extra = 0)
        then
            v_padlen := v_passlen;
        else
            v_padlen := v_passlen - v_extra + 8;
        end if;
    end if;
    v_password := rpad(p_password,v_padlen);
    -- Encrypt the the password
    dbms_obfuscation_toolkit.DES3Encrypt (
        input_string     => v_password,
        key_string       => v_key,
        encrypted_string => v_userpass,
        which            => 1);
    return v_userpass;
exception
    when OTHERS then
        errm := SQLERRM;
        raise_application_error (-20001,errm);
end;
```

13. Then we will create a function that checks the application user's password and ensures that it matches the one supplied.

### is_password_correct_vpd.sql

```
create or replace function is_password_correct
(
    p_userid    IN varchar2,
    p_password  IN varchar2
)
return varchar2
is

    v_userpass     varchar2(2000);
    v_user_role    varchar2(2000);
    v_password     varchar2(2000);
    errm           varchar2(2000);
    v_key          varchar2(2000) :=
       'adfwff2dwcc3299fmc0cecc0fc';
begin
    -- First get the encrypted password from the table
    select userpass, user_role
    into   v_userpass, v_user_role
    from   app_users
    where  userid = p_userid;
    -- Decrypt the string to get the password
    -- Note the key used.
    dbms_obfuscation_toolkit.DES3Decrypt (
        input_string     => v_userpass,
        key_string       => v_key,
```

```
    -- Compare the passwords
    v_password := rtrim(v_password);
    if (v_password = p_password)
    then
        -- set the context attributes
        set_claim_app_ctx ('app_user_id', p_userid);
        set_claim_app_ctx ('app_user_role',
                                 v_user_role);
        dbms_session.set_identifier(p_userid);
        return 'YES';
    else
        return 'NO';
    end if;
exception
    when OTHERS then
        errm := SQLERRM;
        raise_application_error (-20001,errm);
end;
```

14. Grant the privilege and create the synonym.

```
connect sys/**** as sysdba
create public synonym is_password_correct
for secuser.is_password_correct
/
grant execute on secuser. is_password_correct to public
/
```

15. Now create the application users that will be used by the application.

```
insert into app_users
values
('MARK',
get_app_password ('FUNNY4EVER'),
'JUNIOR_CLAIM_VIEWER'
);
insert into app_users
values
('ANTHONY',
get_app_password ('TAKES4EVER'),
'JUNIOR_CLAIM_ANALYST'
);
insert into app_users
values
('ANNIE',
get_app_password ('2BORNOT2B'),
'CLAIM_SUPERVISOR'
);
```

16. Create the tables that will hold the authority data for the claims.

```
create table claim_value_policy
(
    username varchar2(20),
    max_claim_amount number
)
/
```

```
create table claim_provider_policy
(
    username      varchar2(20),
    access_type   varchar2(10),
    provider_id   number
)
/
```

17. Insert data into these authorization tables.

```
insert into claim_value_policy
values
('MARK',1500);

insert into claim_value_policy
values
('ANTHONY',2500);

insert into claim_value_policy
values
('ANNIE',3500);
```

18. Insert data into the *claim_provider_policy* table in such a way that it look like this.

```
USERNAME             ACCESS_TYP PROVIDER_ID
-------------------- ---------- -----------
ANNIE                SELECT         1234567
ANNIE                SELECT         2345678
ANNIE                SELECT         3456789
MARK                 SELECT         1234567
ANTHONY              SELECT         2345678
ANTHONY              SELECT         3456789
MARK                 SELECT         2345678
MARK                 SELECT         3456789
MARK                 INSERT         1234567
MARK                 UPDATE         1234567
MARK                 UPDATE         2345678
```

19. Then create the policy functions of the table *claims*. First, the SELECT function is created.

### select_auth_claims.sql

```
create or replace function select_auth_claims
(
    p_schema_name    in varchar2,
    p_object_name    in varchar2
)
return varchar2
is

    l_ret        varchar2(2000);
begin
    if p_schema_name = user
    then
```

```
        for prov_rec in
        (
            select provider_id
            from claim_provider_policy
            where username in (
                sys_context('claim_app_ctx',
                    'app_user_id'),
                user)
            and access_type = 'SELECT'
        ) loop
            l_ret := l_ret||','||prov_rec.provider_id;
        end loop;
        l_ret := ltrim(l_ret,',');
        l_ret := 'PROVIDER_ID IN ('||l_ret ||')';
    end if;
    return l_ret;
end;
```

20. Next, create the insert policy function.

### insert_auth_claims.sql

```
create or replace function insert_auth_claims
(
    p_schema_name     in varchar2,
    p_object_name     in varchar2
)
return varchar2
is

    l_ret         varchar2(2000);
begin
    if p_schema_name = user
    then
        l_ret := '1=1';
    else -- if the user is different from the owner
        for prov_rec in
        (
            select provider_id
            from claim_provider_policy
            where username in (
                sys_context('claim_app_ctx',
                    'app_user_id'),
                user)
            and access_type = 'INSERT'
        ) loop
            l_ret := l_ret||','||prov_rec.provider_id;
        end loop;
        l_ret := ltrim(l_ret,',');
        l_ret := 'PROVIDER_ID IN ('||l_ret ||')';
        if l_ret = 'PROVIDER_ID IN ()' then
            l_ret := '1=1';
        end if;
```

```
end;
```

21. Then create the update policy function.

### update_auth_claims.sql

```
create or replace function update_auth_claims
(
    p_schema_name     in varchar2,
    p_object_name     in varchar2
)
return varchar2
is
    l_ret         varchar2(2000);
begin
    if p_schema_name = user
    then
        l_ret := '1=1';
    else -- if the user is different from the owner
        for prov_rec in
        (
            select provider_id
            from claim_provider_policy
            where username in (
                sys_context('claim_app_ctx',
                   'app_user_id'),
                user)
            and access_type = 'UPDATE'
        ) loop
            l_ret := l_ret||','||prov_rec.provider_id;
        end loop;
        l_ret := ltrim(l_ret,',');
        l_ret := 'PROVIDER_ID IN ('||l_ret ||')';
    end if;
    return l_ret;
end;
```

22. Finally, issue the delete policy function.

### delete_auth_claims

```
create or replace function delete_auth_claims
(
    p_schema_name     in varchar2,
    p_object_name     in varchar2
)
return varchar2
is
    l_ret         varchar2(2000);
```

```
    then
        l_ret := '1=1';
    else -- if the user is different from the owner
        for prov_rec in
        (
            select provider_id
            from claim_provider_policy
            where username in (
                sys_context('claim_app_ctx',
                    'app_user_id'),
                user)
            and access_type = 'DELETE'
        ) loop
            l_ret := l_ret||','||prov_rec.provider_id;
        end loop;
        l_ret := ltrim(l_ret,',');
        l_ret := 'PROVIDER_ID IN ('||l_ret ||')';
    end if;
    return l_ret;
end;
```

23. The policy to limit the records based on the value of the claim is set up next.

### check_claim_value_policy

```
create or replace function check_claim_value_policy
(
    p_schema_name     in varchar2,
    p_object_name     in varchar2
)
return varchar2
is
    l_ret            varchar2(2000);
    l_max_claim_amount number;
begin
    l_ret := NULL;
    if p_schema_name = user
    then
        l_ret := '1=1';
    else -- if the user is different from the owner
         begin
            select max_claim_amount
            into l_max_claim_amount
            from claim_value_policy
            where username in (
                sys_context('claim_app_ctx',
                    'app_user_id'),
                user);
            l_ret := 'CLAIM_AMOUNT <= '||
                l_max_claim_amount;
        exception
            when NO_DATA_FOUND then
                l_ret := NULL;
```

```
        end;
    end if;
    return l_ret;
end;
```

24. After the policy functions are created, the policy itself must be created and applied to the table *claims*.

### add_policies.sql

```
begin
dbms_rls.add_policy (
    object_schema     => 'CLAIM_SCHEMA',
    object_name       => 'CLAIMS',
    policy_name       => 'CLAIM_SELECT_POLICY',
    function_schema   => 'SECUSER',
    policy_function   => 'SELECT_AUTH_CLAIMS',
    statement_types   => 'SELECT'
);
dbms_rls.add_policy (
    object_schema     => 'CLAIM_SCHEMA',
    object_name       => 'CLAIMS',
    policy_name       => 'CLAIM_INSERT_POLICY',
    function_schema   => 'SECUSER',
    policy_function   => 'INSERT_AUTH_CLAIMS',
    statement_types   => 'INSERT',
    update_check      => TRUE
);
dbms_rls.add_policy (
    object_schema     => 'CLAIM_SCHEMA',
    object_name      => 'CLAIMS',
    policy_name       => 'CLAIM_UPDATE_POLICY',
    function_schema   => 'SECUSER',
    policy_function   => 'UPDATE_AUTH_CLAIMS',
    statement_types   => 'UPDATE',
    update_check      => TRUE
);
dbms_rls.add_policy (
    object_schema     => 'CLAIM_SCHEMA',
    object_name      => 'CLAIMS',
    policy_name       => 'CLAIM_VALUE_POLICY',
    function_schema   => 'SECUSER',
    policy_function   => 'CHECK_CLAIM_VALUE_POLICY',
    statement_types   => 'UPDATE',
    update_check      => TRUE
);
end;
```

25. Finally, it's time to check whether these settings work.

```
connect appuser/every1knows
select
    is_password_correct('MARK','FUNNY4EVER')
```

```
from
    dual;

IS_PASSWORD_CORRECT('MARK','MARK')
----------------------------------
YES
```

26. Check the session context settings.

```
select
    sys_context('claim_app_ctx','app_user_id')
from
    dual;

SYS_CONTEXT('CLAIM_APP_CTX','APP_USER_ID')
------------------------------------------
MARK

select
    sys_context('claim_app_ctx','app_user_role')
from
    dual;

SYS_CONTEXT('CLAIM_APP_CTX','APP_USER_ROLE')
--------------------------------------------
JUNIOR_CLAIM_ANALYST
```

27. Activate the role authorized for this application user, MARK.

```
execute set_user_role
```

28. Check the role that is active now.

```
select * from session_roles
/

ROLE
------------------------------
JUNIOR_CLAIM_ANALYST
```

29. Now, check the table to see if the VPD works.

```
select * from claim_schema.claims
/

C SSN        MEMBER_ID PROVIDER_ID CLAIM_AMOUNT PAID_AMOUNT S
-- --------- ---------- ----------- ------------ ----------- -
 1 123456789      12345     1234567         1200        1200 P
 3 234567891      12345     2345678         1400        1300 P
```

And it did! We just created a highly secure system using shared user ids and application ids, making all groups – developers, DBAs, architects and security people – very happy.

# Oracle Policy Manager

The *Oracle Policy Manager* provides a nice GUI interface to manage policies and application contexts. Unfortunately, the tool is not integrated into Oracle Enterprise Manager as of Oracle 9i. This is invoked from the command line as:

```
oemapp opm
```

This brings up the main screen of the tool as shown in Figure 5.3. As you can see, the policy groups, policies under that group, and application contexts are displayed. For each application context, the trusted package can be seen here or set here.

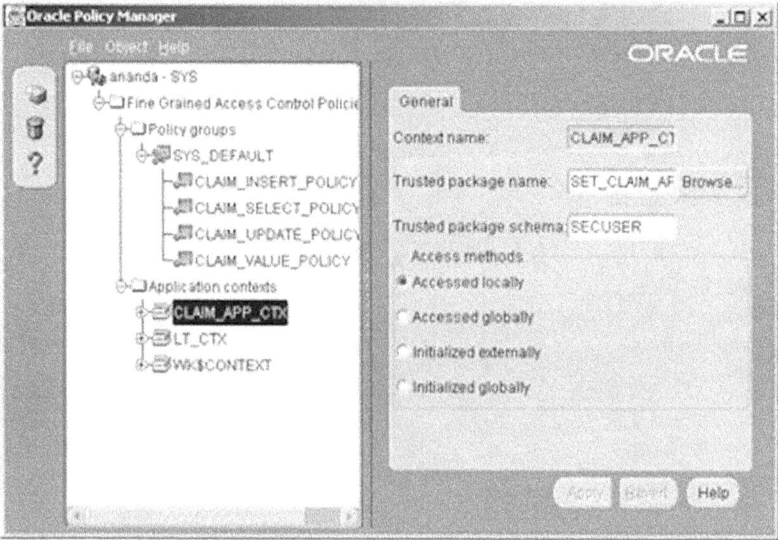


**Figure 5.3** *Oracle Policy Manager*

Clicking on one of the policies, CLAIM_VALUE_POLICY, we can see or edit the policy parameters. The screen is shown in Figure 5.4. As you can see, almost all policy attributes, except the statements on which they are evaluated, are displayed. The statements they are applied to are shown on the tab named *Enforcement.*

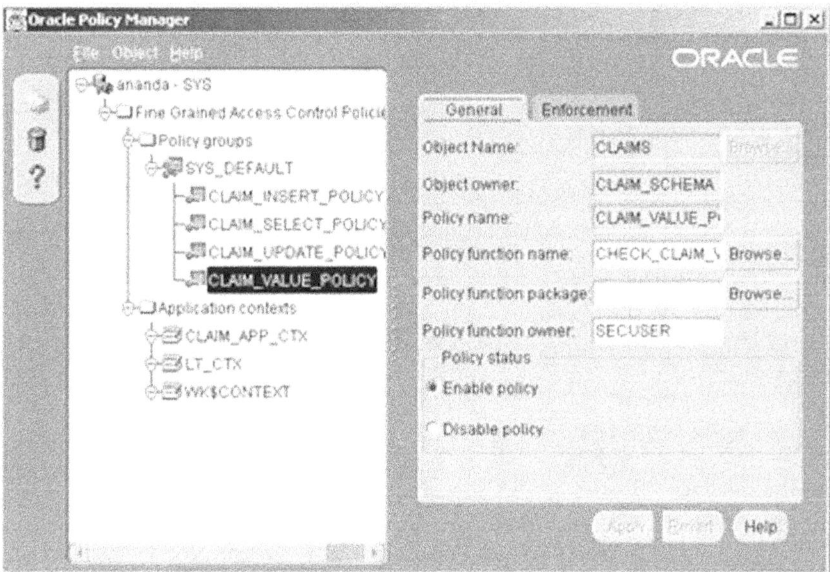


**Figure 5.4** *Setting Policy Values*

The OPM tool, like the other OEM tools, has a help system that displays small help text when the mouse is held over the fields.

# VPD in Other Oracle Tools

Other Oracle tools such as Export, Import, SQL*Loader, etc. are also affected by VPD. These are nothing but regular users using a tool to query data, so the VPD engages to filter out rows that are not supposed to be accessible by the user. Let's examine the issues and what to expect.

## Export/Import

While exporting in conventional mode, the effect is nothing more than a single user querying the data, as if from SQL*Plus, so the records are always filtered. Here is an example of the export against the table *claims:*

```
exp judy/**** tables=claims file=d.dmp

Export: Release 9.2.0.2.1 - Production on Fri Jun 20 17:39:31 2003

Copyright (c) 1982, 2002, Oracle Corporation.  All rights reserved.

Connected to: Oracle9i Enterprise Edition Release 9.2.0.2.1 - Production
```

```
With the Partitioning, OLAP and Oracle Data Mining options
JServer Release 9.2.0.2.0 - Production
Export done in WE8MSWIN1252 character set and AL16UTF16 NCHAR character set

About to export specified tables via Conventional Path ...
EXP-00079: Data in table "CLAIMS" is protected. Conventional path may only
be exporting partial table.
. . exporting table                        CLAIMS          3 rows exported
EXP-00081: Exporting access control for table/view "CLAIMS" as non-DBA.
EXP-00081: Exporting access control for table/view "CLAIMS" as non-DBA.
EXP-00081: Exporting access control for table/view "CLAIMS" as non-DBA.
Export terminated successfully with warnings.
```

Note how only 3 rows are shown. That is what Judy was supposed to see, and that is what was exported.

Two important points are to be noted here:

- Note the output: "EXP-00079: Data in table "CLAIMS" is protected." This means the *claims* table is protected by a policy, and the table rows returned may be partial. The user should be aware of this.
- *Direct path exports* act in a slightly different manner. Since they bypass the SQL buffer, the VPD will not be able to modify the query, and therefore the VPD cannot apply. However, since the policy is defined on the table, bypassing the VPD should not compromise security. Rather, Oracle decides to go for a conventional path export, even if a direct path is specified. This is also shown in the above output, "Conventional path may only be exporting partial table."

What if you want to export all the rows? There are two options to achieve that:

- Temporarily disable the policy
- Use a user with the EXEMPT ACCESS POLICY system privilege.

Similar to Import, the policy is also enforced if the INSERT policy is defined on the table. If a data row is inserted that does not satisfy the policy function, the Oracle error "ORA-28115: policy with check option violation" is returned.

## SQL*Loader

SQL*Loader tries to load the tables using a call to INSERT INTO … statement, which invokes the policy function for INSERT. Therefore any record that does not satisfy the policy function is rejected, and the log file shows:

```
Record 3: Rejected - Error on table CLAIM_SCHEMA.CLAIMS.
ORA-28115: policy with check option violation
```

While doing a direct path export, the SQL buffer is also bypassed. However, unlike import, SQL*Loader does not just switch over to conventional path load. Rather it errors out:

```
sqlldr judy/**** control=load_claims.ctl data=claims_data.txt direct=yes

SQL*Loader: Release 9.2.0.2.1 - Production on Fri Jun 20 18:29:33 2003

Copyright (c) 1982, 2002, Oracle Corporation.  All rights reserved.

SQL*Loader-951: Error calling once/load initialization
ORA-00604: error occurred at recursive SQL level 1
ORA-28113: policy predicate has error
```

Naturally, the error is subtle but required, otherwise, we will not be able to enforce the security policies and may provide covert channels for hackers to break in.

## Direct Path Insert

Finally, the last place for such an insert is direct path insert. If Nathan inserts the data like this:

```
insert /*+ APPEND */ into claim_schema.claims
select * from claim_schema.claims
where provider_id = 2345678
/
insert /*+ APPEND */ into claim_schema.claims
                                       *
ERROR at line 1:
ORA-28115: policy with check option violation
```

The insert is immediately rejected. All the channels to bypass the data are blocked. The only way to invoke the SQL loader direct path is to temporarily disable the policy.

# Potential Problems and Concerns

Like any other feature, VPD also has some features of which you should be aware. Luckily, most of these features are not overly problematic, but they must be fully comprehended before they are put into widespread use.

## Referential Integrity Constraints

Referential integrity constraints pose some important, but not necessarily serious, issues you have to understand. This is perhaps better explained by an example.

Assume we have another table named *claim_line* that holds line items in individual claims defined as follows

```
Name                  Null?     Type
-----------------     --------  ------------
CLAIM_ID              NOT NULL  NUMBER
LINE_ID               NOT NULL  NUMBER
PROCEDURE_CODE                  CHAR(4)
CLAIM_AMOUNT                    NUMBER(5)
PAID_AMOUNT                     NUMBER(5)
```

The primary key columns are (CLAIM_ID, LINE_ID). The CLAIM_ID column is a foreign key referencing table *claims*. Since this table contains sensitive information on procedures performed on the patient (PROCEDURE_CODE), and this information is specifically protected by HIPAA, we have defined certain policies that prevent everyone from seeing the table rows. The policy states that Senior Analysts can see all rows of *claims* but only CAIM_LINE record with "procedure_code != '040'," which is *HIV Testing*.

Assume a claim with CLAIM_ID = 1 has two records in *claim_line* table with procedure codes 010 and 040. The senior claim analyst is supposed to see only the one with the procedure code 010, not the other. Now, he or she deletes the row from the *claims* table with CLAIM_ID=1. This operation is permissible by the policy. If the referential integrity constraint is defined with ON DELETE CASCADE, the operation will delete the rows from the *claim_line* table too, but one of the two child records doesn't exist as far as the user is concerned. So, it will raise an error immediately.

This will let the user know that the CLAIM_ID 1 has a procedure code with value 040, meaning the member was tested for HIV. This could be a compliance hole, a clear violation of the privacy policy mandated by HIPAA. You should be aware of this possibility while designing the VPD system.

# Troubleshooting

## ORA-28110

**ORA-28110: Policy function or package has error** occurs when a policy function has some error such as a compilation problem. The solution is to recompile the package or the function after fixing the underlying problem.

## ORA-28112

**ORA-28112: failed to execute policy function** occurs when the policy function encounters some runtime errors, typically unhandled exceptions. Fortunately, the error will produce a trace file in the *user_dump_dest* directory that can be examined and the error can be corrected.

## ORA-28113

**ORA-28113: policy predicate has error** occurs when the policy function returns a predicate that is wrong in syntax. Fortunately, this also generates a trace file in the *user_dump_dest* directory. For example, one error looks like this

```
*** SESSION ID:(8.4395) 2003-06-20 18:32:00.000
*** 2003-06-20 18:32:00.000
------------------------------------------------
Error information for ORA-28113:
Logon user      : SYSTEM
Table/View      : CLAIM_SCHEMA.CLAIMS
Policy name     : CLAIM_SELECT_POLICY
Policy function: SECUSER.SELECT_AUTH_CLAIMS
RLS predicate   :
PROVIDER_ID IN ()
ORA-00936: missing expression
```

The error is very clear; the predicate PROVIDER_ID IN () is syntactically wrong in a where condition. This can be fixed by examining the function and what it returns.

## ORA-28116

**ORA-28116: insufficient privileges to do direct path access** typically occurs when you do a SQL*Loader direct path load from a user who is subjected to policy function. The only ways to bypass this is to either load in conventional path, or temporarily disable the policy to load.

# Debugging With Events

The exact working of the VPD can be easily seen by setting an event in the session to dump the contents into a trace file. In Nathan's case, we can debug the exact statement that is passed to Oracle.

```
connect nathan/***
connected.
alter session
   set events
```

```
'10730 trace name context forever, level 12'
/

Session altered.

select * from claim_schema.claims;

….
```

This produces a trace file in the *user_dump_dest* directory. Upon examining the file we can see that the contents look like this

```
*** 2003-06-20 20:01:20.000
*** SESSION ID:(25.1245) 2003-06-20 20:01:20.000
---------------------------------------------
Logon user      : NATHAN
Table/View      : CLAIM_SCHEMA.CLAIMS
Policy name     : CLAIM_SELECT_POLICY
Policy function: SECUSER.SELECT_AUTH_CLAIMS
RLS view :
SELECT
"CLAIM_ID","SSN","MEMBER_ID","PROVIDER_ID","CLAIM_AMOUNT","PAID_AMOUNT","STA
TUS" FROM "CLAIM_SCHEMA"."CLAIMS"  "CLAIMS" WHERE (PROVIDER_ID IN
(1234567,2345678,3456789))
```

The exact statement that is passed to the database is clearly shown, and that will help debug any issues with the VPD rewriting the query.

## Summary

In this chapter, we explored the concepts of Virtual Private Database (VPD) and Application Contexts, and how they are used to secure a database. HIPAA regulations clearly mandate that the data be accessible to only those who are authorized to use it. Instead of creating a separate database for each user, or creating several views to portray different user security requirements, VPD provides a way to instantly partition your existing tables into secured tables visible differently to different people.

In the other sections, we have seen how an application user authentication can be used in a secured way, and how that can still be used for VPD, even though the database user is different from the application user. The application user model described here will be used throughout the book for secured identity management without invoking the Oracle Advanced Security option.

# Oracle Encryption

CHAPTER

## What is Encryption?

I have a tough time remembering numbers – any number – ATM Card PIN, Social Security Number, telephone numbers, pretty much anything that starts or ends with or is enclosed by numbers. So I have a simple infrastructure – I write the numbers on the objects they are used with, in code – a code only I can decipher. In other words, I encrypt them to be decrypted using the original algorithm used to encrypt them.

In our effort to prevent and discourage hackers from obtaining valuable information from the database, we have discussed the essential steps to take to prohibit unauthorized access to the database and the tables. But what if the hacker somehow gets in? In a recent report by a prestigious research company, and also reported by other independent studies, most of unauthorized data access is done from inside, not outside.

In a typical setup, the database is behind a firewall and is not necessarily open to external traffic – making it difficult, if not impossible, for hackers to break in from outside. However, lax security policies or employees with their own agenda can "sniff in" the sensitive data. Sometimes the urge to do that is purely benign – perhaps for a conversation piece in a cocktail party; but sometimes the intent is to obtain sensitive information. In an insurance company, the information contained within the annals of the database can be quite valuable, such as the history of diseases a member may have been tested for or diagnosed with. This information is defined within HIPAA as Patient Health Information (PHI) and has been explicitly identified as data that is to be protected.

This calls for the last line of defense for protecting the sensitive data from prying eyes – making the data useless for the unauthorized user – or encrypting it. In the case of the insurance database, the sensitive information such as diagnosis codes or physician comments could be stored as encrypted. In the case of hospitals, the information could be even more sensitive – in addition to the diagnosis codes, there are data about the patient's credit card information, employer information, health history, and much more. Of course, it is probably impractical to encrypt all the information that needs to be protected. So a decision must be made to choose the most important data to protect.

There are several ways data can be encrypted. There are third party tools that encrypt the data before it gets to Oracle. Similarly, the data is decrypted after it is fetched from the database. However, they are outside the scope of the database. Although it is valuable and practical – the cost may be prohibitive, and may not be justifiable. Fortunately, Oracle provides certain encryption routines to be used by the users. This book explores those options and explains how to use them.

In all of the Oracle-supplied encryption routines, the concept is fundamentally simple – the data is fed along with the encryption key, and out pops the encrypted data. When the need comes to decipher the data, the encrypted information and the key both are fed into the routine, and the raw information comes out.

However, the common element in both cases is the *key*, called the encryption key. This key is literally the *key* to get to the data, and thus becomes valuable and must be strongly protected. If this key is lost, the encrypted data will not be decipherable in any way. And, of course, if the hackers get this key, they can decrypt the sensitive data. Needless to say, the challenge is to somehow store the key in a secured manner so that unauthorized users don't have access to it, but authorized users should have no problem in using it to decrypt the data.

# Types of Encryption

## DES

There are several encryption schemes in use today – with varying strengths and difficulty in deciphering the contents. The most popular is the standard called DES (Digital Encryption Standard). It was introduced by the American National Standards Institute (ANSI) over 20 years ago and has been the de facto standard or encryption, particularly in the financial services industry. It uses a 64-bit key to encrypt the data. Actually only 56 bits of the 64 bits are used, but the user has to supply all the 64 bits. So the hacker has to try $2^{56}$, or 72,057,594,037,927,936 combinations to guess the encrypted data.

## DES3

The DES standard was difficult enough to crack at the time it was introduced; but for today's powerful machines, the encryption is rather prone to cracking by brute force. To address the problem the standard was enhanced to DES3 (Triple DES algorithm), which encrypts the DES encrypted data to make it more difficult to crack. It can pass the DES encrypted data up to three times through its encryption routine. Therefore, the hacker must try $2^{112}$ times for a two-pass scheme, or $2^{168}$ times for a three pass one. Needless to say, this is more difficult to crack and is used frequently.

## Hashing

Hashing is making a string of characters from an input string based on some calculations. This is primarily used for check summing methods, where checksums (hashed) before and after the transit are compared to make sure that the string was not tampered with while in transit. This also provides a tool to have some type of encryption. Please note that this is not an encryption in the strictest sense of the term; it is not encrypted with a key big enough to withstand deciphering programs, but the concept is similar and is discussed briefly here. Also, there is no equivalent of decryption – or *de-hashing*. So it is not used to encrypt data.

# Oracle's Built-in Tools

Oracle has a suite of tools to implement encryption inside the database. The primary package in providing the APIs is the *dbms_obfuscation_toolkit*. In this chapter, we will explore this package.

## DES3 Encryption

Before starting to explain the concepts and usage, it might be helpful to see an actual example of the encryption routine in action. If we need to encrypt a value 'TOOSENSITIVEINFO', we would call

```
declare
    v_encrypted_data      varchar2(2000);
begin
    dbms_obfuscation_toolkit.DES3Encrypt (
        input_string     => 'TOOSENSITIVEINFO',
        key_string       => '1234567890123456',
        encrypted_string => v_encrypted_data
    );
    dbms_output.put_line('Encrypted Value = '||
        v_encrypted_data);
end;
/
```

The output comes back as

```
Encrypted Value = ►└ó├é╩╜Az▐▼τ╤ëf┬

PL/SQL procedure successfully completed.
```

Note the value that comes back as encrypted. It has some types of control characters, but can be easily stored in the database as a varchar2 field. Let's dissect this little piece of code.

The procedure *DES3Encrypt* takes two input and one output parameters. One of the inputs is, of course, the string to be encrypted. The other is the encryption key. In this example, we have used a 16-byte key. In real life examples, you should probably use longer keys to protect better.

To decrypt the encrypted data, we will use the sister procedure, *DES3Decrypt* as follows

```
declare
    v_decrypted_data      varchar2(2000);
begin
    dbms_obfuscation_toolkit.DES3Decrypt (
        input_string     => '►└ó╞é╨╜Az▐▼τ╤ëf┬',
        key_string       => '1234567890123456',
        decrypted_string => v_decrypted_data
    );
    dbms_output.put_line('Decrypted Value = '||
        v_decrypted_data);
end;
/
```

The output comes back as

```
Decrypted Value = TOOSENSITIVEINO

PL/SQL procedure successfully completed.
```

We used the *same* key used to encrypt the original value and we got the results back. This should be enough for you understand the basic workings of the encryption and decryption routines. This type is known as *symmetric encryption model* – the same key is used for both encryption and decryption.

Note, we have used a key of exactly 16 characters. Remember the definition of the Triple DES algorithm? It passes an 8-bit key to the encrypted data through the encryption operation again to get the encrypted data. In this case, the default implementation of the DES3Encrypt procedure passes only once after the original encryption by the 8-bit key; so there are two passes, each with 8 bits. Therefore, the procedure requires a 16-bit key for encryption. If a key of lesser length is specified, the procedure will return an error. Longer strings are accepted but only the first 16 characters are used.

However, DES3 encryption is about three passes, not two. The third pass is made by specifying a parameter in the procedure to value 1, which ups the key requirement to

24 bits. For example, the above encryption routine might be written for Triple DES Encryption as.

```
declare
    v_encrypted_data        varchar2(2000);
begin
    dbms_obfuscation_toolkit.DES3Encrypt (
        input_string      => 'TOOSENSITIVEINFO',
        key_string        => '123456789012345678901234',
        encrypted_string => v_encrypted_data,
        which             => 1
    );
    dbms_output.put_line('Encrypted Value = '||
        v_encrypted_data);
end;
/
```

Note the key supplied is 24-bit, not 8, and the encrypted value will be different from the above case.

The DES3 encryption can be used in many situations to provide strong security for sensitive data. Note the key is the central figure in this scheme, and proper generation of the key is vital to encrypt the data securely.

# *dbms_obfuscation_toolkit*

Now that you understand the concept and application of the package, let's explore what it has to offer. Essentially, it offers encryption and decryption routines for DES and Triple DES and a hashing routine for MD5. We saw the examples of DES3 routines earlier. Let's expand on the features of this tool. The following is an explanation of the procedures inside the package

## DES3Encrypt

This is the primary way to encrypt the data. Interestingly, this is an *overloaded* code, i.e. there are procedures and functions both named after this, and the functions and procedures can take multiple parameters. This may seem like adding to the confusion, but in reality, this may be a boon to work with – since you will have flexibility.

Here is the explanation of the procedure versions of the code. This version takes string values as parameters.

| PARAMETER | DESCRIPTION |
|---|---|

| PARAMETER | DESCRIPTION |
|---|---|
| INPUT_STRING | This is the string to be encrypted in VARCHAR2 datatype. The input must be a multiple of 8 characters, since the encryption algorithm breaks it into blocks of 8 bits and applies the encryption key to it. If the string is not a multiple of 8, it should be padded with blanks to make it that. During decryption, these padded characters must be stripped to arrive at the original value. |
| KEY_STRING | This is the encryption key in the VARCHAR2 datatype. The key must be either 16 characters (if the double pass is used) or 24 (if the triple pass is used). These passes will be explained in the next parameter |
| WHICH | This is the parameter to instruct the encryption routine to make it a double pass of a triple pass. The value of 0 here, the default, makes the encryption double pass. This means, the encryption is done with 8 bits once and then again with 8 bits. In triple pass, the double passed one is encrypted again with 8 bits, making it more difficult to crack. Passing a value of 1 in this parameter indicates triple pass. |
| ENCRYPTED_STRING | This is the only OUT parameter of the procedure, again in VARCHAR2 datatype, which produces the encrypted string. |
| IV_STRING | This is a parameter newly introduced in Oracle 9i. In addition to the key supplied, the parameter *input_vector* can also be passed to further strengthen the encrypted code, as well as provide support to the third party encryption routines where the use of this input vector is common. The default is null. |

**Table 6.1** *Parameters for DES3Encrypt Procedure for VARCHAR2*

Another version of the same procedure takes raw values as parameters.

| PARAMETER | DESCRIPTION |
|---|---|
| INPUT | This is the input value to be encrypted in RAW datatype. |
| KEY | This is the encryption key in the RAW datatype. |
| WHICH | 0 – for double pass and 1 – for triple pass. |

| PARAMETER | DESCRIPTION |
|---|---|
| ENCRYPTED_DATA | This is the only OUT parameter of the procedure, again in RAW datatype. |
| IV | The same as the explanation for IV_STRING in the string version of the procedure, but in RAW datatype. |

**Table 6.2** *Parameters for DES3Encrypt Procedure for RAW*

Here is the function version of the same code using raw data as parameters. This function returns the encrypted value in RAW datatype.

| PARAMETER | DESCRIPTION |
|---|---|
| INPUT | This is the input value to be encrypted in RAW datatype. |
| KEY | This is the encryption key in the RAW datatype. |
| WHICH | 0 – for double pass and 1 – for triple pass. 0 is the default. |
| IV | The same as the explanation for IV_STRING in the string version of the procedure, but in RAW datatype. Default is null. |

**Table 6.3** *Parameters for DES3Encrypt Function for RAW*

As in case of the procedure, the function also has a counterpart using parameters in VARCHAR2 datatype.

**Since the code *DES3Encrypt* is defined as both a function and a procedure, as well as overloaded with several types of parameters, there are actually four declarations for the code segment. Therefore, the calling of this code segment with parameters may not work without naming the parameters. You have to use named parameters, as described in the example in the beginning of the chapter.**

## DES3Decrypt

Similar to the encryption routines, the package also has decryption routines – and there are four declarations to it, just like its encryption counterpart. Here is the explanation of the procedure version using RAW datatypes.

| PARAMETER | DESCRIPTION |
|---|---|

| PARAMETER | DESCRIPTION |
|---|---|
| INPUT | This is the input value to be decrypted in RAW datatype. |
| KEY | This is the encryption key in the RAW datatype. |
| DECRYPTED_DATA | This is the only OUT parameter of the procedure, again in RAW datatype. This returns the decrypted raw data. |
| WHICH | 0 – for double pass and 1 – for triple pass. |
| IV | The same as the explanation for IV in the encryption routines, in RAW datatype. The default is a null value. |

**Table 6.4** *Parameters for DES3Decrypt Function for RAW*

The parameters are very similar to the ones found in encryption routines. An example of the decryption routine is provided at the beginning of the chapter.

The *DESEncrypt* and *DESDecrypt* code segments, available both as functions and procedures and with overloaded parameters using varchar2 and raw datatype, do the same thing as the DES3 counterparts, only do it in one pass, using a 64-bit key. Actually, the 8 bits of the 64 bits are thrown out and only 56 bits are used. Since they use a low length key, they are more amenable to breakage. In addition, the *iv* and *iv_string* parameters are not available in these stored codes.

## RAW or VARCHAR2

As you have noticed earlier, the functions and procedures have been overloaded with parameters both in RAW and VARCHAR2. Which one should be used?

The use of varchar2 parameters makes it simpler to use; but may prove difficult to use in some situations. From the example given at the beginning of the chapter note that the encrypted data are in special characters which are not printable. Sometimes this can cause problems, such as in string assignments in some native languages. Also, when Oracle Globalization (a.k.a. National Language System - NLS) is used, the use of these special characters may pose some problems – especially while exporting and importing the data. Therefore, it is better to use the raw datatypes, since Oracle will handle the explicit conversion and these problems will not arise.

However, the use of raw datatypes poses another problem – the storage of these values in tables. Using RAW columns in tables is not the most convenient feature to use – and therefore database administrators and developers alike may eschew it.

To use the raw datatypes, there is another useful feature that can convert the raw data into hexadecimal format, which can be easily stored as a string.

The following code converts the value of the variable of raw datatype to a character format.

```
v_char_var := utl_raw.cast_to_varchar2(v_raw_var)
```

To convert a varchar2 value to raw, use the other function:

```
v_raw_var := utl_raw.cast_to_raw(v_char_var)
```

A raw value can be further converted into a hexadecimal value using the function `RAWTOHEX`, and a hexadecimal value can be converted into raw using the corresponding function, *hextoraw*.

## Key Generation

The other component we will have to worry about is the actual key that is used to encrypt and decrypt. The key must be such that it is not easily guessed, and since no one is expected to remember it, it may not be a string of human comprehensible characters. It can be just any arbitrary string of characters. The best option to generate a key is using the new code segment *DES3GetKey* in the package *dbms_obfuscation_toolkit*. As in all other codes in this package, the *DES3GetKey* code is also implemented as both a procedure and a function and overloaded with both VARCHAR2 and RAW datatypes. Here is the explanation of the parameters to the procedure version in the RAW format.

In the procedure version of the VARCHAR2 format, the parameters are the same, except *seed* is renamed to *seed_string*. Of course, the datatypes change from RAW to VARCHAR2.

Here is an example of how the procedure is used:

```
declare
    v_key_raw  raw (2000);
    v_key      varchar2 (2000);
    v_seed     varchar2 (2000) := 'Seed';
    v_seed_raw raw (2000);
begin
    v_seed := rpad(v_seed, 80);
    v_seed_raw := utl_raw.cast_to_raw (v_seed);
    dbms_obfuscation_toolkit.DES3GetKey(
        which=> 1,
        seed => v_seed_raw,
        key  => v_key_raw
    );
    v_key := rawtohex(v_key_raw);
    dbms_output.put_line('The key is '||v_key);
end;
/
```

Let's analyze the code. The seed to be passed has to be in raw. So, we added the *utl_raw.cast_to_raw* to the seed value passed as a string. The seed must be at least 80 characters, so we add blank characters to the variable V_SEED to make it at least 80 characters.

The output comes back as:

```
The key is 4B547B479B25967365D3717112A52C954883F02416296F7A
```

This is a key we can use to encrypt all the data. Subsequent calls to the above code will produce different results, so the key value can be different each time.

If your database is 8i, then you don't have the luxury of using this procedure/function. However, you can easily create your own as in the code example given below. This uses the *dbms_random.random* function to randomize a number from which the character string is constructed. From the random number obtained, we will take the 3 numbers from the third position and check if they exist within 33 and 125, the allowable numbers for ASCII printable characters. If they fall within that range, we will get the ASCII character for that number and append to the key string. The idea behind selecting from the middle of the number is simply to make sure that we will get a number beginning with zero, or in effect, a two digit number. Selecting the first three numbers from the random number will never yield a two-digit number.

### get_key_8i.sql

```
create or replace function get_key_8i
return varchar2
is
    filled    boolean;
    int_num   number(14);
    v_key     varchar2(24);
    counter   number := 0;
begin
    loop
        exit when filled;
        int_num := to_number(substr(to_char
                (abs(dbms_random.random)),3,3));
        if int_num between 33 and 125 then
             counter := counter + 1;
             if counter = 24 then
                 filled := true;
             end if;
             v_key := v_key ||chr(int_num);
        end if;
    end loop;
    return v_key;
end;
```

So, we now have a procedure to generate the key and encrypt the data, the two very important steps in building an encryption system. The next step is to build one.

# Building an Encrypted System

In the example system, we will take the case of the table *claim_line* into account. Some of the information in the table is identified as PHI, and therefore may be a good candidate for encryption. One such field is procedure codes (*procedure_code*). This field holds the diagnosis of diseases or other diagnostic information done on the user, and is therefore extremely sensitive as per HIPAA regulations. Other fields in other tables may be Credit Card Numbers, Social Security Numbers, etc.

The usual approach is to generate a specific key for a specific value, and store that key in a separate place. To make it simple, we can use a single key for a single record of *claim_line* table, regardless of how many columns are to be encrypted.

Our key holding table will then have to hold the row identifier of the claim line table, and the key used to encrypt data in that row. The row identifier could be the primary key, or some other set of columns to uniquely identify a row. To make it more generic, we can have a single table to hold all the keys or all the tables, partitioned on the *table_name* column. For the sake of this example, assume there is one table to hold keys per the source table to be encrypted. That table, named *claim_line_keys* could be defined as

```
CLAIM_ID                    NUMBER
LINE_ID                     NUMBER
KEY_VALUE                   VARCHAR2(200)
```

There are two ways to handle the encryption in the table *claim_line*.

**View Method** - The table could be renamed to *claim_line_clear* and a view named *claim_line* be created. The PROCEDURE_CODE column of the view could display the data in encrypted manner. No one should have access to the original table. All the applications, the users, etc. should refer to the view.

When the applications need to insert data into the table, there could be an INSTEAD OF trigger defined on the view that decrypts the data and stores the original value in the CLEAR table, which contains the data in the unencrypted manner.

**Direct Encryption** - When the data is entered into the *claim_line* table, or the field PROCEDURE_CODE is updated, the changed data could be encrypted before putting it into the table, so that the field PROCEDURE_CODE contains encrypted values. In this manner the query to the table will always return an encrypted value. The user must decrypt this to get the actual value.

The inserts and updates can be handled in a slightly simpler manner, using triggers to update the value before the database value is written.

Either method is easy to accomplish and may prove better or worse depending on your specific situation. We will use the direct update of the table approach as an example.

Our redesigned table CLAIM_LINE looks like this

```
CLAIM_ID            NOT NULL NUMBER
LINE_ID             NOT NULL NUMBER
PROCEDURE_CODE               VARCHAR2(200)
CLAIM_AMOUNT                 NUMBER(5)
PAID_AMOUNT                  NUMBER(5)
```

Notice that *procedure_code* is now 200 characters long, enough to hold the encrypted value.

To hold the keys, we will design another table *claim_line_keys* as follows.

```
CLAIM_ID      NOT NULL NUMBER
LINE_ID       NOT NULL NUMBER
KEY_STRING    NOT NULL VARCHAR2(80)
```

The primary key is (CLAIM_ID, LINE_ID) and the key to encrypt the corresponding procedure code is stored in the column KEY_STRING.

The decryption will work as per Figure 6.1. We will get the encrypted value and the corresponding key, and feed them to the decryption process to get the original value.

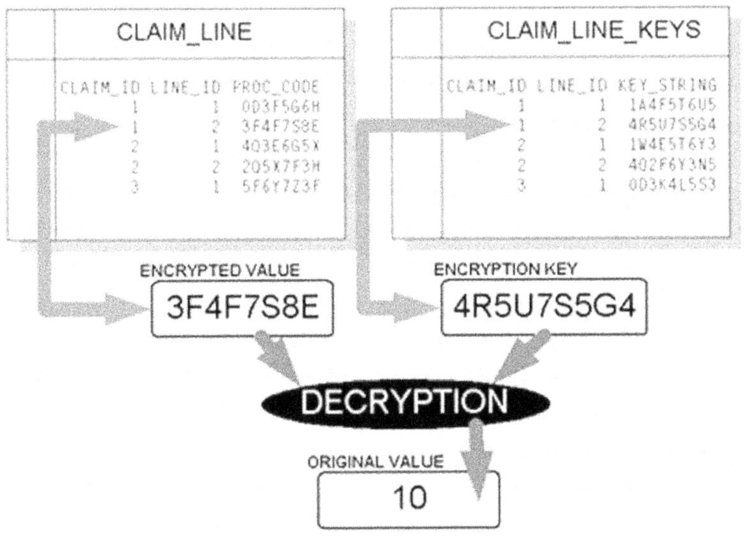


**Figure 6.1** *The claim_line Decryption Process*

## Key Generation

The first task is to generate the key for the encryption. Either of the two methods described earlier can be used. We will create a function to return the key. For simplicity, the *DES3GetKEy* procedure of the package is used here; but the other method can be used as well.

### get_key.sql

```
create or replace function get_key
(
   p_seed          in varchar2 := 'Seed'
)
return raw
is
   v_key_raw  raw (2000);
   v_seed_raw raw (2000);
   v_seed     varchar2(2000) := p_seed;
begin
   v_seed := rpad(v_seed, 80);
   v_seed_raw := utl_raw.cast_to_raw (v_seed);
   dbms_obfuscation_toolkit.DES3GetKey(
       which=> 1,
       seed => v_seed_raw,
       key  => v_key_raw
```

```
end;
```

This function will return a different and randomized key every time it is called.

## The Encryption Process

The next step is to create a function that returns the encrypted value from an input value.

### get_encrypted_value.sql

```
create or replace function get_encrypted_value
(
    p_input_value in varchar2,
    p_key         in raw
)
return raw
is
    v_iv            raw (2000) := null;
    v_inlen         number;
    v_padlen        number;
    v_extra         number;
    v_input_value   varchar2(2000);
    v_ret           raw(2000);
    v_input_raw     raw(2000);
begin
    --
    -- Next,we will pad the value to make the
    -- length a multiple of 8.
    v_inlen := length (p_input_value);
    if (v_inlen < 8)
    then
        v_padlen := 8;
    else
        v_extra := mod(v_inlen, 8);
        if (v_extra = 0)
        then
            v_padlen := v_inlen;
        else
            v_padlen := v_inlen - v_extra + 8;
        end if;
    end if;
    v_input_value := rpad(p_input_value, v_padlen);
    --
    -- The input value has to be converted to RAW
    v_input_raw := utl_raw.cast_to_raw (v_input_value);
    --
    -- Now we have to encrypt the value
    dbms_obfuscation_toolkit.DES3Encrypt (
```

```
        which          => 1,
        iv             => v_iv,
        encrypted_data => v_ret
    );
    return v_ret;
end;
```

This function takes an input value and a key, and throws out an encrypted value.

## Decryption Routine

The other side of the coin is the routine to decrypt the data that has been encrypted earlier. This can be set up as follows.

### get_decrypted_value.sql

```
create or replace function get_decrypted_value
(
    p_input_value in raw,
    p_key         in raw
)
return varchar2
is
    v_decrypted      raw (2000);
    v_ret            varchar2(2000);
    v_iv             raw (2000) := null;
begin
    dbms_obfuscation_toolkit.DES3Decrypt (
        input          => p_input_value,
        key            => p_key,
        which          => 1,
        iv             => v_iv,
        decrypted_data => v_decrypted
    );
    v_ret := utl_raw.cast_to_varchar2(v_decrypted);
    return v_ret;
end;
```

Note that we have used the *input vector* (IV) in both cases. The explanation of using that will be revealed later.

## Updating the Existing Data

The *claim_line* table currently looks like this

```
CLAIM_ID LINE_ID PROCEDURE_CODE CLAIM_AMOUNT PAID_AMOUNT
-------- ------- -------------- ------------ -----------
       1       1 01                     1200        1000
       1       2 03                     1300        1200
```

The column PROCEDURE_CODE must be expanded to hold the encrypted value. The column is expanded to VARCHAR2(200), assuming 200 is the maximum value of the encrypted value.

Now we will update the existing records to the encrypted value and store their keys in the keys table.

### update_encrypted_data.sql

```
declare
    v_key  raw (80);
begin
    for inrec in (
        select
            claim_id,
            line_id,
            procedure_code
        from claim_line)
     loop
        v_key := get_key;
        update claim_line
        set procedure_code =
            get_encrypted_value(procedure_code, v_key)
        where claim_id = inrec.claim_id
        and line_id = inrec.line_id;
        insert into claim_line_keys
        values
        (inrec.claim_id, inrec.line_id, v_key);
     end loop;
end;
```

This will make the PROCEDURE_CODE values in the *claim_line* to be encrypted with some key and the key will be stored in the *claim_line_keys* table.

We will have to write another function to produce the actual value of PROCEDURE_CODE.

### get_procedure_code.sql

```
create or replace function get_procedure_code
(
    p_claim_id in number,
    p_line_id  in number
)
return varchar2
is
    v_enc_proc_code     varchar2(200);
    v_key               varchar2(200);
    v_dec_proc_code     varchar2(200);
begin
    select procedure_code
    into v_enc_proc_code
    from claim_line
    where claim_id = p_claim_id
    and line_id = p_line_id;
    --
    select key_value
    into v_key
    from claim_line_keys
    where claim_id = p_claim_id
    and line_id = p_line_id;
    v_dec_proc_code := get_decrypted_value
    (v_enc_proc_code, v_key);
    --
    return v_dec_proc_code;
end;
```

All these procedures can be owned by the user SECUSER, and execute privileges only can be given to the user APPUSER on the functions GET_PROCEDURE_CODE.

## Triggers

Our objective is to make the process of storing the data in encrypted manner and retrieving in decrypted manner as transparent as possible. For this reason, we will create triggers that will encrypt the input value automatically. The first trigger we will create is the BEFORE INSERT ROW type.

### tr_rbiu_claim_line.sql

```
create or replace trigger tr_rbiu_claim_line
before insert or update on claim_line
for each row
declare
    v_key   raw (80);
```

```
    if INSERTING then
            v_key := get_key;
            :new.procedure_code := get_encrypted_value (
                    :new.procedure_code, v_key);
            insert into claim_line_keys
            values
            (:new.claim_id, :new.line_id, v_key);
    end if;
    if UPDATING then
            select key_value
            into v_key
            from claim_line_keys
            where claim_id = :new.claim_id
            and line_id = :new.line_id;
            :new.procedure_code := get_encrypted_value (
                    :new.procedure_code, v_key);
    end if;
end;
```

This will update the value with an encrypted value, if it already exists, or will insert the value with encryption, even if the user inserts the value in clear text.

```
SQL> select get_procedure_code (1,2) from dual;

GET_PROCEDURE_CODE(1,2)
---------------------------------------------------
04

SQL> update claim_line set procedure_code = '05'
2> where claim_id = 1 and line_id = 2;

1 row updated.
```

Check if the update was successfully applied. Note we did the update in clear text.

```
SQL> select get_procedure_code (1,2) from dual;

GET_PROCEDURE_CODE(1,2)
---------------------------------------------------
05
```

Let's check the insert now.

```
SQL> insert into claim_line values
  2  (1,4,'03',1400,1300);

1 row created.

SQL> select get_procedure_code (1,4) from dual;

GET_PROCEDURE_CODE(1,4)
----------------------------------------------------------
03
```

And it worked. Even if the user entered the password in clear text, the trigger encrypted it and stored it in the database.

# Enhancements

## Extra Security through Application User Management

Remember the use of the input vector (IV) variables used earlier? We simply used them and set them to null in our processing. However, they will perform a very important task to make our application even more secure. Please note, this parameter is available in Oracle 9i and up only.

In Chapter 4, we demonstrated a new model of application user password management. In this mode, the application user authenticates him or herself against the database by calling a function, *is_password_correct* and passing the application user ID and password as parameters. The function returns YES if the combination is correct and NO if it is not.

The function also sets the application context attributes to the values obtained from the *app_users* table. The user will not be able to set these attributes directly; only the calling of the password authentication function can do that. This made the application user management a great tool for secured applications.

Based on the context attribute APP_USER_ROLE, the user could then call another procedure called *set_user_role*, which sets his or her authorized roles. Note how powerful this setup is, and how securely it handled the application user authentication. We can use it to our advantage in this case of encryption, too. The input vector is yet another lock on the encryption process. We will use a value here, instead of the value used earlier, NULL, in the encryption and decryption processes.

But what does that achieve? If the user has to supply the input vector (IV), the value could as well be unsecured.

That's where the design excels. The user never has to supply his or her IV in the process. It will be set automatically as a context attribute by the password authentication process. The function will have a call similar to:

```
set_claim_app_ctx ('input_vector',
    'some_string_that_can_be_set_here');
```

This will set the attribute INPUT_VECTOR in the context *claim_app_ctx* to a value *some_string_that_can_be_set_here*. Inside the encryption and decryption routines shown earlier in this chapter, we will make additional calls to check this value by:

```
v_iv := sys_context ('claim_app_ctx', 'input_vector')
```

This will store the value of the attribute, if set, to the variable V_IV, which could then be converted to raw and used in the encryption and decryption. The modified decryption process is shown in Fig 6.2.

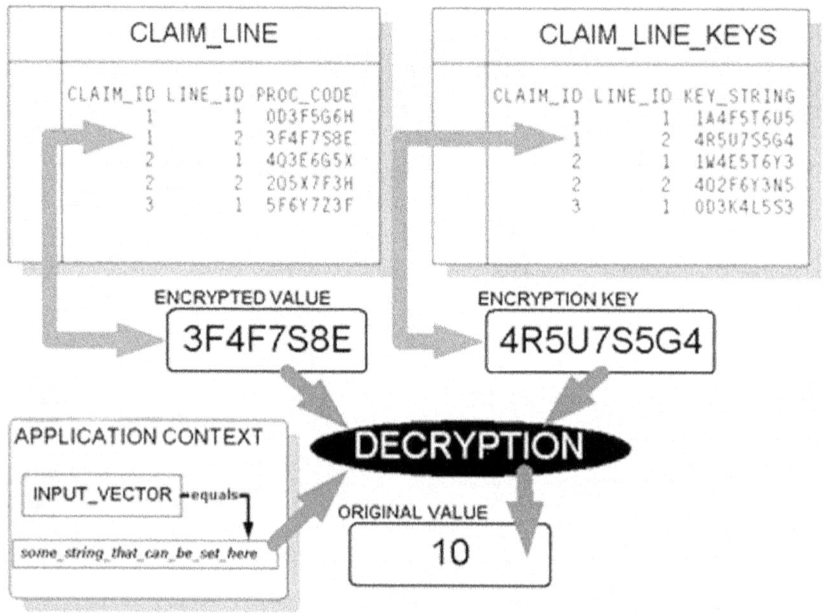


**Figure 6.2** *Decryption Process with Input Vector*

Using an IV in the encryption process will require the same IV to be applied during the decryption process. If the user somehow gets into the database, learns the keys and tries to steal the procedure codes, he or she will not be successful. Reason: the IV value, which is another key in the process, will *not* be set in that manner.

As we saw in Chapter 4, the only way the application context attributes can be set is through a *trusted* procedure, *never independently*. This will prevent the hacker from setting the value of *input_vector* to the expected string *some_string_that_can_be_set_here* and therefore the decryption will never be successful. Similarly, if the hacker tries to set another value of the input vector in the encryption process, he or she will not be successful, either.

With this change in design, let's rewrite our routines. First, we have to modify the *is_password_correct* function to set the context attribute. Merely adding a line among the lines already there makes the change. The entire function is not being reproduced here.

```
-- set the role and the context
set_claim_app_ctx ('app_user_id', p_userid);
set_claim_app_ctx ('app_user_role', v_user_role);
set_claim_app_ctx ('input_vector',
    'some_string_that_can_be_set_here');
dbms_session.set_identifier (p_userid);
```

The added line is shown inside the box above.

The next step is to change the codes in the functions for encryption and decryption.

## Encryption

Using the new variable input vector, we will rewrite the encryption routine described earlier.

### get_encrypted_value_with_iv.sql

```
create or replace function get_encrypted_value
(
    p_input_value in varchar2,
    p_key         in raw
)
return raw
is
    v_iv            raw (2000);
    v_iv_string     varchar2(2000);
    v_inlen         number;
    v_padlen        number;
    v_extra         number;
    v_input_value   varchar2(2000);
    v_ret           raw(2000);
    v_input_raw     raw(2000);
begin
    --
    -- Next,we will pad the value to make the
```

```
    if (v_inlen < 8)
    then
        v_padlen := 8;
    else
        v_extra := mod(v_inlen, 8);
        if (v_extra = 0)
        then
            v_padlen := v_inlen;
        else
            v_padlen := v_inlen - v_extra + 8;
        end if;
    end if;
    v_input_value := rpad(p_input_value, v_padlen);
    --
    -- The input value has to be converted to RAW
    v_input_raw := utl_raw.cast_to_raw (v_input_value);
    --
    -- Now we have to find out the session context
    -- attribute input_vector
    --
    select sys_context ('claim_app_ctx','input_vector')
    into v_iv_string
    from dual;
    v_iv := utl_raw.cast_to_raw (v_iv_string);
    --
    -- Now we have to encrypt the value
    dbms_obfuscation_toolkit.DES3Encrypt (
        input          => v_input_raw,
        key            => p_key,
        which          => 1,
        iv             => v_iv,
        encrypted_data => v_ret
    );
    return v_ret;
```

Note how we have selected the session context attribute and applied that to the *input_vector* shown in bold in the script.

## Decryption

### get_decrypted_value_with_iv.sql

```
create or replace function get_decrypted_value
(
    p_input_value in raw,
    p_key         in raw
)
return varchar2
is
    v_decrypted     raw (2000);
```

```
    v_iv_string     varchar2(2000);
begin
    select sys_context ('claim_app_ctx', 'input_vector')
    into v_iv_string
    from dual;
    v_iv := utl_raw.cast_to_raw(v_iv_string);
    dbms_obfuscation_toolkit.DES3Decrypt (
        input           => p_input_value,
        key             => p_key,
        which           => 1,
        iv              => v_iv,
        decrypted_data => v_decrypted
    );
    v_ret := utl_raw.cast_to_varchar2(v_decrypted);
    return v_ret;
end;
```

Note how the session context attribute has been selected and used here. The relevant piece of the code is shown in bold.

## Testing

After setting all these up, it is time to test the setup to make sure everything is working as per our expectation. We will use SQL*Plus to test this.

```
SQL> set serveroutput on
SQL> var k varchar2(2000)
SQL> var d varchar2(2000)
SQL> var e varchar2(2000)
SQL> variable v varchar2(2000)
SQL> exec :k := get_key

PL/SQL procedure successfully completed.

SQL> print k

K
------------------------------------------------
27F96A49CFB9841ACD6D932D492FD35F1718186409E26C83
```

We got the key in a variable for easy use. Next, check to make sure that no context attributes have been set.

```
SQL> select * from session_context;

no rows selected
```

This is as per expectation. No session context attributes have been set since no trusted procedures have been executed. Next, authenticate the user MARK, with a password 5UCC355. The details of how to do that have been discussed in Chapter 4.

```
SQL> exec :v := is_password_correct ('MARK','5UCC355')

PL/SQL procedure successfully completed.

SQL> print v

V
---
YES
```

This means the user has been successfully authenticated. This process also sets the session context attributes confirmed as follows.

```
SQL> select * from session_context;

NAMESPACE     ATTRIBUTE     VALUE
------------- ------------- ------------------------------
CLAIM_APP_CTX APP_USER_ROLE JUNIOR_CLAIM_ANALYST
CLAIM_APP_CTX APP_USER_ID   MARK
CLAIM_APP_CTX INPUT_VECTOR some_string_that_can_be_set_here
```

The last context, INPUT_VECTOR is of importance to us. The authentication process correctly put the value we expected there. Now, let's encrypt some values.

```
SQL> exec :e := get_encrypted_value ('01',:k)

PL/SQL procedure successfully completed.

SQL> print e

E
----------------
6FDA3673BA40DE3F
```

This returned some value for encrypted string. Let's try to decrypt that.

```
SQL> exec :d := get_decrypted_value (:e, :k)

PL/SQL procedure successfully completed.

SQL> print d

D
--
01
```

Voila! We successfully decrypted that. But we were supposed to decrypt that anyway, weren't we? What value have we added to the process by introducing the concept of input vector and by using the application contexts? Let' examine it.

If a user bypasses the application authentication process, most likely that user is either a DBA or a malicious hacker. In this case, the application context cannot be set properly, since the user did not invoke the application user authentication process. Therefore, the session context retrieval will fail and the user will not be able to decrypt the value, even if he posses the encryption string! Let's see this in action.

The user logs in to SQL*Plus but does not call *is_password_correct* function, i.e. bypasses the regular authentication method. The user also somehow learns the encryption key. The encrypted procedure code and encryption keys are as given in the example above.

```
SQL> variable v varchar2(2000)
SQL> var k varchar2(2000)
SQL> var d varchar2(2000)
SQL> var e varchar2(2000)
SQL> set serveroutput on
SQL> select * from session_context;

no rows selected
```

This is expected. Since the user did not call the function to authenticate himself or herself, the application contexts are not set, and in particular, the attribute *input_vector* is not set. Then the hacker calls the function to decrypt the value using the encrypted value and the encryption key.

```
SQL> exec :d := get_decrypted_value ('6FDA3673BA40DE3F',
'27F96A49CFB9841ACD6D932D492FD35F1718186409E26C83')

PL/SQL procedure successfully completed.

SQL> print d

D
-------
B"÷°Ö╜
```

Note the resultant output. This is not '01', the correct value; rather some jumbled up characters. This is due to the fact that the value of the *input_vector* is NULL. Without the required value of *'some_string_that_can_be_set_here'*, the decryption will never be successful. In addition, the user can never set the value of *input_vector* directly, due to the dependence on the trusted procedure.

We have achieved the objective of securing the data using not just authentication, but by removing any possibility of malicious users bypassing the normal channels and obtaining data.

This is an important aspect to understand and utilize in your overall security design. Using authentication, *input_vector* and a context-based key as described above, you can cover almost all possible routes to unauthorized data access.

# Key Management

The next thorny issue to be handled is how to manage the several keys that will be used to authenticate data. In the method described above, this issue is moot since the key is an integral part of the data itself. In other cases, where the data needs to be encrypted with a less dynamic scheme, or where the encryption key and the table data are disjointed, the issue of key management comes up.

One option is to have a single key, which is 24 bytes long and use it to encrypt everything. This is, of course, the simplest but not the safest. If the hacker learns the key, all of the data will be exposed. But with proper safeguarding, this option may be a viable one.

Other options for handling multiple keys are described here.

## Database

The key can be stored in the database in a safe schema, similar to the application user management schema we saw earlier. The applications can ask for the key whenever it needs to en/decrypt anything. Although this seems simple, in practice this may create more problems. The biggest of all is how to manage the key updates. A simple task like changing keys will have to go through a process of re-encrypting the data and updating the entire table, a task that may be close to impossible in an active system.

## Filesystem

The key can be stored in an operating system file, which can be retrieved at runtime and then supplied to the database during the decryption or encryption process. One advantage of this scheme is the security it offers from the DBA. Traditionally in any scheme involving only the database, the DBA can still query all tables and procedures, and therefore can learn the key to decrypt the data. By placing it in the OS, only a privileged set of users will be able to access it, not even the DBA.

However, this option also fraught with other problems – the most important of which is reliability. The key is not part of the database anymore and is not backed up, recovered or otherwise in sync with the stages of the database. If they key is lost, the data inside the database is lost forever.

### Users

This is perhaps the best in terms of security. The user who is supposed to encrypt and decrypt has to supply the key at runtime. However, the biggest problem in this scheme is the chance that the user may lose the key and therefore render the database useless. Apart from that, the other serious problem is the fact that the key must be shared among a group of people who might have to operate on the data. This increases the security hole, the very thing we are supposed to prevent using encryption.

Based on the above analysis, it would seem that the dynamic encryption scheme is the best of the all solutions.

## Securing the Code

The other weak link in the security chain is the code used to encrypt and decrypt. This is particularly true if the key is embedded inside the procedure or function. Even if the key is not present in the program, the code logic may give away several valuable features of the security scheme and should be protected. The feature Oracle provides to encrypt the code itself is known as WRAP. You would invoke the following to wrap a SQL file *get_encrypted_data.sql*

```
wrap iname=get_encrypted_data.sql
```

This will generate another file named *get_encrypted_data.plb*, which will contain encrypted contents of the file. An example is provided in Figure 6.3. This is part of the wrapped file. Note the syntax used for creating a function or procedure is intact, but everything else is replaced by seemingly random characters. This file can be directly run to create the function.

```
create or replace function get_encrypted_data wrapped
0
abcd
abcd
abcd
abcd
abcd
abcd
abcd
```

```
abcd
abcd
abcd
abcd
abcd
abcd
abcd
abcd
3
8
9200000
1
4
0
1d
2 :e:
1FUNCTION:
1GET_ENCRYPTED_DATA:
1P_INPUT:
```

**Figure 6.3** *Part of the Wrapped PL/SQL file.*

One word of caution here – *wrap* is an one-way encryption process for the files; there is no *unwrap* function. So never throw away your original file. The wrapping is done to make sure that someone peeking into the *dba_source* view will not be able to see the code in clear text.

# A Word on MD5 Procedures

If you look into the source code for the *dbms_obfuscation_toolkit* package specification, you might notice some functions and procedures named *MD5*. Each procedure is also overloaded with both RAW and VARCHAR2 parameter datatypes, and therefore there are four declarations of MD5 available in the package.

These code segments are not documented, probably because they are not encryption mechanisms. The MD5 programs are used to create a hash or *digested* value from the input, not encrypt it, hence the name MD, short for *Message Digest.* This hashed value cannot be reversed to the original value, or *un-hashed*, or *undigested*. This property of one way hashing makes it an unsuitable candidate for encryption, and therefore is not covered in this book in detail. However, for the sake of completeness, the usage has been explained here.

MD5 routines can be used to create hash values for integrity checking purposes. For instance, while transmitting the data over a network, the hashed value of the data can also be sent, perhaps separately. Upon receiving the data and the hash, the target system may hash the data again and compare that with the hash it received to make sure the data is intact. This process is known loosely as *checksumming*. MD5 is a great way to provide checksumming functionality in your application.

As in the case of the *DES3Encrypt* and *DES3Decrypt* procedures, since it has two functions and two procedures defined with the same name and with the same number of inputs, a regular call to the procedure will return an error.

```
SQL> variable v varchar2(2000)
SQL> exec :v := dbms_obfuscation_toolkit.md5 ('ARUP' )

ERROR at line 1:
ORA-06550: line 1, column 13:
PLS-00307: too many declarations of 'MD5' match this call
ORA-06550: line 1, column 7:
PL/SQL: Statement ignored
```

The problem is the way *MD5* is defined. There are two functions named *MD5*, with input parameters RAW in one and VARCHAR2 in the other. To correct the problem use:

```
SQL> exec :v := dbms_obfuscation_toolkit.md5 -
2> (input_string=> 'ARUP')
```

Note the use of named parameter as the input. This makes sure the correct parameter name is used.

# Conclusion

In conclusion, we want to stress that encryption alone is not a solution to data security, it must be used in conjunction with other access control mechanisms provided by Oracle. However, sometimes the needs of specific situations do warrant utilization of encryption routines. While HIPAA does not specifically state any necessity of encryption, the security mandates it places on PHI information, such as procedures done on the patients or diagnosis, indirectly places emphasis on encryption.

In this chapter you should have leaned the usage of Oracle's built-in encryption tool *dbms_obfuscation_toolkit*. You also learned how to build a secure authentication and encryption system so that back channels are not allowed to decrypt sensitive data.

# Oracle Network Security

CHAPTER

## Securing the Network

A network is the glue that connects the clients to the servers, the applications to the database, and one database to another. This component does not provide the management functions for the data contained within. It simply provides a transportation system for the flow of the data – something like a roadway system.

Without the network, databases are akin to islands, adequately secured, but disconnected – in other words, practically useless. Standalone servers are sometimes useful, such as batch programs running on the database server itself. This scenario is extremely rare, and with the commoditization trend of the server market, this phenomenon is probably very short lived. In a vast majority of cases, the server interacts with the application clients located on separate hardware, and the data is exchanged among the clients using the network.

The very purpose of networks, to transport data, opens up a huge security hole. So far, we have discussed ways to secure the database, our house, but not the path that leads to our house. The path, comparable to the network, can be subject to all sorts of security hazards, people could be kidnapped on their way to or from our house, strangers could waylay legitimate visitors and break into our house. Malicious people could place Trojan horses that we so willingly invite to our secured house only to find that attackers come from within it.

Being a link in the processing chain that connects the database to the users, our security is only as good as the most vulnerable of all. In the efforts to strengthen the security of the system, it's not enough to fortify the fortress, but also the *path* that leads to other friendly fortresses. We must secure the network.

## A Network Primer

Although this is not a book about networking, it has been our experience that most Oracle DBAs and architects understand very little of this important component of the enterprise infrastructure. Part of it is the specialized knowledge that is a prerequisite for these concepts to be grasped, but for the most part, it is just plain apathy. Networking is perceived as a beast not to be disturbed if it is running. In this section, we will cover, very briefly, the concepts of networking that are relevant to our discussion.

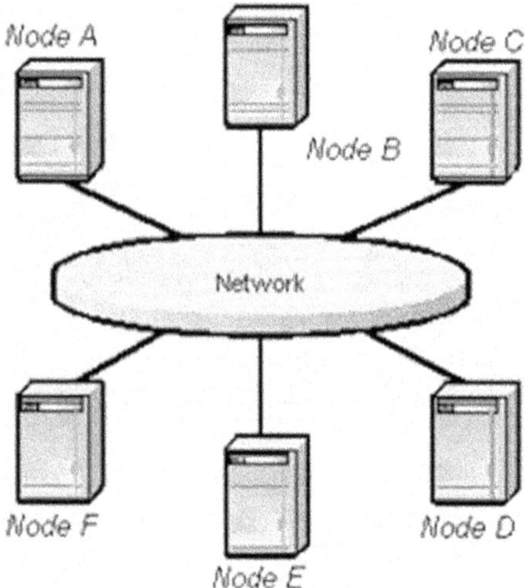


**Figure 7.1** *A Simple Network*

Consider Figure 7.1 for a simple network. The computers are all connected to each other using a single wire that runs from computer to computer. The computers, called *nodes* on the network, can talk to each other using the common roadway that runs among them.

When node A wants to send some data to node C, the data is placed in a virtual container known as a *packet* and placed on the network. But how does the node C know that this is a packet destined for it? The packet has an address where the name of the node is specified. The packet nevertheless moves to all the nodes on the network, and the nodes examine the header of the packet to see the addressee. Since they are not the addressees, they place the packet back in the network and off it goes to the next one.

The process of placing the data in a packet and placing the address, etc. is done by a special component called *network management layer*. Upon receiving the packet, the receiver unpacks the actual data inside it. But how does it know how the sender packed it in the first place? The creation of the packet is not random, rather is governed by a set of standardized rules.

This set of rules is known as a *protocol*. Since all the nodes understand and follow these common rules, i.e. run the same protocol, communication is simple and possible. One of these protocols, the most popular one, is known as *TCP/IP* (**T**ele**C**ommunication **P**rotocol/**I**nternet **P**rotocol).

Needless to say, this process is not very efficient. In a large network, if all the nodes pick a packet up to examine the addressee, the packets will take a long time to reach their destination. Therefore, another strategy is used in large networks.

A special component receives all the packets from the senders, decodes the addresses and then sends the packets to the respective addressees – much like the postal system. This operation is called either *routing* or *switching*, depending upon the exact operation used and this special component is known as a *router* or a *switch*. This has been explained in Figure 7.2.

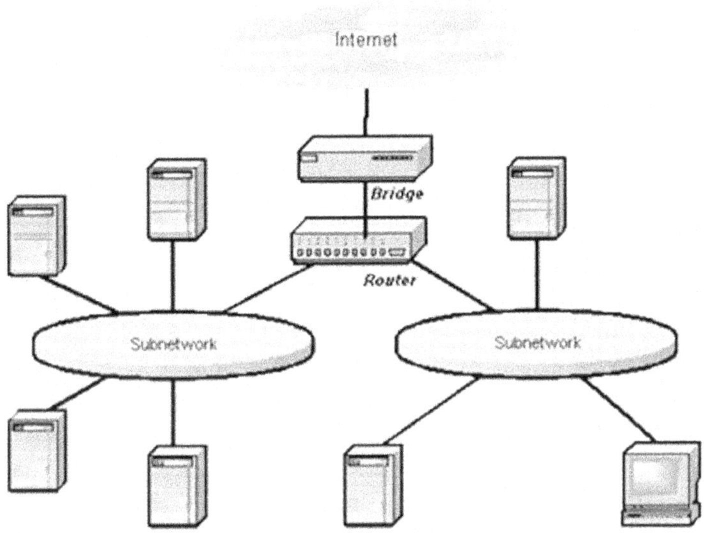


**Figure 7.2** *Networks with Switches and Routers*

However, in a very large network, this switch quickly becomes a bottleneck, as all the packets must be sourced through it. Therefore, a large network may have several switches. The switches themselves may be connected to each other, too, through another special component known as a *bridge*. The bridges themselves may be connected to a much larger network, the Internet. The special bridge that connects the company's network, or the Local Area Network (LAN), is known as a *gateway*.

It is this gateway that provides the means of exchange between the LAN and the Internet. It's sort of like keeping the main door to your house always open. But since this is the gateway to communication with the outside world, it is in need of monitoring.

Besides monitoring the gateway for traffic, another component is used to keep the data traffic within the company inside the network, and not allowing outside data traffic to come inside. This component is called a *Firewall*. Firewalls prevent outsiders, including potential hackers, from getting inside the network.

Please note that this is a very simplistic view and explanation of a network in operation. Real life cases are very complex, and the definitions of components such as routers and switches are governed by the internal workings beyond the scope of this book. The explanation was provided as a background to discuss the potential threats to the infrastructure – how they originate and how to prevent them.

# What are the Threats

With this background in place, let's discuss the various threats that we need to address. Here are some of the threats in brief.

## Sniffing

This is literally eavesdropping on a conversation. A hacker drops in a line in the wires that run between two computers, routes the packets to himself or herself, reads the contents, and sends the packets on their way as shown in Figure 7.3. This process is known as *sniffing*. Since the data is not altered in anyway, this may not be threat to data authenticity, but certainly to the privacy that HIPAA so fiercely attempts to protect.

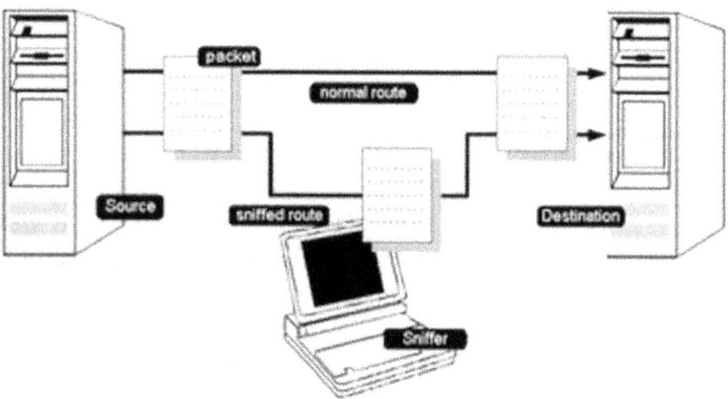


**Figure 7.3** *Sniffing*

In the simple network shown in Figure 7.1, it is quite easy to eavesdrop, since all the packets are routed to all the computers anyway. A malicious user might instruct the network software to examine not only the addresses, but also the contents, therefore stealing the information in the process. In a larger network as shown in Figure 7.2, this may be difficult since the switch will send only the correct packets to a hacker's computer, not all.

Ironically, sniffing is actually a genuine need, especially in cases where the network management functions must be diagnosed and debugged for any problems. To meet this end, several tools are available to perform this important yet potentially malicious function. In cases of switched networks, there are tools available that do the routing of the packets to be sniffed.

## Spoofing

This is a more threatening approach in hacking. The hacker not only steals the packets, but also alters their contents to suit his or her own purpose. As shown in Figure 7.4, the hacker waylays the packet that has the claim amount as 1200, makes it 1000, and sends the packet on its way to the destination. The amount 1000 has a better chance of being accepted than 1200, so this act may be very profitable to the hacker. This could be applied in bank transactions where the hacker alters the transaction amounts to come to a better, but not so honorable, end-state.

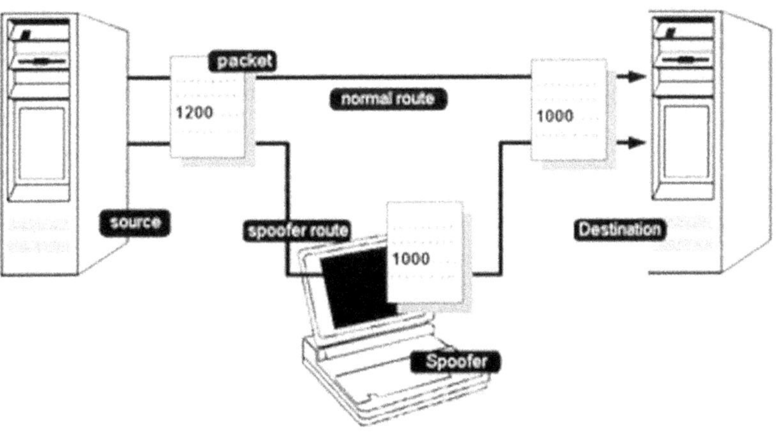


**Figure 7.4** *Spoofing*

Spoofing can be prevented in several ways, such as tweaking the network management software itself or by employing proper techniques in the Oracle Network design. Much of our discussion here is based on this design.

There are several threats to the network layer itself, but most of them are related to the underlying network protocol, and some to the operating system that uses services at the ends. These are mostly handled by the system and network administrators, and are therefore beyond the scope of this book. In this chapter, we will discuss only those threats relevant to Oracle DBAs and architects, and how they are handled.

# Oracle Network Management

Before starting the discussion on security, let's briefly explore the mechanism of network management in Oracle. A complete discussion of the topic is available in the Networking Manuals, and they are not being repeated here. Rather we will highlight the most important parts of the process, and how they fit together to bring the client to the server.

As we discussed earlier, the actual task of moving the data between two machines is left to the services provided by the networking software. Oracle software uses these underlying services to establish the communication between the components.

Oracle uses a common set of services known as *Transparent Network Substrate* (TNS) to handle communication within Oracle components. It is important to remember this model of network communication. You will see the acronym TNS jumping up at many places, especially in error messages. TNS uses the underlying protocol, which could be TCP/IP, SPX/IPX, DECNET, AppleTALK, or something else. This combination of TNS and the underlying networking protocol makes the diagnosis of problems quite challenging, but Oracle does provide some tracing facilities to make it easier.

Let's now examine the way a network connection is handled in Oracle. Refer to Figure 7.5 for the operation.

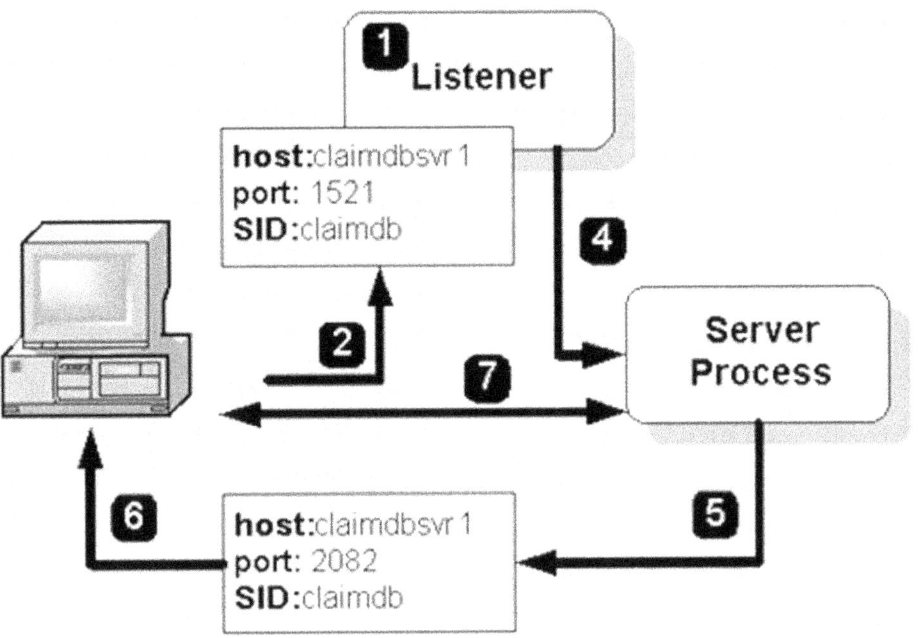


**Figure 7.5** *Database Connection In Dedicated Server*

1. When the client requests a connection to the database, the request is handled by a process called *listener*. This process continuously polls the requests comings to a specific place, called a port. Typically, port numbers 1521 and 1526 are used for Oracle connections. A listener may be listening at port 1521, for instance.

2. A client sends a request to connect to a specific database service (either through a system identifier, or through a service name, or both), with the host address and the port number a listener might be listening to. The client uses a connect string which defines the host's address, the port number and the SID/service name.

3. After receiving the request, the listener validates the request, i.e. verifies that it has come from a valid source, that the SID supplied is the one it is listening for, and all such details. If all are accepted, this request is fulfilled.

4. The next event depends on the database connection configuration, whether it runs in dedicated or shared server mode. In this figure, we have assumed the dedicated server model for connections. The listener then spawns off a database server process to satisfy the request of the user. This server process handles all the requests of the client.

We will make a slight digression here. The server process is a separate process under UNIX operating systems. In Windows, this is a separate thread under the process *oracle.exe.*

5. The server process will need to communicate to the client through a certain doorway, or a port. This port number is not the same as the port number the listener was listening on, i.e. 1521. Rather it is a port assigned dynamically from a pool of unused numbers, e.g. 1609.

6. The listener passes the information on the port where this newly created server process will listen to the client process.

7. After this event, the role of listener is complete. The client process then communicates to the server process through this port 1609. For instance, the client may ask for all the records of the table claims. The server process validates the request, and if the client is authorized, gets the data from the database block buffers or from the disk, and passes to the client process. Under no circumstances does the client process handle the Oracle software code directly. Since there is a server process for each client process handling the request, this is known as a two-task processing model.

The processing is a little different under shared server, or multi-threaded server model as in Figure 7.6.

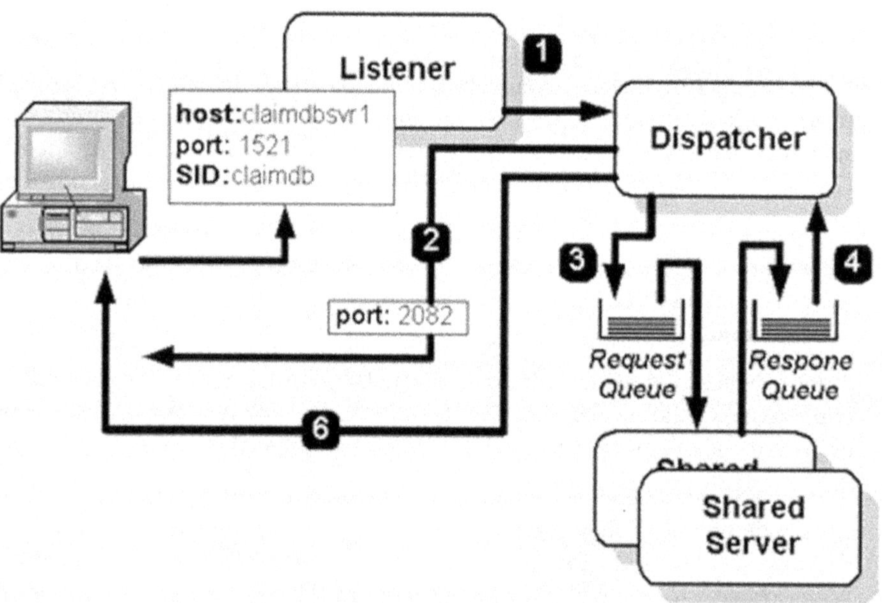


**Figure 7.6** *Connection Process through Shared Servers*

1. After getting the connection request, the listener process does not create a server process, rather passes the connection to a separate process called dispatcher. Note that this is not the same as the previous model, where the address of the server process is passed to the client process. Rather the listener actually hands over the client process request to the dispatcher.
2. In the same manner as in dedicated server mode, the listener passes the port number of the dispatcher handling the request to the client process, and asks it to communicate directly to the dispatcher. Note that the port number of the dispatcher is not the same as the listener port. Once again, after this event, the role of the listener is complete.
3. The dispatcher finds out the least loaded shared server from the pool of servers, and passes the connection to the shared server process to fulfill the request. However, this is rather complex considering the fact that the shared server may be servicing other clients, too. So the dispatcher places the request of the user in a queue called Request Queue.
4. The shared server picks up the request from the queue and fulfils the request. The results are placed in a queue called Response Queue.
5. The dispatcher is notified of the completion of the request.
6. The dispatcher then notifies the client process to get the results from the response queue.

Note, in this process, the dispatcher plays a very important role in the communication between the client and the server processes. Accordingly, these processes are part of the overall connection. This alliance of the client process, the dispatcher and the server process is known as a virtual circuit. The view *v$circuit* gives the information on the virtual circuits. Also, note the important difference – the client process knows only the address of the dispatcher process, not the shared server process, which is equivalent to the server process. The dispatcher is a middleman in all communication between the clients and the servers.

Armed with this information, we can then try to fortify our defenses against the threats discussed above.

# Listener Security

We saw the role the listener process plays in the communication process. Apparently, it does nothing more than simply creating the server process, and then passing its address to the client process - in case of dedicated server mode - or passing the address of the least loaded dispatcher to the client process. However, as the functions imply, the listener does some serious undercover work to put things together. To bequeath or redirect the processes, the listener process has to have some operating system level permission to do what it plans to do. The hackers use this capability of the listener to mount attacks.

Oracle MetaLink has examples of what types of attack are possible and what has been done to prevent them. The good news is that applying the listener patches for that particular attack can prevent all of these known potential attacks.

For instance, one attack sends a large string to the listener to execute. Upon receiving the string, the listener can't handle the size of the data coming in and therefore errors out with a buffer overflow condition. The hacker exploits this to bring down the listener, to achieve what is known as a *Denial of Service* attack. After this vulnerability was discovered, Oracle immediately released a patch that prevented the listener from accepting strings of large size, foiling the attacker's strategy of making the buffer overflow.

Oracle makes known to the community the vulnerabilities and the solutions through an alert system. These alerts can be found at Oracle Technology Network's Security Alerts (http://otn.oracle.com/deploy/security/alerts.htm), for which you do not have to be an Oracle customer under support contract. A sample shot of the website is given in Figure 7.7.

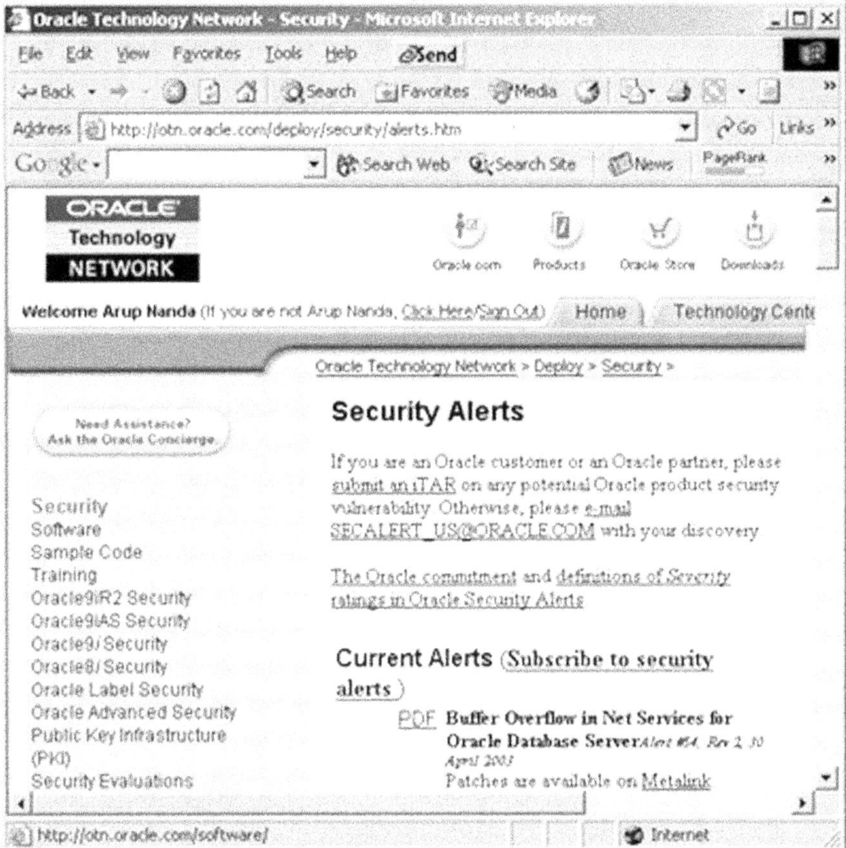


**Figure 7.7** *Security Alerts in Oracle Technology Network Website*

However, the patches are downloaded from Oracle MetaLink, for which you need to have a valid Oracle Support contract. Since these potential holes have been sealed by these patches, the problems will cease to exist simply by applying the patches.

For this reason, the security patches must be applied as soon as they are released. If you have applied them, then the vulnerabilities are no longer applicable. Therefore, this book does not discuss the details of a problem that no longer exists. If you are still interested to know how these vulnerabilities are manifested and resolved, you can visit the webpage to see the details.

We strongly advise you to apply these security patches, if not the regular patchsets, without testing.

**Visit the Oracle security alerts website and apply the security-related patches as soon as they are available.**

## Listener Password

Most of the attacks in the listener are executed either by passing a malicious command to be executed in the operating system, or by modifying the listener settings. The former is handled by applying the security patches as suggested by the alerts. The latter can be handled by securing the listener itself.

Most of the settings in the listener can be set via the command line, from the LSNRCTL prompt. Hackers use this to pass a damaging command. For instance, the hacker may send the command STOP, to stop the listener process. Of course, this does not damage the database itself, but all the client connections subsequent to this operation will fail, same as in a Denial of Service attack. This is as bad as the database being down itself.

Another tactic hackers employ is using the SERVICES command that shows all the relevant information about the listener process, the database services it is listening for, the status of these services, etc. This information may be useful to launch future attacks and should not be shown in an unauthorized manner.

Both of these potential vulnerabilities can be resolved simply by placing a password for the listener. If a password is set for the listener, any command other than START, STATUS and HELP will first require a correct password.

Setting a password for listener is the least security you should have for the listener. By default, it doesn't have any password and many DBAs simply do not create one. Part of the reason is the perceived complexity in specifying and using a password. Here is an explanation of setting the password of a listener.

When the listener is first created, there is no password. The password is set by the command from the lsnrctl prompt

```
LSNRCTL> change_password
```

This will prompt for the old and new passwords, and when entered, they are not displayed on the screen. When the listener is initially created, the password is not set, or null. So, just press the return key when prompted for the old password.

Once the passwords are changed, you have to supply the password before doing any administrative work, such as changing a parameter or stopping the listener. The password is set by the command SET PASSWORD <*password*>. For instance, to stop the listener, you would use the following commands in LSNRCTL utility, assuming the password is t0p53r3t.

```
LSNRCTL> set password
Password: Enter t0p53cr3t here; it will not be displayed.
The command completed successfully
LSNRCTL> stop
Connecting to
(DESCRIPTION=(ADDRESS=(PROTOCOL=TCP)(HOST=PROLIGENCE1)(PORT=1521)))
The command completed successfully
LSNRCTL>
```

This will make the work of the hacker impossible unless the password is known.

The password feature in listener control is a little cumbersome to understand. In this section, we will unveil some of these idiosyncrasies and how to resolve them.

## Entering Passwords

The password can be set either by specifying it through the command CHANGE_PASSWORD, or through a parameter in the *listener.ora* file. We saw how to do that through the CHANGE_PASSWORD command earlier. If the password is changed this way, it should not be specified in the *listener.ora* file. The password is not displayed anywhere. When supplying the password in the listener control utility, you must supply it at the Password: prompt as shown above. You cannot specify the password in one line as shown below.

```
LSNRCTL> set password t0p53cr3t
LSNRCTL> stop
Connecting to (DESCRIPTION=(ADDRESS=(PROTOCOL=IPC)(KEY=EXTPROC)))
TNS-01169: The listener has not recognized the password
LSNRCTL>
```

The password has to be specified on the prompt as follows.

```
LSNRCTL> set password
Password: Enter t0p53cr3t here; it will not be displayed.
The command completed successfully
LSNRCTL> stop
```

The other method of setting the password is through the parameter file. In the file *listener.ora*, insert the following line.

```
passwords_listener = t0p53cr3t
```

To specify passwords for other listeners, use the name appended to the word passwords above. For example,

```
passwords_listener1 = t0p53cr3t
```

sets the password for listener1. In this method, setting the password has to be passed in one line such as:

```
LSNRCTL> set password t0p53cr3t
```

The method of getting a prompt and entering the non-displayed password will not work.

However, when the password is changed in the case where the password is explicitly mentioned in the parameter file, the operation will never be successful.

```
LSNRCTL> set password manager1
The command completed successfully
LSNRCTL> change_password
Old password:
New password:
Reenter new password:
Connecting to (DESCRIPTION=(ADDRESS=(PROTOCOL=TCP)(HOST=DBDEV1)(PORT=1526)))
TNS-01169: The listener has not recognized the password
LSNRCTL> set password
Password:
The command completed successfully
LSNRCTL> change_password
Old password:
New password:
Reenter new password:
Connecting to (DESCRIPTION=(ADDRESS=(PROTOCOL=TCP)(HOST=DBDEV1)(PORT=1526)))
TNS-01169: The listener has not recognized the password
LSNRCTL>
```

Regardless of how you enter the password, through a single line or on the prompt, the change will not be successful. To change the password, you have to remove the line *passwords_listener* in the file *listener.ora* and then change the password.

## Encrypted Passwords

The other option in specifying the password of the listener is to record the password encrypted in the parameter file. This is done by recording the configuration changes automatically in the parameter file as described below.

```
LSNRCTL> set save_config_on_stop on
Connecting to (DESCRIPTION=(ADDRESS=(PROTOCOL=IPC)(KEY=EXTPROC)))
```

```
LISTENER parameter "save_config_on_stop" set to ON
The command completed successfully
LSNRCTL> set password t0p53cr3t
The command completed successfully
LSNRCTL>
```

The commands will instruct the listener to save the configuration to the file after stopping the listener, as mentioned by the command set *save_config_on_stop* on. This will place the following lines in the file `listener.ora`

```
#----ADDED BY TNSLSNR 05-JUL-2003 00:12:48---
SAVE_CONFIG_ON_STOP_LISTENER = ON
#--------------------------------------------

#----ADDED BY TNSLSNR 05-JUL-2003 00:13:49---
PASSWORDS_LISTENER = 8D5438362F7F2951
#--------------------------------------------
```

Note how the password has been recorded in the file, but in an encrypted manner.

In this setup, where the encrypted password is mentioned in the parameter file, setting the password is like the case where the password is not specified in the parameter file.

Similarly, while changing the password, you can change it using the CHANGE_PASSWORD command. There is no need to remove the line from the parameter file.

## How to Check If the Password is Set

From the listener control prompt, issue the command STATUS. If the Security setting is shown as ON, then the password is set for the listener. This is shown below with the relevant display indicated by a sign ☜.

```
LSNRCTL> status
Connecting to (DESCRIPTION=(ADDRESS=(PROTOCOL=TCP)(HOST=ANANDA)(PORT=1521)))
STATUS of the LISTENER
------------------------
Alias                     LISTENER
Version                   TNSLSNR for 32-bit Windows: Version 9.2.0.1.0 -
Produc
tion
Start Date                05-JUL-2003 15:23:19
Uptime                    0 days 6 hr. 24 min. 56 sec
Trace Level               off
Security                  ON ☜
SNMP                      OFF
Listener Parameter File   d:\ora9\network\admin\listener.ora
Listener Log File         d:\ora9\network\log\listener.log
Services Summary...
```

```
  ANANDA               has 1 service handler(s)
  ANANDA               has 2 service handler(s)
  ANANDA               has 2 service handler(s)
The command completed successfully
LSNRCTL>
```

## In Summary

If the password is specified in the parameter file in clear text, then the user must enter his or her password at the LSNRCTL prompt:

```
LSNRCTL> set password password
```

But if the password is changed through the CHANGE_PASSWORD command, and there is no mention of password in the parameter file, or the parameter file has an encrypted password due to the save on stop parameter, the password has to be entered from the prompt as follows

```
LSNRCTL> set password
Password: <password>
```

These idiosyncrasies are not well documented in any Oracle manual and therefore should be considered while managing listener passwords.

## External Procedures

One of the features introduced to the database in Oracle 8 is the ability to call external C programs from within the database. This was done to extend the functionality of the PL/SQL routines that can be written in C to perform complex calculations, such as mathematical modeling, or interaction with filesystems. However, the way it was done opened up many security holes.

The functionality exploits the ability of the listener to issue operating system commands. The external procedures are supposed to issue the commands to the listener on a special IPC pipe named EXTPROC. The specification exists in the *listener.ora* file as

```
(ADDRESS_LIST =
  (ADDRESS = (PROTOCOL = IPC)(KEY = EXTPROC))
```

These external procedures operate by instructing the listener to issue these operating system commands on their behalf. Since the listener runs with the privilege of the operating system user oracle, the only limit to which commands can be executed by the external procedures is the limit on what the oracle account can do. This means the datafiles could potentially be deleted. Hackers can also use this feature to open up your server's filesystem and write malicious data, threatening data integrity.

External procedure service in listener is created by default. In most shops we have seen, this functionality is not used at all. But since the *listener.ora* file has it, the default listener is already listening for it, and stopping the listener, which is not an option, is the only way it can be deactivated.

There are two ways to handle this potential threat. If this is not used in your organization, remove it completely from the *listener.ora* file and restart the listener.

If the external procedures are to be used, remove the entry from *listener.ora* and place it in a separate listener. For instance, your original *listener.ora* file is probably similar to the following.

```
LISTENER =
  (DESCRIPTION_LIST =
    (DESCRIPTION =
      (ADDRESS_LIST =
        (ADDRESS = (PROTOCOL = IPC)(KEY = EXTPROC))
      )
      (ADDRESS_LIST =
        (ADDRESS = (PROTOCOL = TCP)(HOST = ANANDA)(PORT = 1521))
      )
      (ADDRESS_LIST =
        (ADDRESS = (PROTOCOL = IPC)(KEY=ANANDA))
      )
    )
  )

SID_LIST_LISTENER =
  (SID_LIST =
    (SID_DESC =
      (SID_NAME = PLSExtProc)
      (ORACLE_HOME = d:\ora9)
      (PROGRAM = extproc)
    )
    (SID_DESC =
      (GLOBAL_DBNAME = ANANDA)
      (ORACLE_HOME = d:\ora9)
      (SID_NAME = ANANDA)
    )
  )
```

This can be changed to

```
LISTENER =
  (DESCRIPTION_LIST =
    (DESCRIPTION =
      (ADDRESS_LIST =
        (ADDRESS = (PROTOCOL = TCP)(HOST = ANANDA)(PORT = 1521))
      )
```

```
        (ADDRESS_LIST =
          (ADDRESS = (PROTOCOL = IPC)(KEY=ANANDA))
        )
      )
    )

LISTENER_EXTPROC =
    (DESCRIPTION_LIST =
      (DESCRIPTION =
        (ADDRESS_LIST =
          (ADDRESS = (PROTOCOL = IPC)(KEY=EXTPROC))
        )
      )
    )

SID_LIST_LISTENER =
    (SID_LIST =
        (SID_DESC =
            (GLOBAL_DBNAME = ANANDA)
            (ORACLE_HOME = d:\ora9)
            (SID_NAME = ANANDA)
        )
    )

SID_LIST_LISTENER_EXTPROC =
    (SID_LIST =
        (SID_DESC =
            (SID_NAME = PLSExtProc)
            (ORACLE_HOME = d:\ora9)
            (PROGRAM = extproc)
        )
        )
```

This will define two different listeners, LISTENER and LISTENER_EXTPROC, both of which are listening for regular database connections on port 1521, and then external procedures, respectively. The second listener could be down for most cases, and brought up only when needed. In case of a threat or suspicion of attack, the listener could be immediately brought down blocking hacking paths, but allowing other connections at the same time.

**Avoid the default setup of the same listener monitoring database connections on ports as well as external procedures. Isolate external procedures to a separate listener that can be handled independently to control the risk.**

## Restricted Parameter Setting

One of the biggest problems in the listener parameters setting is the way the listener parameters can be easily changed by the SET command, such as

```
LSNTCTL> set rawmode on
LSNRCTL> services
```

This command will let the hacker know a whole lot of things helpful in launching an attack. For instance, with the non-RAW mode, the SERVICES command will produce the following output.

```
Connecting to (DESCRIPTION=(ADDRESS=(PROTOCOL=TCP)(HOST=ANANDA)(PORT=1521)))
Services Summary...
Service "ANANDA" has 2 instance(s).
  Instance "ANANDA", status UNKNOWN, has 1 handler(s) for this service...
    Handler(s):
      "DEDICATED" established:0 refused:0
         LOCAL SERVER
  Instance "ANANDA", status READY, has 1 handler(s) for this service...
    Handler(s):
      "DEDICATED" established:0 refused:0 state:ready
         LOCAL SERVER
```

In RAW mode, the output of SERVICES command is

```
Connecting to (DESCRIPTION=(ADDRESS=(PROTOCOL=TCP)(HOST=ANANDA)(PORT=1521)))
Services Summary...
(SERVICE=(SERVICE_NAME=ANANDA)(INSTANCE=(INSTANCE_NAME=ANANDA)(NUM=1)(INSTAN
CE_STATUS=UNKNOWN)(HANDLER=(HANDLER_DISPLAY=DEDICATED
SERVER)(HANDLER_INFO=LOCAL
SERVER)(HANDLER_MAXLOAD=0)(HANDLER_LOAD=0)(ESTABLISHED=0)(REFUSED=0)(HANDLER
_ID=6822DEBD0821-484B-8427-
E204F5FE1EFD)(PRE=any)(HANDLER_NAME=DEDICATED)(SESSION=NS)(ADDRESS=(PROTOCOL
=beq)(PROGRAM=oracle)(ENVS='ORACLE_HOME=d:\ora9,ORACLE_SID=ANANDA')(ARGV0=or
acleANANDA)(ARGS='(LOCAL=NO)'))))(NUMREL=1))(INSTANCE=(INSTANCE_NAME=
ANANDA)(NUM=2)(HANDLER=(HANDLER_DISPLAY=DEDICATED
SERVER)(STA=ready)(HANDLER_INFO=LOCAL
SERVER)(HANDLER_MAXLOAD=149)(HANDLER_LOAD=10)(ESTABLISHED=0)(REFUSED=0)(HAND
LER_ID=E898681A4553-439B-8D5C-083DBDF02884)(PRE=any)(HANDLER_NAME=DEDICATED)
(SESSION=NS)(ADDRESS=(PROTOCOL=BEQ)(PROGRAM=oracle)(ARGV0=oracleananda)(ARGS
='(LOCAL=NO)'))))(NUMREL=1)))
```

Note the detailed information produced, which can help the hacker is designing a strategy. Since one way we counter the threat is by displaying the minimum information, how do we prevent the hacker from issuing a SET command?

The answer is to set a parameter in *listener.ora* to ON, as follows:

```
ADMIN_RESTRICTIONS_LISTENER1 = ON
```

where LISTENER1 is the name of the listener. This can be changed to reflect the name of the listener to which this restriction is. While this parameter is set to ON, the SET command will fail. The only way to change a parameter is to change it in the *listener.ora* file, and then recycling the listener via a stop-start sequence or by the RELOAD command. A typical hacker will not be able to issue the RELOAD as easily as the SET command; therefore, this protection is adequate enough. Of course, this should definitely be in place if the listener does not have a password.

The apparent downside to this setting may seem to be the need to bounce the listener while setting innocuous settings such as log level or trace level. However, bouncing the listener is not as involved as bouncing the database, and this argument does not hold ground.

 **It is preferable to set the administration restrictions on the listener, in addition to the password setting.**

## Checking for Attempted Break-ins

The reason you want to password protect the listener is to make sure no unauthorized person tries to modify the listener. However, listener password management is not as robust as that inside the database – there are no expiry dates for the password, no format validations, etc. This may tend to make the password a little weaker, and make it more prone to break-ins through brute force. Hackers try all the possible passwords they can guess to finally hit upon the correct one.

However, every unsuccessful attempt is clearly recorded in the log file of the listener. Here is an example of the *listener.log* that displays an attempted access with an incorrect password:

```
05-JUL-2003 21:14:39 * services * 1169
❶ TNS-01169: The listener has not recognized the password
05-JUL-2003 21:14:46 * services * 1169
❷ TNS-01169: The listener has not recognized the password
05-JUL-2003 21:14:55 *
❸
(CONNECT_DATA=(CID=(PROGRAM=)(HOST=)(USER=ananda))(COMMAND=services)(ARGUMEN
TS=64)(PASSWORD=xxxxxxxx)(SERVICE=LISTENER)(VERSION=153092352)) * services *
0
```

The first two lines state that the password entered did not match to the correct one, and the third line was correct. By examining the listener logs regularly, you can identify possible break-ins.

 **Check the *listener.log* regularly for attempts to guess the password. If such an attempt is discovered, immediately change the password.**

# Node Filtering

Using nothing but regular Oracle*Net (or Oracle*Net, as it is called in Oracle 9i and up), you can easily set up a rudimentary firewall-like system to accept connections from a set of trusted clients and servers, and reject connections from known potentially unsafe machines. A typical setup might be the situation shown in figure 7.8, where a set of client application servers and a database server provide the functionality for the users.

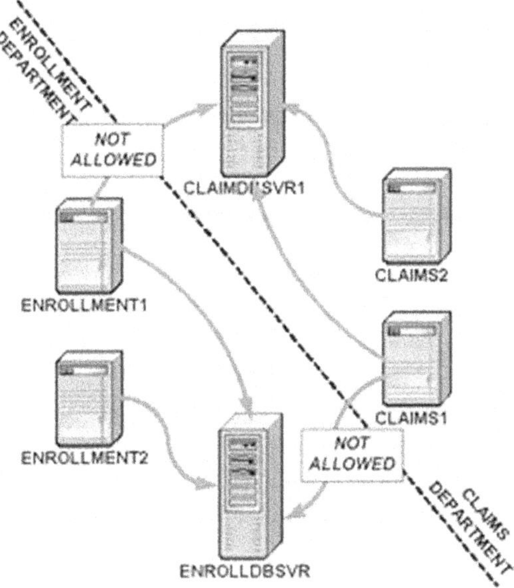


**Figure 7.8** *Typical Client and Server Restrictions Based on Departments*

In this network, the application servers CLAIMS1 and CLAIMS2 access the database on server CLAIMDBSVR. Since we know that no client machines other than the ones shown here are going to access the server database, the Oracle*Net listener on the database server can be configured to accept connections only from these machines. The network also has some other servers, such as the application servers ENROLLMENT1 and ENROLLMENT2 accessing the database on server ENROLLDBSVR. The listener on CLAIMDBSVR can be configured so that the connection requests from ENROLLMENT1 and ENROLLMENT2 are rejected and CLAIMS1 and CLAIMS2 are accepted.

This can be done suing a facility called Valid Node Checking in Oracle*Net. A set of parameters can be placed in some parameter files on the server with the following lines.

```
tcp.validnode_checking = yes
tcp.excluded_nodes = (enrollment1, enrollment2)
tcp.invited_nodes = (claims1, claims2)
```

The location of these parameters varies from version to version. In Oracle 8i, these are set in a file named *protocol.ora*; in Oracle 9i, these are set in *sqlnet.ora*. Both of these files are located in the directory specified by the environmental variable *tns_admin*, which defaults to $ORACLE_HOME/network/admin in UNIX or %ORACLE_HOME%\network\admin in Windows.

 **Important: The parameters are set in *sqlnet.ora* in Oracle9i and *protocol.ora* in Oracle 8i.**

These parameters are intuitively self-explanatory. The first line "tcp.validnode_checking = yes" specifies that the nodes are to be validated before accepting the connection.

The second line specifies that the nodes enrollment1 and enrollment2 are not allowed to connect to the listener. The nodes are indicated either by IP Address (e.g. 192.168.1.100), or the node names as shown above. A single line that is separated by commas specifies the list of node names. The single line is important – you can't break the line.

The third line states that the nodes claims1 and claims2 are allowed. This is important if you specify some node named in the excluded list, but then specify that node as allowed in the invited list. If this list is specified, then it takes precedence over the excluded list.

After making the change in *protocol.ora* (in Oracle 8i) or *sqlnet.ora* (in Oracle 9i and above), stop and restart the listener. The values take effect only during the startup of the listener. After this change, if a user, regardless of the authentication in the database or authority level, connects from the node enrollment1, he or she receives the error

```
$ sqlplus nathan/5ucc355@claimdb

SQL*Plus: Release 9.2.0.2.0 - Production on Wed Jul 2 11:57:06 2003

Copyright (c) 1982, 2002, Oracle Corporation.  All rights reserved.
```

```
ERROR:
ORA-12537: TNS:connection closed

Enter user-name:
```

The error message is a little less intuitive It does not explicitly state the nature of the error.

The same user connecting from node CLAIMS1 will succeed. In this case, the listener simply rejects the connection originating from the node ENROLLMENT1, regardless of the user.

This principle can be extended to cover a variety of friend or foe servers and clients. However, there is no way to specify a wild card character in the node list. For this reason, this method is not very suitable for excluding a list of servers from a network or sub-network. This can be used where the list of machines accessing the network is relatively small and the machines are in a sub-network, behind a firewall. Since the names of the machines are known, the list of allowed and excluded nodes can be easily set up, and this approach can be used.

## Summary

- Node Validation can be used to instruct listeners to accept or reject a connection from a specific client.
- The parameter file is *sqlnet.ora* in Oracle 9i and *protocol.ora* in Oracle8i.
- The nodes must be explicitly specified by name or by IP Address; no wildcards are supported.

## Node Checking Coexistence

Sometimes you may want to have a setup where the validation check of the nodes should be excluded for certain clients and in some situations. In essence, you may want to have the infrastructure for both the node checking and non-checking for a database.

This is accomplished through multiple listeners. The listener performs node validation checking. Therefore, if we configure one listener that does the checking and one that does not, we can establish this setup. However, the parameter file where the check is enforced is the same for a single Oracle Home, regardless of how many listeners are configured. So, in order to use the listeners in different configurations, we need to define a second Oracle Home and create a listener listening on a separate port. This is illustrated in the figure 7.9.

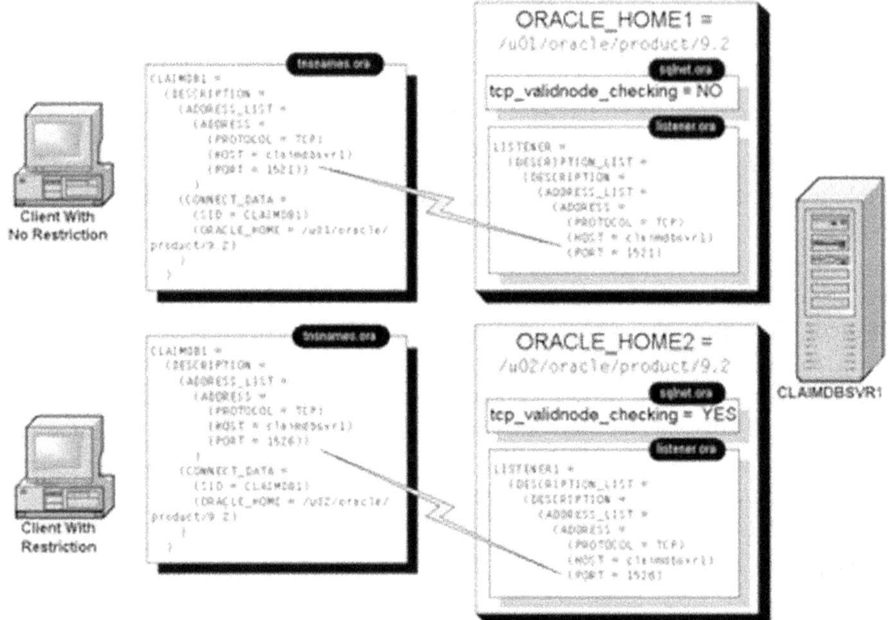


**Figure 7.9** *Using Node Validation and No Validation on the Same Host.*

The server CLAIMDBSVR1 has two Oracle Homes. Assuming the server is UNIX, these homes are:

```
ORACLE_HOME1 - /u01/oracle/product/9.2
ORACLE_HOME2 - /u02/oracle/product/9.2
```

All products are installed on Home1 and all databases use this home. Since we are interested in the listener only, the second home needs to contain only the networking libraries, binary, etc. There is no need to install anything else on the second home; and this keeps the size of this home to a minimum.

The next task is to place the following parameters on the file *sqlnet.ora* in the TNS_ADMIN directory of the second home, located in /u02/oracle/product/9.2/network/admin.

```
tcp.validnode_checking = yes
tcp.excluded_nodes = (enrollment1, enrollment2)
tcp.invited_nodes = (claims1, claims2)
```

These lines are not present in the file *sqlnet.ora* under the directory /u01/oracle/product/9.2/network/admin.

The next step is to configure two listeners. Since they should be listening on separate ports, we will configure a listener that allows unrestricted access as listener1, listening on port 1521. The other listener will be named listener2 and will listen on port 1526. On the first Oracle Home, under the directory for TNS_ADMIN, typically /u01/oracle/product/9.2/network/admin, modify the file *listener.ora* to look like the following.

```
LISTENER1 =
  (DESCRIPTION_LIST =
    (DESCRIPTION =
      (ADDRESS_LIST =
        (ADDRESS =
          (PROTOCOL = TCP)
          (HOST = claimdbsvr1)
          (PORT = 1521)
        )
      )
    )
  )

SID_LIST_LISTENER1 =
  (SID_LIST =
    (SID_DESC =
      (GLOBAL_DBNAME = CLAIMDB1)
      (ORACLE_HOME = /u01/oracle/product/9.2)
      (SID_NAME = CLAIMDB1)
    )
  )
```

Configure the second listener by modifying the file *listener.ora* under the second Oracle Home, /u02/oracle/product/9.2/network/admin to look like the following:

```
LISTENER2 =
  (DESCRIPTION_LIST =
    (DESCRIPTION =
      (ADDRESS_LIST =
        (ADDRESS =
          (PROTOCOL = TCP)
          (HOST = claimdbsvr1)
          (PORT = 1526)
        )
      )
    )
  )

SID_LIST_LISTENER2 =
  (SID_LIST =
    (SID_DESC =
      (GLOBAL_DBNAME = CLAIMDB1)
      (ORACLE_HOME = /u01/oracle/product/9.2)
      (SID_NAME = CLAIMDB1)
```

```
    )
  )
```

Notice, the port is 1526 and the Oracle Home is still the same, pointing to the original one under /u01. The listener name has been changed to listener2 from listener1, and the rest of the file is pretty much the same.

Once configured, start the listeners from the command line as:

```
Lsncrctl start listener1
Lsncrctl start listener2
```

This will start both listeners.

On the client side, configure the service name entries in the *tnsnames.ora* file under the network/admin directory under the Oracle Home. Any client who will have unrestricted access to the server without any validation check should have an entry in the file as follows.

```
CLAIMDB1 =
  (DESCRIPTION =
    (ADDRESS_LIST =
      (ADDRESS =
        (PROTOCOL = TCP)
        (HOST = claimdbsvr1)
        (PORT = 1521)
      )
    )
    (CONNECT_DATA =
      (SID = CLAIMDB1)
    )
  )
```

This will let the users connect to the listener listening on port 1521, meaning they will bypass the node validation checking. The clients for whom access should be restricted should have an entry in the *tnsnames.ora* file similar to the following.

```
CLAIMDB1 =
  (DESCRIPTION =
    (ADDRESS_LIST =
      (ADDRESS =
        (PROTOCOL = TCP)
        (HOST = claimdbsvr1)
        (PORT = 1526)
      )
    )
    (CONNECT_DATA =
      (SID = CLAIMDB1)
    )
  )
```

The entry is identical to the one above, except the port, which is 1526. The listener listening on that port does the node checking, and thus allows or rejects connections based on the clients from which they originate.

This setup can be an immense help in cases where the sub-networks are established to prevent connections from outside, yet allow free access from the inside. Instead of creating a multitude of sub-networks, the node checking can be turned on to dynamically allow or reject connections from client machines.

# Troubleshooting

Things may not turn out to be as smooth as the example has shown. One of the common problems is that the exclusion may not seem to work, even though the files may be present and the parameters seem to be defined properly.

To diagnose the issue, you need to turn tracing on for the connection process. Tracing the process can be done in several levels, and in this case, we need to have that for the level called support, or 16. In the file *sqlnet.ora* place the following line:

```
trace_level_server = support
```

This causes the connection process to write detailed information in a trace file under the directory $ORACLE_HOME/network/trace. Sometimes the directory is specified differently by a parameter in the file *sqlnet.ora* as:

```
trace_directory_server = /tmp
```

This will cause the trace information to be written to the directory /tmp instead of the one mentioned earlier.

After setting the parameters as above, attempt the connection again. There is no need to bounce the listener. The connection attempt will create trace files similar to *svr_0.trc* to be written in the proper directory.

Open this file in an editor. Parts of the file are explained below.

```
[01-JUL-2003 18:27:04:483] Attempted load of system pfile source
/u02/oracle/product/9.2/network/admin/sqlnet.ora
[01-JUL-2003 18:27:04:483] Parameter source loaded successfully
[01-JUL-2003 18:27:04:483]
[01-JUL-2003 18:27:04:483]  -> PARAMETER TABLE LOAD RESULTS FOLLOW <-
[01-JUL-2003 18:27:04:483] Successful parameter table load
[01-JUL-2003 18:27:04:483]  -> PARAMETER TABLE HAS THE FOLLOWING CONTENTS <-
[01-JUL-2003 18:27:04:483]   tcp.validnode_checking = yes
[01-JUL-2003 18:27:04:483]   trace_level_server = support
```

```
[01-JUL-2003 18:27:04:483]   tcp.invited_nodes = (192.168.128.123,
192.168,128.1
22, 127.0.0.1)
[01-JUL-2003 18:27:04:484]   NAMES.DIRECTORY_PATH = (TNSNAMES)
[01-JUL-2003 18:27:04:484]   tcp.excluded_nodes = (172.21.5.196)
[01-JUL-2003 18:27:04:484] --- PARAMETER SOURCE INFORMATION ENDS ---
```

These lines indicate that

- The parameter file /u02/oracle/product/9.2/network/admin/sqlnet.ora was read by the listener.
- The parameters were loaded successfully.
- The contents of the parameter were read as we mentioned them.
- The names of the excluded and invited nodes are displayed.

If the information is not displayed as see, here, the problem could be in the way the parameter file is written, most likely a typographical error such as a missing parenthesis. This error should be fixed before proceeding further.

If the parameters are loaded properly, the next thing is to check the section where the node validity checking is done. This section of the file looks like this.

```
[01-JUL-2003 18:27:04:489] ntvllt: Found tcp.invited_nodes. Now loading...
[01-JUL-2003 18:27:04:489] ntvllhs: entry
[01-JUL-2003 18:27:04:489] ntvllhs: Adding Node 192.168.128.123
[01-JUL-2003 18:27:04:489] ntvllhs: Adding Node 192.168
[01-JUL-2003 18:27:04:489] ntvllhs: Adding Node 128.122
[01-JUL-2003 18:27:04:489] ntvllhs: Adding Node 127.0.0.1
[01-JUL-2003 18:27:04:489] ntvllhs: exit
[01-JUL-2003 18:27:04:489] ntvllt: exit
[01-JUL-2003 18:27:04:489] ntvlin: exit
[01-JUL-2003 18:27:04:489] nttcnp: Validnode Table IN use; err 0x0
```

The first line indicates that the parameter *tcp.invited_nodes* was found. Next, the entries in that list are read and displayed one after the other. This is the most important clue. If the addresses are written incorrectly, or the syntax is wrong, this in indicated in the trace files by not specifying the node names checked. The last line in this section shows that the ValidNode table as read and used has an error code of 0x0 (in hexadecimal, equating to zero), i.e. it has no errors.

If there is a problem in the way the valid node parameters were written in the parameter file, the trace file would have shown something different. For instance, say the parameters were written as

```
tcp.excluded_nodes = (172.21.5.196
```

Note how a parenthesis is left out, indicating a syntax problem. However, this does not affect the connection. Listener simply ignores the error and allows the connection without doing a valid node checking. Upon investigation, we find in the trace file the root of the problem. The trace file shows the following information.

```
--- PARAMETER SOURCE INFORMATION FOLLOWS ---
[02-JUL-2003 13:49:05:453] Attempted load of system pfile source
/u201/oracle/product/9.2/network/admin/sqlnet.ora
[02-JUL-2003 13:49:05:453] Load contained errors
[02-JUL-2003 13:49:05:453] Error stack follows:
NL-00422: premature end of file
NL-00427: bad list

[02-JUL-2003 13:49:05:453]
[02-JUL-2003 13:49:05:453]  -> PARAMETER TABLE LOAD RESULTS FOLLOW <-
[02-JUL-2003 13:49:05:453] Some parameters may not have been loaded
[02-JUL-2003 13:49:05:453] See dump for parameters which loaded OK
```

This clearly shows that the parameter file had errors that prevented the loading of the parameters. For this reason, the valid node checking is turned on and in use, but there is nothing in the list of the excluded nodes as shown in the following line from the trace file.

```
[02-JUL-2003 13:49:05:463] nttcnp: Validnode Table IN use; err 0x0
```

Since the error is 0x0, i.e. no error is reported by the validity checking routine.

The subsequent lines on the trace file show other valuable information. For instance this line:

```
[01-JUL-2003 18:27:04:492] nttbnd2addr: using host IP address:
192.168.128.133
```

shows that the IP address of the server that the listener was supposed to route the connection to was 192.168.128.133.

If all goes well, the listener allows the client to open a connection. The following line confirms this.

```
[01-JUL-2003 18:27:04:494] nttcon: NT layer TCP/IP connection has been
established.
```

As the line says, the TCP/IP connection has been established. If any other problems exist, the trace file will show information helpful for diagnosis.

> Valid Node Checking can be a quick and easy solution for implementing database security inside a sub-network, without the additional overhead of maintaining several sub-networks.

## Connection Manager

Originally introduced as a tool to coordinate connections to the database from several clients, the tool known as Connection Manager has many more capabilities, including a very useful and effective security application.

It is essentially a middleware tool that sits between the clients and the database servers and redirects the connections. Two uses of the tool have been shown in Figure 7.10, *Connection Concentration* and *Multiprotocol Support.*

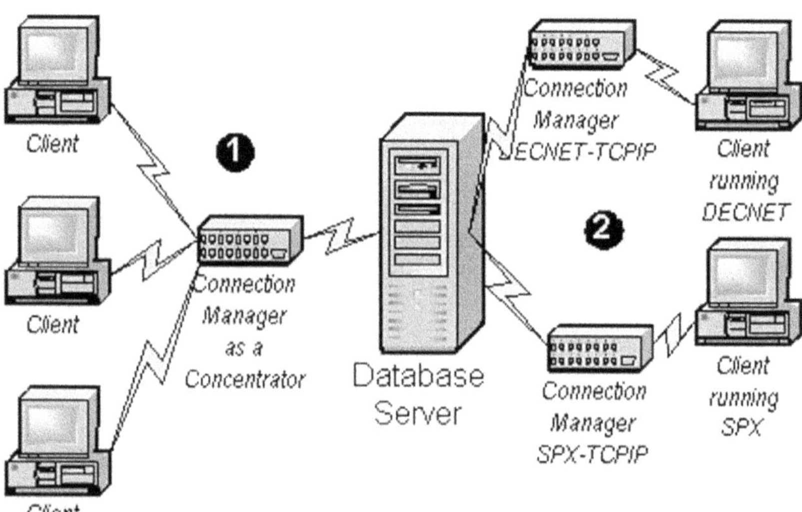


**Figure 7.10** *Connection Manager*

- As shown in the figure, on the left side, a database services many different client processes. Since the clients may be active only a fraction of the time, the database can support the load of, say, 10,000 clients, but that will translate to 10,000 network connections, which may introduce problems specific to its own nature – such as network bandwidth depletion, increase in latency, etc. Introducing a middle tier, the Connection Manager, alleviates this problem. This server accepts the connections from the client and connects to the database server only once, providing a conduit to the connections from the clients. The server has only one connection to the CM server, or perhaps a connection to a set of CM servers, but not to all the clients. This concept of sharing the connection comes in handy when managing a large number of clients serviced by a single database server.

- Another use of the CM is the Network Protocol Bridge. Typically, the listener on a database server uses a well-known protocol, TCP/IP, which cannot service clients using another protocol from the Novell Netware, SPX, or DECNET from HP, or some other protocol. The listener must be configured to listen to all these different protocols, and those protocols must be installed on the server machine. That may be impossible to attain. A connection manager server that has both protocols can be placed in between and can act as a bridge as shown in Figure 7.10 on the right side.

The other two uses of Connection Manager are very helpful in security and will be discussed later.

## Workings of Connection Manager

The next step is to quickly build a CM server used to service a database instance. The setup needs a parameter definition file of its own, *cman.ora*, which cannot be created via the GUI tools, it must be created manually. The location of the file is the directory specified by the environmental variable *tns_admin*, which defaults to $ORACLE_HOME/network/admin. The file has three distinct sections to handle three different things.

### Address Section

In this section, the host where the CMAN server is running, the port it is listening to and the protocol it is expecting are mentioned. As example is shown below.

```
CMAN =
   (ADDRESS_LIST =
      (ADDRESS =
         (PROTOCOL=TCP)
         (HOST=cman.proligence.com)
         (PORT=1610)
      )
   )
```

Here the CMAN server is expecting TCP/IP protocol messages from host cman.proligence.com on port 1610. Any port can be used, but traditionally, 1610 and 1630 are ports used for CMAN, just as 1521 and 1526 are used for listener processes.

If you have a multi-protocol setup so that CMAN can act as a bridge, another ADDRESS entry for that protocol can be entered in the ADDRESS_LIST.

## Profile Section

The next section sets the parameters for the different behavioral aspects of the CMAN process. An example is given below.

```
CMAN_PROFILE =
   (PARAMETER_LIST =
      (MAXIMUM_RELAYS=64)
      (LOG_LEVEL=4)
      (TRACING=YES)
      (RELAY_STATISTICS=YES)
      (SHOW_TNS_INFO=YES)
      (USE_ASYNC_CALL=YES)
      (AUTHENTICATION_LEVEL=0)
   )
```

Most of the parameters can be left at their default values. Some important ones are discussed below.

*tracing* indicates that the CMAN server should write some detailed traces to the trace directory which defaults to $ORACLE_HOME/network/trace, or can be specified by a parameter in this file TRACE_DIRECTORY.

*authentication_level* is an important one. If the clients are authenticated with Oracle Advanced Security, this parameter should be set to 1, i.e. true. The CMAN server will expect an authentication routine to be performed. If no such authentication used, then this parameter should be set to 0, or false.

## Rules Section

The third section specifies the rules to accept or reject connections coming from specific clients to specified servers that are very important to our security setup. An example of this file is given below.

```
CMAN_RULES =
   (RULE_LIST =
      (RULE =
         (SRC = app1.claim.proligence.com)
         (DST = claimdbsvr1.proligence.com)
         (SRV = claimdb1)
         (ACT = accept) ❶
      )
      (RULE =
         (SRC = app1.enroll.proligence.com)
         (DST = claimdbsvr1.proligence.com)
         (SRV = claimdb1)
         (ACT = reject) ❷
      )
)
```

In the segment above, we have defined two rules. In the first one, we have asked all connections originating from the client machine app1.claim to freely be accepted into the destination server claimdbsvr1 for the database claimdb1. This is indicated by the parameter ACT being set to accept, as shown in the indicator ❶ above. The other rule says that for the same destination, any connections coming from the client app1.enroll should be immediately disallowed, as shown in indicator ❷ above. The number of rules can be defined for any number of servers and clients as needed with a single RULE tag inside the RULE_LIST.

However, you must be wondering why this is all necessary when we can easily use the Node Filtering technique described earlier. Node filtering is easier to set up, and does not need a separate process (CMAN) be run, so why go to the trouble of setting these complicated parameter files?

The answer lies in the limitations of the Node Filtering technique - it can't handle wildcards in a client name or IP Address. Each IP address must be specified in full. In a typical organization, this becomes rather impossible with so many clients.

The number of characters allowed in a single line limits the maximum number of servers that can be placed in the parameter file. Therefore, not too many client names can be specified through the node filtering technique, and this is yet another limitation that large corporations may find unacceptable.

Connection Manager answers the second limitation by allowing as many rules to be defined as needed. As for the first one, the use of wildcards is permitted. A wild card is designated by the letter x. For instance, in the above definition, if we wanted to reject any connection coming from the sub-network enroll.proligence.com, which includes app1, app2 and so on, instead of defining a rule for each client, we could specify a rule:

```
(RULE =
   (SRC = x.enroll.proligence.com) ☜
   (DST = claimdbsvr1.proligence.com)
   (SRV = claimdb1)
   (ACT = reject)
)
```

Note how the wildcard x has been specified in the line indicated. This will prevent a connection from any client where the last part of the name matches enroll.proligence.com. The same technique can be used in IP Addresses, e.g. 192.168.1.x. Sometimes, the use of IP addresses may be easier due to careful sub-domaining and a more intuitive IP address depending on the sub-network the client is on.

## Managing the Processes

CMAN uses two processes, similar to the listener process, CMGW and CMADMIN, both controlled by an executable CMCTL. To start the processes, you would call the CMCTL executable from the command line which will bring up the CMCTL prompt:

```
CMCTL for DEC OSF/1 AXP: Version 8.1.7.4.0 - Production on 06-JUL-2003
11:46:32

(c) Copyright 1998 Oracle Corporation.  All rights reserved.

Welcome to CMCTL, type "help" for information.

CMCTL>
```

From this prompt, you could control the CMAN processes. To start the processes, you would use:

```
CMCTL> start
ADMIN Status:
(STATUS=(VERSION=8.1.7.4.0)(STARTED=06-JUL-2003 11:45:29)(STATE=RUNNING))
CMAN Status:
(STATUS=(VERSION=8.1.7.4.0)(STARTED=06-JUL-2003 11:45:31)(STATE=running))
CMCTL>
```

Note the two processes have started as indicated by the two displayed lines. To know the status of these two at any point in time, you would issue the command STATUS. However, to get a better display on the processes, you could set the display mode to VERBOSE as indicated below.

```
CMCTL> set displaymode verbose
Current display mode is VERBose

CMCTL> status

STATUS of the cman
-----------------------------------------
CMAN  Version              8.1.7.4.0
Start-up time              06-JUL-2003 11:45:31
Current state              running

STATUS of the cman_admin
-----------------------------------------
ADMIN Version              8.1.7.4.0
Start-up time              06-JUL-2003 11:45:29
Current state              RUNNING

CMCTL>
```

To instruct the processes to start accepting the connections, you would use the command ACCEPT_CONNECTION. To stop accepting connections, you would use:

```
CMCTL> accept_connections off

Profile of the CMAN
----------------------------------------
Current state              offline
```

CMAN responds with the status as offline.

## Client Setup

Next comes the setup of the client to access CMAN services. The regular service name in the *tnsnames.ora* file may look like this.

```
CLAIMDB1 =
    (DESCRIPTION =
        (ADDRESS_LIST =
            (ADDRESS =
                (PROTOCOL = TCP)
                (HOST = claimdbsvr1.proligence.com)
                (PORT = 1521)
            )
         )
         (CONNECT_DATA =
            (SERVICE_NAME = CLAIMDB1)
         )
    )
```

We need to modify this to the following.

```
CLAIMDB1 =
    (DESCRIPTION =
        (ADDRESS_LIST =
            (ADDRESS = ❶
                (PROTOCOL = TCP)
                (HOST = cman.proligence.com)
                (PORT = 1610)
            )
            (ADDRESS =
                (PROTOCOL = TCP) ❸
                (HOST = claimdbsvr1.proligence.com)
                (PORT = 1521)
            )
         )
         (SOURCE_ROUTE= YES) ❷
         (CONNECT_DATA =
            (SERVICE_NAME = CLAIMDB1)
         )
```

)

Let's examine this file in detail. Notice we have inserted a new address indicated by ❶ to specify the address of the CMAN server and the port it listens on. The port 1610 was specified in the configuration file for the CMAN server, *cman.ora*.

There is a new parameter, indicated by ❷ *source_route* = YES. This instructs the CMAN server to contact the listener on the address specified by the other address block indicated by ❸. In this case, the listener on claimdbsvr1 listening on port 1521 is contacted as shown in the address block ❸. The client now connects to the database as specified by the *service_name* parameter as above. The important point to note here is that the connections are sourced through the connection manager, i.e. the client connects to the CMAN server, and CMAN in turn connects to the database on behalf of the client. This process is known as *relaying*.

Now that you understand how to setup and use the Connection Manager to establish access control polices in the network, you can use this powerful tool to establish access control policies for the databases and the networked clients.

Note, you could have connection manager running, and at the same time have the client connect directly to the listener on the server without problems. Sometimes it may be necessary to temporarily bypass CMAN problems from trusted clients such as dedicated batch processing servers. In such a case, you could still have some protection from unauthorized access by configuring the node filtering technique.

 **Use Connection Manager to deny access to the database from untrusted clients and servers. This will act as a small, yet effective, firewall.**

# Firewalls

We have discussed firewalls in earlier chapters. Essentially, they provide a barrier that does not allow anyone from outside to come in contact with the machines inside the firewall, while the machines inside can freely communicate among themselves. By preventing the access of the machines from outside, potential attacks can be thwarted.

However, some form of access to the outside world is needed to function properly; otherwise, the organization will become an island. To allow for the normal flow of business, some ports are opened up in the firewall through which outsiders can access the machines inside. Typically, these ports are tightly controlled and monitored, and are configured to allow only certain services to pass through – such as an http request or ftp request. This is known as opening up a hole in the firewall.

Since the Oracle listener listens to the port 1521, the most convenient way to allow Oracle connections to flow through the firewall seems to be opening up the port 1521 on the firewall. However, that will not enable Oracle connections to flow through, as we will see in the subsequent paragraphs.

From the initial discussion on Oracle Network operations, we have seen that the listener simply listens to port 1521, to which the clients first connect. After the request is granted, the listener either creates a server process (in the dedicated server mode), or contacts the least loaded dispatcher (in the shared server mode), to service the request of the client. In either case, it passes the address of the appropriate process to the client. Since all communication must be tunneled through a port, a port is dynamically created for the client. Note the word *dynamically,* meaning the port numbers are assigned out of a pool of available ones – typically over the number 1024 - and the exact number will not be known until runtime. For instance, the port number assigned could be 1321, which is not open in the firewall, so the client process trying to connect to the port will fail. Opening up the listener ports will not be enough to tunnel connections through the firewall.

On the other hand, if you open up all possible ports on the firewall, these ports could be subject to break-in, and the whole purpose of having a firewall is defeated.

The other problem in using a firewall is *Network Address Translation* (NAT). Most firewalls are configured in such a way that there are two IP addresses for a server, depending upon whether the server is accessed from inside or outside the firewall. For instance, the server claimdbsvr1 may have an IP address of 192.168.1.31 within the company network, but from outside it is seen as 12.129.211.121 (this is a fictitious IP address used for illustration only and any resemblance to a real one is purely coincidental). When the clients from outside the firewall connect to the server 12.129.211.121, the firewall translates the address to 192.168.1.31. This helps hide the machines inside the firewall, and prevents some form of hacker attacks.

However, it is this property that is a stumbling block in network connections. From the discussion on networking, remember that the listener passes to the client a port number and the host address. Refer to figure 7.11 for the problem.

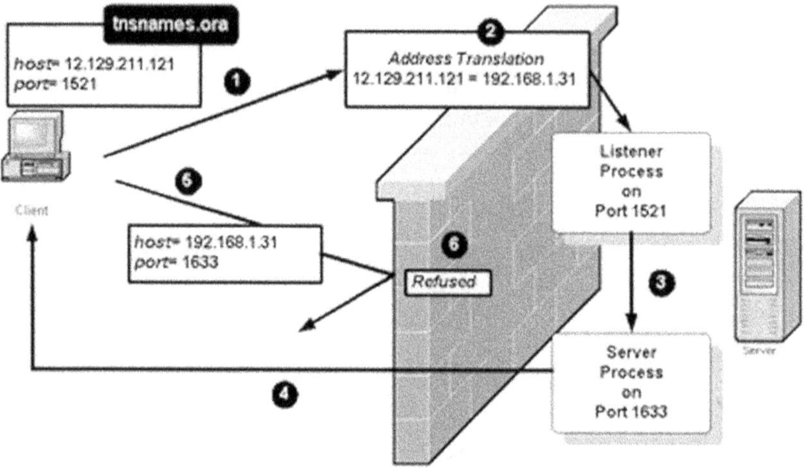


**Figure 7.11** *Using Network Address Translation in a Firewall Will Cause Oracle Connections to Fail.*

1. Client connects to listener on host with the IP address 12.129.211.121 on port 1521.
2. The firewall translates the IP address to 192.168.1.31 and passes on the request to the listener.
3. The listener accepts the connection and either creates a server process or uses one of the existing dispatchers, depending on whether the database is running in dedicated or shared server mode, respectively.
4. This process, the port number and host name is passed on to the client, and the packet is redirected to the port.

   Here is an important point to note – the host IP address passed is the real one, 192.168.1.31, not 12.129.211.121. In addition, the port number is also the port number dynamically generated; say, 1633, not 1521.
5. The client tries to start communication through this port 1633 on host 192.168.1.31,
6. The firewall sees that the client is trying to access the internal IP Address and blocks the call. The connection fails. Even if the ports are unrestricted on the firewall, the host name translation fails, and the connection from the client cannot be fulfilled.

This is another problem in using a firewall and Oracle combination.

## In summary:

There are two problems in using a firewall and Oracle combination.

- Port number is dynamically generated and is generally blocked on the firewall.
- Network address translation gives the client an IP address that is blocked by the firewall.

# Solutions to Firewall Problems

Let's talk about solutions to these problems.

## Oracle Server in DMZ

The server running the database should not be exposed to the firewall at all. Instead, the accesses to the database must be made from application servers, and these can be placed in the Demilitarized Zones (DMZ), along with the database servers. This protects the listener process from being attacked directly, one of the major concerns in the security setup. This is shown in Figure 7.12.

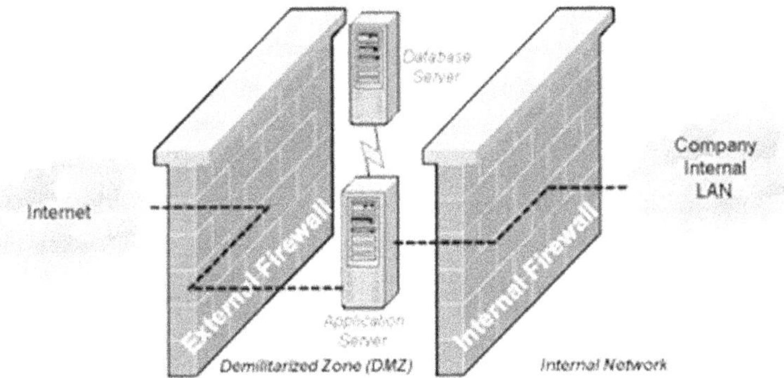


**Figure 7.12** *Database Servers in DMZ Setup*

For a vast majority of organizations, this setup is feasible and desirable. Most likely, there is never a need to expose the database server machine to the firewall. The only outsiders who might interact with the database generally do that through a web server, or some other application server, which requires a separate server anyway. Moreover, it is certainly not desirable to run the application/web server and the database on the same physical machine. Therefore, this model of isolated servers is possible and should be aimed at. A firewall should never allow connections to flow directly to the database server itself. Within the DMZ, the database server can have either Connection Manager and/or Node Filtering to accept connections only from the trusted application/webservers.

## Transparent Proxying

Another method used in firewall and Oracle combination is proxy ports. There are commercially available products that can accept the port requested from the client and temporarily open up that port to the client so that the connection can go through. One such firewall product is Side Winder G3 from Secure Computing. This is not intended to be an endorsement of the product.

## Port Forwarding

This method uses the Secure Shell (SSH) protocol to tunnel requests through the firewall. SSH is a protocol similar to the telnet one, except that security is added with encryption and checksumming to prevent tampering. SSH is the accepted way to handle traffic in the Internet world. There is a key provision in SSH called port forwarding that is used here to achieve our objective.

Typing "ssh" on the command line, we can see all the available options, of which two are relevant to us at this moment.

- -L listen-port:host:port Forward local port to remote address
- -R listen-port:host:port Forward remote port to local address

These cause SSH to listen for connections on a port, and forward them to the other side by connecting to host:port.

Setting these options allows the service to listen on a specific port, but after getting the request, send it to a separate port. This operation of port forwarding is completely transparent to the client trying to connect. For added security, we can have a server handle this port forwarding, say portforward.proligence.com. The application server is claimapp1.proligence.com and the database server is claimdbsvr1.proligence.com.

You can run this on the server claimapp1

```
ssh -L 8080:claimdbsvr1:1521 portforward
```

This will cause all the traffic going to port 8080 to be routed to the port 1521 on the server claimdbsvr1 instead. The firewall need be opened on port 1521 only, but only from the PORTFORWARD server. The application will connect to the PORTFORWARD server, so the *tnsnames.ora* entry will have to be changed as follows.

```
CLAIMDB1 =
    (DESCRIPTION =
        (ADDRESS_LIST =
            (ADDRESS =
                (PROTOCOL = TCP)
                (HOST = portforward.proligence.com)
                (PORT = 8080)
            )
         )
         (CONNECT_DATA =
            (SERVICE_NAME = CLAIMDB1)
         )
    )
```

The applications will be now connected through this SSH port forwarder.

## Preventing Port Redirection

The third method is preventing TNS from providing a different port to the client. This approach is not recommended, but can be used in some cases.

Under Windows, there is a key USE_SHARED_SOCKET under the tree HKEY_LOCAL_MACHINE\Software\Oracle that controls the port redirection. If this key is set to TRUE, then listener handles all connections. Remember from our earlier discussion on the networking connection model that the listener's role is completed when the client connects. Under this approach, even if the listener goes down, the connections are not affected. By setting the registry key, all connections flow through the listener process, making it a single point of failure. If the listener service dies, so do all the sessions. In addition, the listener also becomes a single point of contention with request and response queues processed serially.

Under UNIX flavored servers, the Multithreaded mode can be set up to redirect only to specific ports using the *init.ora* parameter *mts_dispatchers*. This parameter allows definition of dispatchers redirecting connections only to a specific port, and those ports can be opened up in the firewall.

However, bear in mind the more ports open on the firewall, the greater the chance of an attack. Therefore, this solution is not recommended. Besides, it uses the MTS mode of connections, not necessarily a better setting compared to the dedicated server model, especially in transaction intensive systems.

## Connection Manager

This is another way to configure tunneling of Oracle*Net traffic through a firewall. From our earlier discussion on CMAN, you learned that it is a middleware server that accepts connection requests from clients and if valid, sends them to the database listener port. When the database responds, the message is not sent directly to the clients, rather it goes to the CMAN server, which in turn forwards it to the client.

This indicates an important aspect of the communication – as far as the client is concerned, the only host and port number it should be interacting with are the CMAN server and the port where it listens. In the section on CMAN, we configured it to listen on port 1610 and the host was cman.proligence.com. This server should be inside the firewall with the database, and the only port that should be opened is 1610, not 1521.

Since the database and CMAN server are both inside the firewall, network address translation does not occur. Therefore, the first problem in using a firewall does not arise. Secondly, the only ports that the client uses to send and receive data are the ones used by CMAN server, and only these should be opened. This resolves the second problem of dynamically generated port numbers.

Of all the approaches, the best is the first one, where the application and the database servers are inside the DMZ, and the database is never exposed to the firewall. The listener has been subjected to attacks in the past, and although there have been patches to thwart attacks, bear in mind that these are effective against only the attacks that are known today. There could be vulnerabilities that are yet to be identified, and a malicious hacker could discover and exploit them to launch attacks.

# Advanced Networking Option

## Checksumming and Encryptions

From the earlier discussion on network security, note the various types of threats possible in the network itself. The options described above present some very common and preventable threats, but they fail to address other and more difficult potential threats from hackers. Spoofing and sniffing can result in compromised network traffic that can be as relatively harmless as stolen data, or as dangerous as altered data. For instance, via spoofing, a thief could steal a packet from a bank transaction and alter the contents to make the amount of deposit bigger. Alternatively, the packet could be retransmitted to make the deposit process twice, doubling the amount.

Data stealing can be prevented, to some extent, by making the transmitted packets unreadable for the non-authorized user, using encryption. Note that this is not encryption of the data in the database, but of the data that is sent in a packet. A sniffer can sniff these packets, but the payload inside will not make sense to the hacker unless he or she knows the encryption key.

Introducing checksumming can prevent the other threat of data manipulation. A checksum is a string that can be derived from some data using some algorithm. If the checksum is run on the same data again, the result will be exactly the same. This principle is used to ascertain the authenticity of the data transmitted.

A very simple example can be used here to illustrate the concept. You gave your nanny a raise of $ 21 per week and ask her to tell your spouse the amount. How do you make sure she will tell the real amount $21, not $31? You have an arrangement with your spouse that in addition to the amount, you will also provide a magic number. This number is a rounded whole number obtained by dividing the number by 4, which comes out to be 5 (21 divided by 4 is 5.25; so 5 is the rounded whole number). If the nanny tells your spouse the amount as $31, the magic number will not be 5, it would be 8, alerting your spouse to the fact that the data has been compromised.

This magic number is also called a checksum. It is calculated before the transmission and is sent separately to the destination. At the destination, the checksum is calculated again and compared to that from the source. If the data has been tampered with in any manner, the checksums will not match. Of course, there is a slight possibility that two very different data items will produce the same checksum, but that is where the modern algorithms excel – in reducing that probability.

Checksumming and encryption are two different ways to ensure the security of the transmitted data. Although the underlying principle is similar, the usage and purpose are different for each. In addition, each can be independently turned on or off, i.e. we could have checksumming but no encryption and vice versa. Therefore, they have been discussed separately.

## Checksumming

Oracle's answer to checksumming is in the Advanced Networking Option (ANO) or Advanced Security Option (ASO). Unfortunately, it is not part of the Oracle database software itself; rather, it is a separately licensable product with an additional price tag.

One very common checksumming algorithm is MD5, which Oracle has licensed and made available as a part of the product itself. The other algorithm is SHA1. The idea is to set checksumming on both the client and the server so that the communication between them will also include the checksum information, and that will ensure data integrity.

To configure the checksumming, all you need to do is to place the appropriate parameters in the `sqlnet.ora` file of the client as shown below.

```
SQLNET.CRYPTO_CHECKSUM_TYPES_CLIENT = (MD5,SHA1)
SQLNET.CRYPTO_CHECKSUM_CLIENT = REQUESTED
```

Similarly on the server's *sqlnet.ora*, place the following lines.

```
SQLNET.CRYPTO_CHECKSUM_TYPE_SERVER = (SHA1,MD5)
SQLNET.CRYPTO_CHECKSUM_SERVER = REQUESTED
```

These lines indicate that the clients will attempt to use both the MD5 and SHA1 checksumming, and the server will accept that. Note how the order of the algorithms varies in the server and the client. In this case, the order in the server takes precedence – the client will try SHA1 first, and then MD5.

The parameter *crypto_checksum_client* is a means to let the other side know what to expect in checksumming, whether it is turned on or off. The valid values of this parameter are ACCEPTED, REJECTED, REQUESTED and REQUIRED.

If any one of the parties has the setting REQUIRED, and the other has REJECTED, the connection will not be successful.

In other cases, the connection will not fail but the checksumming may not be active depending on the combination. For instance, if the server's setting is ACCEPTED, checksumming is active if the client setting is either REQUIRED or REQUESTED, but it is inactive if the client setting is ACCEPTED. The status of the checksumming in various combinations of this parameter is shown in Table 7.1.

| _SERVER | _CLIENT | | | |
|---|---|---|---|---|
| | ACCEPTED | REJECTED | REQUESTED | REQUIRED |
| ACCEPTED | INACTIVE | INACTIVE | ACTIVE | ACTIVE |
| REJECTED | INACTIVE | INACTIVE | INACTIVE | *Failure* |
| REQUESTED | ACTIVE | INACTIVE | ACTIVE | ACTIVE |
| REQUIRED | ACTIVE | *Failure* | ACTIVE | ACTIVE |

**Table 7.1** *Status of checksumming in various combinations of the parameter crypto_checksum_*.*

The default value is REJECTED, which means that the checksum is neither sent to the receiver nor accepted from the sender. If one of the parties, the client or the server, asks for checksumming, and the other party has the default setting, then the connection will fail. Therefore, we have set the parameter to REQUESTED in the example above. In this setting, if the other party has specified anything but REJECTED, the checksumming is activated.

The other important parameter is *sqlnet.crypto_seed.* While generating the cryptographic keys, most of the algorithms use seed values to arrive at the key. This seed decides how random the checksum value is going to be. The default is often sufficient, but you could always use your own value. There is no fixed format – any ASCII character is acceptable and must be at least 10 and at most 70 characters long.

When checksumming is active, the sender breaks the data into packets and labels them with sequence strings so that the receiver can piece them together to make it whole. The MD5 algorithm makes a hash calculation of the data in each packet to get the checksum, and adds that value to the end of the packet. The server makes the same hash calculation and compares with the checksum received. If they match, the data integrity is ensured.

## Encryption

The other side of the security in transit is the encryption of the data. In Chapter 6, on database encryption, we introduced the concept. Without repeating that, we will explore the process more in terms of how it applies to encryption in networks. Any encryption is based on a key, which is used to encrypt and decrypt the data. If this key becomes known, the encrypted data becomes easily accessible, so this key has to be difficult to guess. The size of the keys is specified in bits – the longer the better for encryption.

Again, Oracle has several of its native encryption algorithms adapted from popular standards. These standards are

**RC4** – This is a stream based ciphering scheme, i.e. each byte is encrypted as it comes in. The keys could be 40, 56, 128 or 256 bits long. The length of the encrypted data is the same as the original data.

**DES** – Since RC4 does the encryption one byte at a time, there could be a huge performance hit. To alleviate this problem and increase the performance, block-ciphering schemes have been developed, where a whole block of data is encrypted at one time. Generally, the blocks are composed of 8 bytes. If the data length is not divisible by 8, extra spaces are added to make it evenly divisible by 8. This process, although faster, makes the encrypted data longer than the original, hence extra bytes have to be sent across the network. However, with today's high-speed networks, this may cease to be a concern. DES is a block-ciphering scheme using 40 and 56 bits.

**Triple DES** – The DES standard was unbreakable for quite some time. However, with the power of modern computers, the scheme's 40 or 56 bit encryption can become vulnerable. Therefore, another scheme, called Triple DES, was created. In this scheme, the data is first encrypted with a 64-bit key, then decrypted using the encrypted value as a key, which yields a very different value, and then encrypted again with the key. This makes the key very difficult to crack. These schemes come in 112 and 168 bit versions.

Similar to checksumming, encryption is also set in the `sqlnet.ora` file in form or two parameters.

```
SQLNET.ENCRYPTION_TYPES_CLIENT = (3des112,rc4_40)
SQLNET.ENCRYPTION_CLIENT = REQUESTED
```

There is a set of two similar parameters for server, too. The encryption schemes used can be one of the following

| VALUE | SCHEME | KEY SIZE |
|---|---|---|
| 3DES112 | Triple DES | 112 |
| 3DES168 | Triple DES | 168 |
| DES | DES | 56 |
| DES40 | DES | 40 |
| RC4_40 | RC4 | 40 |
| RC4_56 | RC4 | 56 |
| RC4_128 | RC4 | 128 |
| RC4_256 | RC4 | 256 |

The value of the parameter *encryption_client* and *encryption_server* decide whether the encryption is active or not as per the same algorithm for checksumming described in Table 7.1.

 **Advanced Networking Option or Advanced Security Option provides much-needed security to data in transit, not just data at rest. For a network that can be attacked, it is highly recommended that the ASO be installed and the bare minimums, like checksumming and encryptions, be enabled.**

# Final Checklist

From the discussion of various security aspects described above, here is a checklist you could use to verify that the network is secure. For more information on any of the items on the checklist, refer to the relevant section in this chapter.

- All security patches from MOSC related to Oracle*Net have been applied.
- Listener password is set.
- A procedure is in place to change the password periodically. An example may be coinciding it with server password changes.
- Permissions of directories admin, log and trace under the directory $ORACLE_HOME/network do not allow any privileges to others. This protects the various parameter files, as well as any information that may be present in the log and trace files.
- The trace directories do not contain any files that are not being used now for some diagnosis.
- In *listener.ora*, parameter *admin_restrictions* is set to ON.
- Listener logging is turned on in *listener.ora*. This is important for identifying attempts to guess the password.
- External procedures are removed from the *listener.ora* file.
- If external procedures are necessary, they are in a different listener.
- Node filtering is turned on and is configured properly so that only trusted clients can connect.
- A procedure is in place to check the listener log for attempted break-ins regularly.

Ideally, the database server should never be exposed to the firewall. That perhaps brings the one requirement to the very top of the list – Do have a firewall! However, if the database server is exposed to the firewall for business reasons, then the following checklist applies.

- Only the ports listened to by the listener are open on the firewall.
- Connection Manager is set up and configured to allow only acceptable connections from trusted sources.
- Application/Webserver and database server are both inside the DMZ.
- Oracle Advanced Security is setup.
- Encryption is configured for Oracle*Net.

- Checksumming is configured for Oracle*Net.

Working with this bare minimum-security checklist, you can secure the network from a majority of attempted break-ins and achieve the policies HIPAA has laid out. For most situations, these measures are adequate. However, bear in mind that a house is as stable as the foundation upon which it is built. If the underlying network is built or managed unsafely, security of the Oracle Network is only as good as that of the foundation Therefore, basic security starts with a very good design of the network itself.

# Conclusion

In our journey to building a secured database system compliant with HIPAA, the Gramm-Leach-Bliley Act, the Safe Harbor Act, and the VISA USA Cardholder Security Agreement, or just your own organization's mandated security, we have leaned how to secure the last frontier of security in an Oracle database world – the networks. Starting with a simple discussion to introduce the concept of general networking – then moving into Oracle*Networking, we strived to instill in the reader a sense of awareness of inner mechanisms of these components, and we provided tools to achieve the objective of securing the system.

This concludes our discussion on Security as applicable to Oracle databases. The next Section of the book will cover the other important aspect of any security system – Auditing.

# Oracle Auditing

# General Oracle Auditing

CHAPTER

## Introduction

So far, in the previous chapters, we have been discussing two very important supporting pillars of the security infrastructure:

**Authentication** – establishing that a user is indeed the one he or she is claiming to be, and

**Authorization** – making sure the user does only up to what is permitted to him or her, nothing beyond that.

Together, these two define the major parts of the security landscape. The third aspect of the security framework deals with *security by detection*. Security by detection is a system that captures traces of the work by the users that can be used to reconstruct what was actually done, not what *could have been* done, which is covered by authorization.

The very knowledge that the work is recorded and can be traced back to their identity is sometimes a deterrent powerful enough to dissuade potential miscreants and users with malicious intent. Specifically, disgruntled employees and other regular users who may not have a direct need to access the data probably will not attempt to steal or soil data due to the fear of detection.

This is similar to placing a surveillance camera in a store. The very presence of it discourages shoplifting and vandalism. The fact that the actions are repeated and can be replayed is a strong deterrent that this third support structure of the security framework tries to achieve. The process of recording the actions by users is known as **auditing** and the information that shows the actions is known as the **audit trail**.

Besides being a strong deterrent to potential miscreants, auditing also exposes whether the *legitimate* users accessed some data that might be considered sensitive. This is where the HIPAA law clearly spells out the need to audit data access – particularly for the data that is considered to be in the domain of Patient Health Information (PHI).

A legitimate user may be authorized to access a particular piece of data such as a patient's HIV diagnosis record under certain situations – such as while handling claims related to the diagnosis. However, if the user accesses the same data at any other time – that is a clear violation of the HIPAA laws, and possibly an indication of unauthorized access.

With this dual intent, we will devote this part of the book to how to record the activities of all types of users, whether legitimate or not, to satisfy regulatory requirements as well as trace user actions to identify possible fraud. The most basic of the needs is to audit the object accesses and record the user's interaction with the database.

# Here Comes AUDIT

Oracle provides a built-in tool to audit access to the database objects and some rudimentary database accesses. The tool, implemented via a single SQL command, is AUDIT. Based on the clause present after the command, it can write an audit trail for a vast majority of cases and satisfy a variety of requirements. The DBA can instruct the RDBMS engine to audit certain events on specified objects. In this section, we will learn how to set it up to satisfy the requirements of HIPAA.

## Preparing for Auditing

Before the AUDIT can be used, the first important job is to identify the location of the audit trail. The location could be either the operating system filesystem or a database table. The initialization parameter file parameter *audit_trail* determines this.

```
audit_trail = db
```

The above statement causes the audit trails to go into the database table named *aud$*, which is owned by the user SYS. Being owned by SYS, it cannot be manipulated by other users.

The following statement sets the trail to go to the operating system files instead. Again, using the initialization parameter file parameter *audit_trail*:

```
audit_trail = os
```

The location of the files is indicated by another initialization file parameter *audit_file_dest* as shown below. In this example, the directory where the audit records will be generated will be /u01/oracle/audit.

```
audit_file_dest=/u01/oracle/audit
```

By default, if the audit trail is set to the filesystem, the destination will be $ORACLE_HOME/rdbms/audit.

This is an important point to remember. Some audit records are generated by default, whether audit trail is specified or not. One such example is when a user logs in as sysdba or as INTERNAL. Oracle automatically creates an OS file as an audit record. The contents of one such file is shown below.

```
Audit file /u01/oracle/product/9.2/rdbms/audit/ora_10010.aud
Oracle9i Enterprise Edition Release 9.2.0.3.0 - Production
With the Partitioning, OLAP and Oracle Data Mining options
JServer Release 9.2.0.3.0 - Production
ORACLE_HOME = /u01/oracle/product/9.2
System name:  OSF1
Node name:  smiley.proligence.com
Release:  V5.1
Version:  1885
Machine:  alpha
Instance name: TEST9
Redo thread mounted by this instance: 1
Oracle process number: 8
Unix process pid: 10010, image: oracle@smiley.proligence.com (TNS V1-V3)

Sat Jun 21 03:34:08 2003
ACTION : 'CONNECT'
DATABASE USER: '/'
PRIVILEGE : SYSDBA
CLIENT USER: oracle
CLIENT TERMINAL:
STATUS: 0
```

These small audit files are written to the default directory mentioned above and quickly fills up the ORACLE_HOME directory or file system, most likely without the express knowledge of the DBA. This should be carefully monitored. Files should be moved or simply deleted to make room in this very important filesystem.

 **Note: There is no equivalent system for writing audit records to a file system in Windows. The parameter *audit_file_dest* does not exist on the Windows platform. All the audit records go to the Event Log.**

In the Windows environment, you would want to check the Event Log. These OS trails are recorded under Application Event Logs. One such log is shown in Figure 8.1.

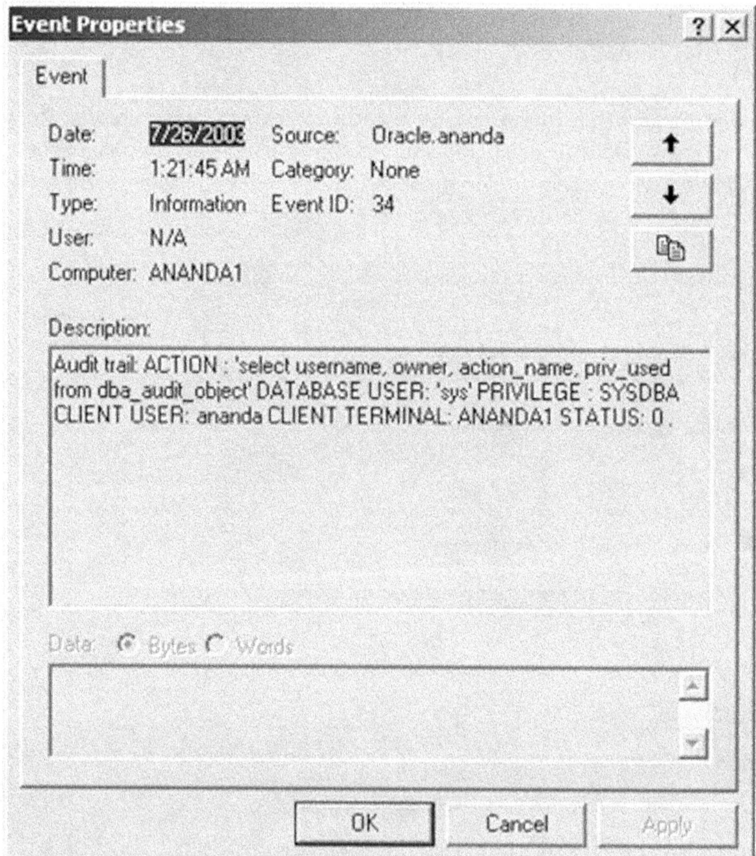


**Figure 8.1** *Windows Event Log Entry For Audits on SYS*

Needless to say, the event log will also get filled up soon with all these entries; therefore they must be purged after backing them up. The events can be written to a file using the menu *Action* → *Save Logfile As* option. Then the event log can be cleared.

To disable auditing, set the parameter *audit_trail* to NONE in *init.ora* and restart the database. Also note that the default setting for *audit_trail* is NONE.

```
audit_trail = none
```

However, this will not turn off the default auditing for SYS or INTERNAL connections. The SYS auditing has been described in detail later in this chapter.

Oracle 10g and beyond supports a new type of auditing known as *Extended Database Auditing*. If specified, the regular AUDIT features also capture the exact SQL statements, even the bind variables. The option is specified at the instance level in the initialization file as

```
audit_trail = db_extended
```

***Warning:*** The SQLTEXT and SQLBIND clob columns are populated only if you set the parameter AUDIT_TRAIL=DB_EXTENDED.
If you set AUDIT_TRAIL=DB, you will NOT get any values for SQLTEXT in the AUD$ table.

Basic database auditing using the DB_EXTENDED setting can be quite useful as it allows the capture of SQL commands issued by users of the database. This is better than redo which only captures the changes to the data not the actual SQL entered. This is how to capture the actual SQL ran by users.

```
USER is "SYS"
SQL> ALTER SYSTEM SET audit_trail=DB_EXTENDED SCOPE=SPFILE;
System altered.
SQL> show parameter audit_trail;

NAME                                 TYPE        VALUE
------------------------------------ ----------- ---------
```

Need to restart!

```
Database closed.
Database dismounted.
ORACLE instance shut down.
```

```

NAME                                 TYPE        VALUE
------------------------------------ ----------- ---------------------------
---
audit_trail                          string      DB_EXTENDED

SQL> audit select on dba_users by access whenever not successful;
Audit succeeded.
SQL> select * from sys.aud$;
no rows selected

SQL> conn scott/tiger@orcl

Connected.

SQL> select * from user_role_privs;
```

```
------------------------------ ------------------------------ --- --- ---
SCOTT                          CONNECT                        NO  YES NO
SCOTT                          PUBLIC                         NO  YES NO
SCOTT                          RESOURCE                       NO  YES NO

SQL> select username, password from dba_users;

select username, password from dba_users

ERROR at line 1:
```

```
SQL> desc sys.aud$;
 Name                                      Null?    Type
 ----------------------------------------- -------- ------------
 SESSIONID                                 NOT NULL NUMBER
 ENTRYID                                   NOT NULL NUMBER
 STATEMENT                                 NOT NULL NUMBER
 TIMESTAMP#                                         DATE
 USERID                                             VARCHAR2(30)
 USERHOST                                           VARCHAR2(128)
 TERMINAL                                           VARCHAR2(255)
 ACTION#                                   NOT NULL NUMBER
 RETURNCODE                                NOT NULL NUMBER
 OBJ$CREATOR                                        VARCHAR2(30)
 OBJ$NAME                                           VARCHAR2(128)
 AUTH$PRIVILEGES                                    VARCHAR2(16)
 AUTH$GRANTEE                                       VARCHAR2(30)
 NEW$OWNER                                          VARCHAR2(30)
 NEW$NAME                                           VARCHAR2(128)
 SES$ACTIONS                                        VARCHAR2(19)
 SES$TID                                            NUMBER
 LOGOFF$LREAD                                       NUMBER
 LOGOFF$PREAD                                       NUMBER
 LOGOFF$LWRITE                                      NUMBER
 LOGOFF$DEAD                                        NUMBER
 LOGOFF$TIME                                        DATE
 COMMENT$TEXT                                       VARCHAR2(4000)
 CLIENTID                                           VARCHAR2(64)
 SPARE1                                             VARCHAR2(255)
 SPARE2                                             NUMBER
 OBJ$LABEL                                          RAW(255)
 SES$LABEL                                          RAW(255)
 PRIV$USED                                          NUMBER
 SESSIONCPU                                         NUMBER
 NTIMESTAMP#                                        TIMESTAMP(6)
 PROXY$SID                                          NUMBER
 USER$GUID                                          VARCHAR2(32)
 INSTANCE#                                          NUMBER
 PROCESS#                                           VARCHAR2(16)
 XID                                                RAW(8)
 AUDITID                                            VARCHAR2(64)
 SCN                                                NUMBER
 DBID                                               NUMBER
 SQLBIND                                            CLOB
```

Now the auditor can select the actual SQL ran by the user.

```
SQLTEXT
------------------------------------------------------------
```

The extra audit information recorded using Extended database audit would be very useful to an Oracle forensics incident handler trying to deal with a hacked server. However Extend audit is quite a performance intensive way to audit. In fact many DBA?s will not use audit at all due to the performance hit. This is why basic audit is currently disabled by default, by Oracle in 10g.

Oracle 11g has audit switched on by default and the performance disadvantage has been greatly reduced. This means that Extended audit could be recorded which would be very useful especially if it was archived and then referred back to in the case of either a suspected incident or the disclosure of a new vulnerability so that access to this vulnerability could be backtracked.

One problem is that database audit is insecure as it is easy to delete by a user with DBA privileges given that the audit trail is simply a table in that database. This is why many DBA?s log to the OS as it is more difficult to get to from the DB. Oracle will always Audit privileged connections and startup/shutdowns to the OS which is often called Mandatory Audit. However the attacker who has gained DBA could still use UTL_FILE to delete the OS based logs as described in the previous sections.

It would be preferable to be able to send audit to a separate log host that could NOT be accessed using the Oracle DBA credentials which may have been gained by the attacker. The need for a separate party to validate data in the DB is echoed by this paper describing a digital notarization service and the concerns over timestamp integrity.

The audit trails now provide a lot more information. The *aud$* table has been expanded with several additional columns.

| COLUMN NAME | DESCRIPTION |
|---|---|
| NTIMESTAMP# | Oracle 9i introduced a new timestamp datatype, which can theoretically store to a dimension of a millisecond. This column stores the extended timestamp in that format. |

| COLUMN NAME | DESCRIPTION |
|---|---|
| PROXY$SID | The SID of the session, if the user is connected using a proxy authorization. Typically users authenticated through external mechanisms such as directory are connected through proxy users. |
| USER$GUID | If the user is authenticated via a means other than database authentication, e.g. through a directory, then this column shows the global user ID of the user. These types of users are known as Enterprise Users. |
| INSTANCE# | In Real Application Clusters, this column stores the instance number to which the user was connected when the audit trail was triggered. |
| PROCESS# | The operating system process identifier of the user's process is stored here. |
| TRAN_ID | The transaction id, if it is a transaction that triggered the audit event, is stored here. This has the format u.s.q where "u" is the rollback (or UNDO) segment number, "s" is the slot number and "q" is the sequence number in that slot. |
| AUDITID | Audit Identifier |
| SCN | The System Change Number where this particular audit entry occurred. This is very useful in reconstructing the exact replica of the database at the time of the audit trail creation using the flashback database feature. |
| DBID | The Database Identifier. |

| COLUMN NAME | DESCRIPTION |
|---|---|
| SQLTEXT | The exact SQL text entered by the user is captured in this column. This column is populated only if extended auditing is enabled. |
| SQLBIND | If the SQL text contains some bind variables, the variables and their values are stored in this column. |

These new columns are also visible in the view *dba_audit_trail*, although in a much more user-friendly manner. Here are the additional columns of the view, new in 10g and beyond.

| COLUMN NAME | DESCRIPTION |
|---|---|
| EXTENDED_TIMESTAMP | The Extended Timestamp. |
| PROXY_SESSIONID | The SID of the proxy user session. |
| GLOBAL_UID | The global user ID of the enterprise user. |
| INSTANCE_NUMBER | The instance number if using RAC. |
| OS_PROCESS | The OS Process Id. |
| TRANSACTIONID | The transaction id. |
| SCN | The System Change Number. |
| SQL_BIND | The bind variables and the value they are set to. |
| SQL_TEXT | The SQL statement that triggered the audit. |

Using Extended Audit Functionality, several types of events can be audited, without any additional coding.

# Filesystem Based Audit Trail

Generally the files generated as an audit trail are named after the process ids. The location of these files are defined by the initialization parameter *audit_file_dest*, which defaults to $ORACLE_HOME/rdbms/audit. Preferably, this should be changed to a different place, somewhere outside the $ORACLE_HOME. These files tend to grow substantially and might fill up the Oracle Home. Ideally, this should be in a separate filesystem by itself such as:

```
audit_file_dest = /u02/ora_audit
```

The directory permissions should be set as Read/Write for owner and none for group and others (600). This will disable any other users ability to manipulate the files.

# Database Resident Audit Trail

The special table named *aud$* holds the audit trail generated. This table is automatically generated during the database creation process. All other dependent views and action code tables are created by running the file $ORACLE_HOME/rdbms/admin/cataudit.sql.

The raw table *aud$* is not very user friendly – the columns are not very intuitive and the table is not logically divided by the different types of information it contains. Therefore, there are several views that have been created on this table to present a more user-friendly view into the table. These views are present with the word AUDIT in them and are available for the user and the DBA views with prefixes – USER and DBA, respectively. Since there is no context where an equivalent one will be useful for ALL views, there is none with that prefix. These views will be better explained as we go through this chapter.

***dba_audit_trail*** – This is a view based on the *aud$* table which decodes most of the values inside the table to present it in a user understandable manner. For instance, the column SPARE1 in *aud$* actually stores the Operating System User Name. The column OS_USERNAME in this view gets its value from that column in the *aud$* table. Similarly, the column ACTION# column holds the user's action in a numeral form. For example, 108 indicates granting system privilege. The view decodes the numerical representation for the actions and presents the information in the column ACTION_NAME. Therefore, this view is actually more useful for analysis than the *aud$* table itself.

The following views are based on the *dba_audit_trail* view.

***user_audit_trail*** – This view is based on all the columns of the *dba_audit_trail* view, but presents information on the current logged in user only. Unlike other data dictionary view, there is no equivalent *all_audit_trail* view, as it is not relevant in this case.

***dba_audit_exists*** – This is an audit trail of the entries where the operation failed due to non-existing objects. This is actually filtered from the view *dba_audit_trail* where the return code is a value other than zero.

***dba_audit_session*** – This records all database connect and disconnect activity. It also records if the action failed, for example, failure due to a security violation.

***dba_audit_statement*** – This view contains information about users entering statements that do not actually access the data inside an object, e.g. ALTER SYSTEM, GRANT, REVOKE on objects, etc.

***dba_audit_object*** – Finally, this view shows all the audit records that were based on database object accesses – e.g. a user selected from a table, or altered another table, etc.

# Types of Auditing

The general Oracle auditing can be broadly divided into three categories based on the event on which they are fired. Before discussing that, another important concept related to auditing, which is present in all these three categories, must be discussed.

## By Session/Access

When an action is made on an object, the action can cause the audit trail to be updated for each time it is issued, or just once per session. For instance, the user issues the following statements:

```
select first_name||' '||last_name from members where member_id = 102;
select plan_code from members where SSN = '123456789';
select SSN from members where last_name = 'DOE';
```

Note the table MEMBER was accessed *three* times by the user in this single session. The choice can be made to write three records into the audit trail, or just one. Sometimes it may not make sense to write audit trails three times. Although the information accessed and the records retrieved may be different, the audit facility does not capture that, so writing three records is not going to be useful for determining accountability any more than capturing only one record.

Therefore, the frequency of capturing the auditing information becomes important in some cases. The frequency that the audit trail is updated can be set by using one of the options shown below:

**BY ACCESS** – This specifies that audit records be written every time the object is accessed.

**BY SESSION** – This specifies the audit record be written only once per session.

In subsequent parts of this chapter we will see this clause in action.

## On Success

Most of the information captured in auditing is to satisfy the requirements of accountability, i.e. the audit trail captures that fact that Judy updated the CLAIMS table. However, another important objective of auditing is to act as a surveillance tool to capture attempted break-ins that must be investigated. Capturing the audit trail when an action is not successful can identify attempted break-ins.

For instance, Judy does not have update privileges on the CLAIMS table and any attempt to update it may be construed as an attempt to break-in. Some attempted access may happen inadvertently, but a sequence of repeated attempts may be a sign of desperate attempts and must be investigated.

To facilitate this effort, Oracle also provides an option to generate audit trails when the audited action is: 1) only successful, 2) only unsuccessful, or 3) both. By default the audit is triggered on both successful and unsuccessful attempts, but they can also be limited to only one option. A clause added to the end of the statement determines this. For instance, if the auditing is to be enabled for successful attempts only, the clause WHENEVER SUCCESSFUL is used. When only the unsuccessful ones are to be audited, the clause WHENEVER NOT SUCCESSFUL is used. An example is given below.

```
audit update on claim_schema,claims by access
whenever not successful;
```

In this statement we want to capture audit records only if they are not successful. Subsequence paragraphs will illustrate this clause in its proper context.

## Statement Auditing

Statement auditing enabled recording of any action due to the execution of an SQL statement such as "audit create procedure." Whenever a user executes the statement, the audit record is generated. Let's see an example. We want to audit when user CLAIM_SCHEMA creates a procedure; so we will issue:

```
audit create procedure by claim_schema;
```

Any time the user CLAIM_SCHEMA tries to create a procedure, the action is logged, regardless of whether it was successful.

In general the syntax for statement level auditing is:

```
AUDIT
```

```
statement_list|ALL
[BY SESSION|ACCESS|<sername>|<proxyuser>]
[ON BEHALF OF <user_list>|ANY] Useful only if the Proxyuser is used.
[WHENEVER [NOT] SUCCESSFUL]
```

where:

**statement_list** is a list of statements that trigger auditing. If more than one auditable statement is provided, they are separated by commas:

```
audit create table, create sequence by judy;
```

The allowable statements vary from version to version. The valid list of statements can be found in a sys owned table called *stmt_audit_option_map*. The keyword ALL can be used as well to enable auditing for all allowed statements.

**username** is the name of the user whose actions are to be audited. It is optional and if omitted the action is audited for the statement by any user.

**proxyuser** is provided when proxy usernames are used to authenticate users. The optional clause ON BEHALF OF is used.

**Finally**, the clause WHENEVER SUCCESSFUL or NOT SUCCESSFUL can be used.

Table 8.1 shows all options available for statement auditing that can be used in the *statement_list* as of Oracle 9i Release 2.

| ALTER ANY CLUSTER | ALTER ANY DIMENSION | ALTER ANY INDEX |
|---|---|---|
| ALTER ANY LIBRARY | ALTER ANY OUTLINE | ALTER ANY PROCEDURE |
| ALTER ANY ROLE | ALTER ANY SEQUENCE | ALTER ANY SNAPSHOT |
| ALTER ANY TABLE | ALTER ANY TRIGGER | ALTER ANY TYPE |
| ALTER DATABASE | ALTER PROFILE | ALTER RESOURCE COST |
| ALTER ROLLBACK SEGMENT | ALTER SEQUENCE | ALTER SESSION |
| ALTER SYSTEM | ALTER TABLE | ALTER TABLESPACE |
| ALTER USER | ANALYZE ANY | AUDIT ANY |
| BACKUP ANY TABLE | BECOME USER | CLUSTER |

| COMMENT ANY TABLE | COMMENT TABLE | CONTEXT |
|---|---|---|
| CREATE ANY CLUSTER | CREATE ANY CONTEXT | CREATE ANY DIMENSION |
| CREATE ANY DIRECTORY | CREATE ANY INDEX | CREATE ANY LIBRARY |
| CREATE ANY OUTLINE | CREATE ANY PROCEDURE | CREATE ANY SEQUENCE |
| CREATE ANY SNAPSHOT | CREATE ANY SYNONYM | CREATE ANY TABLE |
| CREATE ANY TRIGGER | CREATE ANY TYPE | CREATE ANY VIEW |
| CREATE CLUSTER | CREATE DATABASE LINK | CREATE DIMENSION |
| CREATE DIRECTORY | CREATE LIBRARY | CREATE PROCEDURE |
| CREATE PROFILE | CREATE PUBLIC DATABASE LINK | CREATE PUBLIC SYNONYM |
| CREATE ROLE | CREATE ROLLBACK SEGMENT | CREATE SEQUENCE |
| CREATE SESSION | CREATE SNAPSHOT | CREATE SYNONYM |
| CREATE TABLE | CREATE TABLESPACE | CREATE TRIGGER |
| CREATE TYPE | CREATE USER | CREATE VIEW |
| DATABASE LINK | DEBUG ANY PROCEDURE | DEBUG CONNECT ANY |
| DEBUG CONNECT SESSION | DEBUG CONNECT USER | DEBUG PROCEDURE |
| DELETE ANY TABLE | DELETE TABLE | DEQUEUE ANY QUEUE |
| DIMENSION | DIRECTORY | DROP ANY CLUSTER |
| DROP ANY CONTEXT | DROP ANY DIMENSION | DROP ANY DIRECTORY |
| DROP ANY INDEX | DROP ANY LIBRARY | DROP ANY OUTLINE |
| DROP ANY PROCEDURE | DROP ANY ROLE | DROP ANY SEQUENCE |

| | | |
|---|---|---|
| DROP ANY SNAPSHOT | DROP ANY SYNONYM | DROP ANY TABLE |
| DROP ANY TRIGGER | DROP ANY TYPE | DROP ANY VIEW |
| DROP DIRECTORY | DROP PROFILE | DROP PUBLIC DATABASE LINK |
| DROP PUBLIC SYNONYM | DROP ROLLBACK SEGMENT | DROP TABLESPACE |
| DROP USER | ENQUEUE ANY QUEUE | EXECUTE ANY LIBRARY |
| EXECUTE ANY PROCEDURE | EXECUTE ANY TYPE | EXECUTE LIBRARY |
| EXECUTE PROCEDURE | EXEMPT ACCESS POLICY | EXISTS |
| FLASHBACK ANY TABLE | FORCE ANY TRANSACTION | FORCE TRANSACTION |
| GLOBAL QUERY REWRITE | GRANT ANY OBJECT PRIVILEGE | GRANT ANY PRIVILEGE |
| GRANT ANY ROLE | GRANT DIRECTORY | GRANT LIBRARY |
| GRANT PROCEDURE | GRANT SEQUENCE | GRANT TABLE |
| GRANT TYPE | INDEX | INSERT ANY TABLE |
| INSERT TABLE | LOCK ANY TABLE | LOCK TABLE |
| MANAGE ANY QUEUE | MANAGE TABLESPACE | MATERIALIZED VIEW |
| NETWORK | NOT EXISTS | ON COMMIT REFRESH |
| PROCEDURE | PROFILE | PUBLIC DATABASE LINK |
| PUBLIC SYNONYM | QUERY REWRITE | READUP |
| READUP DBHIGH | RESTRICTED SESSION | RESUMABLE |
| ROLE | ROLLBACK SEGMENT | SELECT ANY DICTIONARY |
| SELECT ANY SEQUENCE | SELECT ANY TABLE | SELECT SEQUENCE |
| SELECT TABLE | SEQUENCE | SYNONYM |
| SYSDBA | SYSOPER | SYSTEM AUDIT |
| SYSTEM GRANT | TABLE | TABLESPACE |

| TRIGGER | TYPE | UNLIMITED TABLESPACE |
|---|---|---|
| UPDATE ANY TABLE | UPDATE TABLE | USER |
| VIEW | WRITEDOWN | WRITEDOWN DBLOW |
| WRITEUP | WRITEUP DBHIGH | |

**Table 8.1** *Statements Valid in Auditing*

## Privilege Auditing

Suppose a user ALLPOWERFUL has been granted the system privilege CREATE ANY TABLE. Using that privilege, the user creates a table *claim_master* in CLAIM_SCHEMA's schema. This is a special kind of activity – the object *claim_master* is owned by CLAIM_SCHEMA, but is created by ALLPOWERFUL. The Privilege Auditing records these types of statements in the audit trail. A simple example is shown below. The following query is used to start auditing whenever the user ALLPOWERFUL uses the CREATE ANY TABLE system privilege.

```
audit create any table by allpowerful by session;
```

The user issues the following command to create a table CLAIM_MASER in the CLAIM_SCHEMA's schema. It uses the system privilege CREATE ANY TABLE, not CREATE TABLE.

```
create table claim_schema.claim_master (………);
```

The user then issues the following statement to create a table *claim_master* in its own schema:

```
create table claim_schema.claim_master (………);
```

In this second statement, the user does not use CREATE ANY TABLE, but CREATE TABLE.

If the auditing options are set for CREATE ANY TABLE and not CREATE TABLE, only the first statement will be audited, not the second.

Let's see the effects of the privileges used in auditing. In this example the user CLAIM_SCHEMA creates a table as:

```
create table sometab1 (col1 number);
```

Now, the user ALLPOWERFUL creates another table in CLAIM_SCHEMA's schema as follows.

```
create table claim_schema.sometab2 (col1 number);
```

Since the user has the CREATE ANY TABLE system privilege, he can create a table in any other user's schema.

Note the important point here. The owner of both these new tables is CLAIM_SCHEMA, although one is created by ALLPOWERFUL. Since we have set up auditing on the privilege CREATE ANY TABLE and that was precisely what the user used, the audit records for these two actions will be different.

Next, the user ALLPOWERFUL creates yet another table in his own schema.

```
create table sometab3 (col1 number);
```

This statement does not need the system privilege CREATE ANY TABLE, but just CREATE TABLE.

In each of these cases the auditing actions will be different. Let's see how. Check the audit records generated by issuing the following query:

```
select username, owner, action_name, priv_used
from dba_audit_object
where obj_name like 'SOMETAB%'
/
```

And the result comes back as:

```
USERNAME         OWNER            ACTION_NAME      PRIV_USED
---------------  ---------------  ---------------  ----------------
CLAIM_SCHEMA     CLAIM_SCHEMA     CREATE TABLE     CREATE TABLE
ALLPOWERFUL      CLAIM_SCHEMA     CREATE TABLE     CREATE ANY TABLE
ALLPOWERFUL      ALLPOWERFUL      CREATE TABLE     CREATE TABLE
```

We have several important points to be noted on the results.

- In the first record, the USERNAME column is CLAIM_SCHEMA, as the user himself issued the statement to create the object in his own schema. Therefore the value of the OWNER column is also CLAIM_SCHEMA.
- In the second record, however, the USERNAME column shows ALLPOWERFUL, the user who actually issued the statement. The object was created in the schema of CLAIM_SCHEMA; so the OWNER is different.
- The user CLAIM_SCHEMA created the table using the privilege CREATE TABLE, therefore the column PRIV_USED reflects that. In the second case, the user ALLPOWERFUL used the privilege CREATE ANY TABLE, the same is reflected in the appropriate column.
- In the third case, the user ALLPOWERFUL used the privilege CREATE TABLE to create the table; so the PRIV_USED column recorded that.

Even though the results were similar, the auditing process captured the exact way these objects were created. This is a very powerful feature to capture the actions of the users regardless of what objects resulted. The model can also be used to check if a user with sweeping privileges, such as SELECT ANY TABLE, attempted to select data from other tables. The username will be recorded in the audit tables.

This can be used to enforce HIPAA mandated security requirements effectively. As we discussed in the earlier chapters, we determined that no user, except SYS and SYSTEM, should have sweeping privileges. But if one does, for business reasons, auditing can easily point out the objects that were accessed using these privileges and then a case can be made to assign specific grants.

The general syntax of the Privilege Auditing is:

AUDIT
*<privilege_list>*|ALL PRIVILEGES
[BY *<username>*|*<proxyuser>*]

```
[ON BEHALF OF <userlist>|ANY]  Useful only if the Proxyuser is used.
[BY SESSION|ACCESS]
[WHENVER [NOT] SUCCESSFUL]
```

where:

**privilege_list** is the list of privileges that can be audited. If more than one privilege is given, they are separated by commas. The allowable privileges are shown in Table 8.2. This is available in the view *system_privilege_map*.

**ALL** - If all the privileges used by a user are to be audited, then the key clause ALL PRIVILEGES can be used.

**username** is the name of the user for which the audit is enabled.

## Examples

To enable auditing on CREATE TABLE and CREATE PROCEDURE by user CLAIM_SCHEMA, use the statement:

```
Audit create table, create procedure by claim_schema by session;
```

To enable auditing of all privileges possible for the same user, use the following:

```
audit all privileges by claim_schema by session;
```

If the auditing on CREATE ANY TABLE is enabled for all users, the BY *<username>* clause should be omitted, as in:

```
audit create table by access whenever successful;
```

This will audit the statement on all users. The following statement creates an audit record when user Judy wants to connect but was not successful due to some problem, such as invalid password.

```
audit create session by judy by session whenever not successful;
```

Table 8.2 below shows the list of allowed privileges that can be specified in the *<privilege_list>*.

| ADMINISTER DATABASE TRIGGER | ADMINISTER RESOURCE MANAGER | ADMINISTER SECURITY |
|---|---|---|

| | | |
|---|---|---|
| ALTER ANY CLUSTER | ALTER ANY DIMENSION | ALTER ANY EVALUATION CONTEXT |
| ALTER ANY INDEX | ALTER ANY INDEXTYPE | ALTER ANY LIBRARY |
| ALTER ANY OPERATOR | ALTER ANY OUTLINE | ALTER ANY PROCEDURE |
| ALTER ANY ROLE | ALTER ANY RULE | ALTER ANY RULE SET |
| ALTER ANY SECURITY PROFILE | ALTER ANY SEQUENCE | ALTER ANY SNAPSHOT |
| ALTER ANY TABLE | ALTER ANY TRIGGER | ALTER ANY TYPE |
| ALTER DATABASE | ALTER PROFILE | ALTER RESOURCE COST |
| ALTER ROLLBACK SEGMENT | ALTER SESSION | ALTER SYSTEM |
| ALTER TABLESPACE | ALTER USER | ANALYZE ANY |
| AUDIT ANY | AUDIT SYSTEM | BACKUP ANY TABLE |
| BECOME USER | COMMENT ANY TABLE | CREATE ANY CLUSTER |
| CREATE ANY CONTEXT | CREATE ANY DIMENSION | CREATE ANY DIRECTORY |
| CREATE ANY EVALUATION CONTEXT | CREATE ANY INDEX | CREATE ANY INDEXTYPE |
| CREATE ANY LIBRARY | CREATE ANY OPERATOR | CREATE ANY OUTLINE |
| CREATE ANY PROCEDURE | CREATE ANY RULE | CREATE ANY RULE SET |
| CREATE ANY SECURITY PROFILE | CREATE ANY SEQUENCE | CREATE ANY SNAPSHOT |
| CREATE ANY SYNONYM | CREATE ANY TABLE | CREATE ANY TRIGGER |
| CREATE ANY TYPE | CREATE ANY VIEW | CREATE CLUSTER |

| | | |
|---|---|---|
| CREATE DATABASE LINK | CREATE DIMENSION | CREATE EVALUATION CONTEXT |
| CREATE INDEXTYPE | CREATE LIBRARY | CREATE OPERATOR |
| CREATE PROCEDURE | CREATE PROFILE | CREATE PUBLIC DATABASE LINK |
| CREATE PUBLIC SYNONYM | CREATE ROLE | CREATE ROLLBACK SEGMENT |
| CREATE RULE | CREATE RULE SET | CREATE SECURITY PROFILE |
| CREATE SEQUENCE | CREATE SESSION | CREATE SNAPSHOT |
| CREATE SYNONYM | CREATE TABLE | CREATE TABLESPACE |
| CREATE TRIGGER | CREATE TYPE | CREATE USER |
| CREATE VIEW | DEBUG ANY PROCEDURE | DEBUG CONNECT ANY |
| DEBUG CONNECT SESSION | DEBUG CONNECT USER | DELETE ANY TABLE |
| DEQUEUE ANY QUEUE | DROP ANY CLUSTER | DROP ANY CONTEXT |
| DROP ANY DIMENSION | DROP ANY DIRECTORY | DROP ANY EVALUATION CONTEXT |
| DROP ANY INDEX | DROP ANY INDEXTYPE | DROP ANY LIBRARY |
| DROP ANY OPERATOR | DROP ANY OUTLINE | DROP ANY PROCEDURE |
| DROP ANY ROLE | DROP ANY RULE | DROP ANY RULE SET |
| DROP ANY SECURITY PROFILE | DROP ANY SEQUENCE | DROP ANY SNAPSHOT |
| DROP ANY SYNONYM | DROP ANY TABLE | DROP ANY TRIGGER |
| DROP ANY TYPE | DROP ANY VIEW | DROP PROFILE |

| | | |
|---|---|---|
| DROP PUBLIC DATABASE LINK | DROP PUBLIC SYNONYM | DROP ROLLBACK SEGMENT |
| DROP TABLESPACE | DROP USER | ENQUEUE ANY QUEUE |
| EXECUTE ANY EVALUATION CONTEXT | EXECUTE ANY INDEXTYPE | EXECUTE ANY LIBRARY |
| EXECUTE ANY OPERATOR | EXECUTE ANY PROCEDURE | EXECUTE ANY RULE |
| EXECUTE ANY RULE SET | EXECUTE ANY TYPE | EXEMPT ACCESS POLICY |
| FLASHBACK ANY TABLE | FORCE ANY TRANSACTION | FORCE TRANSACTION |
| GLOBAL QUERY REWRITE | GRANT ANY OBJECT PRIVILEGE | GRANT ANY PRIVILEGE |
| GRANT ANY ROLE | INSERT ANY TABLE | LOCK ANY TABLE |
| MANAGE ANY QUEUE | MANAGE TABLESPACE | ON COMMIT REFRESH |
| QUERY REWRITE | READUP | READUP DBHIGH |
| RESTRICTED SESSION | RESUMABLE | SELECT ANY DICTIONARY |
| SELECT ANY SEQUENCE | SELECT ANY TABLE | SYSDBA |
| SYSOPER | UNDER ANY TABLE | UNDER ANY TYPE |
| UNDER ANY VIEW | UNLIMITED TABLESPACE | UPDATE ANY TABLE |
| WRITEDOWN | WRITEDOWN DBLOW | WRITEUP |
| WRITEUP DBHIGH | | |

**Table 8.2** *System Privilege Auditing Options*

## Shortcuts

Sometimes you may want to audit a group of options on all objects of a specific type. For instance, you want to audit CREATE, DROP and TRUNCATE on all tables by user JUDY whenever they are not successful. You could issue:

```
audit create table by judy whenever not successful;
```

```
audit drop table by judy whenever not successful;
audit truncate table by judy whenever not successful;
```

Or you could just issue:

```
audit table by judy whenever not successful;
```

This will audit the statements CREATE, DROP and TRUNCATE only, not other statements such as INSERT, DELETE, ALTER, etc. Therefore it is important to remember which of the operations are audited and which are not. The shortcuts and their actions have been given in table 8.3 below. The general syntax is:

AUDIT *<shortcut>* ......

The available shortcuts have been described in Table 8.3 below.

| IF THE SHORTCUT IS | THEN THE AUDITING OPTIONS ARE SET FOR |
|---|---|
| CLUSTER | CREATE CLUSTER<br>AUDIT CLUSTER<br>DROP CLUSTER<br>TRUNCATE CLUSTER |
| CONTEXT | CREATE CONTEXT<br>DROP CONTEXT |
| DATABASE LINK | CREATE DATABASE LINK<br>DROP DATABASE LINK |
| DIMENSION | CREATE DIMENSION<br>ALTER DIMENSION<br>DROP DIMENSION |
| DIRECTORY | CREATE DIRECTORY<br>DROP DIRECTORY |
| INDEX | CREATE INDEX<br>ALTER INDEX<br>DROP INDEX<br>ANALYZE ANY |
| NOT EXISTS | This is a special case of shortcut. If this is set, any SQL statement failing due to the non-existence of an object triggers and audit record. |

| IF THE SHORTCUT IS | THEN THE AUDITING OPTIONS ARE SET FOR |
|---|---|
| PROCEDURE | CREATE FUNCTION<br>CREATE LIBRARY<br>CREATE PACKAGE<br>CREATE PACKAGE BODY<br>CREATE PROCEDURE<br>DROP FUNCTION<br>DROP LIBRARY<br>DROP PACKAGE<br>DROP PROCEDURE<br>JAVA STORED PROCEDURES |
| PROFILE | CREATE PROFILE<br>ALTER PROFILE<br>DROP PROFILE |
| PUBLIC DATABASE LINK | CREATE PUBLIC DATABASE LINK<br>DROP PUBLIC DATABASE LINK |
| PUBLIC SYNONYM | CREATE PUBLIC SYNONYM<br>DROP PUBLIC SYNONYM |
| ROLE | CREATE ROLE<br>ALTER ROLE<br>DROP ROLE<br>SET ROLE |
| ROLLBACK SEGMENT | CREATE ROLLBACK SEGMENT<br>ALTER ROLLBACK SEGMENT<br>DROP ROLLBACK SEGMENT |
| SEQUENCE | CREATE SEQUENCE<br>DROP SEQUENCE |
| SESSION | The connections and disconnections by users are audited. |
| SYNONYM | CREATE SYNONYM<br>DROP SYNONYM |
| SYSTEM AUDIT | This is also a special case of auditing. When a user issues the AUDIT command itself, or NOAUDIT, this setting triggers an audit record to be generated. |

| IF THE SHORTCUT IS | THEN THE AUDITING OPTIONS ARE SET FOR |
|---|---|
| SYSTEM GRANT | Whenever the user grants a system privilege to another user or itself, this setting triggers an audit trail. |
| TABLE | CREATE TABLE<br>DROP TABLE<br>TRUNCATE TABLE |
| TABLESPACE | CREATE TABLESPACE<br>ALTER TABLESPACE<br>DROP TABLESPACE |
| TRIGGER | CREATE TRIGGER<br>ALTER TRIGGER<br><br>Important: Only the statements that enable or disable a trigger by the ALTER TRIGGER command are logged, not altering the trigger body.<br><br>DROP TRIGGER<br>ALTER TABLE<br><br>Only the trigger related statements in ALTER TABLE, such as adding or dropping triggers are audited. |
| TYPE | CREATE TYPE<br>CREATE TYPE BODY<br>ALTER TYPE<br>DROP TYPE<br>DROP TYPE BODY |
| USER | CREATE USER<br>ALTER USER<br>DROP USER |
| VIEW | CREATE VIEW<br>DROP VIEW |

**Table 8.3** *Shortcuts and their Auditing Actions*

Oracle also provides another type of shortcut to audit some commonly used system privileges. They are referred to as DBA, RESOURCE and CONNECT to record groups of privileges.

 **Note: The words CONNECT, RESOURCE, and DBA should not be confused with the database roles of the same names. These are just shortcuts to a group of privileges.**

The following example shows how the shortcuts are used:

```
audit connect;
```

This will enable auditing for CREATE SESSION, since CONNECT is a shortcut for it. The shortcut RESOURCE enables auditing on the following:

- ALTER SYSTEM
- TABLE
- CLUSTER
- TABLESPACE
- ROLLBACK SEGMENT
- TYPE
- SYNONYM
- VIEW
- SEQUENCE
- DATABASE LINK
- PROCEDURE

So when you use AUDIT RESOURCE, the auditing is enabled for all objects mentioned above.

The third shortcut, DBA does the same as enabling auditing on the following:

- SYSTEM AUDIT
- USER
- PUBLIC SYNONYM
- PUBLIC DATABASE LINK

- ROLE
- SYSTEM GRANT

These three shortcuts can be used to enable auditing quickly. It may not be practical to audit everything these shortcuts offer since some may be left out. If necessary, one convenient way may be to enable auditing by the shortcut and then selectively disable auditing. For instance, if all the audit options in the shortcut RESOURCE are necessary, except VIEW, they can all be enabled by AUDIT RESOURCE and then the undesired one can be disabled by the NOAUDIT VIEW command.

This shortcut concept may not be particularly useful and can be prone to mistakes. Remember from the above discussion that a shortcut TABLE refers to only CREATE TABLE, DROP TABLE and TRUNCATE TABLE. This shortcut does not include other important operations such as ALTER TABLE, even though the user may expect it to. It is perhaps best to avoid shortcuts at least to avoid confusion, if nothing else.

## Object Auditing

This type of auditing is based on specific objects and the actions made on them, not general statements, or using privileges. An example may make it clearer:

```
audit select on claim_schema.claims by access;
```

This will enable audit trails when any user selects from the table CLAIMS. Note the important difference here – there is no user specified. Just the object is specified and the frequency of triggering – by session or by access. So any user who selects from this table will trigger auditing.

In general, the audit command takes the following form:

```
AUDIT
<statement_list>|ALL
[ON <objectname>|DEFAULT]
[BY SESSION|ACCESS]
[WHENEVER [NOT] SUCCESSFUL]
```

Where:

**statement_list** are the allowable statements that can be audited. The list is different in every version; a recent list for each version may be found in the data dictionary view *stmt_audit_option_map*. Table 8.1 has a list of such statements. If more than one statement is given, they are separated by comma.

If all statements are required to be audited on an object, the keyword ALL can be used.

**objectname** is the name of the object on which the actions are to be audited. A list of object names can be given also, separated by commas. The objects can also be specified in the *<owner>.<objectname>* format

## Examples

To enable audit on all types of privileges on the object, use the clause ALL PRIVILEGES in the statement. An example is given below for illustration.

```
audit all privileges;
```

The use of ON DEFAULT specifies that those auditing options be turned on for any objects of that type created after this statement is given. For instance, if we want to enable select auditing on all tables created, we would issue:

```
audit select on default by access;
```

The setting of auditing on default objects can be seen from the data dictionary view *all_def_audit_opts*, as shown below:

```
select * from all_def_audit_opts
/

ALT AUD COM DEL GRA IND INS LOC REN SEL UPD REF EXE
--- --- --- --- --- --- --- --- --- --- --- --- ---
-/- -/- -/- -/- -/- -/- -/- -/- -/- A/A -/- -/- -/-
```

Note how the SEL column shows by access on both successful and unsuccessful attempts.

# Checking for Unsuccessful Actions

If the action is not successful, and the action is audited for non-success, then an audit record is generated. The view *dba_audit_exists* shows those records. For instance, assume we set up auditing for CREATE TABLE by any user for both success and non-success. We would issue the following two statements consecutively.

```
connect claim_schema/claim_schema
create table mytab1 (col1 number)
/
create table mytab1 (col1 number)
/
```

Note how the attempt was made to create the same table again, and it will fail with the following message:

```
ORA-00955: name is already used by an existing object
```

The success and failure of these two statements will be logged in the audit table. The failure of the statement can be seen from records in the *dba_audit_exists* as follows:

```
select ACTION_NAME, returncode
from dba_audit_exists
where owner = 'CLAIM_SCHEMA'
and obj_name = 'MYTAB1';
```

The result comes back as:

```
ACTION_NAME                  RETURNCODE
---------------------------- ----------
CREATE TABLE                        955
```

The only record here is the failure of the second statement. The RETURNCODE field is the important since it records the exact error condition that caused this failure. In this case, it is 955, which corresponds to the ORA-00955 thrown earlier.

It is important to note that not all types of errors are reported in this view. For instance ORA-955 is reported, but "ORA-1950 no privileges on tablespace XXX" is not reported. Reported audit records are in the *dba_audit_trail* and *dba_audit_object* views.

This may cause some confusion while searching for unsuccessful operations in the database. It may be worthwhile to query only the view *dba_audit_trail* for everything, including unsuccessful operations.

## Auditing for SYS Connections

This is a thorny issue is Oracle security. When a user with SYSDBA privileges connects to the database, the action is expected to be for administrative reasons only, such as shutdown, startup, add a service to the listener, etc. Generally, we would not expect these actions to be audited and therefore not picked up by the auditing mechanism.

However, the user who is connected as SYSDBA is a regular user, just like any other user, but with all powerful *do anything* privileges. This user could potentially alter the data in a table in any schema. Since the action is not audited, the trace of this data manipulation is hidden. In case of an investigation later, the audit trails will have no record of such manipulations – a huge security hole.

Sine HIPAA regulations expect accountability for data changes at any level, regardless of who made them, it becomes necessary to audit the actions of such privileged users for any data changes. Unfortunately, in Oracle 8i and below, the actions of a user connected as SYSDBA is not recorded, except the mandatory audit trail in the OS filesystem that merely states that the SYSDBA connection was established, nothing else. The actions conducted by the user after connecting as SYSDBA are not recorded.

In Oracle 9i and up, the facility is available. All actions by the user connected a SYSDBA, such as changing data, etc., can recorded in the audit trail. This is independent of the setting in the *audit_trail* parameter. It is done through the initialization parameter *audit_sys_operations*. By default it is set to FALSE. The following setting in the initialization parameter file will enable SYSDBA auditing:

```
audit_sys_operations = TRUE
```

This is a static parameter that cannot be set using the ALTER SYSTEM command since the database must be bounced for it to take effect.

When this is set to TRUE, all actions by the user connected as SYSDBA and SYSOPER are audited in the operating system file. Some very important points must be observed in this regard, and are perhaps better explained through examples.

Let's create three users with three different privileges as follows.

```
create user sysdba1 identified by sysdba1
/
grant create session, sysdba to sysdba1
/
create user sysoper1 identified by sysoper1
/
grant create session, sysoper to sysoper1
/
create user regulardba1 identified by regulardba1
/
grant create session, dba to regulardba1
/
```

Now we will see what actions from these users will trigger auditing and how the information is presented.

## Case 1: User Connecting as SYSDBA

Let's test for the user SYSDBA1 connecting as SYSDBA.

```
connect sysdba1/sysdba1 as sysdba
select * from claim_schema.claims
/
```

Now check the audit records generated. This time, for the sake of diversity, let's check this in the Windows environment. From the Event Viewer, check the event logs. There should be two entries. If you open those entries, you will notice that one is for SYSDBA connection as shown in Figure 8.2.

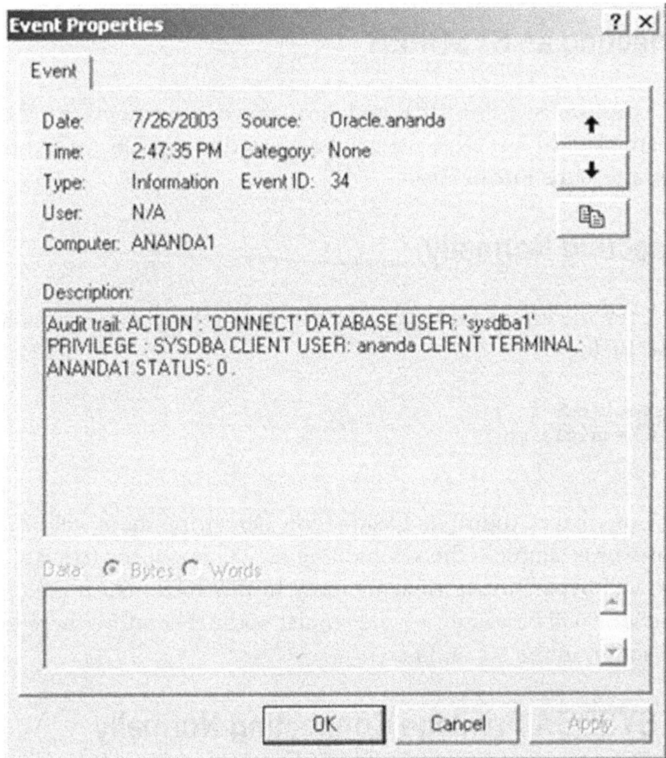


**Figure 8.2** *Event Log Entry for SYSDBA Connection*

Note the information inside the event log entry.

```
Audit trail: ACTION : 'CONNECT' DATABASE USER: 'sysdba1' PRIVILEGE : SYSDBA
CLIENT USER: ananda CLIENT TERMINAL: ANANDA1 STATUS: 0.
```

It shows that the Windows user "ananda" connected as the Oracle user "sysdba1" using the privilege "SYSDBA". The connection came from the client terminal "ANANDA1".

The next entry corresponds to the selection from claims. Without reproducing the entire picture, only the lines from the event log are shown here.

```
Audit trail: ACTION : 'select * from claim_schema.claims' DATABASE USER:
'sysdba1' PRIVILEGE : SYSDBA CLIENT USER: ananda CLIENT TERMINAL: ANANDA1
STATUS: 0 .
```

Note how the exact action performed by the user, i.e. "select * from claim_schema.claims" is recorded in detail.

## Case 2: User Connecting as SYSOPER

If the user SYSOPER1 connects as SYSOPER and performs the same actions, the event log will record them also. In UNIX, a file will be created in the OS Audit Log Directory that will show the same information.

## Case 3: User Connecting Normally

In the third case, we will see the effects of a regular DBA user connecting normally, *not* as SYSDBA or SYSOPER.

```
connect regulardba1/regulardba1
select * from claim_schema.claims
/
```

If you check the Event Log or the Audit File Destination Directory, there will be no entries. Why so? The answer is simple – the sys auditing facility is not for regular users; but for users who will bypass the normal auditing. In the third case, if the auditing is set up, the actions will be caught by the regular audit. Therefore there is no need to catch the same action in the sys audits.

## Case 4: User with SYSDBA Privilege Connecting Normally

The fourth case is also interesting. The user SYSDBA1 now connects normally and performs the same select query.

```
connect sysdba1/sysdba1
select * from claim_schema.claims
/
```

The query will fail since the user did not connect as SYSDBA and does not have any other privilege to perform the query. If you examine the audit destination, you will also find that there is no audit record for these actions. The reason is also simple to understand – the user connected normally, not as SYSDBA, and therefore the action was not audited. In the first case, the user did connect as SYSDBA, triggering the audit. The mere possession of the SYSDBA privilege does not trigger the sys auditing; hence the privilege must be used.

## In Summary

- Only the users who connected as SYSDBA, SYSOPER are audited.
- A user who has the SYSDBA privilege, but connects normally, is not audited in this setup. For the auditing to be triggered, the user has to connect as SYSDBA.
- The user SYS is audited. In Oracle 9i, the user SYS can connect only as SYSDBA; so there is no possibility of user SYS connecting normally.
- The audit records go to the filesystem (in UNIX) or Event Log (in Windows), not to the database tables, even if the parameter *audit_trail* is set to DB. The location in UNIX is the filesystem specified by the initialization parameter *audit_file_dest*, which defaults to $ORACLE_HOME/rdbms/audit.
- This parameter is independent of the other audit parameter *audit_trail*. The SYSDBA auditing can be enabled or disabled regardless of whether regular auditing is set.

## The Use of SYS Auditing

Since the SYS user is audited and the audit record goes into a filesystem area, not the database object like a table, the security is more pronounced. If this filesystem area is somehow protected so that the regular DBA user does not have read or write access to it, only the auditors or other security personnel have access. The information can be considered more secure than the regular database auditing, which can be tampered with by anyone with a DBA role. In Windows NT, the event log is generally not available to the regular user and therefore the trail is protected.

Since auditing SYS user actions must be accounted for, it is recommended that this auditing be enabled. The logs (in UNIX) and Event Log (in Windows) should be periodically archived to an offline medium and purged from the system.

# Data Dictionary Views for Auditing

We have covered some data dictionary tables in line with the descriptions above. Some additional important tables have been described here.

***audit_actions*** – This table contains the auditable action and its associated numeric code. This numeric Action# is referenced in the *aud$* table. Table 8.4 has a listing of all auditable actions.

***stmt_audit_option_map*** – This data dictionary table lists all the options in auditing SQL statements. Table 8.2 has a listing of all options that are available.

***system_privilege_map*** – So far we have talked about auditing on objects. Auditing can also be set on system privileges like ALTER SYSTEM. The system privilege statements that can be audited have been given in Table 8.2. This may seem similar to the table *stmt_audit_option_map*, but there is a very subtle but important difference. The table *stmt_audit_option_map* holds statements that can be audited, such as 'create procedure'. However, there is also a system privilege called 'create procedure'. When that is granted to a user, the audit action triggered is different and that is what is stored in the table *system_privilege_map*. These differences are explained elsewhere in this chapter.

## Checking the Audit Trail

The raw audit trail is written in the table *aud$*, which may not be user-friendly. We briefly mentioned some of the views designed to facilitate the interpretation of the information contained in this table at the beginning of the chapter. Here we will discuss these in detail.

### *dba_audit_trail*

This view reports all the records of the table *aud$* after interpreting the columns, i.e. decoding the codes to proper descriptions, such as decoding the action codes to the names of those actions. Here are the columns of this view in detail.

| COLUMN NAME | DESCRIPTION |
|---|---|
| OS_USERNAME | The operating system user who logged on. |
| USERNAME | The database user who logged on. |
| USERHOST | The host name of the machine from which the user logged on. In Windows, it is null. |

| COLUMN NAME | DESCRIPTION |
|---|---|
| TERMINAL | The terminal of the host machine from where the user logged on. In Windows, it is the machine name. |
| TIMESTAMP | The timestamp of the audit event. |
| OWNER | If the audit event was based on an object, the owner of the object is recorded here. |
| OBJ_NAME | The name of the object is recorded here if the audit is based on a database object. |
| ACTION | The numeric code of the action performed by the user. This description of this code is found in the table *audit_actions*. |
| ACTION_NAME | The operation performed that was captured by the audit, e.g. CREATE TABLE or ALTER SESSION. This is actually decoded from joining the tables *aud$* and *audit_actions* on the ACTION# column. Table 8.4 has a list of these action names. |
| NEW_OWNER | If an object is renamed, the owner of the new object is recorded here. |
| NEW_NAME | If an object is renamed, the new name is recorded here. |
| OBJ_PRIVILEGE | If the audited action was either a GRANT or a REVOKE of some privilege on an object, this column records what object privileges were acted upon. |
| SYS_PRIVILEGE | Similar to above, except that the system privileges are described. |
| ADMIN_OPTION | Indicates if the privilege was granted with ADMIN OPTION. |
| GRANTEE | If the audited action is a grant of some privilege or a role, the name of the grantee, which could be a user or a role is recorded here. |
| AUDIT_OPTION | When the statement AUDIT triggers the auditing action, the option is recorded here. |

| COLUMN NAME | DESCRIPTION |
|---|---|
| SES_ACTIONS | If the auditing action is on an object, the audit information is recorded in a long string here. This has been described below in detail. |
| LOGOFF_TIME | If the auditing was for user sessions, the column records the timestamp when the session ended. |
| LOGOFF_LREAD | Logical blocks read when the session was active. |
| LOGOFF_PREAD | Physical blocks read by the session |
| LOGOFF_LWRITE | Logical blocks written by the session. |
| LOGOFF_DLOCK | If the session detected deadlocks, the number of such events is recorded here. |
| COMMENT_TEXT | This is important for authentication purposes. Described in detail below. |
| SESSIONID | The Audit Session Id of that session. Remember, this is the Audit Session Id, not the Session Id from *v$session* view. |
| ENTRYID | A single statement may trigger several types of audited events, e.g. a select * from dual may trigger Oracle check whether a cached cursor similar to the query exists or not. All these entries are assigned one unique entry id within a session id. |
| STATEMENTID | A single session may have several audited statements – such as, the user created a table, altered another, selected yet another, etc. Each of these statements is assigned one statement id that is unique in that session id. If the audited event is not a statement, then the statement id is 0. |

| COLUMN NAME | DESCRIPTION |
|---|---|
| RETURNCODE | The return code of the action – 0 if everything went smoothly. If an error occurs, the returncode is the Oracle error number. For instance, if the action is CREATE TABLE and the table already exists, the error is "ORA-00955: name is already used by an existing object", and the returncode in this view is set to 955. |
| PRIV_USED | This field records the system privilege used to conduct the action. For instance, a user may have CREATE ANY TABLE system privilege. If he creates a table in his own schema, the privilege used is CREATE TABLE; but if he used it to create a table in a different user's schema, then the privilege CREATE ANY TABLE is used. This column records the exact privilege used. |
| CLIENT_ID | The Client Identifier for that session, which is relevant only in Oracle 9i and above. This has been described in detail later in this chapter. |
| SESSION_CPU | The CPU time consumed by this session. |

The three columns referenced above have been described in detail here.

**SES_ACTIONS** – This is a long string that shows the actions made on the object. The string is 19 characters long, of which only the first 13 are relevant. These 13 characters represent the result of an action on the object. For instance, the first character is for ALTER. If this character shows S, then the object was altered successfully. A value of F indicates a failed alter on the object. It both success and failure results exist for the ALTER – the character is B (for both).

The other characters represent the following

| POSITION | AUDITED ACTION |
|---|---|
| 1 | ALTER |
| 2 | AUDIT |
| 3 | COMMENT |
| 4 | DELETE |

| | |
|---|---|
| 5 | GRANT |
| 6 | INDEX |
| 7 | INSERT |
| 8 | LOCK |
| 9 | RENAME |
| 10 | SELECT |
| 11 | UPDATE |
| 12 | REFERENCES |
| 13 | EXECUTE |

For instance, if the string is as follows:

```
S------------
```

An S in the first place means the ALTER was successfully executed on the table. All other fields are hyphens, i.e. no activity occurred corresponding to those fields.

## Important Point about Action and Ses_Action

Sometimes the record may show a different value when Action = SELECT and the SES_ACTION field is null. Additionally, another record may exist for another table with SES_ACTIONS set to "---------S---------", which also indicates SELECT (S in 10th place). This could appear confusing. The ACTION field has the value of SESSION REC in the second case.

This can be easily understood by the applicability of audit in various situations. If a table is specifically being audited for SELECT, as in Object Auditing, a record with ACTION value SELECT will be generated. That is not statement auditing, therefore the SES_ACTIONS field is left null. In the second case, the auditing is of Statement in nature, with the statement SELECT TABLE being audited, therefore ACTION shows a more general SESSION REC and the SELECT tab on the SES_ACTIONS is set to S.

**COMMENT_TEXT** – This holds miscellaneous comments on the connection or the session, more specifically, the connection information on the session, i.e. how the user was authenticated. A typical line may look like:

```
Authenticated by: DATABASE; Client address:
(ADDRESS=(PROTOCOL=tcp)(HOST=x.y.z.w)(PORT=1791))
```

Let's analyze the various parts of this message. It shows the user was connected through database authentication and shows the client address (masked in this example). Note the port number is 1791. We don't have such a port defined; the only defined ports are 1521 and 1526. Where did it come from? It comes from the dynamic ports allocated by the listener. This phenomenon has been described in depth in the Chapter on Network Security.

**ACTION and ACTION_NAME** – These hold the Action# and the decoded Action Description as defined in the table *audit_actions*. The following Table 8.4 has a list of the actions audited.

| | | |
|---|---|---|
| ALTER CLUSTER | ALTER DATABASE | ALTER DIMENSION |
| ALTER FUNCTION | ALTER INDEX | ALTER JAVA |
| ALTER OPERATOR | ALTER OUTLINE | ALTER PACKAGE |
| ALTER PACKAGE BODY | ALTER PROCEDURE | ALTER PROFILE |
| ALTER RESOURCE COST | ALTER ROLE | ALTER ROLLBACK SEG |
| ALTER SEQUENCE | ALTER SESSION | ALTER SNAPSHOT |
| ALTER SNAPSHOT LOG | ALTER SUMMARY | ALTER SYSTEM |
| ALTER TABLE | ALTER TABLESPACE | ALTER TRIGGER |
| ALTER TYPE | ALTER TYPE BODY | ALTER USER |
| ANALYZE CLUSTER | ANALYZE INDEX | ANALYZE TABLE |
| ASSOCIATE STATISTICS | AUDIT DEFAULT | AUDIT OBJECT |
| CALL METHOD | COMMENT | COMMIT |
| CREATE CLUSTER | CREATE CONTEXT | CREATE CONTROL FILE |
| CREATE DATABASE | CREATE DATABASE LINK | CREATE DIMENSION |
| CREATE DIRECTORY | CREATE FUNCTION | CREATE INDEX |
| CREATE INDEXTYPE | CREATE JAVA | CREATE LIBRARY |

| | | |
|---|---|---|
| CREATE OPERATOR | CREATE OUTLINE | CREATE PACKAGE |
| CREATE PACKAGE BODY | CREATE PROCEDURE | CREATE PROFILE |
| CREATE PUBLIC DATABASE LINK | CREATE PUBLIC SYNONYM | CREATE ROLE |
| CREATE ROLLBACK SEG | CREATE SCHEMA | CREATE SEQUENCE |
| CREATE SNAPSHOT | CREATE SNAPSHOT LOG | CREATE SUMMARY |
| CREATE SYNONYM | CREATE TABLE | CREATE TABLESPACE |
| CREATE TRIGGER | CREATE TYPE | CREATE TYPE BODY |
| CREATE USER | CREATE VIEW | DELETE |
| DISABLE ALL TRIGGERS | DISABLE TRIGGER | DISASSOCIATE STATISTICS |
| DROP CLUSTER | DROP CONTEXT | DROP DATABASE LINK |
| DROP DIMENSION | DROP DIRECTORY | DROP FUNCTION |
| DROP INDEX | DROP INDEXTYPE | DROP JAVA |
| DROP LIBRARY | DROP OPERATOR | DROP OUTLINE |
| DROP PACKAGE | DROP PACKAGE BODY | DROP PROCEDURE |
| DROP PROFILE | DROP PUBLIC DATABASE LINK | DROP PUBLIC SYNONYM |
| DROP ROLE | DROP ROLLBACK SEG | DROP SEQUENCE |
| DROP SNAPSHOT | DROP SNAPSHOT LOG | DROP SUMMARY |
| DROP SYNONYM | DROP TABLE | DROP TABLESPACE |
| DROP TRIGGER | DROP TYPE | DROP TYPE BODY |
| DROP USER | DROP VIEW | ENABLE ALL TRIGGERS |

| | | |
|---|---|---|
| ENABLE TRIGGER | EXECUTE PROCEDURE | EXECUTE TYPE |
| EXPLAIN | GRANT OBJECT | GRANT ROLE |
| INSERT | LOCK | LOGOFF |
| LOGOFF BY CLEANUP | LOGON | NETWORK ERROR |
| NOAUDIT DEFAULT | NOAUDIT OBJECT | NO-OP |
| PL/SQL EXECUTE | RENAME | REVOKE OBJECT |
| REVOKE ROLE | ROLLBACK | SAVEPOINT |
| SELECT | SESSION REC | SET ROLE |
| SET TRANSACTION | SYSTEM AUDIT | SYSTEM GRANT |
| SYSTEM NOAUDIT | SYSTEM REVOKE | TRUNCATE CLUSTER |
| TRUNCATE TABLE | UPDATE | UPDATE INDEXES |
| USER COMMENT | VALIDATE INDEX | |

**Table 8.4** *Auditable Actions*

The following views are based on the *dba_audit_trail* view. All these views have some columns of the view *dba_audit_trail*, and the column names and their explanations are the same as the parent view.

***user_audit_trail*** This view is based on all the columns of the *dba_audit_trail* view, but presents information on the current logged in user only. Unlike other data dictionary view, there is no equivalent *all_audit_trail* view, as it is not relevant in this case. This view contains those records from *dba_audit_trail* for which the object owner or the audited user is the logged in user.

***dba_audit_exists*** This is an audit trail of the entries where the operation failed due to non-existing objects. This is actually filtered from the view *dba_audit_trail* where the return code is something other than zero. Only the following return codes are captured in this view.

1, 942, 943, 951, 955, 957, 959, 1418, 1430, 1432, 1433, 1434, 1435, 1452, 1471, 1534, 1535, 1543, 1758, 1917, 1918, 1919, 1920, 1921, 1922, 2019, 2024, 2239, 2264, 2266, 2273, 2289, 2292, 2297, 2378, 2379, 2382, 4042, 4043, 4080, 4081, 12006 and 12325

Some of these error codes are well known, e.g.1 indicates Unique Key violation, 942 indicates invalid table name or lack of privileges to access the table/view, etc.

***dba_audit_session*** This records all activities where the users connected and disconnected from the database. It also records if the action failed due to various reasons such security violations or invalid passwords. These audit records are indicated by action#s 100, 101 and 102 in the table *aud$*, also known as SESSION REC as a descriptive name.

## Example

The following query shows the clients that could not be connected to the database and the Oracle error.

```
select
   os_username,
   username,
   userhost||'-'||terminal client,
   action_name,
   returncode
from
   dba_audit_session
where
   returncode != 0
/
```

The output comes back as:

```
OS_USERNAME USERNAME     CLIENT     ACTION_NAME RETURNCODE
----------- ------------ ---------- ----------- ----------
jdoe        CLAIM_SCHEMA cap1-pts/5 LOGON             1017
```

Here we see that the operating system user jdoe tried to login as CLAIM_SCHEMA from the terminal pts/5 on machine cap1. The return code was 1017, which is the Oracle error for "invalid username/password; logon denied". This proves that the user supplied a wrong password for CLAIM_SCHEMA. Does this smell of attempted break-in? It could. There could be a simple explanation – the user forgot the password of CLAIM_SCHEMA and at the second attempt provided the correct one. A series of repeated attempts, however, would arouse suspicion.

Another thing to note here is the OS user jdoe was doing this. Is jdoe authorized to connect to CLAIM_SCHEMA? If jdoe is a DBA, or an application owner, this may not arouse any suspicion, but if that user is really a claim analyst, he or she has no reason to connect to the CLAIM_SCHEMA user, and this event certainly needs more investigation.

***dba_audit_statement*** This view contains information where the user entered statements that did not particularly access the data inside an object, e.g. ALTER SYSTEM, GRANT, REVOKE on objects, etc. Here is a complete list of the statements that are captured in this view:

| ACTION# | STATEMENT |
|---:|---|
| 17 | GRANT OBJECT |
| 18 | REVOKE OBJECT |
| 30 | AUDIT OBJECT |
| 31 | NOAUDIT OBJECT |
| 49 | ALTER SYSTEM |
| 104 | SYSTEM AUDIT |
| 105 | SYSTEM NOAUDIT |
| 106 | AUDIT DEFAULT |
| 107 | NOAUDIT DEFAULT |
| 108 | SYSTEM GRANT |
| 109 | SYSTEM REVOKE |
| 114 | GRANT ROLE |
| 115 | REVOKE ROLE |

***dba_audit_object*** This view shows all the audit records that were based on database object accesses – e.g. a user selected from some table, or altered another table, etc. It has some columns of the *dba_audit_trail* view, filtered by the actions that are related to objects only.

## Checking the Settings for Auditing Objects

The data dictionary view *dba_obj_audit_opts* records all the objects and the audit settings on all the possible statements that could be made against them. Please note that this records all the objects, whether or not there is an audit event set. Therefore, this view tends to return a large number of records for each object in the database.

A smaller view, *user_obj_audit_opts* holds the same structure, but only for the user logged in.

The view shows the audit options set for the object, one column per each type of statement. For instance, if we decide to audit all ALTER statements on table CLAIMS owned user CLAIM_SCHEMA, we would issue:

```
AUDIT ALTER ON CLAIM_SCHEMA.CLAIMS BY SESSION;
```

After this, we can see what audit options exist for this object by issuing:

```
select ALT from dba_obj_audit_opts
where owner = 'CLAIM_SCHEMA'
and object_name = 'CLAIMS';
```

The result comes back as:

```
ALT
---
S/S
```

Note the column name, ALT, that signifies the audit options for the ALTER statements on the object. A separate column exists for each of the statements. A complete list is provided in Table 8.5, where the columns of this view have been described.

Note the value is shown as "S/S". It means that the options are set to record the statement when the statement is successful (the letter S in the first position) and unsuccessful (the other letter S in the second position). Since we did not specify which to audit, the default of both was applied.

If we decide not to audit the object, we can specify:

```
noaudit alter on claim_schema.claims;
```

Now, if we check the settings again:

```
select ALT from dba_obj_audit_opts
where owner = 'CLAIM_SCHEMA'
and object_name = 'CLAIMS';
```

The result comes back as:

```
ALT
---
-/-
```

Note, the values have hyphens in them, meaning the audit action is not set. If while setting the audit, we specify to audit only when the attempt is unsuccessful, we can set:

```
audit alter on claim_schema.claims by session whenever not successful;
```

```
select ALT from dba_obj_audit_opts
where owner = 'CLAIM_SCHEMA'
and object_name = 'CLAIMS';

ALT
---
-/S
```

Note the first position, which shows the setting for auditing successful attempts, shows a hyphen ("-"), since we did not set it. The second position, for unsuccessful attempts, shows "S", meaning it has been set.

Another type of auditing is set for ACCESS as in:

```
audit select on claim_schema.claims by access;
```

In this case the values in this column are recorded as A, as shown in the following query:

```
select SEL from dba_obj_audit_opts
where owner = 'CLAIM_SCHEMA'
and object_name = 'CLAIMS';
```

The result comes back as:

```
SEL
---
A/A
```

It shows the first letter A, for successful attempts and the second letter A, for unsuccessful ones, exactly like the BY SESSION option.

Table 8.5 below shows the columns of this view and their description.

| COLUMN NAME | DESCRIPTION |
| --- | --- |
| OWNER | The owner of the object on which this auditing option is set. |
| OBJECT_NAME | The name of the object. |
| OBJECT_TYPE | The type of the object, e.g. TABLE, VIEW, PROCEDURE, etc. |

| COLUMN NAME | DESCRIPTION |
|---|---|
| ALT | If the auditing options for ALTER statements on the object is set. The format is as described earlier, *<frequency>/<frequency>*, where *<frequency>* is either 'A' (for BY ACCESS) or 'S' (for BY SESSION). If not set, that particular value is a hyphen "-". The left character represents successful execution and the right one failure. |
| AUD | Auditing option for the issuance of the AUDIT command on that object. |
| COM | Auditing options for creation of comments on this object. |
| DEL | Auditing options for DELETE on this object. |
| GRA | Auditing options for GRANTs performed on this object. |
| IND | Auditing options for INDEX operations on this object. |
| INS | Auditing options for INSERTs to this object. |
| LOC | Whenever a lock is attained on this object, this auditing option specifies whether a record is written or not. |
| REN | Auditing option when the object is renamed. |
| SEL | Auditing option when the object is SELECTed from. |
| UPD | Auditing option when an UPDATE is issued on the object. |
| REF | If the table is a referenced in a foreign key relationship, then this audit option can be set. |
| EXE | Auditing EXECUTE operations on the object. It is valid for only procedures, packages, and type bodies. |
| CRE | Auditing options when a CREATE statement is issued for that object. |
| REA | Auditing option for READ on the object. Relevant only for directory objects. |
| WRI | Auditing options for writing operations. |

**Table 8.5** *Columns of the view dba_obj_audit_opts*

## An Alternative View

The biggest problem with this view is the way the information is presented. The information is shown in fields as letters and this view contains a line for each of the objects in the database, whether or not it has auditing enabled. To search if there is auditing enabled for an object for any of the options, you would have to write a query similar to the following:

```
select *
from dba_obj_audit_opts
where owner = 'claim_schema'
and object_name = 'claims'
and object_type = 'table'
and alt != '-/-'
and aud != '-/-'
….
and so on for all the columns.
```

This query is rather complicated and cumbersome to write, prone to errors, and inconvenient. Upon selecting the view definition query from the view *dba_views* for the view *dba_obj_audit_opts*, we can see that it is based on the individual data dictionary tables that store the objects, e.g. *tab$* for tables, *procedure$* for procedures, etc. The column AUDIT$ in all these data dictionary tables stores the information of the audit setting, if set. For instance, if the audit option by access is set for ALTERs on table CLAIM_SCHEMA, the column AUDIT$ for that table in the table *tab$* is set to

```
AA----------------------------
```

Note how the first two characters are "A" and "A" and the rest are all hyphens, indicating that the audit option on ALTER on this table is set by access (as shown by A), for both successful and unsuccessful (A in both places) and no other audit option is set (as shown by hyphens).

This information can be used to our advantage. Here we will create another view, called *only_obj_audit_opts*, which will contain records only if the audit options are present. The structure is identical to the *dba_obj_audit_opts* view, but the records are filtered. This new view is created with the following listing. It is an adaptation of the original view with our changes highlighted.

### present_dba_obj_audit_opts.sql

```
create or replace view present_dba_obj_audit_opts
(
   username,
   object_name,
   object_type,
   ALT, /* Alter */
   AUD, /* Audit */
   COM, /* Comment */
   DEL, /* Delete */
   GRA, /* Grant */
   IND, /* Index */
   INS, /* Insert */
   LOC, /* Lock */
   REN, /* Rename */
   SEL, /* Select */
   UPD, /* Update */
   REF, /* Reference */
   EXE, /* Execute */
   CRE, /* Create */
   REA, /* Read */
   WRI  /* Write */
)
as
select u.name, o.name, 'TABLE',
   substr(t.audit$,1,1)||'/'||substr(t.audit$,2,1),
   substr(t.audit$,3,1)||'/'||substr(t.audit$,4,1),
   substr(t.audit$,5,1)||'/'||substr(t.audit$,6,1),
   substr(t.audit$,7,1)||'/'||substr(t.audit$,8,1),
   substr(t.audit$,9,1)||'/'||substr(t.audit$,10,1),
   substr(t.audit$,11,1)||'/'||substr(t.audit$,12,1),
   substr(t.audit$,13,1)||'/'||substr(t.audit$,14,1),
   substr(t.audit$,15,1)||'/'||substr(t.audit$,16,1),
   substr(t.audit$,17,1)||'/'||substr(t.audit$,18,1),
   substr(t.audit$,19,1)||'/'||substr(t.audit$,20,1),
   substr(t.audit$,21,1)||'/'||substr(t.audit$,22,1),
   substr(t.audit$,23,1)||'/'||substr(t.audit$,24,1),
   substr(t.audit$,25,1)||'/'||substr(t.audit$,26,1),
   substr(t.audit$,27,1)||'/'||substr(t.audit$,28,1),
   substr(t.audit$,29,1)||'/'||substr(t.audit$,30,1),
   substr(t.audit$,31,1)||'/'||substr(t.audit$,32,1)
from sys.obj$ o, sys.user$ u, sys.tab$ t
where o.type# = 2
  and not (o.owner# = 0 and o.name = '_default_auditing_options_')
  and o.owner# = u.user#
  and o.obj# = t.obj#
  and (t.audit$ like '%S%' or t.audit$ like '%A%')
union all
select u.name, o.name, 'VIEW',
   substr(v.audit$,1,1)||'/'||substr(v.audit$,2,1),
   substr(v.audit$,3,1)||'/'||substr(v.audit$,4,1),
   substr(v.audit$,5,1)||'/'||substr(v.audit$,6,1),
   substr(v.audit$,7,1)||'/'||substr(v.audit$,8,1),
   substr(v.audit$,9,1)||'/'||substr(v.audit$,10,1),
```

```
   substr(v.audit$,15,1)||'/'||substr(v.audit$,16,1),
   substr(v.audit$,17,1)||'/'||substr(v.audit$,18,1),
   substr(v.audit$,19,1)||'/'||substr(v.audit$,20,1),
   substr(v.audit$,21,1)||'/'||substr(v.audit$,22,1),
   substr(v.audit$,23,1)||'/'||substr(v.audit$,24,1),
   substr(v.audit$,25,1)||'/'||substr(v.audit$,26,1),
   substr(v.audit$,27,1)||'/'||substr(v.audit$,28,1),
   substr(v.audit$,29,1)||'/'||substr(v.audit$,30,1),
   substr(v.audit$,31,1)||'/'||substr(v.audit$,32,1)
from sys.obj$ o, sys.user$ u, sys.view$ v
where o.type# = 4
  and o.owner# = u.user#
  and o.obj# = v.obj#
  and (v.audit$ like '%S%' or v.audit$ like '%A%')
union all
select u.name, o.name, 'SEQUENCE',
   substr(s.audit$,1,1)||'/'||substr(s.audit$,2,1),
   substr(s.audit$,3,1)||'/'||substr(s.audit$,4,1),
   substr(s.audit$,5,1)||'/'||substr(s.audit$,6,1),
   substr(s.audit$,7,1)||'/'||substr(s.audit$,8,1),
   substr(s.audit$,9,1)||'/'||substr(s.audit$,10,1),
   substr(s.audit$,11,1)||'/'||substr(s.audit$,12,1),
   substr(s.audit$,13,1)||'/'||substr(s.audit$,14,1),
   substr(s.audit$,15,1)||'/'||substr(s.audit$,16,1),
   substr(s.audit$,17,1)||'/'||substr(s.audit$,18,1),
   substr(s.audit$,19,1)||'/'||substr(s.audit$,20,1),
   substr(s.audit$,21,1)||'/'||substr(s.audit$,22,1),
   substr(s.audit$,23,1)||'/'||substr(s.audit$,24,1),
   substr(s.audit$,25,1)||'/'||substr(s.audit$,26,1),
   substr(s.audit$,27,1)||'/'||substr(s.audit$,28,1),
   substr(s.audit$,29,1)||'/'||substr(s.audit$,30,1),
   substr(s.audit$,31,1)||'/'||substr(s.audit$,32,1)
from sys.obj$ o, sys.user$ u, sys.seq$ s
where o.type# = 6
  and o.owner# = u.user#
  and o.obj# = s.obj#
  and (s.audit$ like '%S%' or s.audit$ like '%A%')
union all
select u.name, o.name, 'PROCEDURE',
   substr(p.audit$,1,1)||'/'||substr(p.audit$,2,1),
   substr(p.audit$,3,1)||'/'||substr(p.audit$,4,1),
   substr(p.audit$,5,1)||'/'||substr(p.audit$,6,1),
   substr(p.audit$,7,1)||'/'||substr(p.audit$,8,1),
   substr(p.audit$,9,1)||'/'||substr(p.audit$,10,1),
   substr(p.audit$,11,1)||'/'||substr(p.audit$,12,1),
   substr(p.audit$,13,1)||'/'||substr(p.audit$,14,1),
   substr(p.audit$,15,1)||'/'||substr(p.audit$,16,1),
   substr(p.audit$,17,1)||'/'||substr(p.audit$,18,1),
   substr(p.audit$,19,1)||'/'||substr(p.audit$,20,1),
   substr(p.audit$,21,1)||'/'||substr(p.audit$,22,1),
   substr(p.audit$,23,1)||'/'||substr(p.audit$,24,1),
   substr(p.audit$,25,1)||'/'||substr(p.audit$,26,1),
   substr(p.audit$,27,1)||'/'||substr(p.audit$,28,1),
   substr(p.audit$,29,1)||'/'||substr(p.audit$,30,1),
   substr(p.audit$,31,1)||'/'||substr(p.audit$,32,1)
from sys.obj$ o, sys.user$ u, sys.library$ p
```

```
  and o.obj# = p.obj#
  and (p.audit$ like '%S%' or p.audit$ like '%A%')
union all
select u.name, o.name, 'PROCEDURE',
   substr(p.audit$,1,1)||'/'||substr(p.audit$,2,1),
   substr(p.audit$,3,1)||'/'||substr(p.audit$,4,1),
   substr(p.audit$,5,1)||'/'||substr(p.audit$,6,1),
   substr(p.audit$,7,1)||'/'||substr(p.audit$,8,1),
   substr(p.audit$,9,1)||'/'||substr(p.audit$,10,1),
   substr(p.audit$,11,1)||'/'||substr(p.audit$,12,1),
   substr(p.audit$,13,1)||'/'||substr(p.audit$,14,1),
   substr(p.audit$,15,1)||'/'||substr(p.audit$,16,1),
   substr(p.audit$,17,1)||'/'||substr(p.audit$,18,1),
   substr(p.audit$,19,1)||'/'||substr(p.audit$,20,1),
   substr(p.audit$,21,1)||'/'||substr(p.audit$,22,1),
   substr(p.audit$,23,1)||'/'||substr(p.audit$,24,1),
   substr(p.audit$,25,1)||'/'||substr(p.audit$,26,1),
   substr(p.audit$,27,1)||'/'||substr(p.audit$,28,1),
   substr(p.audit$,29,1)||'/'||substr(p.audit$,30,1),
   substr(p.audit$,31,1)||'/'||substr(p.audit$,32,1)
from sys.obj$ o, sys.user$ u, sys.procedure$ p
where o.type# >= 7 and o.type# <= 9
  and o.owner# = u.user#
  and o.obj# = p.obj#
  and (p.audit$ like '%S%' or p.audit$ like '%A%')
union all
select u.name, o.name, 'TYPE',
   substr(t.audit$,1,1)||'/'||substr(t.audit$,2,1),
   substr(t.audit$,3,1)||'/'||substr(t.audit$,4,1),
   substr(t.audit$,5,1)||'/'||substr(t.audit$,6,1),
   substr(t.audit$,7,1)||'/'||substr(t.audit$,8,1),
   substr(t.audit$,9,1)||'/'||substr(t.audit$,10,1),
   substr(t.audit$,11,1)||'/'||substr(t.audit$,12,1),
   substr(t.audit$,13,1)||'/'||substr(t.audit$,14,1),
   substr(t.audit$,15,1)||'/'||substr(t.audit$,16,1),
   substr(t.audit$,17,1)||'/'||substr(t.audit$,18,1),
   substr(t.audit$,19,1)||'/'||substr(t.audit$,20,1),
   substr(t.audit$,21,1)||'/'||substr(t.audit$,22,1),
   substr(t.audit$,23,1)||'/'||substr(t.audit$,24,1),
   substr(t.audit$,25,1)||'/'||substr(t.audit$,26,1),
   substr(t.audit$,27,1)||'/'||substr(t.audit$,28,1),
   substr(t.audit$,29,1)||'/'||substr(t.audit$,30,1),
   substr(t.audit$,31,1)||'/'||substr(t.audit$,32,1)
from sys.obj$ o, sys.user$ u, sys.type_misc$ t
where o.type# = 13
  and o.owner# = u.user#
  and o.obj# = t.obj#
  and (t.audit$ like '%S%' or t.audit$ like '%A%')
union all
select u.name, o.name, 'DIRECTORY',
   substr(t.audit$,1,1)||'/'||substr(t.audit$,2,1),
   substr(t.audit$,3,1)||'/'||substr(t.audit$,4,1),
   substr(t.audit$,5,1)||'/'||substr(t.audit$,6,1),
   substr(t.audit$,7,1)||'/'||substr(t.audit$,8,1),
   substr(t.audit$,9,1)||'/'||substr(t.audit$,10,1),
   substr(t.audit$,11,1)||'/'||substr(t.audit$,12,1),
```

```
   substr(t.audit$,17,1)||'/'||substr(t.audit$,18,1),
   substr(t.audit$,19,1)||'/'||substr(t.audit$,20,1),
   substr(t.audit$,21,1)||'/'||substr(t.audit$,22,1),
   substr(t.audit$,23,1)||'/'||substr(t.audit$,24,1),
   substr(t.audit$,25,1)||'/'||substr(t.audit$,26,1),
   substr(t.audit$,27,1)||'/'||substr(t.audit$,28,1),
   substr(t.audit$,29,1)||'/'||substr(t.audit$,30,1),
   substr(t.audit$,31,1)||'/'||substr(t.audit$,32,1)
from sys.obj$ o, sys.user$ u, sys.dir$ t
where o.type# = 23
  and o.owner# = u.user#
  and o.obj# = t.obj#
  and (t.audit$ like '%S%' or t.audit$ like '%A%')
```

This new view *present_dba_obj_audit_opts* will show records for only those objects for which the auditing options are enabled, not all the objects. This will help tremendously while checking quickly for a setting in audit.

A word of caution is in order here. This view is based on Oracle's unpublished data dictionary contents and is not supported by Oracle. The contents may change without notice during database upgrades and therefore this view may not work as per expectations. Please use this at your own risk. The authors do not take any responsibility in supporting this view.

Another way to look up this information is by creating a view on the view *dba_obj_audit_opts* to filter out the objects for which the audit is not set. This view is defined as follows:

### dba_obj_audit_opts_filtered

```
create or replace view dba_obj_audit_opts_filtered
as
select * from dba_obj_audit_opts
where ALT != '-/-'
or AUD != '-/-'
or COM != '-/-'
or DEL != '-/-'
or GRA != '-/-'
or IND != '-/-'
or INS != '-/-'
or LOC != '-/-'
or REN != '-/-'
or SEL != '-/-'
or UPD != '-/-'
or REF != '-/-'
or EXE != '-/-'
or CRE != '-/-'
or REA != '-/-'
or WRI != '-/-'
```

The advantage of this view is its foundation as the original view. Since it does not depend on the data dictionary internals, the applicability is somewhat improved across different versions as well as its supportability in the future versions.

However, there is a serious flaw in this view due to inconsistency in the Oracle database software. Selecting from the view *dba_obj_audit_opts* for some Index Organized Tables, we can see that the audits options are not populated by hyphens, but by *nulls*. To check this, issue this query:

```
select *
from dba_obj_audit_opts
where alt = chr(0)||'/'||chr(0)
/
```

The result comes back as the follows. Only part of the result is shown here.

```
OWNER
------------------------------
OBJECT_NAME                    OBJECT_TY
------------------------------ ---------
ALT AUD COM DEL GRA IND INS LOC REN SEL
--- --- --- --- --- --- --- --- --- ---
UPD REF EXE CRE REA WRI
--- --- --- --- --- ---
SYS_IOT_OVER_31407             TABLE
 /   /   /   /   /   /   /   /   /   /
 /   /   /   /   /   /

QS_WS
SYS_IOT_OVER_31434             TABLE
 /   /   /   /   /   /   /   /   /   /
 /   /   /   /   /   /

QS_WS
SYS_IOT_OVER_31452             TABLE
 /   /   /   /   /   /   /   /   /   /
 /   /   /   /   /   /
```

Note how the auditing options are set as "NULL/NULL", not "-/-" as in other cases. In the view *dba_obj_audit_opts*, since we are looking for non-matches with "-/-", this view will show us the above records too. Therefore, either the view defined by us can be modified to exclude null values or the earlier view *only_audits* can be used instead.

## dba_priv_audit_opts

The view described earlier shows the auditing options set for database objects like tables, views, etc. The other audit options set on system privileges such as CREATE TABLE, etc. are recorded in another view, *dba_priv_audit_opts*. An example may make it clear. Suppose we audit the ALTER SESSION statements issued by user JUDY. We would issue:

```
audit alter session by judy;
```

Then, we could query the view *dba_priv_audit_opts* to find out what audit options have been set.

```
select * from dba_priv_audit_opts;
```

The output comes back as:

```
USER_NAME PROXY_NAME PRIVILEGE
--------- ---------- ----------------------------
SUCCESS              FAILURE
-------------------- ----------------------------
JUDY                 ALTER SESSION                             BY ACCESS
BY ACCESS
```

Note the dissimilarity with the earlier view for objects. This view does not display all the privileges, but only the ones that have been marked for audit. This facility makes it easier to quickly check the audit settings of any system privilege. The following section describes the columns of this view.

| COLUMN NAME | DESCRIPTION |
|---|---|
| USER_NAME | The name of the user for which the privilege auditing is enabled. |
| PROXY_NAME | If the auditing is enabled for a proxy user, not a real one, this column shows that information. |
| PRIVILEGE | The privilege for which the auditing is set. |
| SUCCESS | SET or NOT SET, depending on the auditing action established for successful execution. |
| FAILURE | Similarly, SET or NOT SET, depending on unsuccessful execution. |

If the audit option is not set, the columns SUCCESS and FAILURE will display "NOT SET."

## Special Case DDL Operations

Let's issue the following. Our intention is to audit all tables created by user JUDY.

```
audit create table by judy by session;
```

When we check the view:

```
select * from
dba_priv_audit_opts
where user_name = 'JUDY';
```

We get:

```
USER_NAME  PROXY_NAME PRIVILEGE      SUCCESS    FAILURE
---------- ---------- -------------- ---------- ---------
JUDY                  CREATE TABLE   BY ACCESS  BY ACCESS
```

Note a very important point here. The auditing option was specified as BY SESSION; but the columns show BY ACCESS, not the expected "BY SESSION". Could this be a bug?

Consider the situation for a moment. When the table CLAIMS is created, it's created by default in the current user's schema. The user could drop it and then create a table called CLAIMS again, in the same session. The table created the second time, although it bears the same name, is a different table. Therefore, an audit record should be generated for each occurrence of the creation of the table CLAIMS, not just one for both occurrences. Oracle takes this into account and marks the audit options as BY ACCESS even though the user specified it as BY SESSION. This occurs for all the DDL operations, not just CREATE TABLE.

 **For DDL operations, the audit options are always set as BY ACCESS, even though the user has specified BY SESSION.**

## *dba_stmt_audit_opts*

This view records the audit settings for individual statements, which may or may not be privileges.

To find out what setting for statement auditing exists in a database, use the query:

```
select * from dba_stmt_audit_opts;
```

The output comes back as:

```
USER_NAME  PROXY_NAME AUDIT_OPTION     SUCCESS    FAILURE
---------- ---------- ---------------- ---------- -------
JUDY                  CREATE SESSION   BY ACCESS  NOT SET
NATHAN                CREATE SESSION   BY ACCESS  NOT SET
```

Doesn't this result look deceptively similar to the other view we just saw, *dba_priv_audit_opts*? All the columns are the same, except AUDIT_OPTION. Actually they appear very similar, but hold different information as explained in the following section.

## Difference between Statement and Privilege Auditing

It is important to understand the difference between the statement level audit and the privilege level audit described in these two different views. Most of the information seems to be in both views and therefore may be confusing to the casual observer. However, they record very different types of information.

Some statements can also be privileges. One such example is CREATE TABLE, which can be granted as a privilege to a user. But the user can also issue a statement such as "CREATE TABLE MYTAB …". In the first case, the privilege is granted and the action, if audited, is shown in *dba_priv_audit_opts* view. In the second case, the audit record is shown in the view *dba_stmt_audit_opts*.

Some SQL statements are only statements; not privileges. The following table 8.5 contains a list of such statements.

| | | |
|---|---|---|
| ALTER SEQUENCE | ALTER TABLE | CLUSTER |
| COMMENT TABLE | CONTEXT | CREATE DIRECTORY |
| DATABASE LINK | DEBUG PROCEDURE | DELETE TABLE |
| DIMENSION | DIRECTORY | DROP DIRECTORY |
| EXECUTE LIBRARY | EXECUTE PROCEDURE | EXISTS |
| GRANT DIRECTORY | GRANT LIBRARY | GRANT PROCEDURE |
| GRANT SEQUENCE | GRANT TABLE | GRANT TYPE |
| INDEX | INSERT TABLE | LOCK TABLE |
| MATERIALIZED VIEW | NETWORK | NOT EXISTS |
| PROCEDURE | PROFILE | PUBLIC DATABASE |

| | | |
|---|---|---|
| | | LINK |
| PUBLIC SYNONYM | ROLE | ROLLBACK SEGMENT |
| SELECT SEQUENCE | SELECT TABLE | SEQUENCE |
| SYNONYM | SYSTEM AUDIT | SYSTEM GRANT |
| TABLE | TABLESPACE | TRIGGER |
| TYPE | UPDATE TABLE | USER |
| VIEW | | |

**Table 8.5** *Statements that are not auditable as privileges.*

For instance, we can audit TABLE by the user CLAIM_SCHEMA as follows:

```
audit table by claim_schema by session;
```

We will see this in the statement audit options view:

```
select * from dba_stmt_audit_opts;
```

Selecting the same information from *dba_priv_audit_opts* will not return any rows.

Similarly, there are SQL statements that can only be privileges, not statements issued by users. The following Table 8.6 has a list of those statements. The audit options on these statements are seen in the view *dba_priv_audit_opts*.

| ADMINISTER DATABASE TRIGGER |
|---|
| ALTER ANY EVALUATION CONTEXT |
| ALTER ANY INDEXTYPE |
| ALTER ANY OPERATOR |
| ALTER ANY PROCEDURE |
| ALTER ANY RULE |
| ALTER ANY RULE SET |
| ALTER ANY SECURITY PROFILE |
| ALTER ANY TABLE |
| ALTER DATABASE |
| ALTER PROFILE |
| ALTER SYSTEM |
| ALTER USER |

| AUDIT SYSTEM |
|---|
| AUDIT SYSTEM |
| CREATE ANY EVALUATION CONTEXT |
| CREATE ANY INDEXTYPE |
| CREATE ANY LIBRARY |
| CREATE ANY OPERATOR |
| CREATE ANY PROCEDURE |
| CREATE ANY RULE |
| CREATE ANY RULE SET |
| CREATE ANY SECURITY PROFILE |
| CREATE ANY TABLE |
| CREATE EVALUATION CONTEXT |
| CREATE EXTERNAL JOB |
| CREATE INDEXTYPE |
| CREATE OPERATOR |
| CREATE PUBLIC DATABASE LINK |
| CREATE RULE |
| CREATE RULE SET |
| CREATE SECURITY PROFILE |
| CREATE SESSION |
| CREATE USER |
| DROP ANY EVALUATION CONTEXT |
| DROP ANY INDEXTYPE |
| DROP ANY OPERATOR |
| DROP ANY PROCEDURE |
| DROP ANY RULE |
| DROP ANY RULE SET |
| DROP ANY SECURITY PROFILE |
| DROP ANY TABLE |
| DROP PROFILE |
| DROP USER |
| EXECUTE ANY EVALUATION CONTEXT |
| EXECUTE ANY INDEXTYPE |
| EXECUTE ANY OPERATOR |
| EXECUTE ANY RULE |
| EXECUTE ANY RULE SET |
| EXEMPT ACCESS POLICY |

| GRANT ANY OBJECT PRIVILEGE |
|---|
| GRANT ANY PRIVILEGE |
| GRANT ANY ROLE |
| UNDER ANY TABLEADMINISTER RESOURCE MANAGER |
| UNDER ANY TYPEADMINISTER SECURITY |
| UNDER ANY VIEW |

**Table 8.6** *Privileges, not Statements*

## Using multiple Statement/Privileges

You cannot mix statements and privileges in a single audit statement.

For instance, the following is correct, where two *statements* have been used.

```
audit alter sequence, alter table by claim_schema, judy by access;
```

Or this one, where two *privileges* have been used:

```
audit administer database trigger, alter any role by claim_schema, judy by
access;
```

But this one is not:

```
audit administer database trigger, alter table by claim_schema, judy by
access;
```

This is because, "database trigger" is a pure privilege and "alter table" is a pure statement.

# Useful Scripts for Auditing

To see what statement and privilege auditing options have been set to in the database use the following script.

### show_stmt_priv_audit_opts.sql

```
column username     format a15
column audit option format a20
```

```
column failure       format a10

select
   user_name,
   audit_option,
   success,
   failure
from
   dba_stmt_audit_opts
union
select
   user_name,
   privilege,
   success,
   failure
from
   dba_priv_audit_opts
```

The output is similar to what is shown below.

```
USER_NAME       AUDIT_OPTION         SUCCESS    FAILURE
--------------- -------------------- ---------- ----------
ANANDA          CREATE PROCEDURE     BY ACCESS  BY ACCESS
ANANDA          CREATE SEQUENCE      BY ACCESS  BY ACCESS
ANANDA          CREATE SESSION       BY ACCESS  BY ACCESS
ANANDA          CREATE TABLE         BY ACCESS  BY ACCESS
                CREATE SYNONYM       BY ACCESS  BY ACCESS
JUDY            ALTER ANY RULE       BY SESSION BY SESSION
JUDY            CREATE ANY RULE      BY SESSION BY SESSION
JUDY            CREATE PROCEDURE     BY ACCESS  BY ACCESS
```

Note the fourth record has no user name. This means the CREATE SYNONYM privilege is audited for all users.

To see the object auditing options set for objects, the following script can be used

### show_obj_audit_opts.sql

```
col owner format a10
col object_name format a15
select *
from dba_obj_audit_opts
where alt != '-/-'
aud != '-/-'
com != '-/-'
del != '-/-'
gra != '-/-'
ind != '-/-'
ins != '-/-'
loc != '-/-'
```

```
upd != '-/-'
ref != '-/-'
exe != '-/-'
cre != '-/-'
rea != '-/-'
wri != '-/-'
```

The output is similar to:

```
OWNER        OBJECT_NAME   OBJECT_TY
------------ ------------ ------------
ALT AUD COM DEL GRA IND INS LOC REN SEL UPD REF EXE CRE REA WRI
--- --- --- --- --- --- --- --- --- --- --- --- --- --- --- ---

CLAIM_SCHEMA CLAIMS         TABLE
-/- -/- -/- -/- -/- -/- A/A -/- -/- A/A -/- -/- -/- -/- -/- -/-

CLAIM_SCHEMA CLAIM_LINE     TABLE
-/- -/- -/- A/A -/- -/- A/A -/- -/- A/A A/A -/- -/- -/- -/- -/-
```

Note the column names have been left in their original form. The explanation of the columns has been given in their respective sections.

A value of hyphen ("-") in the field indicates it is not set. The value left of the forward slash ("/") is for SUCCESS, and the one to the right is for FAILURE. A value of "A" indicates the audit records are generated once per access and "S" indicates once per session. For instance in the above output, the value in the INS column for CLAIM_SCHEMA.CLAIMS is "A/A", which indicates the audit records are generated once per insert statement into this table and are triggered when the statement succeeds or not.

# Protecting the Audit Trail

If the audit destination is the database, then the DBA can also select as well as delete the data. This leaves at least one hole in the security framework. To protect the trails in this case, the OS audit destination may be used. A person other than the DBA, typically the security auditor, would protect the destination directory.

The other aspect of securing the trail is to audit the access of the *aud$* table.

```
AUDIT AUD$;
```

This will enable the audit trail for any action on the table *aud$*, which can then be checked later.

# Preserving the Audit Trail

## The Need

To enforce accountability, the audit information is a valuable tool. It throws light on past actions by the user. However, as we saw earlier, this information grows fast in the database because it is a direct result of, and proportional to, the degree of activity in the database. Being inside the SYSTEM tablespace, the *aud$* table contributes significantly to the increased space usage by that tablespace, often running out of room on the filesystem.

This is an interesting challenge. This table is the only table owned by SYS that grows proportionately to the user activity, not necessarily due to data growth. In fact, in a heavily accessed database, this table grows even if the user data size remains constant. If the table can't grow extents, all database activities that are being audited abort with errors. This is the reason the table should be purged periodically. This is the only SYS-owned table against which actions like DELETE and TRUNCATE are allowed.

Before purging the data from this table, an important point must be brought up – audit records are valuable. Even if they have been summarized in some report, it may still be worth keeping the old data intact in the raw form, as the reports may not have extracted every bit of useful information. In the future, this seemingly unimportant information may provide clues to some investigation into malicious activities. Simply archiving the generated reports off to an archival medium like a tape satisfies HIPAA requirements. Although HIPAA does not recommend specifically keeping the raw audit log, it is prudent to archive the raw data, as a substitute or as a complement to the reports, for the following reasons:

- Raw audit logs are smaller in size compared to reports, and therefore cheaper to store.
- Raw audit logs contain all data; nothing is left out, which might be the case in reports.
- Raw audit logs can be used to format reports in any manner required for the investigation. The reports are pretty rigid.
- Raw audit logs can be put into the database as a copy of the *aud$* table, which could then be UNIONed to produce a single coherent report using the scripts already in place. No new scripts will be required.
- Raw audit logs will be exactly that – raw, not cooked. This may add a significant touch of security the auditors crave.

Therefore, it is vital to archive off the *aud$* table in such a way that it can be reinstated later and with no loss of accuracy. We will cover that in this next section.

## New Tablespace and Owner

To prevent overgrowth of the SYSTEM tablespace it seems logical to move the offending object, the table *aud$*, to another tablespace. Since this is the only table that grows by leaps and bounds, and this is the only one that is purged and re-filled, this decision may seem sound.

A word of caution may be in order here. In recent years, Oracle Support has categorically warned against moving this table out of the SYSTEM tablespace. They cite the reason that the Oracle software code makes implicit assumptions about the existence of the table in the SYSTEM tablespace and therefore some tasks, such as recovery, may be affected. However, in our testing and experience, we have not encountered a problem by moving the table out of the SYSTEM tablespace or moving it to a schema other than SYS. While we recommend this approach, you might want to consider the warning from Oracle.

### Steps

1. **Create a New Tablespace**. First, identify the new tablespace where the *aud$* table will go. It is vital to have a separate and exclusive tablespace so the database will be minimally affected if a relocation error is encountered. The tablespace should not be named AUDIT since this is a reserved word. You could use the name AUDIT enclosed by double quotes, e.g. "AUDIT" to get around this limitation, but that may cause confusion later. It is perhaps best to create a tablespace named AUDIT_DATA, or something similar.
2. **Create Index Tablespace**. The *aud$* table has an index named I_AUD1 which also resides in the SYSTEM tablespace. This index must also be moved. Creating an entirely new tablespace is not necessary. The index can be relocated to the same tablespace that the *aud$* table is in, i.e. AUDIT_DATA. However, for administrative reasons, it is a good idea to keep them separate.
3. **Decide on the Schema**. The next task is to decide on the schema. This being a very special table, a special user, such as SYS or SYSTEM, could own it. However, as a normal database practice, avoid manipulating objects owned by SYS and SYSTEM. Therefore the user should be different. Try something like AUDITOR.
4. **Stop Database Activity.** When the table is moved, it is important to stop all activity. The reason being that the actions may be written to the *aud$* table, and

the move process would make the call fail. The database should be stopped and restarted in restricted mode.

5. **Create Temp Table**. As user SYS, create the table *aud_temp* from the original table as shown in the following query. While doing this, it may also be prudent to increase the storage parameters. However, since we have already created the tablespace as Locally Managed with Automatic Allocation of Segments, this action (the changes in storage) is not required for databases created with 9i and above.

```
create table auditor.aud_temp
tablespace audit_data
as
select * from aud$
/
```

6. **Rename**. As user AUDITOR, rename the table to the appropriate value using the following statement:

```
rename aud_temp to aud$
/
```

7. **Create the Index**. As user AUDITOR, create the index on the table.

```
create index i_aud1
on aud$ (sessionid, ses$tid)
tablespace audit_indx
/
```

Again, the storage clause is not required if the ASSM mode and LMT are selected in the tablespace AUDIT_INDX.

8. **Open the database**. Remove the database from RESTRICTED mode.

Now the table *aud$* will be under the AUDITOR schema and will be in tablespace AUDIT_DATA. The index will be in AUDIT_INDX. The growth can be handled easily in this set up and it will be easier to archive and purge data from this table.

## Archival

The next issue is how to handle storage of the data from this audit trail. Remember from the beginning discussions in this section that it is preferable to archive the raw tables used to store audit trails. This can be backed up even if the *aud$* table is in the tablespace SYSTEM and is owned by SYS.

First, determine what will be the archival frequency. For a heavily used database, it may make sense to archive every month, during a monthly maintenance timeslot. After the archival the audit table starts with a clean slate. In a relatively less used database, the frequency could be less, e.g. every six months.

Next determine the location of these audit tables. For our example purpose, we may decide to create a tablespace called AUDIT_ARCH_DATA, locally managed with uniform extents. A similar table *audit_arch_indx* may be created for the index on the archived *aud$* table, if desired.

Find a suitable time to stop the database and shut it down.

Make changes to the initialization file to disable auditing (specifying *audit_trail* = none) and start the database in restricted mode.

Create the replica of the table in the archival tablespace, e.g. if a monthly cycle is followed, use a name such as AUD_0307 for data related to July 2003. The table can be created using the following script:

```
create table aud_0307
tablespace aud_arch_data
nologging
as
select * from aud$
/
```

This will create a table with minimal logging in the desired tablespace.

Next, truncate the original table *aud$*.

```
truncate table aud$;
```

The truncation of table *aud$* is supported. It is the only SYS owned object that can be manipulated by the user. Truncation will reset the high water mark of the table.

Shutdown the database, change the initialization file to reflect *audit_trail* = db and then restart.

The tablespace AUD_ARCH_DATA can be made read-only now and be backed up only once.

```
alter table audit_arch_data read only
/
```

Since it is read-only, there is no need to make subsequent backups.

It may not be necessary to keep this database online. It is conceivable that this table can be exported and the export file preserved.

## Preservation in Archival Media

It may be necessary to protect the material in archival media for quick retrieval. The exported file can be imported back for query if needed. However, import takes time and is not very convenient, particularly with the massive amount of redo log activity. Since the *aud$* table does not have any columns of the LONG data type, it can be exported as a flat file and then loaded back when necessary using SQL*Loader direct load option, or using Oracle 9i's External Table option.

## Online Access

If it is necessary to provide online access to the archived *aud$* table, a different archival strategy should be considered. One way of achieving this is by creating the archived table in a separate tablespace. This tablespace may be placed in a filesystem made of inexpensive hardware, such as Serial ATA, or even Write Once Read Many (WORM) drives such as optical jukeboxes. The Serial ATA devices offer the least dollar per megabyte of storage at respectable access speeds. These devices are being used right now for archiving the log directory and the same concept can be extended to the *aud$* table archival too. Since access to the archived table is limited to SELECTs, and perhaps an occasional TRUNCATE by the DBA, Serial ATA devices provide an adequate solution.

# A Complete System

Next, we will devise a system that will provide all the features we want, at a cost that can be justified. This procedure will also create a HIPAA compliant archival model for the *aud$* table.

## Requirements

- The auditing data needs to be archived and purged off every month. This frequency is based on the load on the system and one month seems to be optimal.
- Ideally, three months worth of audit data should be available. Therefore, every month, the oldest month should be archived and purged. For instance, on July 31st, the data for April should be archived and purged off. Data for May, June and July should be in *aud$* table.
- There will be a small period of inactivity.
- The redo and undo generation should be minimal.

- The archived data should be available for query on request. A small amount of time can be allowed between the request and the expectation for delivery of the data.
- Existing reports based on the data dictionary views such as *dba_audit_session* are already built. The report should not have to be modified to query the archived data.

## Design

These requirements seem reasonable for a security and accountability conscious database implementation. Next, we will see how to set this up.

1. First we will decide on a naming convention for the tablespaces and tables. Since the purge and archival routine has to run every month, we will name tables with the month and year, e.g. AUD<*yy*><*mm*>, where <*yy*> is the two-digit year and <*mm*> is the two-digit month when the data is being archived. The routine run at the end of September 2003 will archive the data from June 2003 and therefore create a table named AUD0306 in tablespace AUD0306.
2. Every month we create a new tablespace, which should be placed in a low throughput and low cost filesystem, say /u200.
3. Next, we will create a table to hold the data from the table *aud$* for the entire month 3 months ago, e.g. of June, if this is run in September. The table is created in NOLOGGING mode to regenerate minimal redo and undo. In this example this table is named AUD0306.
4. Then the data in the archived table should be deleted from the main *aud$* table. A simple DELETE AUD$ will do; but there are two problems:
   - A regular delete generates a lot of redo and undo activity.
   - A regular delete also does not reset the high water mark, so the table is fragmented.

   Therefore, as an alternative, we will create a separate temporary table named *aud_temp* on the same tablespace as the *aud$* table. This table holds the records that are not present in the archived table AUD0306.
5. After this table is created, the original *aud$* table is dropped.
6. The table *aud_temp* is then renamed to the main table *aud$*. The index on it, I_AUD1, is rebuilt.
7. The tablespace AUD0306 is converted to READ ONLY.

8. This tablespace is now *transported* to a separate medium such as a WORM device, which could be as simple as a Writable CD-ROM. The datafiles of the tablespace and the small export dump file are written to the WORM device.

9. The tablespace is then dropped.

These steps have been implemented in the code below. The code has been deliberatively broken into three parts since only the successful execution of the prior part should pave the way for the next part. If an error occurs during any part, it should be stopped.

### archive_audit_1.sh

```
# ---------------------------------------------------
# Filename    : archive_audit_1.sh
# Description : First part of the AUD$ archival and purge
#               process.
# Parameters  : 1. 2-digit Year of the archival process
#               2. 2-digit Month of the process
# Important:
#    Change the variables AUDIT_TS_NAME and
#    ARC_FILE_SYSTEM, SYS_PASSWORD to suit to your site.
# ---------------------------------------------------
#
# Site dependent variables
AUDIT_TS_NAME=SYSTEM
ARC_FILE_SYSTEM=/u201
SYS_PASSWORD=manager
#
ARC_YEAR=$1
ARC_MONTH=$2
ARC_TS_NAME=AUD$ARC_YEAR$ARC_MONTH
ARC_TABLE_NAME=AUD$ARC_YEAR$ARC_MONTH
#
sqlplus /nolog << EOF1
whenever sqlerror exit
connect sys/$SYS_PASSWORD as sysdba
create tablespace $ARC_TS_NAME
datafile '$ARC_FILE_SYSTEM/${ARC_TS_NAME}_01.dbf'
size 10M
autoextend on next 10M
extent management local
uniform size 256K
/
REM
prompt AudArch: Created Tablespace $ARC_TS_NAME
create table $ARC_TABLE_NAME
tablespace $ARC_TS_NAME
nologging
as
select * from AUD$
where timestamp# between
      to_date('$ARC_YEAR$ARC_MONTH','RRMM')
```

```
    to_date('$ARC_YEAR$ARC_MONTH','RRMM'),1)
/
prompt AudArch: Created Table $ARC_TABLE_NAME
create table AUD_TEMP
tablespace $AUDIT_TS_NAME
nologging
as
select * from AUD$
where timestamp# >
  add_months(
     to_date('$ARC_YEAR$ARC_MONTH','RRMM'),1)
/
prompt AudArch: Created Temporary AUD$ table
EOF1
#
Echo Only if all the steps were successful,
Echo execute the second part archive_audit_2.sh
#
```

After completion of this part examine the log file and see if all the steps were successfully executed. Only after you have verified that the first part executed successfully should you move on to the next part, *archive_audit_2.sh*.

## archive_audit_2.sh

```
# ---------------------------------------------------
# Filename    : archive_audit_2.sh
# Description : Second part of the AUD$ archival and
#               purge process.
# Parameters  : 1. 2-digit Year of the archival process
#               2. 2-digit Month of the process
# Assumption  : A file .sys_passwd in this directory
#               containing the password of SYS.
# Important:
#    Change the variables AUDIT_TS_NAME, AUDIT_INDEX_TS
#    and ARC_FILE_SYSTEM, SYS_PASSWORD to suit to
#    your site.
# ---------------------------------------------------
#
# Site dependent variables
AUDIT_TS_NAME=SYSTEM
AUDIT_INDEX_TS=SYSTEM
ARC_FILE_SYSTEM=/u200
SYS_PASSWORD=manager
#
ARC_YEAR=$1
ARC_MONTH=$2
ARC_TS_NAME=AUD$ARC_YEAR$ARC_MONTH
ARC_TABLE_NAME=AUD$ARC_YEAR$ARC_MONTH
#
sqlplus /nolog << EOF1
```

```
drop table AUD$
/
prompt AudArch: Dropped Table AUD$
REM
rename AUD_TEMP to AUD$
/
prompt AudArch: Renamed Table AUD_TEMP to AUD$
REM
create index i_aud1
on aud$ (sessionid, ses$tid)
tablespace $AUDIT_INDEX_TS
nologging
/
prompt AudArch: Created Index I_AUD1
REM
alter tablespace $ARC_TS_NAME readonly
/
prompt AudArch: Tablespace $ARC_TS_NAME made Read Only
EOF1
#
# Export the tablespace as transportable
# Note the password of SYS is passed from a file. This
# eliminates the chance of the password being visible
# by a ps -aef command
#
exp transport_tablespace=Y tablespaces=\($ARC_TS_NAME\)
file=$ARC_FILE_SYSTEM/tts_${ARC_TS_NAME}.dmp < .sys_passwd
#
echo AudArch: Exported Tablesapce as Transportable
echo Files $ARC_FILE_SYSTEM/tts_${ARC_TS_NAME}.dmp and
$ARC_FILE_SYSTEM/${ARCH_TS_NAME}_01.dbf should be put together and form a
set.
echo Only after this part is over successfully, run the
echo Part 3 of the process.
#
```

At this stage the tablespace can be dropped.

## archive_audit_3.sh

```
# ---------------------------------------------------
# Filename    : archive_audit_3.sh
# Description : Third part of the AUD$ archival and
#               purge process.
# Parameters  : 1. 2-digit Year of the archival process
#               2. 2-digit Month of the process
# Assumption  : A file .sys_passwd in this directory
#               containing the password of SYS.
# Important:
#    Change the variable SYS_PASSWORD to suit to
#    your site.
# ---------------------------------------------------
```

```
SYS_PASSWORD=manager
#
ARC_YEAR=$1
ARC_MONTH=$2
ARC_TS_NAME=AUD$ARC_YEAR$ARC_MONTH
sqlplus /nolog << EOF1
whenever sqlerror exit
connect sys/$SYS_PASSWD as sysdba
drop tablespace $ARC_TS_NAME
including contents
and datafiles /* Only in 9i */
/
prompt AudArch: Dropped Tablespace $ARC_TS_NAME
EOF1
```

## Retrieval

When the archived data needs to be retrieved, this process makes it very easy. Since the data was initially exported as transportable, all that needs to be done while importing is to mount the WORM device (or the filesystem containing the archived tablespace) and plug the tablespace into the database using import. Since the tablespace has been named after the year and the month, they will be always unique.

After the tablespace is imported, the table AUD0309, say, will be available. A view named *aud$_combined* may be created using:

```
create view aud$combined
as
select * from aud$
union all
select * from aud0309
/
```

A public synonym *aud$* can then be created for this new view:

```
create public synonym aud$ for sys.aud$_combined
/
```

Now all the reports developed against the data dictionary views will pick up data from this table as well.

# Application Users and Auditing

So far we have discussed auditing user actions assuming that the user connected to the database is an actual user. In some applications, particularly third party applications, the users are authenticated by the application that then connects to the database as a generic user. For instance an application user may be called CLARA, and the application can authenticate her in a variety of ways – against a table containing the user names and their passwords or using domain authentication as in a Windows environment. After authentication the application connects to the database as a generic user, e.g. APPUSER. As far as the application is concerned, the user is CLARA. For the database, the user is APPUSER. Therefore all auditing records show the user as APPUSER, not CLARA, and all audit trails will be recorded as being done by APPUSER. This completely defeats the purpose of auditing and accountability.

The best option is to have separate user accounts and have them authenticated by the database. However, that is not a choice many DBAs have when they inherit applications written long ago.

Another option is to have Oracle Single Sign-On Option (SSO) where a secured application model authenticates the application user once and his identity is passed from tier to tier. This is perhaps the best practical option overall and Oracle is investing heavily in the identity management process – an area that is supposed to mushroom into big business in the next few years. However, the biggest obstacle to this is the infrastructure requirement and complexity it brings to the table. This setup requires Oracle Advance Networking Option (ANO, also known as Advanced Security Option) and may need Oracle Application Server as a middle tier. The ANO is a must have requirement and with it being an add-on option with the increased complexity of operating it, proves it to be quite a challenge.

So, we are left with the task of unearthing a middle ground to identify those application users without using the complicated and expensive ANO. In Chapter 5, we explained a detailed model of securely managing application users using a combination of application authentication functions, roles authenticated by procedures, and application contexts. Please revisit that Chapter for a refresher. Next we will cover how to extend the functionality of auditing.

## Client Identifier

In a previous chapter, we introduced the concept of Client Identifiers, which appeared in Oracle 9i. A user can set the value of a predefined application context attribute called *client_identifier* as shown below.

```
exec dbms_session.set_identifier ('ARUP');
```

This sets an application context attribute named *client_identifier* to the value 'ARUP'. This is unique to a session and stays in the memory attached to that session as long as the session is active. This has nothing to do with any other attribute of the session –

the username, the client IP address, the terminal, or any other details. The same user from another session can set another value of *client_identifier* to identify the session.

The session can check what the current value of the *client_identifier* is by issuing:

```
select sys_context('USERENV','CLIENT_IDENTIFIER')
from dual
/
```

The result comes back as:

```
SYS_CONTEXT('USERENV','CLIENT_IDENTIFIER')
--------------------------------------------
ARUP
```

From another session, if we query the data dictionary view *v$session* for this session, we can see the *client_identifier* of that session as following:

```
select client_identifier
from v$session
where sid  = <the SID of the session>
/
```

We get:

```
CLIENT_IDENTIFIER
-----------------------------------------------
ARUP
```

The usefulness of *client_identifier* does not stop here. Its importance extends into auditing as well. In the *aud$* table, there is a column labeled CLIENTID, which stores this context attribute. In order to understand how it works, let's see an example.

First, we enable auditing on SELECT on table CLAIMS using the following query:

```
audit select on claim_schema.claims by access;
```

Then connecting as user APPUSER, we will select from the table CLAIMS.

```
select * from claim_schema.claims;
```

The result of the query is not shown here, as it's not relevant. This action has caused auditing to be triggered. We will see the auditing information from the trail generated.

```
select client_id
from dba_audit_object
where username = 'APPUSER'
and OBJ_NAME = 'CLAIMS'
```

```
/

CLIENT_ID
------------------
```

The CLIENT_ID column came back as *NULL*, because by default nothing was set in the client identifier. Next, we will issue the same query, but we will set the client identifier as follows:

```
SQL> connect appuser/*****
SQL> exec dbms_Session.set_identifier ('ARUP')

PL/SQL procedure successfully completed.

SQL> select * from claim_schema.claims;
```

When we query the audit trail, we find:

```
select client_id
from dba_audit_object
where username = 'APPUSER'
and OBJ_NAME = 'CLAIMS'
/

CLIENT_ID
--------------------------
ARUP
```

The audit trail captured the client identifier application context. If the user APPUSER logs in from two different places and sets the client identifier unique to each session, the actions go into the audit trail along with the client identifiers.

This concept can be applied in the application user concept. The client identifier can be set to some meaningful value such as the application user. So, if the application user CLARA issues the select query, the client identifier can be set to CLARA, which then goes into the audit trail. At the beginning of every session, the application must call

```
begin
   dbms_session.set_identifier (p_app_user);
end;
```

The application knows the name of the user; so it can assign the value of *p_user_id* variable. After that, every time the audit trail is generated, the client identifier CLARA also tags along.

## Security

So far, it has been simple; but here comes a monkey wrench into the wheel. The whole mechanism is based on two very important assumptions:

- That the user will call the line *dbms_session.set_identifier* as the first task in a session.
- That the user will supply the *correct* name of the application user to the packaged procedure.

These two assumptions are fundamental to the tracking of application users; but unfortunately, these assumptions are easily circumvented. The user may not call the procedure to set the client identifier, either deliberately or inadvertently. Nothing will then go into the CLEINTID column of the *aud$* table, nor will it cause an error. The application will continue to run fine without the vital auditing information. Because of this, the omission may not be even detected.

Similarly the user may not supply the correct value for the application user id. The human user Clara can login as APPUSER and then issue *dbms_session.set_identifier* ('JOE'). This will record all the auditing information as being done by *Joe*, not Clara.

Therefore the above setup in its present form is not adequate. We need some extensive work to make it more secure.

Making the application call the procedures directly can solve the problem. After the application authenticates the user using some mechanism such as Domain Authentication, the username is known. After it connects to the database, the application can execute the procedure *dbms_session.set_identifier* with the proper username. The user has no chance of entering anything in there.

However, what if the user connects to the database outside the application, e.g. using SQL*Plus or some other tools like TOAD? Then the *client_identifier* is not set.

This is where the elaborate application user management functionality described in Chapter 5 comes handy. Instead of repeating those steps here, we will just highlight the important points. All the procedures and functions mentioned here are described in Chapter 5 and are available from the online code depot.

- All the privileges are granted to several roles corresponding to several types of users. All these roles are authenticated by procedures.
- The user APPUSER is granted all these roles, but *none* as default. So when a user logins in APPUSER, none of the roles are enabled, meaning the user can't do anything at that point.

- After the user logs in as *APPUSER*, he has to execute a special function called *is_password_correct* which accepts two parameters – the *application* userid and the password, and returns YES, if correct and NO, otherwise.
- Inside this function, all the roles allocated to that application user are enabled by the *set_role* procedure.
- The user APPUSER is not given execute privileges on the package *dbms_session*. This will prevent the user from calling the procedure *set_identifier* directly.
- The *is_password_correct* function also sets the client identifier.
- Since the user APPUSER must know the application user's password, the chance that someone else would logs in as APPUSER and make changes is eliminated.
- Also, since the client identifier is set automatically and the user can't set it specifically, the authenticity of the client identifier is also maintained.

As you can see, client identifiers provide the missing link between the actual user and the database. This functionality can be extended not just to an application user management, but to auditing as well.

# Other Types of Audit

You might have noticed the central theme of the auditing actions mentioned in the previous sections is auditing access to the object. However, creating a trail of activity is not just about accessing the specific objects; but other things as well – such as data. The Oracle tool AUDIT can't capture changes to the data inside objects like tables.

Similarly, if the source code of a procedural object like a function or procedure is changed, the audit command captures the fact that it was changed, but not what was changed. Typically, the changes to data find their way into the redo logs and then to the archived logs, which can be mined later to identify the changes. The changes can also be captured at the source through triggers. All these options that are beyond the capabilities of the regular audit command have been discussed in subsequent chapters in this book.

Another part of the problem in auditing is when the user only selects, not changes, the data. This does not cause any triggers to fire and this information does not go into the redo log files, and therefore can't be mined later. Unfortunately, prior to Oracle 9i, it was not possible to capture the user's select statements. In some cases, this may not seem important, but in a scenario where you are dealing with data containing PHI, auditing is mandated by HIPAA. Oracle 9i introduced a new feature called *Fine Grained Auditing* (FGA) that allows not merely recording of select statements, but even records selectively based on user defined filtering criteria. In Chapter 11, we will discuss details the FGA and how to use it in complicated situations such as the application user management area.

## Conclusion

In this chapter we explored the Oracle standard auditing techniques and how they can be used to implement a variety of mandated accountability requirements. The majority of the requirements of HIPAA can be fulfilled by these out-of-the-box audit features and should be implemented without haste. Standard auditing does affect performance, but doing it selectively on specific columns, such as those containing PHI information, might not affect the performance as bad as expected and can be tolerable. The most important aspect of auditing is not to collect, but to analyze periodically to assess threats and attempted break-ins.

# Oracle System Event Trigger Auditing

CHAPTER

## Introduction

Some of the most exciting new features within Oracle are the new system-level triggers that were introduced in Oracle8i. What is truly exciting is that we can combine the system-level triggers with STATSPACK extension tables, thereby building a mechanism that will give complete auditing information on user logon and logoff, DDL, and server errors.

Just as an Oracle trigger fires on a specific DM event, system-level triggers are fired at specific system events such as logon, logoff, database startup, DDL execution, and servererror triggers:

- **Database startup triggers** - Database startup triggers can be used to invoke the *dbms_shared_pool.keep* procedure to pin all frequently referenced PL/SQL packages into RAM.
- **Logon triggers** - The logon triggers can be used to store login information directly inside Oracle tables, thereby providing a complete audit of when users enter your system.
- **Logoff triggers** -- Oracle logoff triggers can automatically capture elapsed session duration times for all users who have accessed your Oracle database.
- **Servererror triggers** -- With the servererror trigger, the Oracle administrator can automatically log all serious PL/SQL errors into an Oracle STATSPACK extension table. This table, in turn, has an insert trigger that e-mails the server error to the DBA for immediate notification.
- **DDL triggers** -- Using the DDL trigger, the Oracle DBA can automatically track all changes to the database including changes to tables, indexes, and constraints. The data from this trigger is especially useful for change control and auditing changes to the production environment. This is especially important for Oracle databases that are "certified" by government agencies.

While Oracle provided the functionality for these new triggers, it was not clear how they could be used in order to track system-wide usage. This chapter describes our work in creating end-user log in/log off procedures to facilitate tracing end-user activity. Please be advised that the initial implementation of system level triggers for end-user tracking is quite new, and as such is still a bit lacking in robust functionality.

While the user log on/log off triggers will accurately tell you the time of the user log on and user log off, the code does not capture any information regarding the specific tasks that were performed during the user's session. Also note that these user log on and log off triggers are best used for those types of applications that utilize time stamped users. By time stamped users, we mean those users who are given a unique Oracle user ID when they access the application. Applications that do not utilize the time stamped Oracle user IDs (SAP, PeopleSoft) may not benefit greatly by using these log on and log off triggers.

Now let's take a closer look at how these triggers work with Oracle tables.

# Database Startup Event Triggers

Package pinning has become a very important part of Oracle tuning. With the introduction of system-level triggers in Oracle8i, we now have an easy tool to ensure that frequently executed PL/SQL remains cached inside the shared pool.

Just like using the KEEP pool with the data buffer caches, pinning packages ensures that the specified package always remains in the *Most Recently Used* (MRU) end of the data buffer. This prevents the PL/SQL from being paged-out and re-parsed on reload. The Oracle DBA controls the size of this RAM region by setting the *shared_pool_size* parameter to a value large enough to hold all the PL/SQL.

Pinning of packages involves two areas:

- **Pinning frequently executed packages** -- Oracle performance can be greatly enhanced by pinning frequently executed packages inside the SGA.
- **Pinning the standard Oracle packages** -- These are shown in the code listing below, and should always be pinned to prevent re-parsing by the Oracle SGA.

You can interrogate the *v$db_object_cache* view to see the most frequently used packages, and automatically pin them at database startup time (with an ON DATABASE STARTUP trigger) using *dbms_shared_pool.keep*.

**pin_packs.sql**

```
create or replace trigger
   pin_packs
     after startup on database
begin
   -- Application-specific packages
   dbms_shared_pool.keep('MAIN_PACK');
   dbms_shared_pool.keep('OTHER_PACK');
   -- Oracle-supplied software packages
   dbms_shared_pool.keep('DBMS_ALERT');
   dbms_shared_pool.keep('DBMS_DDL');
   dbms_shared_pool.keep('DBMS_DESCRIBE');
   dbms_shared_pool.keep('DBMS_LOCK');
   dbms_shared_pool.keep('DBMS_OUTPUT');
   dbms_shared_pool.keep('DBMS_PIPE');
   dbms_shared_pool.keep('DBMS_SESSION');
   dbms_shared_pool.keep('DBMS_STANDARD');
   dbms_shared_pool.keep('DBMS_UTILITY');
   dbms_shared_pool.keep('STANDARD');
```

# Extending STATSPACK Tables for System Events

Because the Oracle system-level triggers can interface with Oracle tables, the logical approach is to create Oracle tables to hold the data. The logical place for this data is inside the STATSPACK tablespace that is owned by the PERFSTAT user. Extending Oracle STATSPACK adds additional information to STATSPACK and enhances existing metrics such as cumulative logins in the *stats$sysstat* table.

- **DDL table** -- The code shown below creates an Oracle table to capture all the salient metrics required to do effective change management within an Oracle environment. Note that this table contains the date that the DDL was made, the ID of the user who originated the DDL change, the type of the object, and the object's name. This information can be quite useful for tracking purposes.

**cr_ddl_tab.sql**

```
connect sys/manager as sysdba

drop table perfstat.stats$ddl_log;


create table
   perfstat.stats$ddl_log
(
   user_name          varchar2(30),
```

```
   object_type      varchar2(18),
   owner            varchar2(30),
   object_name      varchar2(128)
)
tablespace perfstat
```

- **servererror table** -- The code below creates an Oracle table that will capture all information related to PL/SQL errors:

### cr_err_tab.sql

```
connect sys/manager as sysdba

drop table perfstat.stats$servererror_log;

create table
   perfstat.stats$servererror_log
(
   error     varchar2(30),
   timestamp date,
   username  varchar2(30),
   osuser    varchar2(30),
   machine   varchar2(64),
   process   varchar2(8),
   program   varchar2(48)
)
tablespace perfstat
;
```

- **login and logoff table** -- We have created a table called *stats$user_log* that can be used to trace both login and logoff events. Notice that this table contains the Oracle user ID, the name of the host server where the connection originated, the last program that was executed by the Oracle user, as well as their login and logoff times. Also, notice a special derived column called ELAPSED_MINUTES that is essentially the time difference (expressed in minutes) between the login time and logoff time.

### cr_user_tab.sql

```
connect sys/manager as sysdba

drop table perfstat.stats$user_log;

create table
   stats_user_log
(
```

```
   host              varchar2(30),
   last_program      varchar2(48),
   last_action       varchar2(32),
   last_module       varchar2(32),
   logon_day         date,
   logon_time        varchar2(10),
   logoff_day        date,
   logoff_time       varchar2(10),
   elapsed_minutes   number(8)
)
tablespace perfstat
```

## Inside the Trigger Definition Scripts

Once we've created the Oracle tables to support the system-level triggers, the next step is to actually write two triggers to add the data to the Oracle STATSPACK extension tables. By storing system event data in Oracle tables, we have the ability to track user behavior over time and audit and monitor important usage trends. Let's examine some working triggers to see how they function:

- **DDL Trigger** -- The DDL trigger executes every time a DDL statement is executed and adds new entries to the *stats$ddl_log* table.

### ddl_trig.sql

```
connect sys/manager as sysdba

create or replace trigger
   DDLTrigger
AFTER DDL ON DATABASE
BEGIN
insert into
   perfstat.stats$ddl_log
(
   user_name,
   ddl_date,
   ddl_type,
   object_type,
   owner,
   object_name
)
VALUES
(
   ora_login_user,
   sysdate,
   ora_sysevent,
   ora_dict_obj_type,
   ora_dict_obj_owner,
   ora_dict_obj_name
);
```

- **Servererror trigger** -- The servererror trigger takes the server error that was generated from Oracle PL/SQL and places it into an Oracle table. Note that by capturing the user ID and the time of the error, the Oracle administrator can build an insert trigger on the stats$ or server error log table and immediately be notified via e-mail when a server error occurs.

### error_trig.sql

```
connect sys/manager

create or replace trigger
   log_errors_trig
after servererror on database
declare
   var_user       varchar2(30);
   var_osuser     varchar2(30);
   var_machine    varchar2(64);
   var_process    varchar2(8);
   var_program    varchar2(48);
begin
   select
      username,
      osuser,
      machine,
      process,
      program
   into
      var_user,
      var_osuser,
      var_machine,
      var_process,
      var_program
   from
      v$session
   where
      sys_context('USERENV','SESSIONID')


   insert into
      perfstat.stats$servererror_log
   values(
      dbms_standard.server_error(1),
      sysdate,
      var_user,
      var_osuser,
      var_machine,
      var_process,
      var_program);
end;
```

- **Logon trigger** -- Next, we need to take look at the login trigger. The code listing below inserts into a table called *stats_user_log*. Inside the logon trigger, notice that only selected columns of the table are populated. At login time the user ID of the person who logs in and the time when they log into the system are populated. The logoff trigger is used to fill in all the additional columns, including the all-important ELAPSED_MINUTES column.

### logon_trig.sql

```
create or replace trigger
   logon_audit_trigger
AFTER LOGON ON DATABASE
BEGIN
insert into stats_user_log values(
   user,
   sys_context('USERENV','SESSIONID'),
   sys_context('USERENV','HOST'),
   null,
   null,
   null,
   sysdate,
   to_char(sysdate, 'hh24:mi:ss'),
   null,
   null,
   null
);
COMMIT;
END;
```

- **Logoff trigger** -- Using the logoff trigger functionality, we obtain information about the time the end user logged off of the system, the last program they were executing, the host they were on, as well as the elapsed time. The code listing below shows how to implement this using an Oracle trigger:

### logoff_trig.sql

```
create or replace trigger
   logoff_audit_trigger
BEFORE LOGOFF ON DATABASE
BEGIN
-- ***************************************************
-- Update the last action accessed
-- ***************************************************
update
stats_user_log
set
last_action = (select action from v$session where
sys_context('USERENV','SESSIONID') = audsid)
where
```

```
-- Update the last program accessed
-- *************************************************
update
stats_user_log
set
last_program = (select program from v$session where
sys_context('USERENV','SESSIONID') = audsid)
where
sys_context('USERENV','SESSIONID') = session_id;
-- *************************************************
-- Update the last module accessed
-- *************************************************
update
stats_user_log
set
last_module = (select module from v$session where
sys_context('USERENV','SESSIONID') = audsid)
where
sys_context('USERENV','SESSIONID') = session_id;
-- *************************************************
-- Update the logoff day
-- *************************************************
update
   stats_user_log
set
   logoff_day = sysdate
where
   sys_context('USERENV','SESSIONID') = session_id;
-- *************************************************
-- Update the logoff time
-- *************************************************
update
   stats_user_log
set
   logoff_time = to_char(sysdate, 'hh24:mi:ss')
where
   sys_context('USERENV','SESSIONID') = session_id;
-- *************************************************
-- Compute the elapsed minutes
-- *************************************************
update
stats_user_log
set
elapsed_minutes =
round((logoff_day - logon_day)*1440)
where
sys_context('USERENV','SESSIONID') = session_id;
COMMIT;
END;
```

Now that we have seen the scripts, let's take a look at how we can get great reports on the behavior of Oracle system events.

# Putting It All Together

With the information captured in the Oracle tables and the system level triggers, we can now add great reports that show the behaviors within our Oracle database. The Oracle administrator is very interested in information that relates to end-user activity. The DBA also wants to be able to track all the significant DDL, server errors, and user login information.

## Servererror Reports

Servererror reports are especially useful for auditing the behavior of PL/SQL in your production environment. Any time an error occurs, the servererror trigger will log the error to a table from which you can create summary reports of all Oracle server errors.

### error_rpt.sql

```
set pages 999;

set lines 80;

alter session set nls_date_format='YY-MM-DD hh24:mi';


break on myday skip 2

-- ***********************************************
-- Servererror report
-- ***********************************************
column   myday       heading 'Date      Hr'   format a13
column   mmessage    heading 'Error|Message'  format a50
column   error_count heading 'Error|Count'    format 999,999

ttitle 'Production Server Error Report|Rollup of errors my day'

select
   to_char(timestamp,'YY-MM-DD')        myday,
   substr(msg,1,50)                     message,
   count(*)                             error_count
from
   perfstat.stats$error_log
group by
   to_char(timestamp,'YY-MM-DD'),
   msg
having
   count(*) > 0
order by
     myday           asc,
```

```
ttitle 'Production Server Error Report|Rollup of errors my day and hour'

select
   to_char(timestamp,'YY-MM-DD HH24') myday,
   substr(msg,1,50)                   message,
   count(*)                           error_count
from
   perfstat.stats$error_log
group by
   to_char(timestamp,'YY-MM-DD HH24'),
   msg
having
   count(*) > 0
order by
     myday          asc,
     error_count    desc
```

Here is a sample of the output:

```
Sat Mar 09                                                      page    1
                         Production Server Error Report
                            Rollup of errors my day

          Error
Date   Hr MESSAGE                                                   Count
----- -- -------------------------------------------------- -------
03-08     ORA-02289: sequence does not exist                        2,421
          ORA-01001: invalid cursor                                   480
          ORA-00054: resource busy and acquire with NOWAIT s          114
          ORA-00942: table or view does not exist                      39
          ORA-00942: table or view does not exist                      10
          ORA-01017: invalid username/password; logon denied            2
          ORA-00920: invalid relational operator                        1
          ORA-01445: cannot select ROWID from a join view wi            1


03-09     ORA-01001: invalid cursor                                    25
          ORA-02289: sequence does not exist                           12
          ORA-00942: table or view does not exist                      11
          ORA-00054: resource busy and acquire with NOWAIT s           10
          ORA-01017: invalid username/password; logon denied            2
```

This report shows daily details, but we can also create a weekly rollup of server errors:

```
Mon Jul 22                                              page    1
                 Production Database Changes
                     Summary DDL Report

                                Changed          Number of
DDL_D USER_NAME                 Object           Production
                                                 Changes
----- -------------------- --------------- ----------
07-21 MWCEDI                    PACKAGE                   6
      MWCEDI                    PACKAGE BODY              6
*****                                            ----------
sum                                                      12
```

```
07-17 MWCEDI              PACKAGE                  3
      MWCEDI              PACKAGE BODY             3
*****                                     ----------
sum                                                6


07-16 EUL_MWC             VIEW                     2
*****                                     ----------
sum                                                2


07-15 MWCEDI              PACKAGE                  5
      MWCEDI              PACKAGE BODY             5
      APPS                VIEW                     1
      MWCEDI              PROCEDURE                1
*****                                     -----------
sum                                               12
```

## Oracle Logon Report

We can use the logon and logoff trigger to store information in *stats$user_log* and write SQL to get detailed reports on average visit length, number of logons per hour, and many other useful statistics.

### user_sum_rpt.sql

```
set pages 999;
set lines 80;

alter session set nls_date_format='YY-MM-DD hh24:mi';

column USER_ID            Heading 'User'            format a10
column AVERAGE_MINUTES    Heading 'Average|Minutes' format 9,999

-- *********************************************************
--  Average duration of visit report
-- *********************************************************

select
  user_id,
  round(avg(elapsed_minutes)) average_minutes
from
   perfstat.stats$user_log
where
   elapsed_minutes is not NULL
group by
   user_id
;

column TOTAL MINUTES    Heading 'Total|Minutes' format 9,999
```

```
break on day skip 2

select
   to_char(logoff_day,'YYYY-MM-DD')  day,
   user_id,
   round(sum(elapsed_minutes))      total_minutes
from
   perfstat.stats$user_log
where
   elapsed_minutes is not NULL
group by
   to_char(logoff_day,'YYYY-MM-DD') ,
   user_id
;

select
   to_char(logon_day,'YYYY-MM-DD')  day,
   count(*)                         number_of_logins
from
   perfstat.stats$user_log
where
   elapsed_minutes is not NULL
group by rollup (
   to_char(logon_day,'YYYY-MM-DD')
   )
```

```
                        Total
Day        User       Minutes
---------- ---------- -------
02-03-06   APPLSYSPUB       0
           APPS           466
           OPS$ORACLE       7
           PERFSTAT        11


02-03-07   APPLSYSPUB       5
           APPS         1,913
           CUSJAN           1
           JANEDI           5
           OPS$ORACLE       6
           PERFSTAT       134
           SYS             58


02-03-08   APPLSYSPUB       1
           APPS         5,866
           OPS$ORACLE      15
           PERFSTAT        44
           SYS              6


02-03-09   APPS             0
           OPS$ORACLE       0
           PERFSTAT        29
```

```
Day        HO NUMBER_OF_LOGINS
---------- -- ----------------
02-03-06   11               37
           12               28
           13               45
           14               38
           15               26
           16               26
           17               25
           18               26
           19               26
           20               26
           21               49
           22               26
           23               24
```

## DDL Reports

This report is critical for the Oracle DBA who must track changes to a production database. This report uses the DDL trigger and produces a complete audit log of all Oracle databases changes.

### ddl_rpt.sql

```
alter session set nls_date_format='YY-MM-DD hh24:mi';

set lines 50

ttitle 'Production Database Changes|Summary DDL Report'

column NBR_Changes heading 'Number of|Production|Changes' format 9,999
column DDL_TYPE    heading 'DDL|Operation' format a8
column USER_NAME   Heading 'User'          format a10
column DDL_DATE    Heading 'Date|of DDL'   format a12
column OBJECT_TYPE Heading 'Object|Type'   format a12
column OWNER       Heading 'Object|Owner'  format a10
column OBJECT_NAME Heading 'Object|Name'   format a40

break on ddl_date skip 2

compute sum of nbr_changes on ddl_date


-- prompt
-- prompt
-- prompt ***********************************************************
-- prompt  List of all  Production Database changes
-- prompt ***********************************************************
-- prompt
-- prompt

set lines 90
```

```
select
   to_char(DDL_DATE,'MM-DD hh24:mi') DDL_DATE,
   user_name,
   DDL_TYPE,
   substr(OBJECT_TYPE,1,12)          OBJECT_TYPE,
   owner||'.'||OBJECT_NAME           OBJECT_NAME
from
   perfstat.stats$ddl_log
where
   object_type not in ('SEQUENCE','SUMMARY')
and
   ddl_type <> 'ANALYZE'
and
   owner <> 'PERFSTAT'
and
   object_name not like '%INTERIM%'
and
   object_name not like '%TEMP%'
and
   object_name not like '%EXPLAIN%'
and
   object_name not like 'MV_%'
and
   object_name not  in ('T1','T2','T3','T4')
--and
--   object_name not like 'EUL%'
--and
--   object_name not like 'MWC%'
--and
--   object_name not like 'AFSHIN%'
--and
--   object_name not like 'CUSTOM%'
and
   ddl_date > sysdate-&1
;
```

Here is a sample of the report:

```
           Date         Type     Object       Object
User       of DDL       of DDL   Type         Name
---------- ------------ -------- ----------- -------------------
SYS        03-07 10:11  DROP     TRIGGER      ERROR_AUDIT_TRIGGER
APPS       03-07 10:12  ALTER    TRIGGER      LOG_ERRORS_TRIG
APPS       03-07 10:14  ALTER    TRIGGER      LOG_ERRORS_TRIG
SYS        03-07 10:23  CREATE   TRIGGER      ERROR_AUDIT_TRIGGER
SYS        03-07 10:24  CREATE   TRIGGER      ERROR_AUDIT_TRIGGER
SYS        03-07 10:25  CREATE   TRIGGER      ERROR_AUDIT_TRIGGER
SYS        03-07 10:27  CREATE   TRIGGER      ERROR_AUDIT_TRIGGER
SYS        03-07 10:28  CREATE   TRIGGER      ERROR_AUDIT_TRIGGER
SYS        03-07 10:33  DROP     TRIGGER      LOG_ERRORS_TRIG
OPS$ORACLE 03-07 12:56  CREATE   TABLESPACE   JANEDI
OPS$ORACLE 03-07 12:57  CREATE   TABLESPACE   JANHF
APPS       03-07 13:10  ALTER    PACKAGE      PA_MC_CURRENCY_PKG
```

```
APPS        03-07 13:10  ALTER    TRIGGER      PA_MRC_DRAFT_INV_ITEM
JANEDI      03-07 14:15  CREATE   TABLE        JAN_EDI_HEADERS
JANEDI      03-07 14:15  CREATE   INDEX        JAN_EDI_HEAD_N1
JANEDI      03-07 14:15  CREATE   TABLE        JAN_EDI_LINES
JANEDI      03-07 14:15  CREATE   INDEX        JAN_EDI_LINE_N1
JANEDI      03-07 14:15  CREATE   TABLE        JAN_EDI_ERRORS
JANEDI      03-07 14:15  CREATE   TABLE        JAN_EDI_GP_ORDERS
JANEDI      03-07 14:15  CREATE   INDEX        JAN_EDI_GP_N1
JANEDI      03-07 14:15  CREATE   INDEX        JAN_EDI_GP_N2
JANEDI      03-07 14:15  CREATE   TABLE        JAN_EDI_GP_ERRORS
JANEDI      03-07 14:15  CREATE   TABLE        JAN_EDI_GP_CONTROLS
JANEDI      03-07 14:15  CREATE   INDEX        JAN_EDI_GP_CNTL_N1
JANEDI      03-07 14:18  ALTER    TABLE        JAN_EDI_HEADERS
JANEDI      03-07 14:18  ALTER    TABLE        JAN_EDI_LINES
JANEDI      03-07 14:18  ALTER    TABLE        JAN_EDI_ERRORS
JANEDI      03-07 14:18  ALTER    TABLE        JAN_EDI_GP_ORDERS
JANEDI      03-07 14:18  ALTER    TABLE        JAN_EDI_GP_ERRORS
JANEDI      03-07 14:18  ALTER    TABLE        JAN_EDI_GP_CONTROLS
OPS$ORACLE  03-07 14:20  ALTER    TABLE        JAN_DEPARTMENTS
OPS$ORACLE  03-07 14:20  ALTER    TABLE        JAN_FORECAST_INTERFACE
OPS$ORACLE  03-07 14:20  ALTER    TABLE        JAN_XREF_LOAD
OPS$ORACLE  03-07 14:20  ALTER    TABLE        JAN_JOBS_INTERFACE
OPS$ORACLE  03-07 14:20  ALTER    TABLE        JAN_ROUTING_COMMENTS
OPS$ORACLE  03-07 14:20  ALTER    TABLE        JAN_EDI_HEADERS
OPS$ORACLE  03-07 14:20  ALTER    TABLE        JAN_EDI_LINES
OPS$ORACLE  03-07 14:20  ALTER    TABLE        JAN_EDI_ERRORS
OPS$ORACLE  03-07 14:20  ALTER    TABLE        JAN_EDI_GP_ORDERS
OPS$ORACLE  03-07 14:20  ALTER    TABLE        JAN_EDI_GP_ERRORS
OPS$ORACLE  03-07 14:20  ALTER    TABLE        JAN_EDI_GP_CONTROLS
SYS         03-07 15:44  CREATE   TRIGGER      ERROR_AUDIT_TRIGGER
SYS         03-07 15:45  CREATE   TRIGGER      ERROR_AUDIT_TRIGGER
OPS$ORACLE  03-08 07:20  DROP     TABLE        ORACHECK_FS_TEMP
OPS$ORACLE  03-08 07:20  CREATE   TABLE        ORACHECK_FS_TEMP
APPS        03-08 11:21  ALTER    TRIGGER      ERROR_AUDIT_TRIGGER
SYS         03-08 11:21  CREATE   TRIGGER      ERROR_AUDIT_TRIGGER
APPS        03-08 11:23  ALTER    TRIGGER      ERROR_AUDIT_TRIGGER
SYS         03-08 11:25  CREATE   TRIGGER      ERROR_AUDIT_TRIGGER
SYS         03-08 12:54  ALTER    TRIGGER      ERROR_AUDIT_TRIGGER
SYS         03-08 12:54  DROP     TRIGGER      ERROR_AUDIT_TRIGGER
SYS         03-08 12:56  CREATE   TRIGGER      ERROR_AUDIT_TRIGGER
OPS$ORACLE  03-09 07:20  DROP     TABLE        ORACHECK_FS_TEMP
OPS$ORACLE  03-09 07:20  CREATE   TABLE        ORACHECK_FS_TEMP
```

Now let's take look at how we can design the user audit table to track user activity.

# Designing a user audit table

The first step is to create an Oracle table that can store the information gathered by the end-user log on/log off triggers. In order to properly design these triggers, we begin by taking a look at the information available inside the system level triggers:

First we gather the information available at log in:

- User ID -- this is the user ID that was used to perform the sign on operation

- Session ID -- this is the Oracle control session ID for the user
- Host -- this is the host name of the computer
- Logon date -- this is an Oracle date data type corresponding to the user log in time, accurate to 1/1000 of a second

Now we gather the information available just prior to user log off. As the user logs off, the Oracle system level trigger provides us with information about the current session:

- Last program -- this provides the name of the last program the user was executing at the time of system log off
- Last action -- this provides the last action performed by the user during the session
- Last module – this provides the name of the last module accessed by the user prior to log off time
- Log off date -- this is an Oracle date data type corresponding to the actual user log off time, accurate to 1/1000 of a second

Now we have the information at log on and log off, but how do we summarize this information and make it accessible to management? Let's take a look at the available options.

## User table normalization

Since the user log on and user log off triggers are separate entities, we have several choices in the design of a table to support this information. We could design two separate tables; a user log on table and a user log off table. However, we would have the difficulty of joining these two tables and correlating which log on corresponds to which log off and so on. This can be a tricky process that presents a lot of opportunity for error. How did user 24 log off before they logged on... and so on… and so on?

In order to get around this table issue, a database design was created whereby a single table is used to record both log on and log off events. This eliminates the need for table joins and the correlation of the data. In addition, we added a field to compute the elapsed minutes for each user's session. This computation done by the trigger saves time and makes for a much more informative report.

**cr_user_tab.sql**

```
create table
   stats$user_log
(
   user_id           varchar2(30),
   session_id           number(8),
   host              varchar2(30),
   last_program      varchar2(48),
   last_action       varchar2(32),
   last_module       varchar2(32),
   logon_day                 date,
   logon_time        varchar2(10),
   logoff_day                date,
   logoff_time       varchar2(10),
   elapsed_minutes      number(8)
)
tablespace perfstat
```

## Designing a log on trigger

Once the table is designed, the next task is to create a system level log on trigger that will fill in as much information as possible at the time of the log on event. The code above illustrates the log on audit trigger that we created. As you can see, we populate this table with three values that are available at log on time:

- User -- this is the Oracle user ID of the person establishing the Oracle session
- Session ID -- this uses Oracle's SYS context function in order to capture the Oracle session ID directly from the *v$session* table
- Host -- this uses Oracle's SYS context function to capture the name of the host from which the Oracle session originated. Please note that capturing the host name is vital for systems using Oracle parallel server or real application clusters, because we can have many sessions connecting from many different instance hosts.
- Log on date -- this captures the date of the actual log on, accurate to 1/1000 of a second. Notice how we partitioned log on date into two separate fields. Having a separate field for log on day and log on time produces a reader friendly report.

### logon_trig.sql

```
create or replace trigger
   logon_audit_trigger
AFTER LOGON ON DATABASE
BEGIN
insert into stats$user_log values(
```

```
    sys_context('USERENV','HOST'),
    null,
    null,
    null,
    sysdate,
    to_char(sysdate, 'hh24:mi:ss'),
    null,
    null,
    null
);
COMMIT;
END;
```

Now that the log on trigger is in place, we have the challenge of creating a log off trigger to capture all the information required to compute the elapsed time for the user session.

## Designing the log off trigger

In order to make a single table function for both log on and log off events, it is first necessary to locate the log on row that is associated with the individual user session. As you might imagine, this is tricky, because you may have many users who are signed on with identical user names. In order to get around this limitation, the Oracle session ID is used. Oracle writes a unique session ID to the *v$session* table for each individual user who is logged on. We can use this session ID as a primary key to update our user audit table with log off information.

Now let's take a look at the information that becomes available to us as a result of using our log off trigger.

We begin by updating the user log table to include the last action performed by the user. Updating the last action is accomplished by using the SYS context function to grab the action column from the *v$session* table.

Next, update the audit table to show the last program accessed during the session. Again, invoke the SYS context function to select the program column from the *v$session* table.

Next, update the last module that was accessed by the user session. This is accomplished by selecting the module column from the *v$session* table and placing it into our user audit table.

The final, and most important step of this procedure, is to insert the log off time and compute the elapsed time for the user session. Updating our user login table with the log off date data type, and then computing the elapsed time achieves this. As noted before, computing the elapsed time for each user session makes each individual record in the *stats$user_log* audit table very useful because it shows the duration of the session.

### logoff_trig.sql

```
create or replace trigger
   logoff_audit_trigger
BEFORE LOGOFF ON DATABASE
BEGIN
-- ***************************************************
-- Update the last action accessed
-- ***************************************************
update
stats$user_log
set
last_action = (select action from v$session where
sys_context('USERENV','SESSIONID') = audsid)
where
sys_context('USERENV','SESSIONID') = session_id;
--***************************************************
-- Update the last program accessed
-- ***************************************************
update
stats$user_log
set
last_program = (select program from v$session where
sys_context('USERENV','SESSIONID') = audsid)
where
sys_context('USERENV','SESSIONID') = session_id;
-- ***************************************************
-- Update the last module accessed
-- ***************************************************
update
stats$user_log
set
last_module = (select module from v$session where
sys_context('USERENV','SESSIONID') = audsid)
where
sys_context('USERENV','SESSIONID') = session_id;
-- ***************************************************
-- Update the logoff day
-- ***************************************************
update
   stats$user_log
set
   logoff_day = sysdate
where
   sys_context('USERENV','SESSIONID') = session_id;
-- ***************************************************
-- Update the logoff time
-- ***************************************************
```

```
set
   logoff_time = to_char(sysdate, 'hh24:mi:ss')
where
   sys_context('USERENV','SESSIONID') = session_id;
-- ****************************************************
-- Compute the elapsed minutes
-- ****************************************************
update
stats$user_log
set
elapsed_minutes =
round((logoff_day - logon_day)*1440)
where
sys_context('USERENV','SESSIONID') = session_id;
COMMIT;
END;
```

Next, we will take a look at a few sample reports. These reports can be enhanced to fit specific needs. As you will see, computing the elapsed minutes is a valuable feature since it produces a more useful report.

## User Activity Reports

Using the user audit table to generate reports can provide a wealth of information. The first report is a summary of total session time.

Start by creating a simple query against the user audit table that will show the day and date, the individual user ID, and the total number of minutes that the user was logged onto the system. While primitive, this shows the total amount of time spent on the system by each user.

This information is especially useful where users are accessing different functional areas of the system. For example, if the user IDs can be correlated directly to screen functions, the Oracle administrator can get a very good idea of the amount of usage within each functional area of the application.

Here is the listing from the *user_sum_rpt.sql* report.

### user_sum_rpt.sql

```
connect perfstat/perfstat;

set pages 999;
set lines 80;
```

```
column TOTAL_MINUTES    Heading 'Total|Minutes' format 9,999

column DAY    Heading 'Day' format a10

break on day skip 2

select
   to_char(logoff_day,'YYYY-MM-DD')  day,
   user_id,
   round(sum(elapsed_minutes))      total_minutes
from
   perfstat.stats$user_log
where
   elapsed_minutes is not NULL
group by
   to_char(logoff_day,'YYYY-MM-DD') ,
   user_id
```

```
                       Total
Day        User       Minutes
---------- ---------- -------
02-03-06   APPLSYSPUB       0
           APPS           466
           OPS$ORACLE       7
           PERFSTAT        11


02-03-07   APPLSYSPUB       5
           APPS         1,913
           CUSJAN           1
           JANEDI           5
           OPS$ORACLE       6
           PERFSTAT       134
           SYS             58


02-03-08   APPLSYSPUB       1
           APPS         5,866
           OPS$ORACLE      15
           PERFSTAT        44
           SYS              6


02-03-09   APPS             0
           OPS$ORACLE       0
           PERFSTAT        29
```

We can use the same table to show the number of users that are on our system at any given hour of the day. This information is especially useful for Oracle administrators who are in charge of tracking user activity. By examining the user audit table for user log on times, we can get an accurate count of generated sessions at any given hour of the day. Below is a sample report showing this information.

```
Day        HO NUMBER_OF_LOGINS
---------- -- ----------------
02-03-06   01                2
           02                3
           03                1
           04                3
           05                6
           06                9
           07               14
           08               19
           09               21
           10               22
           11               26
           12               28
           13               45
           14               38
           15               26
           16               26
           17               25
           18               26
           19               26
           20               26
           21               49
           22               26
           23               24
```

At this point the information can then be taken into an MS Excel spreadsheet, and expanded into impressive line charts. Figure 9.6 shows a nice example.

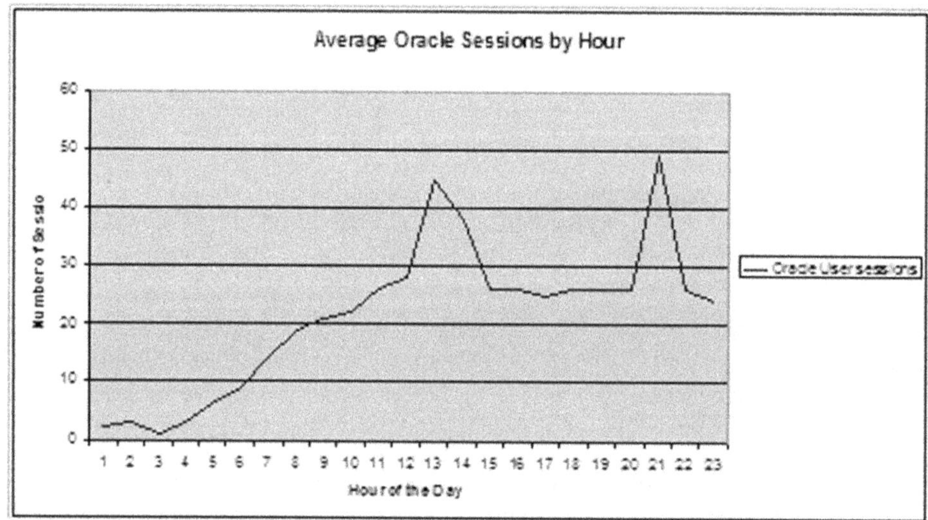


**Figure 9.1 –** *Average Oracle Sessions by Hour*

This produces a very clear graph showing user activity by the hour of the day. Once you get a large amount of user activity in your system, you can also summarize this information by the day of the week, or the hour of the day. This provides a tremendous amount of information regarding the user signature for the system. By signature, we mean trend lines or spikes in user activity. For example, we might see high user activity every Wednesday afternoon at 1:00pm. Using this user audit table, we can quickly identify these user signatures, and adjust Oracle in order to accommodate these changes in usage.

# Conclusion

Related DDL, system errors, and user activity can easily be captured using the system level triggers. However, system level triggers are not as sophisticated as they could be, and Oracle indicates that efforts are underway to enhance system level trigger functionality with the introduction of Oracle10g in 2003.

However, the judicious use of the system log on and system log off triggers can provide a very easy and reliable tracking mechanism for Oracle user activity. For the Oracle administrator who is committed to tracking user activity over long periods, the user audit table can provide a wealth of information, including usage signatures aggregated by the hour of the day and the day of the week.

# Oracle Grants Auditing

CHAPTER

## Introduction

So far, we have discussed how to record the activities of a user after they have occurred. This helps us establish accountability – which itself is a powerful enough deterrent to prevent users from committing any malicious act. In addition, legitimate users will refrain from accessing the sensitive information if it is known that their tracks can be retraced.

However, the goal of security is not to find acts of illegitimate activities, but to prevent them. Simply by preventing the user from doing something he or she is not expected to do, we can establish a perimeter around the data we intend to protect. The way we enforce this perimeter is through granting specific privileges on the objects – either directly to the users or through roles. In auditing, it becomes important to analyze these granted privileges, and to record them. This special act of auditing is not the record of change of data, but the very existence of privileges to do so, and changes to those privileges. This type of auditing is known as Grants Auditing.

There are two different types of requirements for auditing the grants in a database.

- Identifying who has what privilege
- Tracking the granting and revoking of privileges

In the subsequent sections we will cover each type in detail.

The important point here to note here is that we are not, at this time, trying to secure the database. Database security was discussed under General Oracle Security in Chapter 4. In that chapter, you learned how to remove the unneeded privileges and grant only the necessary ones to the appropriate users. Here is the recap of the concepts explained there. Please refer to the Chapter 4 for details on each of these concepts.

- Make sure the accounts created by the Oracle installation are reviewed, and unnecessary accounts are either removed or locked.
- No user should have sweeping privileges, unless specifically required. Sweeping privileges are privileges not normally required by a regular user, e.g. CREATE

TABLE. The online code depot has a script that identifies these grants - *find_sweeping_privs.sql*.

- A regular user who is not required to own objects should not have any schema privileges that can create objects. The online code depot script *find_schema_privs.sql* can be used to identify them.
- No users, except the DBA users, should have any system privileges granted to them with ADMIN OPTION. These privileges and users can be identified using the online code depot script *users_with_sys_grant_admin_option.sql*.
- No user should have object privileges granted with the GRANTABLE option. All privileges should be granted to users directly. The online code depot has a script *users_with_obj_grant_admin_option.sql* which will identify these users and the grants.

After these safety factors are addressed, the database can be considered to be in a relatively safe mode. However, the auditing requirements call for tracking who has what privileges, and this information must be recorded and preserved. It might also help to run security evaluation scripts from time to time to check if recent developments have been introduced to take any corrective actions.

# Checking Grants

In this type of auditing, we will record the privileges granted to the users, and record them to satisfy auditing requirements. The following script can be used to record the current privileges for the users. For the sake of convenience of discussion, the script has been marked with section numbers, referenced later in the chapter.

### check_grants.sql

```
REM ~~~~~~~~~~~~~~~~~~~~~~~~~~~~~~~~~~~~~~~~~~~~
REM Preamble: Setting all the necessary settings
REM ~~~~~~~~~~~~~~~~~~~~~~~~~~~~~~~~~~~~~~~~~~~~

set lines 132
set pages 45
set feed off
set trimspool on

col grantee          format a20
col privilege        format a25
col obj_name         format a30
col grantor          format a20
col grantable        format a3
col object_type      format a20
```

```
col username         format a20
col tablespace_name  format a30
col used_bytes       format 999,999,999
col max_bytes        format a15

col role_admin       format a3
col priv_admin       format a3

col through_role     format a20
col granted_role     format a20

spool grant_check.txt

select
   to_char(sysdate, 'mm/dd/yyyy hh24:mi:ss')
       curr_timestamp
from
   dual
/

REM ~~~~~~~~~~~~~~~~~~~~~~~~~~~~~~~~~~~~~~~~~
REM Section 1
REM ~~~~~~~~~~~~~~~~~~~~~~~~~~~~~~~~~~~~~~~~~
prompt
prompt Roles Granted to Users
prompt ~~~~~~~~~~~~~~~~~~~~~~~~~~~~~~~~~~~~
prompt

select
   grantee,
   granted_role,
   admin_option,
   default_role
from
   dba_role_privs
where
   grantee not in ('SYS','SYSTEM')
order by
   grantee,
   granted_role
/

REM ~~~~~~~~~~~~~~~~~~~~~~~~~~~~~~~~~~~~~~~~~
REM Section 2
REM ~~~~~~~~~~~~~~~~~~~~~~~~~~~~~~~~~~~~~~~~~

prompt
prompt Object Privileges Granted to Roles
prompt ~~~~~~~~~~~~~~~~~~~~~~~~~~~~~~~~~~~~
prompt

select
   p.grantee,
   p.privilege,
   o.object_type,
   p.owner||'.'||p.table_name obj_name,
```

```
from
   dba_tab_privs p,
   dba_objects o
where
   grantee not in ('DBA')
and
   grantee in
      (select role from dba_roles)
and
   o.owner = p.owner
and
   o.object_name = p.table_name
order by
   p.grantee,
   p.owner,
   p.table_name,
   p.privilege
/

REM ~~~~~~~~~~~~~~~~~~~~~~~~~~~~~~~~~~~~~~~~~
REM Section 3
REM ~~~~~~~~~~~~~~~~~~~~~~~~~~~~~~~~~~~~~~~~~

prompt
prompt System Privileges Granted to Roles
prompt ~~~~~~~~~~~~~~~~~~~~~~~~~~~~~~~~~~~~~~~
prompt

select
    grantee,
    privilege,
    admin_option
from
    dba_sys_privs
where
    grantee not in ('DBA')
and
    grantee in
      (select role from dba_roles)
order by
    grantee,
    privilege
/

REM ~~~~~~~~~~~~~~~~~~~~~~~~~~~~~~~~~~~~~~~~~
REM Section 4
REM ~~~~~~~~~~~~~~~~~~~~~~~~~~~~~~~~~~~~~~~~~

prompt
prompt Object Privileges Directly Granted to Users
prompt ~~~~~~~~~~~~~~~~~~~~~~~~~~~~~~~~~~~~~~~~~~~
prompt

select
   p.grantee,
   p.privilege,
```

```
   p.grantor,
   p.grantable
from
   dba_tab_privs p,
   dba_objects o
where
   grantee not in ('SYS','SYSTEM')
and
   grantee in
      (select username from dba_users)
and
   o.owner = p.owner
and
   o.object_name = p.table_name
order by
   p.grantee,
   p.owner,
   p.table_name,
   p.privilege
/

REM ~~~~~~~~~~~~~~~~~~~~~~~~~~~~~~~~~~~~~~~~~~
REM Section 5
REM ~~~~~~~~~~~~~~~~~~~~~~~~~~~~~~~~~~~~~~~~~~
prompt
prompt Object Privileges Granted to Users Through Roles
prompt ~~~~~~~~~~~~~~~~~~~~~~~~~~~~~~~~~~~~~~~~~~~~~~~~~
prompt

select distinct
   drp.grantee                      grantee,
   rtp.privilege                    privilege,
   rtp.owner||'.'||rtp.table_name  obj_name,
   rtp.role                         through_role,
   drp.admin_option                 admin_option,
   drp.default_role                 defult_role
from
    role_tab_privs  rtp,
    dba_role_privs  drp,
    role_role_privs rrp
where
    drp.grantee in (select username from dba_users)
and
    drp.grantee not in ('SYS','SYSTEM')
and
(
    rtp.role = drp.granted_role
    or
    (
        rtp.role = rrp.granted_role
        and
        rrp.role = drp.granted_role
    )
    or
    (
        rtp.role = rrp.granted role
```

```
    )
)
and rtp.role not in
    (
        'SELECT_CATALOG_ROLE',
        'IMP_FULL_DATABASE',
        'EXP_FULL_DATABASE',
        'DBA',
        'XDBADMIN',
        'EXECUTE_CATALOG_ROLE'
    )
/

REM ~~~~~~~~~~~~~~~~~~~~~~~~~~~~~~~~~~~~~~~~~
REM Section 6
REM ~~~~~~~~~~~~~~~~~~~~~~~~~~~~~~~~~~~~~~~~~
prompt
prompt Privileges on Columns of Tables Granted
prompt ~~~~~~~~~~~~~~~~~~~~~~~~~~~~~~~~~~~~~~~
prompt

select
   grantee,
   owner||'.'||table_name obj_name,
   column_name,
   grantor,
   privilege,
   grantable
from
   dba_col_privs
where
   grantee not in ('SYS','SYSTEM')
order by
   grantee,
   owner,
   table_name,
   column_name,
   privilege
/

REM ~~~~~~~~~~~~~~~~~~~~~~~~~~~~~~~~~~~~~~~~~
REM Section 7
REM ~~~~~~~~~~~~~~~~~~~~~~~~~~~~~~~~~~~~~~~~~
prompt
prompt System Privileges Granted to Users
prompt ~~~~~~~~~~~~~~~~~~~~~~~~~~~~~~~~~~~~~~~
prompt

select
    grantee,
    privilege,
    admin_option
from
    dba_sys_privs
where
    grantee not in ('SYS','SYSTEM')
and
```

```
order by
    grantee,
    privilege
/

REM ~~~~~~~~~~~~~~~~~~~~~~~~~~~~~~~~~~~~~~~~~~~~~
REM Section 8
REM ~~~~~~~~~~~~~~~~~~~~~~~~~~~~~~~~~~~~~~~~~~~~~
prompt
prompt System Privileges Granted to Users Through Roles
prompt ~~~~~~~~~~~~~~~~~~~~~~~~~~~~~~~~~~~~~~~~~~~~~~~~
prompt

select distinct
    d.grantee           grantee,
    p.role              through_role,
    p.privilege         privilege,
    d.admin_option,
    d.default_role
from
    role_sys_privs p,
    dba_role_privs d,
    role_role_privs r
where
    d.grantee in
      (select username from dba_users)
and
    d.grantee not in ('SYS','SYSTEM')
and
(
    p.role = d.granted_role
    or
    (
        p.role = r.granted_role
        and
        r.role = d.granted_role
    )
)
and p.role not in
    (
      'SELECT_CATALOG_ROLE',
      'IMP_FULL_DATABASE',
      'EXP_FULL_DATABASE',
      'DBA',
      'XDBADMIN',
      'EXECUTE_CATALOG_ROLE'
    )
/

REM ~~~~~~~~~~~~~~~~~~~~~~~~~~~~~~~~~~~~~~~~~~~~~
REM Section 9
REM ~~~~~~~~~~~~~~~~~~~~~~~~~~~~~~~~~~~~~~~~~~~~~
prompt
prompt Quota on Tablespaces Granted to Users
prompt ~~~~~~~~~~~~~~~~~~~~~~~~~~~~~~~~~~~~~~~~~~~~
prompt
```

```
   username,
   tablespace_name,
   bytes used_bytes,
   decode(max_bytes,-1,'UNLIMITED',
      to_char(max_bytes,'999,999,999.999'))
          max_bytes
from
   dba_ts_quotas
where
   username not in ('SYS','SYSTEM')
order
   by username,
   tablespace_name
/
```

## About this Script

Since this is such a long script, we have referenced the various sections by section numbers. Let's analyze this script in detail.

One of the most powerful features of this script is that these sections can be placed in separate scripts, which can be run independently. In a typical audit, the DBA is expected to run this script in its entirety for the results to be filed, so the script is provided here as a monolithic whole. If desired, especially for ad-hoc reporting, extract the appropriate sections from this script and either run that SQL statement, or place it in a script to be run later from the command line.

The first part of the script, named Preamble, is not really a section. It defines all the necessary settings such as line and page size, etc. If the script is divided into the individual parts, make sure this section is present at the beginning of each script.

### Roles Granted to Users

This section captures roles granted to the users. Along with the necessary information, we can also see if the role is a default role assigned to the user. If that is the case, the role is enabled immediately after the user logs in.

In addition, this also shows if a role is granted to another role. If a second role is granted to a user, then the user inherits the privileges of the first role, too. If the second role is default for the user, then the first role's privileges are enabled at login.

The other significant information it shows is if the role can be granted to others by the user to whom it is granted. If the ADMIN_OPTION is YES, then the role can be granted to others. Typically, in a security conscious environment, you will refrain from granting a role with the admin option. All the users should be granted roles directly by a DBA user, such as SYS or SYSTEM.

This section shows roles granted to both users and roles, so we can identify the cascading grants given to users through roles.

## Object Privileges Granted to Roles

This section shows only the object privileges granted to roles, not users. Object privileges are based on objects, such as execute privilege on a procedure, or select privilege on a table, etc. Figure 10.1 shows a partial output of this section. Here, we see that the role DBA has privileges to execute the package body *dbms_storage_map* owned by SYS, as the first line suggests. Similarly, the other lines show which roles have privileges on which objects.

```
GRANTEE              PRIVILEGE              OBJECT_TYPE        OBJ_NAME                       GRANTOR              GRA
-------------------- ---------------------- ------------------ ------------------------------ -------------------- ---
DBA                  EXECUTE                PACKAGE BODY       SYS.DBMS_STORAGE_MAP           SYS                  NO
DBA                  ALTER                  TABLE              SYS.MAP_OBJECT                 SYS                  NO
DBA                  DEBUG                  TABLE              SYS.MAP_OBJECT                 SYS                  NO
DBA                  DELETE                 TABLE              SYS.MAP_OBJECT                 SYS                  NO
DBA                  FLASHBACK              TABLE              SYS.MAP_OBJECT                 SYS                  NO
DBA                  INSERT                 TABLE              SYS.MAP_OBJECT                 SYS                  NO
DBA                  ON COMMIT REFRESH      TABLE              SYS.MAP_OBJECT                 SYS                  NO
DBA                  QUERY REWRITE          TABLE              SYS.MAP_OBJECT                 SYS                  NO
DBA                  SELECT                 TABLE              SYS.MAP_OBJECT                 SYS                  NO
DBA                  UPDATE                 TABLE              SYS.MAP_OBJECT                 SYS                  NO
DBA                  EXECUTE                PACKAGE            SYS.OUTLN_EDIT_PKG             SYS                  NO
DBA                  EXECUTE                PACKAGE BODY       SYS.OUTLN_EDIT_PKG             SYS                  NO
DBA                  EXECUTE                PACKAGE            SYS.OUTLN_PKG                  SYS                  NO
DBA                  EXECUTE                PACKAGE BODY       SYS.OUTLN_PKG                  SYS                  NO
DBA                  UPDATE                 TABLE              WKSYS.WK$SYS_CONFIG            WKSYS                NO
DELETE_CATALOG_ROLE  DELETE                 TABLE              SYS.FGA_LOG$                   SYS                  NO
EXECUTE_CATALOG_ROLE EXECUTE                PACKAGE            SYS.DBMSZEXP_SYSPKGGRNT        SYS                  NO
EXECUTE_CATALOG_ROLE EXECUTE                PACKAGE BODY       SYS.DBMSZEXP_SYSPKGGRNT        SYS                  NO
EXECUTE_CATALOG_ROLE EXECUTE                PACKAGE            SYS.DBMS_ALERT                 SYS                  NO
EXECUTE_CATALOG_ROLE EXECUTE                PACKAGE BODY       SYS.DBMS_ALERT                 SYS                  NO
EXECUTE_CATALOG_ROLE EXECUTE                PACKAGE            SYS.DBMS_APPLY_ADM             SYS                  NO
EXECUTE_CATALOG_ROLE EXECUTE                PACKAGE BODY       SYS.DBMS_APPLY_ADM             SYS                  NO
EXECUTE_CATALOG_ROLE EXECUTE                PACKAGE            SYS.DBMS_AQ                    SYS                  NO
```

**Figure 10.1** *Output of Section 2 of the Check Grants Script*

The output also shows if the role is grantable to another user. For instance, in the above case, the GRANTABLE column is YES, which means if the DBA role is granted to a user ANANDA, the user ANANDA can grant the execute privilege on the package to another user. Needless to say, this is not desirable, and should not be allowed.

The other important column is GRANTOR. It indicates if the owner of the object granted the privilege, or if someone else with such a privilege made the grant. Sometimes it may be required to identify the source of a grant, not just the existence of it.

## System Privileges Granted to Roles

The above section shows the object privileges. However, the roles might have been granted system privileges, too. Here is a partial output of the script in this section.

```
GRANTEE              PRIVILEGE                 ADM
-------------------- ------------------------- ---
DBA                  ALTER ANY ROLE            YES
DBA                  ALTER ANY RULE            YES
DBA                  ALTER ANY RULE SET        YES
DBA                  ALTER ANY SEQUENCE        YES
DBA                  ALTER ANY SNAPSHOT        YES
DBA                  ALTER ANY TABLE           YES
DBA                  ALTER ANY TRIGGER         YES
DBA                  ALTER ANY TYPE            YES
DBA                  ALTER DATABASE            YES
DBA                  ALTER PROFILE             YES
DBA                  ALTER RESOURCE COST       YES
DBA                  ALTER ROLLBACK SEGMENT    YES
DBA                  ALTER SESSION             YES
DBA                  ALTER SYSTEM              YES
DBA                  ALTER TABLESPACE          YES
DBA                  ALTER USER                YES
```

The important column here is shown by ADM, meaning ADMIN_OPTION. If it shows YES, as in case of the above values, a user with the granted role of DBA can grant the privilege directly to other users. Again, this is not desirable in a security framework. An exception to the rule may be made in some cases, such as for the DBA role, which is special and not granted to any user. Other regular roles should not have ADMIN_OPTION set to YES.

## Object Privileges Directly Granted to Users

In this section we will see the object privileges granted directly to the user, not through a role. A partial output is shown in Figure 10.2.

```
GRANTEE          PRIVILEGE            OBJECT_TYPE        OBJ_NAME                    GRANTOR            GRA
---------------- -------------------- ------------------ --------------------------- ------------------ ---
SECUSER          SELECT               VIEW               SYS.DBA_AUDIT_POLICIES      SYS                NO
SECUSER          EXECUTE              PACKAGE BODY       SYS.DBMS_FGA                SYS                NO
SECUSER          EXECUTE              PACKAGE            SYS.DBMS_FGA                SYS                NO
SECUSER          EXECUTE              PACKAGE BODY       SYS.DBMS_FLASHBACK          SYS                NO
SECUSER          EXECUTE              PACKAGE            SYS.DBMS_FLASHBACK          SYS                NO
SECUSER          EXECUTE              PACKAGE BODY       SYS.DBMS_RLS                SYS                NO
SECUSER          EXECUTE              PACKAGE            SYS.DBMS_RLS                SYS                NO
SECUSER          EXECUTE              PACKAGE BODY       SYS.DBMS_SESSION            SYS                NO
SECUSER          EXECUTE              PACKAGE            SYS.DBMS_SESSION            SYS                NO
SERGEY           ALTER                TABLE              ANANDA.CLAIM                ANANDA             NO
SERGEY           DEBUG                TABLE              ANANDA.CLAIM                ANANDA             NO
SERGEY           DELETE               TABLE              ANANDA.CLAIM                ANANDA             NO
SERGEY           FLASHBACK            TABLE              ANANDA.CLAIM                ANANDA             NO
SERGEY           INDEX                TABLE              ANANDA.CLAIM                ANANDA             NO
SERGEY           INSERT               TABLE              ANANDA.CLAIM
```

**Figure 10.2** *Object Privileges Granted Directly to the Users.*

We can see the privileges granted to the user (GRANTEE) on various objects inside the database. We can also see the GRANTOR of the privilege, if any user other than the owner made the grant, and if the privilege is GRANTABLE, i.e. if the user can grant the same privilege to another user. In an ideal setup, no user should have a GRANTABLE privilege. If a user needs a certain privilege on an object, then it should be directly granted, not through another user.

## Object Privileges Granted to Users through Roles

In the previous section, we saw the privileges granted to users directly. However, they can also be granted some privileges through roles. This sections shows which privileges have been granted to users via roles. Fig 10.3 shows a partial output from the section.

```
GRANTEE              PRIVILEGE                  OBJ_NAME                         THROUGH_ROLE         ADM DEF
-------------------- -------------------------- -------------------------------- -------------------- --- ---
ANANDA               DELETE                     SYS.AUX_STATS$                   GATHER_SYSTEM_STATIS NO  YES
                                                                                 TICS

ANANDA               DELETE                     SYS.FGA_LOG$                     DELETE_CATALOG_ROLE  NO  YES
ANANDA               INSERT                     SYS.AUX_STATS$                   GATHER_SYSTEM_STATIS NO  YES
                                                                                 TICS

ANANDA               SELECT                     SYS.AUX_STATS$                   GATHER_SYSTEM_STATIS NO  YES
                                                                                 TICS

ANANDA               SELECT                     SYS.DBA_WORKSPACES               WM_ADMIN_ROLE        NO  YES
ANANDA               SELECT                     SYS.DBA_WORKSPACE_SESSIONS       WM_ADMIN_ROLE        NO  YES
ANANDA               SELECT                     WMSYS.DBA_WM_SYS_PRIVS           WM_ADMIN_ROLE        NO  YES
ANANDA               SELECT                     WMSYS.DBA_WM_VERSIONED_TABLES    WM_ADMIN_ROLE        NO  YES
ANANDA               SELECT                     WMSYS.DBA_WORKSPACE_PRIVS        WM_ADMIN_ROLE        NO  YES
ANANDA               SELECT                     WMSYS.DBA_WORKSPACE_SAVEPOINTS WM_ADMIN_ROLE          NO  YES
ANANDA               UPDATE                     SYS.AUX_STATS$                   GATHER_SYSTEM_STATIS NO  YES
                                                                                 TICS

APPUSER              DELETE                     BHC.CLAIM                        TCOP_APP_USER_ROLE   NO  NO
APPUSER              DELETE                     BHC.CLAIM_HEADER                 TCOP_APP_USER_ROLE   NO  NO
APPUSER              DELETE                     BHC.CLAIM_LINE                   TCOP_APP_USER_ROLE   NO  NO
APPUSER              INSERT                     BHC.CLAIM                        TCOP_APP_USER_ROLE   NO  NO
APPUSER              INSERT                     BHC.CLAIM_HEADER                 TCOP_APP_USER_ROLE   NO  NO
APPUSER              INSERT                     BHC.CLAIM_LINE                   TCOP_APP_USER_ROLE   NO  NO
APPUSER              INSERT                     CLAIM_SCHEMA.CLAIMS              CLAIM_SUPERVISOR     NO  NO
APPUSER              SELECT                     BHC.CLAIM                        TCOP_APP_USER_ROLE   NO  NO
APPUSER              SELECT                     BHC.CLAIM_HEADER                 TCOP_APP_USER_ROLE   NO  NO
APPUSER              SELECT                     BHC.CLAIM_LINE                   TCOP_APP_USER_ROLE   NO  NO
APPUSER              UPDATE                     BHC.CLAIM                        TCOP_APP_USER_ROLE   NO  NO
APPUSER              UPDATE                     BHC.CLAIM_HEADER                 TCOP_APP_USER_ROLE   NO  NO
APPUSER              UPDATE                     BHC.CLAIM_LINE                   TCOP_APP_USER_ROLE   NO  NO
APPUSER              UPDATE                     CLAIM_SCHEMA.CLAIMS              JUNIOR_CLAIM_ANALYST NO  NO
```

**Figure 10.3** *Object Privileges Granted through a Role*

In addition to the usual columns showing the users and the privileges, we can also see whether the role can be granted to other users (ADMIN_OPTION). The role through which these privileges have come to the users is also shown here (THROUGH_ROLE). Finally, the last column shows if the role is default for the user, i.e. will be active after logging in.

## Privileges on Columns of Tables Granted

In this section, we will see the privileges on column level security granted to users. Although this type of grant can be made to users as well as roles, we will show them both in a single output as follows.

```
GRANTEE              OBJ_NAME                       COLUMN_NAME                    GRANTOR              PRIVILEGE
-------------------- ------------------------------ ------------------------------ -------------------- -------------------------
GRA
---
IMP_FULL_DATABASE    CLAIM_SCHEMA.CLAIMS            CLAIM_ID                       CLAIM_SCHEMA         UPDATE
NO

SECUSER              CLAIM_SCHEMA.CLAIMS            CLAIM_ID                       CLAIM_SCHEMA         UPDATE
NO
```

Included is a column for GRANTOR, i.e. who granted the privilege, if it is someone other than the owner.

## System Privileges Granted to Users

This shows the system privileges, not object privileges, granted to the users directly, not through any roles, etc. The following is a partial output.

```
GRANTEE              PRIVILEGE                ADM
-------------------- ------------------------ ---
ALI                  CREATE SESSION           NO
ALI                  UNLIMITED TABLESPACE     NO
ANANDA               AUDIT ANY                NO
ANANDA               DROP ANY TABLE           NO
ANANDA               GRANT ANY PRIVILEGE      NO
ANANDA               UNLIMITED TABLESPACE     NO
ANDREY               CREATE SESSION           NO
ANONYMOUS            CREATE SESSION           NO
APPUSER              CREATE SESSION           NO
APPUSER              UNLIMITED TABLESPACE     NO
BHC                  CREATE SESSION           NO
BHC                  UNLIMITED TABLESPACE     NO
```

In addition to the user who has been granted the privilege (GRANTEE) and the privilege granted, the output also shows if the privileges are granted with ADMIN_OPTION. If it's YES, then the grantee can grant the same privilege to another user. In an ideal situation, you would never have a user with a privilege that can be administered by that user.

## System Privileges Granted to Users through Roles

In the previous section, we saw the privileges granted to users directly. However, they can also be granted some privileges through roles. This sections shows which privileges have been granted to users via roles. Here is a partial output from the section.

```
GRANTEE      THROUGH_ROLE PRIVILEGE                ADM DEF
------------ ------------ ------------------------ --- ---
BHC          CONNECT      ALTER SESSION            NO  YES
BHC          CONNECT      CREATE CLUSTER           NO  YES
BHC          CONNECT      CREATE DATABASE LINK     NO  YES
BHC          CONNECT      CREATE SEQUENCE          NO  YES
BHC          CONNECT      CREATE SESSION           NO  YES
BHC          CONNECT      CREATE SYNONYM           NO  YES
BHC          CONNECT      CREATE TABLE             NO  YES
BHC          CONNECT      CREATE VIEW              NO  YES
BHC          RESOURCE     CREATE CLUSTER           NO  YES
BHC          RESOURCE     CREATE INDEXTYPE         NO  YES
```

In addition to the usual columns showing the users and the privileges, we can see here whether the privileges can be granted to others (ADMIN_OPTION). The role through which these privileges have come to the users is also shown here

(THROUGH_ROLE). Finally, the last column shows if the role is default for the user, i.e. will be active after logging in.

## Quota on Tablespaces Granted to Users

This is not strictly a privilege, but is important to list as a part of the overall privilege management system. The following is a partial output from this section.

```
USERNAME             TABLESPACE_NAME    USED_BYTES MAX_BYTES
-------------------- ----------------- ---------- ---------
HR                   EXAMPLE            1,638,400 UNLIMITED
ODM                  ODM                5,439,488 UNLIMITED
ODM_MTR              ODM                4,259,840 UNLIMITED
OE                   EXAMPLE            6,946,816 UNLIMITED
OEM_ANANDA           OEM_REPOSITORY    33,488,896 UNLIMITED
OEM_ANANDA           TEMP                       0 UNLIMITED
OLAPSYS              CWMLITE           13,303,808 UNLIMITED
PERFSTAT             USERS                589,824 UNLIMITED
PM                   EXAMPLE            3,342,336 UNLIMITED
QS                   EXAMPLE            1,572,864 UNLIMITED
QS_ADM               EXAMPLE                    0 UNLIMITED
QS_CB                EXAMPLE                    0 UNLIMITED
QS_CBADM             EXAMPLE              851,968 UNLIMITED
QS_CS                EXAMPLE              655,360 UNLIMITED
QS_ES                EXAMPLE            1,179,648 UNLIMITED
QS_OS                EXAMPLE            1,179,648 UNLIMITED
QS_WS                EXAMPLE            1,179,648 UNLIMITED
SECUSER              USERS                458,752 UNLIMITED
SH                   EXAMPLE          125,763,584   102,400
```

It shows the allowed quota on the tablespaces (MAX_BYTES) for the users, and how much of the tablespace is filled up by the user (USED_BYTES). If the quota is unlimited, that is shown.

## View *table_privileges*

There is a view named *table_privileges*, to show different permissions for various objects. Unfortunately this view is de-supported, but is available as of Oracle 9.2 for backward compatibility with Oracle 6. This view may actually provide an easier to understand portrayal of the permissions and grants than that of the *dba_tab_privs* view. It has been explained here, in addition to *dba_tab_privs*, for the sake of completeness. Please note that in future versions, this may not exist.

The following table shows the columns of the view *table_privileges*.

| COLUMN | DESCRIPTION |
|---|---|

| COLUMN | DESCRIPTION |
|---|---|
| GRANTEE | The user or the role to whom the privilege has been granted. |
| OWNER | The owner of the table object on which the privilege is granted. |
| TABLE_NAME | The name of the object. As it has been seen before, this column name is actually a misnomer. It shows the name of the object, which may be a table, a view, a procedure, or any other type of object, not necessarily a table. |
| GRANTOR | The user who granted the privilege to the grantee. It is not necessarily the same as the object owner. |
| SELECT_PRIV | Shows if Select Privilege is granted. |
| INSERT_PRIV | Shows if Insert Privilege is granted. |
| DELETE_PRIV | Shows if Delete Privilege is granted. |
| UPDATE_PRIV | Shows if Update Privilege is granted. |
| REFERENCES_PRIV | Shows if References Privilege is granted. Used for creating Referential integrity constraints on the table. |
| ALTER_PRIV | Shows if Alteration Privilege is granted. |
| INDEX_PRIV | Shows if Index Creation Privilege is granted. |

**Table 10.1** *Columns of View table_privileges*

Using the script *check_grants.sql* or its sections separately, we can quickly create a baseline of the privileges that exist in the database. These scripts can be periodically run, and the output generated can be preserved, after being certified by the auditors. This alone satisfies a number of HIPAA regulations.

However, this is, as already said, just a baseline. There is nothing that prevents an authorized user from altering these grants after the baseline is generated. Therefore, the auditor somehow has to guarantee that the grants are not altered after they are issued. Even if they are altered, they must be audited so that the changes can be reconciled. The next section discusses how to track (or audit) the changes to the grants.

## Tracking Grants

The simplest way to track the grant and revocation of privileges is by auditing the GRANT statement itself. For instance, if we wanted to track all types of grants on the table CLAIMS, we can issue

```
audit grant on claim_schema.claims by access;
```

This audits all grants made by a non-SYS user on the table *claims* owned by CLAIM_SCHEMA. To confirm the setting, check the view *dba_obj_audit_opts* as follows.

```
select GRA
from dba_obj_audit_opts
where and owner = 'CLAIM_SCHEMA'
and object_name = 'CLAIMS'
/
```

This query returns

```
GRA
---
S/S
```

It means the grants are audited whether successful or not. In this setting, if the user CLAIM_SCHEMA issues the following statement to grant selection on this table to JUDY:

```
grant select on claims to judy
/
```

This grant will trigger an audit record to be generated and placed in the *aud$* table. The record is visible from the *dba_audit_trail* view, too, but there is a special view named *dba_audit_statement* that is used solely for this purpose. To see this audit, we will issue

```
select
   timestamp,
   username,
   action_name,
   obj_privilege, owner, obj_name, grantee from
 dba_audit_statement
/
```

The query returns:

```
TIMESTAMP USERNAME     ACTION_NAME    OBJ_PRIVILEGE
--------- ------------ -------------- ----------------
```

```
OWNER            OBJ_NAME         GRANTEE
---------------- ---------------- --------------------

20-AUG-03 CLAIM_SCHEMA GRANT OBJECT    ---------Y------
CLAIM_SCHEMA     CLAIMS           JUDY
```

Note the various columns of the result. They show that the user CLAIMS_SCHE MA (Column: USERNAME) granted some object privilege (Column: ACTION_NAME) on CLAIM_SCHEMA's object CLAIMS (Column: OBJ_NAME) to user JUDY (Column: GRANTEE).

The query answered the most of the essential questions. However, note that while it accurately recorded that a user did some object grant, it did not say which specific grant. The column that shows this is OBJ_PRIVILEGE.

This column shows a value "---------Y------" a series of hyphens with a single Y in between. This set of characters show which type of grant was performed on this table. This shows Y in the 10th position, meaning the grant was on SELECT statement. The above example would be deciphered as the user issued a grant select on table CLAIMS to JUDY.

The position of the characters in the string shown by OBJ_PRIVILEGE identifies the type of grant. Table 10.2 shows the position and what each position represents.

| POSITION | AUDITED STATEMENT |
|---|---|
| 1 | ALTER |
| 2 | AUDIT |
| 3 | COMMENT |
| 4 | DELETE |
| 5 | GRANT |
| 6 | INDEX |
| 7 | INSERT |
| 8 | LOCK |
| 9 | RENAME |
| 10 | SELECT |
| 11 | UPDATE |
| 12 | REFERENCES |
| 13 | EXECUTE |

**Table 10.2** *Significance of Characters in OBJ_PRIVILEGE*

If the position contains a hyphen, the corresponding statement was not granted. A value of Y indicates it was granted and a value of N indicates it was revoked.

If multiple privileges are granted on the table, then each of the corresponding characters in the string are populated. For instance, if the owner grants SELECT, INSERT and DELETE to JUDY in one statement, the audit record will look like

```
---Y--Y--Y------
```

Here, the positions 4, 7 and 10 are populated, indicating that the statement granted the privileges of DELETE, INSERT and SELECT.

If a user who has the GRANT ANY OBJECT PRIVILEGE grants the privileges, then the audit record shows that fact, too. In this example, the user ANANDA has the above-mentioned system privilege and it issues:

```
grant select on claim_schema.claims to judy
/
```

Checking the audit records:

```
select priv_used from dba_audit_statement
/
```

We see:

```
PRIV_USED
----------------------------------------
GRANT ANY OBJECT PRIVILEGE
```

Note how the column value clearly shows which privilege was used, i.e. GRANT ANY OBJECT PRIVILEGE. When the user CLAIM_SCHEMA issues the same grant statements, this column, PRIV_USED, is not populated, simply because the user granted on his or her own table, so no special privileges were necessary. Therefore, the PRIV_USED column provides valuable information required to firmly establish accountability.

Table 10.3 below shows the various columns of the view *dba_audit_statement* and their descriptions.

| COLUMN | DESCRIPTION |
|---|---|
| OS_USERNAME | The Operating System username |
| USERNAME | The database username |

| COLUMN | DESCRIPTION |
|---|---|
| USERHOST | The host name from where the user is connected. |
| TERMINAL | The terminal number. In case of Windows, this shows the machine name. The USERHOST column shows nothing. |
| TIMESTAMP | The Timestamp when it occurred. |
| OWNER | The owner of the object on which the audit occurred. |
| OBJ_NAME | Name of the object on which the auditing occurred. However, this also shows non-objects such as roles, as we will see later. |
| ACTION_NAME | The action performed that triggered the audit. The action may not be complete, i.e. it might show GRANT OBJECT that indicates some type of object privilege (select, insert, etc.) was issued on the object. The actual grant is shown in the OBJ_PRIVILEGE column and the object is shown in the OBJ_NAME column. |
| NEW_NAME | If the object is renamed, and the operation is audited, this column shows the new name. |
| OBJ_PRIVILEGE | The Object Privilege granted that triggered the audit. It has been explained earlier in detail. |
| SYS_PRIVILEGE | If the auditing event triggered by granting a System Privilege, then the privilege is shown here. |
| ADMIN_OPTION | If the grant is given with an ADMIN OPTION clause, this column is populated. |
| GRANTEE | The user or role this privilege was granted or revoked from. |
| AUDIT_OPTION | Audit option set with the statement. |
| SES_ACTIONS | Session Actions, in the format similar to OBJ_PRIVILEGE. |
| COMMENT_TEXT | If this field is populated, it yields some information about the way the user was authenticated. |

| COLUMN | DESCRIPTION |
|---|---|
| SESSIONID | The auditing session id as selected from *v$session* view. |
| ENTRYID | The entry id inside a single session, relevant only if the session has more than a single entry. |
| STATEMENTID | The statement inside a session. One statement may cause multiple actions. |
| RETURNCODE | The result of the action. Typically it's zero (0), for a successful action. If the action fails due to some reason, it's set to the Oracle error number. |
| PRIV_USED | If the privilege used by the user is something special, then it's mentioned here. For instance, is user SCOTT drops his own table EMP, there is no special privilege required, and this field is left null. But if user FRED, who has DROP ANY TABLE privilege, drops Scott's table EMP, then the special privilege is used, and is recorded in this column. |
| CLIENT_ID | If the session sets the client identifier using DBMS_APPLICATION_INFO, it's shown here. |
| SESSION_CPU | The amount of CPU consumed by the session. |

**Table 10.3** *Columns of View dba_audit_statement*

The view captures audit records only on certain types of statements. As you can see, the view is specifically for grants and audit related records, the kind we are interested in.

```
ALTER SYSTEM
AUDIT DEFAULT
AUDIT OBJECT
GRANT OBJECT
GRANT ROLE
NOAUDIT DEFAULT
NOAUDIT OBJECT
REVOKE OBJECT
REVOKE ROLE
SYSTEM AUDIT
SYSTEM GRANT
SYSTEM NOAUDIT
SYSTEM REVOKE
```

Please note: all types of audit records are visible in the view *dba_audit_trail*, regardless of their nature.

## Tracking Role Grants

A special type of auditing is required for granting roles to users. The auditing event is known as SYSTEM GRANT, given as follows.

```
audit system grant by access;
```

This tracks all role grants to users. For instance, is the user Nathan is granted the role JUNIOR_CLAIM_VIEWER as:

```
grant JUNIOR_CLAIM_VIEWER to nathan;
```

The action is captured in the audit records and can be accessed by issuing:

```
select
   timestamp,
   username,
   action_name,
   obj_name,
   grantee,
   priv_used
from dba_audit_statement
/
```

The results come out as:

```
TIMESTAMP USERNAME                       ACTION_NAME
--------- ------------------------------ -----------
OBJ_NAME
-----------------------------------------------------
GRANTEE                        PRIV_USED
------------------------------ ---------------------
25-AUG-03 ANANDA                         GRANT ROLE
JUNIOR_CLAIM_VIEWER
NATHAN                         GRANT ANY ROLE
```

Note the important points here – the ACTION_NAME column shows GRANT ROLE, and the role name is shown in the column OBJ_NAME, as the value JUNIOR_CLAIM_VIEWER. Therefore, the column OBJ_NAME does not show only objects, but grants as well. This is an important fact to remember.

These audit trails clearly show when the privileges were granted or revoked, and by whom. Combining this information with the regular audits, we can identify another important requirement of HIPAA and other security regulations, namely whether the user had any possibility of accessing the data at any point in time. It will also capture any malicious activity in the past. For instance, the user APPUSER is not expected to update the table CLAIMS. However, due to an honest mistake or a deliberate act, the user was granted the privilege for a very short time, during which the user updated some key values, and then the privilege was revoked. A later analysis will reveal that the user does not have update privileges on CLAIMS, so there would be no questioning the possibility of such an act. Although the AUDIT record will show that the update occurred, the analysis will raise more questions than answers, due to this ambiguity. However, if the grants auditing is enabled, the act of granting and revoking the privilege will be captured too, and the act can be discovered and explained.

## Conclusion

Auditing Grants is a very important part of the security framework applicable to any database, not just those under the HIPAA regulations. In this chapter we learned how to:

- Record the present privileges granted to the users through a single script that can be run periodically.
- Record the changes made to these grants using AUDIT functionality, which will produce a track record of the changes.

In the next chapter we will explore the hitherto impossible task of auditing select statements using an Oracle feature called Fine Grained Auditing (FGA).

# Fine Grained Auditing

CHAPTER

## Introduction

So far, we have explored using AUDIT functionality to record the fact that a user accessed a certain table and performed a certain operation on it, e.g. selected from it or updated some records, etc. However, the other important aspect of the operation – *what* was updated or selected – has remained unrecorded. The AUDIT functionality cannot record the access at that granular level.

To some extent, the activities can be recorded in that granular detail using triggers on the tables and using LogMiner, as we saw in an earlier chapter. The LogMiner extracts the information about the changes from the archived log files, indicating the user and other information. This is an unobtrusive operation, i.e. it does not affect online transaction processing. The triggers can be placed on tables to record the changes. While they affect the online activity on the tables, they offer flexibility in recording the activities *at the source*, not after the fact, as in the case of LogMiner. This provides valuable flexibility, such as recording the old values before change and triggering alarms based on the changes audited.

However, both of these methods fail to address the auditing requirements when the data is selected, not *changed*. A mere selection without any change is not a transaction from Oracle's point-of-view, and thus is not captured by the redo log files, nor is it found in the archived log files. The LogMiner, then, cannot find them. Similarly, there is no triggering statement that gets triggered by the SELECT statement. Therefore, the trigger mechanism can't be used for SELECTs capturing the action.

Until Oracle 9i, there was no method by which a SELECT statement could be audited granularly to show what the user selected. Oracle 9i introduced a new tool named Fine Grained Auditing (FGA) that is used to capture the details of the select only queries issued by users. The tool gives a new edge to the auditing tools available to the DBA to satisfy the requirements of a number of compliance bodies such as HIPAA. Under the HIPAA law, the data selected from the tables should also be audited – to record the tracks of who is accessing what information, particularly sensitive data such as Patient Health Information (PHI), among others. Oracle FGA addresses this issue.

In this chapter we will study the FGA in detail and see how the tool can be used to satisfy the requirements of HIPAA. After completing this chapter, you will be able to build the necessary infrastructure to achieve that objective using the scripts provided.

# Fine Grained Auditing

The concept can be better explained by an example. Extending from the earlier examples, the same table CLAIMS is used. In that table, we will record the audit if anyone selects from the table. This can be done by issuing

```
begin
   dbms_fga.add_policy (
      object_schema=>'CLAIM_SCHEMA',
      object_name=>'CLAIMS',
      policy_name=>'LARGE_CLAIM'
  );
end;
```

This statement creates an FGA policy named LARGE_CLAIM on the table *claims*. Note this policy is different from the policy defined in Virtual Private Database (VPD). Even though both are called policies, VPD policies restrict the rows visible to the users whereas FGA policies define how the select statements are recorded. They are very different concepts.

After this statement is executed, any select statement on the *claims* table is audited. For instance, if JUDY selects from this table as:

```
select * from claim_schema.claims;
```

The operation is audited. The audit records can be seen by issuing:

```
select db_user, os_user, policy_name,
to_char(timestamp,'mm/dd/yyyy hh24:mi:ss'),
sql_text
from dba_fga_audit_trail
where object_schema = 'CLAIM_SCHEMA'
and object_name = 'CLAIMS';
```

The results come back as:

```
DB_USER OS_USER POLICY_NAME     TO_CHAR(TIMESTAMP,'
------- ------- ------------- -------------------
SQL_TEXT
---------------------------------------------------
JUDY    ananda  LARGE_CLAIM    08/17/2003 23:24:13
select * from claim_schema.claims
```

Note how the Database user JUDY is recorded, with the Operating system user, the timestamp and the SQL Text that is issued by the user. The statement was audited due to the existence of the policy LARGE_CLAIM as shown in the appropriate column.

The auditing of select statement, hitherto impossible, is possible now using the Fine Grained Auditing. Hopefully this example shows the power and functionality of this new tool.

Similarly, the view *dba_fga_audit_trail* also has some additional columns to support the added functionality.

| COLUMN NAME | DESCRIPTION |
|---|---|
| STATEMENT_TYPE | The type of statement – INSERT, UPDATE, DELETE, or SELECT that triggered the auditing. |
| EXTENDED_TIMESTAMP | The extended timestamp of the trail entry. See the corresponding entry in Table 13.1 for more explanation. |
| PROXY_SESSIONID | If the user is an enterprise user and connects using a proxy user, the SID of the session of the proxy user connection is shown here. |
| GLOBAL_UID | If the user is an enterprise user, the global user ID. |
| INSTANCE_NUMBER | The instance number if using RAC |
| OS_PROCESS | The Operating System process id. |
| TRANSACTIONID | The transaction identifier, if the statement is part of a transaction. |
| STATEMENTID | The statement id. For more detailed explanation, see the chapter on Auditing. |
| ENTRYID | The entry identifier in the audit trail. See the Chapter on Auditing for more details. |

## Behavior in Views

FGA functions even if a view is used on the base table. Therefore, there is no need to create anther policy on the view. This leads to simplified administration. Consider the following, where the user creates a view on this table.

```
create view vw_claims as select * from claims;
```

Now if JUDY selects from the view instead of the table:

```
select * from claim_schema.vw_claims;
```

This statement triggers an auditing record to be generated. If we execute the same statement we used earlier to get the data from *dba_fga_audit_trail*,

```
select db_user, os_user, policy_name,
to_char(timestamp,'mm/dd/yyyy hh24:mi:ss'),
sql_text
from dba_fga_audit_trail
where object_schema = 'CLAIM_SCHEMA'
and object_name = 'CLAIMS';
```

The results come back as:

```
DB_USER OS_USER POLICY_NAME     TO_CHAR(TIMESTAMP,'
------- ------- -------------- -------------------
SQL_TEXT
---------------------------------------------------
JUDY    ananda  LARGE_CLAIM    08/17/2003 23:24:13
select * from claim_schema.claims

JUDY    ananda  LARGE_CLAIM    08/17/2003 23:33:13
select * from claim_schema.vw_claims
```

Note how the selection from the view is captured as well. Interestingly, the auditing records show that the base table *claims* was accessed (the OBJECT_NAME column is *claims*), not the view, although the SQL statement gives the truth away.

If we need to audit only the selections from the view, and not from the table, we could set up the policy in that way, as in the following example:

```
begin
   dbms_fga.add_policy (
      object_schema=>'CLAIM_SCHEMA',
      object_name=>'VW_CLAIMS',
      policy_name=>'VW_CLAIM'
  );
end;
/
```

This policy explicitly shows selection on the views only, not on the underlying table. After setting up the policy, if Judy selects from the view, and we select the audit records:

```
select
   db_user,
   object_name,
   policy_name,
   to_char(timestamp,'mm/dd/yyyy hh24:miss'),
   sql_text
from dba_fga_audit_trail
where object_schema = 'CLAIM_SCHEMA'
/
```

We will see:

```
DB_USER OBJECT_NAME POLICY_NAME TO_CHAR(TIMESTAMP,'
------- ----------- ----------- -------------------
SQL_TEXT
---------------------------------------------------
JUDY    VW_CLAIMS   VW_CLAIM     08/17/2003 23:24:13
select * from claim_schema.vw_claims
```

Note the use of the view name in the OBJECT_NAME column, instead of the base table name. In addition, there is no other record for the selection from the base table.

> **If a policy is defined on a base table, the FGA record will be generated even if the table is selected indirectly, such as where a view based on that table is queried. If the policy is specifically defined on the view, then the audit record is generated if the view is queried, not the table. When a table is queried by Oracle indirectly, such as in enforcing a Foreign Key constraint, the FGA auditing is not enabled.**

# Prerequisite

The FGA can work only in Cost Based Optimizer. This means the *optimizer_mode* and *optimizer_goal* in both session and system (where appropriate) levels should not be set to RULE. Also, the tables should be properly analyzed, with at least estimated statistics. Additionally, the statement should not have the RULE hint in it.

The FGA will *appear* to work under the Rule Based Optimizer (RBO), but the results will be inaccurate with a large number of false positives. Do not use FGA under RBO.

# The *dbms_fga* Package

The central mechanism for the FGA is implemented in the package *dbms_fga*, where all the APIs are defined. Typically, a user other than SYS is given the responsibility of maintaining these policies. With the convention followed earlier, we will go with the user SECUSER, who is entrusted with much of the security features championed in this book. The following statement grants the user SECUSER enough authority to create and maintain the auditing facility.

```
grant execute on dbms_fga to secuser
/
```

The biggest problem with this package is that the polices are not like regular objects with owners. While a user with execute permission on this package can create policies, he or she can drop policies created by *another* user, too. This makes it extremely important to secure this package and limit the use to only a few users who are called to define the policies, such as SECUSER, a special user used in examples throughout this book.

Now, let's explore the procedures in the package in detail.

## *add_policy*

We saw earlier how to add a policy to a table or view, but only three parameters of the procedure were used. There are several other very important parameters, as described below.

### Audit Condition

HIPAA requirements generally call for specific auditing, not a broad record-everything policy. For instance, you may want to audit only when someone selects claims for amounts more than $500. If the user selects any claim below that amount, it is not worth keeping an auditing record.

FGA can easily handle this. The parameter *audit_condition* that was not used in the earlier example can be used to trigger auditing selectively. To satisfy the requirement, we could specify the parameter

```
audit_condition=>'CLAIM_AMOUNT>500'
```

in the *dbms_fga.add_policy* procedure. By default, all access queries are audited, regardless of the data returned. The above parameter will restrict the auditing information. Even if the query does not specify the clause, if any of the rows returned contain a claim amount of more than 500, the auditing is triggered.

The parameter can also be provided in multiple conditions, e.g.

```
audit_condition=>'CLAIM_AMOUNT>500 OR PAID_AMOUNT>500'
```

Here the auditing will be triggered if either of the conditions CLAIM_AMOUNT>500 or PAID_AMOUNT>500 is satisfied in the retrieved data.

## Relevant Columns

Once again, HIPAA requirements could determine the change in strategy. Typically, the law might ask that access only to certain columns be audited, for example to sensitive columns containing Personal Health Information. In your case, the columns are perhaps Social Security Number (SSN), procedures conducted on the patient in that claim, etc. The requirement might state to audit the query only if these columns are accessed. The parameter in the function ADD_POLICY that does this is set as shown below.

```
audit_column => 'SSN, PROC_CODE'
```

In this example, the audit records are triggered only if the columns SSN and PROC_CODE are selected in the query. These columns are referred to as *Relevant Columns*. By default, all the columns of the object are relevant. Specifying this parameter can limit the amount of audit generated.

Based on these two parameters, a complete example of adding a policy is shown below.

```
begin
   dbms_fga.add_policy (
      object_schema=>'CLAIM_SCHEMA',
      object_name=>'CLAIMS',
      policy_name=>'LARGE_CLAIM',
      audit_condition=>
        'CLAIM_AMOUNT>500 OR PAID_AMOUNT>500',
      audit_column=>
        'SSN, PROC_CODE'
  );
end;
/
```

Note the columns referenced in the *audit_column* and *audit_condition* parameters are different. This might create some confusion on how various situations are handled. It can be understood by using a few simple rules.

- If the query selects the columns mentioned in the *audit_column* parameter, then check the next step; otherwise, this is not a candidate for auditing.
- If the query selects rows that satisfy the clause in the *audit_condition*, then the statement is audited; otherwise, this is not audited.

Sometimes the query might reference the columns implicitly, not explicitly naming them. The auditing is triggered in that case, too. For instance, the following query is audited based on the policy defined earlier.

```
select * from claims;
```

Even though the columns are not named, the fact that all columns are selected triggers the audit. Another case is

```
select claim_id from claims where ssn = '123456789';
```

The following table shows the expected audit triggering in different scenarios.

| USER SELECTED RELEVANT COLUMNS | THE AUDIT CONDITION IS EVALUATED TO TRUE | IS THE ACTION AUDITED? |
|---|---|---|
| Yes | Yes | Yes |
| Yes | No | No |
| No | Yes | No |
| No | No | No |

For instance, in the following example, assume the policy has been defined with the two important parameters as:

```
audit_condition=>
  'CLAIM_AMOUNT>500',
audit_column=>
  'SSN, PROC_CODE'
```

The user issues several statements as shown in the following table. The issuance of an audit record and the reason for it is explained after each statement.

| | |
|---|---|
| 1 | `SELECT CLAIM_AMOUNT`<br>`FROM CLAIMS`<br>`WHERE CLAIM_ID = 123456`<br>`This returns a row where claim amount is 600`<br><br>**Not Audited**. Although the audit condition is true (CLAIM_AMOUNT > 500), the query did not specify any of the relevant columns, SSN and PROC_CODE. So it's not audited. |
| 2 | `SELECT SSN`<br>`FROM CLAIMS`<br>`WHERE CLAIM_ID = 123456`<br><br>The value of claim amount is 600 for this claim.<br><br>**Audited**. The audit condition is true (CLAIM_AMOUNT > 500), the query contained the relevant columns SSN or PROC_CODE. So it is audited. |
| 3 | `SELECT PROC_CODE`<br>`FROM CLAIMS`<br>`WHERE CLAIM_ID = 456789`<br><br>This returns a row where claim amount is 400<br><br>**Not Audited**. Although the selected columns are in the relevant list, the audit condition is false (CLAIM_AMOUNT is not greater than 500). So it is not audited. |
| 4 | `SELECT CLAIM_AMOUNT`<br>`FROM CLAIMS`<br>`WHERE CLAIM_ID = 456789`<br><br>This returns a row where claim amount is 400<br><br>**Not Audited.** Neither the audit condition is evaluated to true (CLAIM_AMOUNT is not greater than 500) nor the relevant columns are in the query. This is not audited. |

| | |
|---|---|
| 5 | `SELECT * FROM CLAIMS WHERE CLAIM_ID = 123456`<br><br>The claim amount of this claim is 600<br><br>**Audited.** Although the relevant columns SSN or PROC_CODE are not explicitly specified, the SELECT * selects them, so the columns are *implicitly* selected. Hence it's audited. |
| 6 | `SELECT COUNT(*) FROM CLAIMS`<br><br>**Not Audited.** The relevant columns are not selected, not even implicitly; hence the action is not audited. |

**Table 11.3** *Effects of Statements on Auditing*

Hopefully this table will provide clear examples for when the auditing engages and when it does not. Following this table, you can devise a fine-grained auditing system for your database with the specific requirements in mind.

# FGA for DML statements

Fine Grained auditing has been expanded to a full solution for all types of database access, starting in Oracle 10g. In Oracle 9i, only select statements could be audited; 10g has expanded this functionality to audit even DML statements such as insert, update and delete. To support this, a new parameter has been introduced in the *add_policy* procedure of the package *dbms_fga.*

The following code sample was used to turn on auditing for a certain table.

```
begin
   dbms_fga.add_policy (
      object_schema=>'CLAIM_SCHEMA',
      object_name=>'CLAIMS',
      policy_name=>'LARGE_CLAIM',
      audit_condition=>
        'CLAIM_AMOUNT>500 OR PAID_AMOUNT>500',
      audit_column=>
        'SSN, PROC_CODE'
  );
end;
/
```

This was used to turn auditing on only for select statements against the table. The same can be now be rewritten as:

```
begin
   dbms_fga.add_policy (
      object_schema=>'CLAIM_SCHEMA',
      object_name=>'CLAIMS',
      policy_name=>'LARGE_CLAIM',
      audit_condition=>
        'CLAIM_AMOUNT>500 OR PAID_AMOUNT>500',
      audit_column=>
        'SSN, PROC_CODE',
      statement_types => 'SELECT'
  );
end;
/
```

To audit insert, delete, and update for the same table on the same policy condition and columns, we can use:

```
begin
   dbms_fga.add_policy (
      object_schema=>'CLAIM_SCHEMA',
      object_name=>'CLAIMS',
      policy_name=>'LARGE_CLAIM',
      audit_condition=>
        'CLAIM_AMOUNT>500 OR PAID_AMOUNT>500',
      audit_column=>
        'SSN, PROC_CODE',
      statement_types => 'SELECT,INSERT,UPDATE,DELETE'
  );
end;
/
```

The above code writes an entry into the table *fga_log$* when the table is subjected to insert, update, delete, and select statements; when the auditing condition is satisfied and the audit columns are referenced.

This newly introduced facility is extremely helpful in cases where row level auditing was captured using table-level triggers in the prior releases. Using the DML FGA policies, the row level triggers can be retired.

Since FGA can also execute a procedure known as handler module when the audit conditions are satisfied, the policy can be extended to perform other tasks, not just writing to the audit trails. Some of these tasks are sending emails, or setting a column to a certain value that has an indicator to cause a future job to be kicked off, etc.

To support the new functionality, the view *dba_audit_policies* has been changed. Here is a description of the view in Oracle 10g.

```
OBJECT_SCHEMA       NOT NULL VARCHAR2(30)
OBJECT_NAME         NOT NULL VARCHAR2(30)
POLICY_NAME         NOT NULL VARCHAR2(30)
POLICY_TEXT                  VARCHAR2(4000)
POLICY_COLUMN                VARCHAR2(30)
PF_SCHEMA                    VARCHAR2(30)
PF_PACKAGE                   VARCHAR2(30)
PF_FUNCTION                  VARCHAR2(30)
ENABLED                      VARCHAR2(3)
SEL                          VARCHAR2(3)
INS                          VARCHAR2(3)
UPD                          VARCHAR2(3)
DEL                          VARCHAR2(3)
```

The last four columns highlighted in bold are new in this release and they indicate the triggering event of this policy. For instance, if a policy is defined for SELECT statements, the column SEL will show YES, else it will show NO. Similarly, INS, UPD and DEL show triggering settings for Insert, Update and Delete, respectively.

## Handler Procedure

The third set of parameters passed to *dbms_fga.add_policy* is related to handler procedures. When the audit condition is triggered on the table or view, the default action is to write the records into the audit trail. However, at the same time, the procedure defined as the handler procedure is executed, if mentioned. In the above case, the following is an example of the handler procedure as a parameter to the *dbms_fga.add_policy* procedure.

```
handler_schema  => 'SECUSER',
handler_module  => 'EMAILER'
```

Here a procedure named EMAILER, owned by SECUSER, is defined as the handler module. When the audit condition is satisfied on the table, the procedure EMAILER is *automatically* called. Imagine this as a *trigger* on the select statement. Ordinarily, triggers are based on some transactional statements such as insert, update, delete, etc.; but this is an example where the concept of triggers can be extended to the select statements, too.

The handler functions are useful in many cases. In the above definition, we can place some logic inside the procedure EMAILER to check other conditions, such as coming from a specific IP Address, and generating emails to alert someone on possible unauthorized access.

An important point to note here is that the handler procedure may be defined in another schema, not necessarily in the same one as that of the table. This ability is particularly well suited for secured applications since no user need be given execute privilege on this procedure, and hence no user can call this procedure independently to create serious damage.

The ability of the handler procedure to execute when an audit condition is satisfied can be exploited by creating a user-defined audit functionality as shown later in this chapter.

## Multiple Policies

A table may have several FGA policies defined on it. All the policies are independently evaluated and handled. For all the policies in which the conditions evaluate to true, the corresponding handler functions are triggered. This may cause some confusion in handling the policies, but in most cases this provides flexibility to the setup. The individual policies can be enabled or disabled based on requirements, without affecting the others.

# Managing Policies

All the administrative operations for policies are done using procedures defined in the supplied package *dbms_fga*. Here are the common operations.

## Dropping Policies

The policies can be dropped by the following command.

```
begin
   dbms_fga.drop_policy (
      object_schema=>'CLAIM_SCHEMA',
      object_name=>'CLAIMS',
      policy_name=>'CLAIM_AMOUNT');
end;
```

### Potential Problem Due To Bug

You should be aware of a bug 2713401 that prevents the policy from being dropped. In this bug, attempts to drop the policy using the above statement will fail with "ORA-28102: policy does not exist" error message. Remember, this is a bug, so it might have been fixed in later releases. If the bug affects your particular release, please read on in this section; otherwise, please skip it.

In order to correct the problem, the best approach is to call Oracle Support and have them address the problem. In development systems, however, here is a solution you could try. We urge you to strongly consider against running it on production, as it is unsupported by Oracle, but it seems to work and can be attempted in development. The authors do not assume any responsibility for any damage caused by intentional application to production or otherwise.

As user SYS, issue the following:

```
begin
   dbms_fga.add_policy (
      object_schema=>'CLAIM_SCHEMA',
      object_name=>'CLAIMS',
      policy_name=>'CLAIM_AMOUNT');
end;
/
```

Note we just created a policy with the same name. Ordinarily, it wouldn't have worked, but it did, due to the bug. At this time, if you select the rows from *fga$* table, you will see two rows for this policy name. One of them should be dropped as in the following.

```
DELETE FGA$
WHERE PNAME = 'CLAIM_AMOUNT'
AND ROWNUM < 2;
```

Now the policy can be dropped normally using *dbms_fga.drop_policy* procedure.

Again, use this trick at your own risk, this is unsupported by Oracle Support.

## Enabling/Disabling Policies

A policy can be disabled, without being dropped. This can be useful in several situations where the policy needs to be temporarily suspended.

```
begin
   dbms_fga.disable_policy (
      object_schema=>'CLAIM_SCHEMA',
      object_name=>'CLAIMS',
      policy_name=>'CLAIM_AMOUNT');
end;
```

To enable it, use the corresponding:

```
begin
   dbms_fga.enable_policy (
      object_schema=>'CLAIM_SCHEMA',
      object_name=>'CLAIMS',
      policy_name=>'CLAIM_AMOUNT');
end;
```

These four procedures inside the *dbms_fga* package handle all operations inside the FGA framework.

# User Defined Audit Handler

If a user queries the table, and the policy condition as well as the columns are satisfied, by default, the action is written into the table *fga_log$* owned by SYS. However, it is not mandatory that the records be written into this table alone. In some cases, as we will see, it may be desirable to have a separate table to record the audit functionality.

## Why a User Defined Audit Table

**Maintainability** – The file grained audit functionality, just like the regular audit, also needs sophisticated archival and purge setups, where the trails can be preserved for analysis later. The best method to achieve this is using a partitioned table for the audit trails. When the time comes to purge, the partition can be simply dropped. If it needs to be preserved, the partition can be converted to a table, and the table can be archived via export or via transportable tablespace. Since partitioning the table *fga_log$* is not supported, the next best option is to create a user defined audit table and record there manually.

**Extended Functionality** – The audit handler can do a lot of things in addition to storing the audit record, such as send an e-mail when a certain audit event occurs, e.g. when someone selects from the highly sensitive procedure codes outside business hours. This functionality may seem a little extreme, but in situations where an immediate action is required based on some auditing event, the functionality can be implemented using the handler function.

## Creating a user Defined Auditing System

First we will create a table to hold the audit records.

### fga_audit.sql

```
/*----------------------------------------------------
Purpose: Creates the table FGA_AUDIT, to store the
         user defined audit records.
----------------------------------------------------*/
```

```
    audit_session_id  number(30),
    entry_id          number(30),
    timestamp         date,
    owner             varchar2(20) not null,
    object_name       varchar2(30) not null,
    policy_name       varchar2(20) not null,
    username          varchar(30),
    os_username       varchar2(30),
    auth_type         varchar2(30),
    client_identifier varchar2(100),
    client_info       varchar2(64),
    sql_text          varchar2(64),
    host              varchar2(54),
    instance_num      number(2),
    ip_address        varchar2(30),
    terminal          varchar2(10),
    dba_flag          varchar2(1),
    scn               number(10)
)
tablespace users
partition by range (timestamp)
(
    partition p1 values less than
       (to_date('04/01/2003','mm/dd/yyyy')),
    partition p2 values less than
       (to_date('07/01/2003','mm/dd/yyyy')),
    partition p3 values less than
       (to_date('10/01/2003','mm/dd/yyyy')),
    partition pm values less than
       (maxvalue)
)
```

## Notes on the table

- The columns of the table are explained in detail later in this section, to set them in the context of the values that go into them.
- The important point here is the partitioning of the table. One of the reasons for rolling out a user defined audit handler is to make the archival and purging of this audit table possible. The most convenient and least expensive way to do that is to partition the table along the timestamp column. Here, we have assumed the data is partitioned quarterly. Since the table always grows, the older partitions are never referenced and can be dropped. Later in this chapter we will discuss the details of the archival-purge process.

Next, we will create the audit handler procedure as follows. Before that we have to grant execute privileges on the built-in package *dbms_flashback* to SECUSER. Since we are capturing the System Change Number (SCN) for when this query occurred, we will need to get that value from the procedure *get_system_change_number* in the package *dbms_flashback*, and that is why we need the execute privileges on this package.

```
connect sys/**** as sysdba
grant execute on dbms_flashback to secuser
/
```

The handler procedure must have only three parameters in exactly the same order as shown below and with the datatype VARCHAR2 for all three.

- Owner of the object on which the audit is defined
- Name of the object
- The name of the policy that is applied to trigger this audit

With this information, we will create the handler procedure as shown in the code below.

### fga_auditor.sql

```
/*--------------------------------------------------------
Purpose: Creates the procedure FGA_AUDITOR, as a handler
         Function in user defined auditing
---------------------------------------------------------*/

create or replace procedure fga_auditor
(
   p_owner     in varchar2,
   p_object    in varchar2,
   p_policy    in varchar2
)
is
begin
   insert into fga_audit
   (
      audit_session_id,
      entry_id,
      timestamp,
      owner,
      object_name,
      policy_name,
      username,
      os_username,
      auth_type,
      client_identifier,
      client_info,
      sql_text,
      host,
      instance_num,
      ip_address,
      terminal,
      dba_flag,
```

```
   values
   (
      sys_context('USERENV','SESSIONID'),
      sys_context('USERENV','ENTRYID'),
      sysdate,
      p_owner,
      p_object,
      p_policy,
      sys_context('USERENV','SESSION_USER'),
      sys_context('USERENV','OS_USER'),
      sys_context('USERENV','AUTHENTICATION_TYPE'),
      sys_context('USERENV','CLIENT_IDENTIFIER'),
      sys_context('USERENV','CLIENT_INFO'),
      sys_context('USERENV','CURRENT_SQL'),
      sys_context('USERENV','HOST'),
      sys_context('USERENV','INSTANCE'),
      sys_context('USERENV','IP_ADDRESS'),
      sys_context('USERENV','TERMINAL'),
      decode(sys_context('USERENV','ISDBA'),
         'TRUE','Y','FALSE','N'),
      dbms_flashback.get_system_change_number
   );
end;
```

## Notes on this Procedure

- Most of the information about the session comes from the built-in function *sys_context*. The exact output of each of these functions is explained later under the description of the columns of the table *fga_audit*.
- The System Change Number is captured from the packaged function *dbms_flashback.get_system_change_number*. We assume that the user SECUSER has been given execute grants on this function.

Then we will add the policy to the table as shown below.

```
begin
   dbms_fga.add_policy (
      object_schema => 'CLAIM_SCHEMA',
      object_name   => 'CLAIMS',
      policy_name   => 'CLAIM_AMOUNT',
      audit_condition =>
         'CLAIM_AMOUNT > 2000 OR PAID_AMOUNT > 2000',
      audit_column    => 'CLAIM_AMOUNT, PAID_AMOUNT',
      handler_schema  => 'SECUSER',
      handler_module  => 'FGA_AUDITOR'
   );
end;
/
```

Now this will make the records go into the table *fga_audit in addition* to the *fga_log$* table. Since we are primarily interested in the table *fga_audit*, we can purge the table *fga_log$* periodically and more aggressively by using TRUNCATE.

Let's examine the information captured in the *fga_audit* table. Selecting all the columns of the table *fga_audit*, here is the output.

```
AUDIT_SESSION_ID   ENTRY_ID TIMESTAMP OWNER
---------------- ---------- --------- -------------------
OBJECT_NAME                     POLICY_NAME
------------------------------- --------------------
USERNAME                        OS_USERNAME
------------------------------- -------------------------
AUTH_TYPE
-------------------------------
CLIENT_IDENTIFIER
---------------------------------------------------------
CLIENT_INFO
---------------------------------------------------------
SQL_TEXT
----------------------------------------------------------
HOST                                        INSTANCE_NUM
-------------------------------------------- ------------

IP_ADDRESS                      TERMINAL   D        SCN
------------------------------- ---------- - ----------
             977          6 06-AUG-03 CLAIM_SCHEMA
CLAIMS                          CLAIM_AMOUNT
JUDY                            ananda
DATABASE
Client_Identifier
Client_Info
select * from claims where member_id = 12345
PROLIGENCE\ANANDA1                                     1
127.0.0.1                       ANANDA1    N    1553620
```

Note how the information of interest is captured in detail. Here it shows that this audit record was generated from session id 977. This particular record was the sixth (ENTRYID=6) audit entry in that session. The user JUDY issued the statement "select * from claims where member_id = 12345." Judy was authenticated by the database (AUTH_TYPE=DATABASE), i.e. the user has a password that was used to connect to the database. She did not connect using EXTERNAL accounts.

The OS userid was ananda. Hmm! Is Judy's Windows login ananda? Most likely not. Perhaps Judy just logged in from some Windows user named ananda. The terminal from where the user connected was PROLIGENCE\ANANDA1. Again this raises suspicion as this does not seem like Judy's PC name. The IP Address shown here is actually changed to protect the identity. In this case the user issued the *dbms_session.set_identifier* to set the client identifier to a value *Client_Identifier*, which shows up under the CLIENT_IDENTIFIER column here.

The user also called the procedure *dbms_application_info.set_client_info* to set the value *Client_Info*. This database is a single instance one, so the INSTANCE_NUM column will always show 0, but this would have shown other instance numbers if the connection came from them. When the query was issued, the System Change Number (SCN) was 1553620. Finally, the policy that triggered this audit record was CLAIM_AMOUNT.

One of the most important pieces of information from the above display is about the object being accessed. Note the statement was "select * from claims where member_id = 12345." However, *what* was *claims*? Was it a table, a view or a synonym? If it was a synonym, what did it point to? A synonym called *claims* pointing to table *claims* owned by CLAIM_SCHEMA is *very different* from *claims* owned by ANOTHER_SCHEMA. The columns OWNER and OBJECT_NAME specify exactly which object was accessed during the query.

The various columns of the table *fga_audit* have been described in the table below.

| COLUMN NAME | DESCRIPTION |
|---|---|
| AUDIT_SESSION_ID | The audit session id, the same as the session id that is in the regular *audit* table. |
| ENTRY_ID | The entry serial number in the same session, similar to the entry id in the regular *audit* table. |
| TIMESTAMP | The timestamp of the entry of the audit record in this table. |
| OWNER | The owner of the object on which this audit record was generated. |
| OBJECT_NAME | The name of the object on which this audit record was generated. |
| POLICY_NAME | The name of the policy on that object which triggered the audit record to be generated. |
| USERNAME | The name of the database user that issued the statement being audited. |
| OS_USERNAME | The Operating system user ID. |
| AUTH_TYPE | The way the database user was authenticated, i.e. by Database, or Externally, etc. |

| COLUMN NAME | DESCRIPTION |
|---|---|
| CLIENT_IDENTIFIER | If the Client Identifier is set using the *set_identifier* procedure in the *dbms_session*, then this field is populated with the value. This is very useful in cases where an application user is used, and the client identifier is used to track the actual user logged in. |
| CLIENT_INFO | If the user sets the client info using the *set_client_info* procedure of the package *dbms_application_info*, then that value is populated here. |
| SQL_TEXT | The exact SQL Text that triggers the auditing is captured here. |
| HOST | The name of the host from where the user is logged in. |
| INSTANCE_NUM | In case of Real Application Clusters (RAC) environment, it might be helpful to know which instance the user was connected to while issuing the SQL statement that triggered the audit. The instance number, as defined in the initialization parameter file is shown here. |
| IP_ADDRESS | The IP Address of the host from where the user was connected is shown here. |
| TERMINAL | The terminal ID of the host from where the user was connected. |
| DBA_FLAG | If the user is DBA and the DBA role is enabled, then it might be useful to know if a DBA role was used to query some application tables. If the DBA user issued a statement that triggered this audit record, this column is set to Y, otherwise it is N. |
| SCN | The System Change Number at the time of the query submission. It is useful to identify the exact data the user saw at that time, not just the data visible now. |

**Table 11.4** *Columns of Table fga_audit*

## Extending Functionality

Anther reason for using the user created auditing as above is to extend the functionality. The handler package and procedure passed to the parameter *handler_module* in the procedure *add_policy* is not just for writing to a table. It can also be used to perform anything else, anything that stored procedures can do. As mentioned earlier, this procedure can be thought of as a *trigger*, triggered by the SELECT statement on the query, similar to the DELETE, UPDATE and INSERT statements. Whenever the condition is satisfied for the audit, the procedure is fired.

One of the most common applications of this procedure is to create an alerting mechanism for when a certain auditing condition is triggered. For instance, the requirements may call for alerting the auditor by e-mail when someone other than the auditor selects some claim information with procedures performed on an HIV patient, a specific data element protected by HIPAA regulation. This kind of functionality can be easily created using the handler function.

# Data Dictionary Tables and Views

## *dba_audit_policies*

The table that holds the policies defined on the table is *fga$* owned by SYS. However, like most other tables used for holding database configurations and settings, this table is excessively normalized and not very user friendly due to the cryptic column names. Therefore, Oracle provides another view called *dba_audit_policies* to show the policies defined on an object. Here are the columns of the view and their descriptions.

| COLUMN NAME | DESCRIPTION |
|---|---|
| OBJECT_SCHEMA | Owner of the object |
| OBJECT_NAME | Name of the object |
| POLICY_NAME | Name of the policy |
| POLICY_TEXT | The SQL text for the policy condition |
| POLICY_COLUMN | The relevant columns on which the policy is set. |
| PF_SCHEMA | Owner of the handler package, if the policy has one. |
| PF_PACKAGE | If the policy is has a handler package, this is the package name. |

| COLUMN NAME | DESCRIPTION |
|---|---|
| PF_FUNCTION | If defined through a function, this column is the function name. |
| ENABLED | If the policy is enabled or not. Shown as YES or NO. |

**Table 11.1** *Columns of View dba_audit_policies*

## An Alternative View

The view *dba_audit_policies* shows the policies and their functions, but the relevant columns are shown in a format that can't be used directly in a DDL statement. To facilitate the process, we will define another view called *dba_fga_audit_opts* to show the same information from the same source, but in a slightly different manner. Here is the script to create the view.

### dba_fga_audit_opts

```
create or replace view dba_fga_audit_opts
 as
 select
    u.name          as object_schema,
    o.name          as object_name,
    f.pname         as policy_name,
    replace(f.ptxt,'''','''''')
                          as policy_text,
    f.pcol             as policy_column,
    f.pfschma     as pf_schema,
    f.ppname      as pf_package,
    f.pfname       as pf_function,
    decode(enable_flag,
       0, 'NO',
       1, 'YES')     as enabled
 from
    sys.user$ u,
    sys.obj$ o,
    sys.fga$ f
 where
    u.user# = o.owner#
 and
```

Note the columns are identical in name and meaning in the other view *dba_audit_policies*, except the column POLICY_COLUMN, which is denoted in a more accurate fashion when quotes are concerned. For instance, if the POLICY_COLUMN is denoted as

```
policy_column => 'STATUS=''ACTIVE'''
```

Then the column POLICY_COLUMN in *dba_audit_policies* shows

```
STATUS = 'ACTIVE'
```

But the corresponding column POLICY_COLUMNS in *dba_fga_audit_opts* shows

```
STATUS = ''ACTIVE''
```

Note how the character value is properly enclosed in two single quotes on each side. This makes it possible for the value to be used directly inside a DDL script without modification.

## fga_log$

The main table to hold to the audit records is *fga_log$* owned by SYS. Here are the columns and their descriptions. This table is important to know, as it is the table manipulated while purging and archiving FGA audit trail data.

| COLUMN NAME | DESCRIPTION |
|---|---|
| SESSIONID | The Audit Session Identifier |
| TIMESTAMP# | The Timestamp in DATE format. |
| DBUID | Database User Id |
| OSUID | OS User ID |
| OSHST | Host Name |
| CLIENTID | Client Identifier, if set. |
| EXTID | If the user is externally identified, this is the External ID of the user. |
| OBJ$SCHEMA | Owner of the table on which this FGA policy is defined and that caused the audit to be generated. |
| OBJ$NAME | Name of the object. |
| POLICYNAME | Name of the policy. |
| SCN | The System Change Number where this select statement occurred. This is very useful in combining this Flashback Queries. |
| SQLTEXT | The text of the SQL statement. |

| COLUMN NAME | DESCRIPTION |
|---|---|
| LSQLTEXT | If the SQL statement is very long, it can't fit within the 4000 character long field SQLTEXT. This field, which is of CLOB data type holds the value. |
| SQLBIND | If a bind variable is used, the value of that variable. |
| COMMENT$TEXT | The Comments. |
| PLHOL | The SQL statement but in LONG format. Due to the presence of this column, this table can't be manipulated in the same way it was possible in AUD$ table. |

**Table 11.2** *Columns of fga_log$ table.*

## *dba_fga_audit_trail*

Like the table *fga$*, *fga_log$* is also not very intuitive or user-friendly, so there are some views defined on it to make the information more presentable and easier to understand. The most common view is *dba_fga_audit_trail*. Here are the columns of the view and their descriptions.

| COLUMN NAME | DESCRIPTION |
|---|---|
| SESSION_ID | The Audit Session Identifier. This is not the same as the Session Identifier from the *v$session* view. |
| TIMESTAMP | The timestamp when the audit record was generated. |
| DB_USER | The Database user. |
| OS_USER | The Operating System User. |
| USERHOST | The host name of the machine from where the user connected. |
| CLIENT_ID | The Client Identifier, if set. |
| EXT_NAME | If the client is externally authenticated, this column holds the external name. |
| OBJECT_SCHEMA | The schema owner of the object on which the access caused the audit to be triggered. |

| COLUMN NAME | DESCRIPTION |
| --- | --- |
| OBJECT_NAME | The name of the object on which the select operation triggered the audit. |
| POLICY_NAME | The name of the policy that triggered the audit. |
| SCN | The System Change Number at which the audit was recorded. |
| SQL_TEXT | The exact SQL statement that triggered the audit statement. |
| SQL_BIND | If the SQL statement used some bind variables, it comes here. |
| COMMENT$TEXT | The comments. |

**Table 11.3** *Columns of view dba_fga_audit_trail*

# Application Users and FGA

Here we will revisit the problem that has been haunting us for several chapters – the use of application users in the database application, as opposed to database users. A typical example is when an application user Judy is not a database user, but rather authenticated by the application – either via checking the password in a table, or via some other mechanism such as checking the Domain password, or LDAP password, etc. The application connects to the database using some default user ID, e.g. APPUSER; and then checks the table obtaining the usernames. Regardless of the method utilized to authenticate the user, the database sees the user as APPUSER, not as Judy. Therefore, even though Fine Grained Auditing is enabled, it yields little information, as the recorded username in all cases is APPUSER, not the user who made the changes. Obviously, this does not establish accountability at all.

The solution to the problem lies in identifying the user's other credentials besides the username in the database – such as the IP address, the OS Username, the host name from where he or she is connected, etc. The trick is to pass these values to the database so that the audit handler can capture them,  and this is achieved through the use of the application contexts described earlier.

## Client Identifier

When the client identifier is set, the value is carried over automatically to the FGA trail log tables. Here is an example of where it is set to value *Some_Identifier*.

```
execute dbms_session.set_identifier('Some_Identifier')
```

At this time, if we see the session in the *v$session* view, we can see the client identifier.

```
select client_identifier
from v$session
where sid = …

CLIENT_IDENTIFIER
-----------------------
Some_Identifier
```

Note this is not the same as Client Info as set by the dbms_application_info package. This column is unique in the way that it shows up in the *fga* table. The column CLIENTID in the table *fga_log$*, the default raw audit table for fine grained auditing, holds the value *Some_Identifier* in this case. The same value shows up in the data dictionary view *dba_fga_audit_trail* column CLIENT_ID. Even though the username shows up as APPUSER or the real database username, if the client identifier is set, the column displays the value and the real user is given away.

The next tricky question is how we can set the client identifier in such a way that it will not be prone to manipulation and can safely point to the real user. If the user is allowed to call the *dbms_session* package to set the client identifier, then it is inherently insecure. The user can set anything in there, even another user. Therefore, we can't let the user set the value. Here are some alternatives for setting this value.

## Set by Application

The application, after connecting to the database as the application user, can call the *dbms_session* package to set the value. Once set, the value will be persistent throughout the session.

However this method is also insecure. The user APPUSER must have the privileges to execute the *dbms_session* package, and thus can call the package outside the application and make changes.

To avoid this security hole, we can revoke execution privileges on *dbms_session* from APPUSER. A detailed approach on how to do this has been described in the Chapter on Virtual Private Database and won't be repeated here. Inside the function *is_password_correct*, the client identifier can be set. This will automatically set the value and the user can't set it outside without calling the function first.

Refer to the script *is_password_correct_vpd.sql* in the online code depot. In that script we set the value of the client identifier to the application user as shown below.

```
dbms_session.set_identifier(p_userid);
```

However, we can assign anything in this value. For instance, we can set the value of the application user as well as the application name to make it more descriptive. This can be done by changing the above line to

```
dbms_session.set_identifier(p_userid||'-claim_app3');
```

Here we assume that the name of the application is *claim_app3*. Sometimes it may be useful to see the value of both the application user and the application name together to ascertain accountability.

## Set by Logon Trigger

The above method works fine if a table in the database authenticates the application user. However, not all applications are designed that way; some applications authenticate users by LDAP, or by Windows Domain, etc. In that case the function *is_password_correct* will not be used, and we can't use the method to set the client identifier.

An alternative method can be used here, via logon triggers. Here we will pass some known facts of the session to the client identifier, such as the OS Username. Here are the steps in detail.

1. First we need to revoke the execute privileges on the package *dbms_session* from public. This package has execute privileges granted to public by default. If you have followed the guidelines mentioned in this book, you should have revoked that. If you haven't, this is the time to revoke it.

   ```
   connect sys/***** as sysdba
   revoke execute on dbms_session from public;
   ```

   Also revoke any execute privileges granted to any role or any user explicitly.

2. Next, we will create a procedure that sets the client identifier. This should not be available to public, so a perfect place for the procedure is the SECUSER schema. Here is the function description:

   ```
   connect secuser/******
   create or replace procedure set_client_id
   as
   begin
      dbms_session.set_identifier (
      sys_context('userenv','os_user'));
   end;
   /
   ```

3. As you can see, the user needs execute privileges on the *dbms_session* package. Following our guidelines earlier in this book, you may have granted that. If not, execute the following SQL to grant that privilege.

```
grant execute on dbms_session to secuser;
```

4. The above procedure wouldn't have been compiled if the grant was not in place. Recompile the procedure to remove the error.

5. Create a database logon trigger to call this procedure.

```
create or replace trigger set_client_id
after logon on database
begin
   secuser.set_client_id;
end;
/
```

The setup is now complete. Anytime a user logs in, the client identifier will be automatically set to the OS user name. Let's test the security of the process. If the user APPUSER executes the package to set the value directly, he or she will get an error, as he or she does not have the execute privileges.

```
SQL> exec dbms_session.set_identifier ('AAAA')
BEGIN dbms_session.set_identifier ('AAAA'); END;

      *
ERROR at line 1:
ORA-06550: line 1, column 7:
PLS-00201: identifier 'DBMS_SESSION' must be declared
ORA-06550: line 1, column 7:
PL/SQL: Statement ignored
```

Similarly, if the user decides to call the procedure instead,

```
SQL> exec secuser.set_client_id ('AAA');
BEGIN secuser.set_client_id ('AAA'); END;

      *
ERROR at line 1:
ORA-06550: line 1, column 7:
PLS-00201: identifier 'SECUSER.SET_CLIENT_ID' must be declared
ORA-06550: line 1, column 7:
PL/SQL: Statement ignored
```

The error message says it all. The user does not have any execute privileges on the procedure. The only way the client identifier can be set is by the logon trigger. We have made sure the client identifier can be set in a secured way.

## Securely Setting the Value

Before concluding our discussion on the client identifier, the only perplexing thing to mention here is to what its value should be set. In the previous example, we have used OS user as a value for the Client Identifier; but the OS user is available anyway in the Fine Grained Auditing log table, so it probably does not achieve a whole lot.

Other values that can be placed here to convey a meaningful client identifier can be some type of proprietary values. For instance, we can encrypt the OS Username, Machine Name, Domain Name, LDAP Key or some other appropriate value and make up a long client identifier. It's not meaningful to see the value on *v$session* view, but when decrypted, it will provide a meaningful picture of the session. If the user does manipulate the value, it will not be decrypted properly as the user does not know the encryption key.

This method can be used inside a procedure owned by a secured user, such as SECUSER. The encryption key is supplied by the application. Here we will use the routines we developed earlier in the Chapter on Encryption.

*get_encrypted_value* – Needs two parameters, the value to be encrypted and the key in RAW datatype. The code can be found in online code depot as *get_encrypted_value.sql*. It returns the encrypted value in hexadecimal representation in VARCHAR2 datatype.

*get_decrypted_value* – Needs two parameters, the value to be decrypted in hexadecimal and the key in RAW datatype. The code can be found in *get_decrypted_value.sql* in the Online Code Depot. The function returns the decrypted value.

The secret to the whole exercise is to have the key supplied by the application. Here we will make up the key as a long list of characters in hexadecimal format. This key is stored in the application code or supplied from a table.

We may decide to store something that is not obtainable in the *sys_context* function. One possibility is using the Domain Name of the user's machine. After the application starts and connects as user APPUSER, or some other generic user, it calls

```
get_encrypted_value('<The Domain Name>',
        hextoraw(
'A8D63820782A4AC510124A64311D1ABC3F6E07429558BE88'
))
```

Note the long key is supplied by the application, along with the Domain Name. The result of the above call is placed in a variable, and this variable is placed in the Client Identifier using SECUSER.SET_CLIENT_ID procedure.

If the domain name is PROLIGENCE.COM, the value will look something like:

```
5E56F606BF398ECF3442BE6708BEBF21
```

which probably means nothing when seen from *v$session*, or from the Fine Grained Auditing tables and views. However, if there is a need to uncover which domain name was used, we could use the function:

```
select  get_decrypted_value(
    '5E56F606BF398ECF3442BE6708BEBF21',
    hextoraw(
'A8D63820782A4AC510124A64311D1ABC3F6E07429558BE88'
    ))
from dual;
```

It returns PROLIGENCE.COM.

Notice, only the application has the key value hard coded inside it, or somehow placed via some sort of table owned by SECUSER; not known to the regular users. Even if a regular user connects as APPUSER and decides to forge identity of the Domain Name to say, ORACLE.COM, he or she will not be successful because he or she does not know the encryption key. The user can call SECUSER.SET_CLIENT_ID to set another client identifier, but it will not be decrypted properly, and will not state ORACLE.COM, unlike what the hacker intended. Therefore, the value can be set and retrieved in a secured manner.

### Potential Threats

This merely ensures that the user does not enter a value that can be considered valid. However, this does not prevent the user from changing the value of the client identifier. It will not be valid, but it will be passed on to the FGA trail tables, and thus the identity of the user can be shrouded. This setup does not help in identifying culprits but makes sure the wrong person is not identified for a malicious act.

**In order to absolutely make sure that the user is identified, you have to user the Oracle Advanced Security option to pass the username from the LDAP server.**

## Application Context

Unlike Virtual Private Database, the Client Identifier method is available only in Oracle 9i.and beyond.  For Oracle 8i, the absence of this variable makes tracking of the usernames difficult. However, FGA is not available in Oracle 8i, so this ceases to be problem.

In VPD, the problem was solved using *application contexts* in Oracle 8i. But even in Oracle 9i, they can be used to enhance the FGA. Earlier, we saw that we could store a long list of information in Client Identifier, such as the Domain Name, Application User Name, Webserver name, among others. Since the value is VARCHAR2, we have to store these values as a long line with some type of delimiters between them, e.g. a pipe character. In this case, a typical Client Identifier value looks like the following

```
PROLIGENCE.COM|ANAN|ws-01.proligence.com
```

This information is valid and useful, but it might be more useful if these values were split into the individual columns instead of clubbed into a single value.

Using our own auditing facility as described earlier in this chapter, we can create columns to hold these values. The users can call the procedure set_claim_app_ctx to set the various attributes of the context as needed.

The procedure was described in Chapter 5, under Virtual Private Database. It's reproduced here.

```
create procedure set_claim_app_ctx

(
    p_attribute_name in varchar2,
    p_attribute_value in varchar2
) is

begin
    dbms_session.set_context(
        'claim_app_ctx',
         p_attribute_name,
         p_attribute_value);
end;
/
```

Then create the context:

```
create context claim_app_ctx
using set_claim_app_ctx
/
```

The application can call the procedures to set the values:

```
set_claim_app_ctx('domain_name','PROLIGENCE.COM')
set_claim_app_ctx('app_username','ANAN')
set_claim_app_ctx('web_server','ws-01.proligence.com')
```

Inside our customer audit handler procedure *fga_auditor*, described earlier in this chapter, we can retrieve these values by issuing

```
sys_context('claim_app_ctx','domain_name')
sys_context('claim_app_ctx','app_username')
sys_context('claim_app_ctx','web_server')
```

which can then be placed in appropriate columns in the custom audit table *fga_audit_log*. If needed, these can be encrypted, too.

# FGA and Flashback Queries

Fine Grained Auditing shows us what query the user issued to select the data, but perhaps the more important question is what data was displayed to the user. Consider the following situation: we have found out from the audit trails that a user has selected the claim amount from the claims table for a claim that was in INACTIVE status. The policy that is defined on claims of INACTIVE status enables the auditing when a user selects the claim. From the audit trails, we saw that the user issued:

```
select claim_amount from claims where claim_id = 1234567;
```

The status value for the claim 1234567 was INACTIVE at that time, which is the reason the FGA handler audited the statement.

Later, the status for this claim was changed to PENDING. At the time the audit record was seen, the status was INACTIVE, not PENDING. So when the auditor issues the same query to see what the user saw:

```
select status from claims where claim_id = 1234567;
```

He or she will see PENDING, not INACTIVE. Although the user saw the claim when it was inactive, the auditor will never ascertain that. This may lead to accountability problems later. Almost always, the audit trails are examined as an after-effect, and the data could have changed since the time the trails were generated. We need to devise a mechanism to let the auditor know what the user saw at that time, not what the value is now.

Fortunately, a feature known as Flashback Queries allows this to be accomplished quite easily. Introduced in Oracle 9i, this tool lets the data be rewound, i.e. the data is shown as a snapshot in some point in the past. Discussing the details of the Flashback Queries is beyond the scope of this book. In this section we will describe how to use this powerful tool to solve this immediate problem.

From the FGA Audit Trails, we know that the audit trails were triggered when the System Change Number (SCN) was 1852891500. To find out all the columns of the claims at that time, we will simply issue:

```
select *
from claim_schema.claims as of scn 1852891500
where claim_id = 1234567;
```

This query selects the records as of SCN 1852891500, not as of now. It will let us know the value of the different columns of that particular claim at the time the user selected the data and the audit record was generated. This will tell us exactly what we want to know.

However, to have a more practical use of the clause in FGA, we will handle it differently. From the Audit Tables, either *dba_fga_audit_trail*, or the user-defined *fga_audit*, the following record is seen.

```
       SCN USERNAME
---------- ------------------------------------------
SQL_TEXT
-----------------------------------------------------
   1553620 CLAIM_SCHEMA
select paid_amount from claims where member_id = 12345
```

It shows that the user issued the mentioned statement while the SCN was 1553620, and the object referenced was owned by CLAIM_SCHEMA. To find out what the user saw at the time, we can issue the following statements in sequence.

```
alter session set current_schema = CLAIM_SCHEMA;
```

This will instruct all the queries to be based on the CLAIM_SCHMEA schema.

```
execute dbms_flashback.enable_at_system_change_number(1553620)
```

This will place the reference time to that point in the past, mentioned by SCN. Now we will execute the SQL query.

```
select paid_amount from claims where claim_id = 1234567;
```

This will return 1200. The queries are repeated as many times as required to find the values at that time. At the end of the session, we can disable the flashback session by:

```
execute dbms_flashback.disable
```

Now all the queries will select the data as of now, not from the past.

This technique can be extended to become a self-sufficient querying system. Consider the following:

```
set linesize 4000
set trimspool on
set pagesize 0
set feedback off
spool show_fga_fb.sql
select 'select * from ('||lsqltext||') as of scn ('||scn||');'
from fga_log$
/
spool off
```

This creates a file *show_fga_fb.sql* with lines similar to the following.

```
select * from (select * from claim_Schema.claims) as of scn 1852891500;
```

The file *show_fga_fb.sql* can then be run to retrieve the values of columns as of a date in the past.

Another variation in the setup can be to include all other relevant details like username, OS username, terminal, timestamp, etc. along with the data selected from the tables. The following query accomplishes the task. If desired, all the relevant details can be placed as needed in the script.

### cr_show_fga_fb.sql

```
set linesize 4000
set trimspool on
set pagesize 0
set feedback off
spool show_fga_fb.sql
select
   'prompt DBSUSER:'||db_user||
   ' OSUSER:'||os_user||
   ' TIMESTAMP:'||timestamp hdr,
   'select * from ('||sql_text||
   ') as of scn ('||scn||');' stmt
from dba_fga_audit_trail
/
spool off
```

Running the script *show_fga_fb.sql* produces a result similar to the following.

```
DBSUSER:CLAIM_SCHEMA OSUSER:ananda TIMESTAMP:18-AUG-03
1 123456789      12345     1234567        1700          1700 P
2 234567891      12345     1234567        2300          1700 P
3 234567891      12345     2345678        1900          1800 P
```

```
DBSUSER:SECUSER OSUSER:ananda TIMESTAMP:18-AUG-03
1 123456789       12345      1234567       1700          1700 P
2 234567891       12345      1234567       2300          1700 P
3 234567891       12345      2345678       1900          1800 P
```

This query returns the values the user saw, not the value as of now. This output can be spooled to a file. This audit record becomes a valuable tool for accountability analysis later, and can satisfy a variety of regulatory requirements, including HIPAA. It also provides a powerful tool to have the accountability analysis for the in-house auditors.

## Preservation of Audit Trail

If the default Fine Grained Auditing is used, the trail is recorded in a table named *fga_log$*, owned by SYS. The simplest way to archive the old data is to export the table with a where clause to filter on dates, and then delete the records exported. However, this method of deleting increases the High Water Mark (HWM) of the table and, over a period of time, the performance of operations on this table becomes so bad that the table needs reorganization, causing downtime for the auditing activity.

The better option is to create a user defined auditing facility as described earlier in this chapter. This facility can write to any table, not just the default *fga_log$* table. Using this, we can set the records to go into a user defined table that is *partitioned.* Partitioning the table is one of the reasons why we want to have a user defined audit trail. An example of the table is given earlier in this chapter.

When the time comes to purge the records, the partition can be simply dropped. Before dropping, the partition can be exchanged with an empty table and this table, which now holds the data from the partition, can be exported so that it can be preserved (archived). This method does not require any extensive reorganization of table.

A suggestion of archival and purging can be obtained from the same topic in Chapter 8 on Oracle Auditing.

## Conclusion

In this chapter, we saw how to use a very powerful tool called Fine Grained Auditing (FGA), introduced in Oracle 9i, to record SELECT statements issued by users. The auditing can be limited to events triggered by specific values in the selected data, or in the specific columns selected, giving the tool a distinct edge in specialized auditing, which was otherwise impossible.

We also saw how to extend the functionality of the tool to cases where the database user is not relevant, such as in case of application-authenticated users. Using application contexts and client identifiers, we learned to capture the statements, too.

Finally, we saw how to use another valuable tool provided by Oracle 9i, Flashback Queries, to identify not only what the user *wanted* to see, but what he or she *actually* saw at that time. This makes it possible to assign accountability to an even greater degree. With this chapter, we complete the section on auditing.

So far, we have explored the various features and tools within Oracle related to security and auditing. In the next chapter, we will bring all the previous chapters together to see how the tools can be used to achieve the security and auditing requirement specifically from the HIPAA perspective.

# HIPAA Compliance & Oracle Solutions

CHAPTER

## Introduction

So far, we have discussed the various facilities and mechanisms provided within Oracle to build and maintain a secured database system. We sincerely hope this information helps in achieving the goal of creating a database compliant with any type of regulatory or internal requirements. The objective of this book was not only to present all such available mechanisms, but also to provide a jumpstart on building the compliance immediately. To that end, we will summarize all concepts explained in earlier chapters and show how they relate to meeting various components of HIPAA regulations.

## HIPAA Requirements

In order to present a holistic and independent view of the requirements, we turned to the independent industry association – Association for Electronic Health Care Transaction, Inc. (www.afehct.org), of Elmsford, NY, which has developed an excellent checklist for HIPAA security compliance. In this chapter we will take that checklist and see how Oracle technology can be used to satisfy the requirements.

## Individual Authentication of Users

| HIPAA REQUIREMENTS | ORACLE SOLUTION |
|---|---|
| Unique individual identifier for each user | This essentially translates to the unique identifier for a user in the database. Even if an LDAP solution is used to authenticate users, the database must have the LDAP user identified. The simplest way to achieve this compliance is to create an individual user id for each named user. If that is not possible, then the next best alternative is to use Single Sign On (SSO) using LDAP and Oracle users identified Externally. If an application using a database table authenticates users rather than LDAP, then a method for secure application user authentication must be followed that is not easy to break and is immune to attacks such as SQL Injection. A mechanism to achieve this is described in Chapter 5. |
| Automatic logoff after specified time | This requires that if a user is idle for some specified time, the connection must be terminated, requiring the user to login again. Idle connections are easy targets for hackers. Chapter 4, the section on Profile Based Security, explains how to achieve this using Oracle Profiles. |

| HIPAA REQUIREMENTS | ORACLE SOLUTION |
| --- | --- |
| Change passwords often (enforced by system) | Even if the hackers crack the password, if they are changed often, the discovery becomes useless. However, most users do not change their password often. This requirement calls for establishing a mechanism that forces the users to change passwords at regular intervals. In Chapter 4, under the section on Profile Enforced Password Management, we have described a method to meet this requirement using Profiles. |
| System generates random password | This requirement makes the assumption that most administrator-assigned passwords are easy to guess, as they are either the same every time or follow a pattern. Therefore, the system assigned passwords should be random. In Oracle, however, the better option is to assign a password and expire it immediately. When the user logs in, he will be prompted for a new password, thus eliminating the need to have a random system generated password. |
| Weak passwords not allowable | Weak passwords, i.e. those are easy to guess and amenable to cracking by hackers, come in many forms. Some are as easy as just common terms: abc123, password, the user's user id, etc. In order to prevent a weak password, Oracle's Password Management Function is handy. It checks the password the user chooses and uses a stored procedure to check to see if it conforms to a standard established by the DBA. This is quite easy to implement and the details can be found in Section Password Management Function in Chapter 4. |

| HIPAA REQUIREMENTS | ORACLE SOLUTION |
|---|---|
| System stores password encrypted | This is not a problem for Oracle user ids, as the password is stored in hash format and cannot be retrieved by the DBA; it can only be changed. However, other types of password management, such as that done through the application using a database table, tend to be stored in clear text. This practice should be prevented and the passwords should be encrypted using Oracle's Obfuscation Toolkit, which is a set of encryption APIs. In Chapter 5, a complete treatise on secure application user management has been provided. |
| Uniform User ID across organization | This requirement calls for assigning a single user id to a physical user, regardless of which system the user accesses. This is desirable for several reasons, the most important being the ability to maintain strong passwords. However, this may be quite difficult to achieve. For instance, co-existence of legacy and open systems requires different ways of handling authentication and is not the same in all cases. In some cases, disparate systems can still be consolidated under a single user authentication system using Single Sign On (SSO). A user might logon to the Company network running Microsoft Windows. The database users can be LDAP users created by the clause "identified externally". This allows all three systems – domain, email and database to have the same user id and password, i.e. the same authentication system. |

| HIPAA REQUIREMENTS | ORACLE SOLUTION |
|---|---|
| Incentives to reduce key account sharing | This follows the same premise as the first requirement – users should have their own user ids, be they in database, in some directory, or in some application user table. This is possible by using unique ids for all users. |
| Single-use or token based passwords | This is not strictly within a database framework. It means the ability to assign a password that can be used only once, after which the password expires. This can be implemented in an indirect way, using triggers to capture when the user logged in and then altering the DBA to expire the account, or change the password. |
| Token card plus password or PIN | This security model requires two forms of authentication –a password and a token card. This combination is challenging for the hackers to break. Oracle Advanced Security provides several options to use Token Card Authentication in addition to passwords. |
| Biometric (fingerprint, retinal scan, etc.) | An alternative to using token cards, etc. is using biometric authentication. Authentication is done using physical attributes such as retinal scans and fingerprints. It authenticates the person, not just the holder of an authentication token. |
| Caller-ID verification of remote location | In this security model, the remote user calls up the system from a known phone number as verified by the caller id service. This model falls in the telephone connectivity software setup, which is outside the Oracle database security framework. |

| HIPAA REQUIREMENTS | ORACLE SOLUTION |
|---|---|
| Telephone callback for remote users | This is also outside the realm of the Oracle database security framework. After a user dials the number for remote connectivity, the number is confirmed by caller id service as that of a known caller. The call is then terminated and the system initiates the call to the remote number to establish the connection. This ensures security even if the remote user somehow masquerades the calling number. |
| Different security for terminals in different locations | This falls under the domain of physical security. A terminal located inside a physically secure data center is less likely to be attacked as opposed to one outside. This has been discussed in depth in Chapter 4 under the section for Physical Security. |
| Comply with Orange Book C2 or better | This is a security specification recommended by an independent party. Oracle database and software is already compliant, so there is no cause of concern for compliance here. |
| Account canceled when employee leaves | This calls for procedural modifications to the security administration. When an employee leaves, there should be a well-defined procedure for the help desk to systematically lock all the accounts used by the employee – email, domain, and database. Often, mostly due to lack of proper procedure, the accounts are left open, which can become prime targets for hackers. |

| HIPAA REQUIREMENTS | ORACLE SOLUTION |
|---|---|
| Emergency access procedures for forgotten password | This is a procedural issue. Forgotten passwords are common among users, and the request to retrieve them costs a lot for the organization. This results in a generic password resetting method used by the help desk. This can be easily integrated with Oracle passwords by changing the password and then expiring it immediately. The user logging in will have to set a new password upon logging in. |
| Policies and procedures in place for Authentication | This is a procedural issue. The organizational audit must ensure that the authentication of users meets certain guidelines to eliminate threats. In all the Chapters on Security in this book, we have covered aspects of authentication schemes and how they can be used. |

## Access Controls

| HIPAA REQUIREMENTS | ORACLE SOLUTION |
|---|---|
| Access control list for each file or database | Access control in a database relates to a defined user and their authorization scheme. In Oracle, it is implemented using privileges and grants to individual users. Careful analysis must establish what users should have access to, what objects must be audited for accuracy, and what changes should be tracked. In Chapter 4, we discussed general Oracle security. In Chapter 10, we explained in detail how to verify existing privileges and track them for auditing purposes.<br><br>Another type of access control is machine-to-machine using the network. In Oracle, several methods can be used to control access among machines – such as Valid Node Checking, Connection Manager Node Checking, SSH Redirections, etc. All these have been discussed in Chapter 7 – Network Security. |
| Access control lists User ID based | This is a subset of the above specification. In a database centric world, this means granting specific privileges to users based on the need and revoking all others. Chapter 4 discusses the privileges granted to users. |
| Role based access profiles | Roles are not users. They are a logical set of privileges that can be granted to users who then get a set of privileges. This makes administration simpler. Chapter 4 explains how to use this type of authorization. |

| HIPAA REQUIREMENTS | ORACLE SOLUTION |
|---|---|
| Access overrides for emergencies | Suppose a need arises where a user needs to perform some action, but that user is not available. Since the password cannot be known by anyone, even the DBA, this may cause a problem. In Oracle, it is possible to operate on objects on other schemas with proper privileges, such as SELECT ANY TABLE, etc. These are system privileges. In Chapter 4, an explanation of such system privileges can be found. If there is an urgent need to login as that user and the password is not known, then the password can be changed, the operation can be performed, and then the password can be changed back using the ALTER USER IDENTIFIED BY VALUES command. |
| Simple access control (All or nothing) | This is what the regular Oracle access control mechanisms provide. If a user has a SELECT privilege on a table, then the user can see all the rows of the table, not a subset. If the access is revoked, then the user can't see any rows of the table. Privileges are explained in Chapter 4. |
| Gross granularity control (Screen based, or application based) | This is used by applications to selectively show rows and columns of tables to the user based on the context and credentials of the user. However, a better approach is to use Oracle views and Virtual Private Database features. The former is explained in Chapter 4 and the latter in Chapter 5. |

| HIPAA REQUIREMENTS | ORACLE SOLUTION |
|---|---|
| Medium granularity control (Record based, or role based algorithm) | Oracle's Virtual Private Database feature, also known as Fine Grained Access Control and Row Level Security, selectively displays the rows based on the credential of the user and other factors such as the context in which the user is requesting the access. The mechanism has been explained in Chapter 5. |
| Fine granularity control (Field based, or User ID based algorithm) | Although Virtual Private Database provides a mechanism to suppress rows the user is not supposed to see, there is no corresponding mechanism to suppress display of columns. So, if the user sees the rows, he sees all the columns of the row, not a few. However the suppression of column values can be achieved by creating a view on the table. An example of this technique has been described in the section on View Based Security in Chapter 4.<br><br>Another option is to grant column level privileges to users to perform certain tasks like updates. This has been explained in the section on Column Privileges in Chapter 4. |
| Multiple parameters (e.g. User ID, role, physical location, function, etc.) | This means the users should be allowed not only if authenticated, but also when other conditions such as coming from a specific IP Address, or machine, time of the day, etc. are satisfied. The ValidNode Checking, as described in Chapter 7, can do a simple check. For example, the database refuses connections coming from a machine other than a list of approved machines. The other mechanisms are trigger based. A database logon trigger checks the conditions such as time of the day, and then decides to allow or disallow the session. Chapter 9 describes how to build such a trigger. |

## Monitoring of Access

| HIPAA REQUIREMENTS | ORACLE SOLUTION |
|---|---|
| System imposed audit trails | This requirement calls for tracking the activities of the users automatically in the database, not by the application. This way the actions are logged regardless of how the actions were performed.<br><br>In Oracle, there are several ways these can be captured. The simplest one is the Audit, described in Chapter 8. However, audit functionality captures only the fact that the object was accessed. For example, the fact that a table was updated would be captured, not specifically which rows were updated, or what the value was before the change. Table triggers that write into a custom audit table as shown in Chapter 9 can do this. Another way to capture the information is from the archived logs using an Oracle tool called LogMiner, as shown in Chapter 9. However, since SELECT statements do not produce redo or cause triggers to fire, these two methods are not useful in capturing the changes. In Oracle 9i and above, Fine Grained Auditing provides the solution for SELECT statements, as explained in Chapter 11. |

| HIPAA REQUIREMENTS | ORACLE SOLUTION |
|---|---|
| Software controlled audit trails | In this method, the application software creates an audit trail of the user's actions. In the case of pre-Oracle9i databases, this is the only way the exact select statements can be captured. However, the ultimate objective is to enable auditing at the database level, not the application or middleware level. |
| Transaction log audit trail | This is close to mining the information contained in transaction logs, such as Oracle's archived logs. LogMiner, explained in detail in Chapter 9, provides the exact functionality. |
| File level audit trail | The requirement here is that access to files be tracked. This is not relevant since there are neither user accessible nor manipulation-enabled files inside an Oracle database. |
| Record level audit trail | Record level audit trails track changes to individual records inside a table. Conventional audits do not provide the functionality. The task calls for creation of table triggers to capture the changes as they occur, and writing to user-defined audit trails, as described in Chapter 9. The other option is to mine information from the archived redo log files using LogMiner, also described in chapter 9. To track SELECT statements, not changes, the Oracle9i Fine Grained Auditing, explained in Chapter 11 can be used. |

| HIPAA REQUIREMENTS | ORACLE SOLUTION |
|---|---|
| Field level audit trail | This calls that changes to specific fields be tracked, not just records. There is no conventional audit facility in Oracle to do so. However using table triggers and using a WHEN clause, the changes to fields can be tracked. This is described in Chapter 9. LogMiner can be used to track changes to fields inside a record, too, as shown in Chapter 9.<br><br>For mere selection of data from the fields, not changes, the Oracle 9i Fine Grained Auditing can actually track access to specific fields using the Policy Columns parameter, as explained in Chapter 11. |
| Write or change data audit trail | Again, all the functionality explained above can be used in this case. |
| Read, display, print data audit trail | Again, all the functionality explained above can be used in this case. |

| HIPAA REQUIREMENTS | ORACLE SOLUTION |
|---|---|
| Automatic display of "last access" to the next user, to allow self-audit by all users. | This requirement states that when the users access the data, they are shown the last time they accessed the same information, similar to how the last login information for the user is shown in UNIX when the user log in. This results in the user himself identifying a possible attack using the userid. However, accesses to Oracle database usually occur transparently, and non-interactively, unlike the UNIX login process. Therefore this functionality does not have a useful place. However, if need be, the users can be allowed to select their own data from the audit tables to examine for possible fraudulent activity. The best course is to build a VPD policy on the AUD$ table to show only the user's own data and let the user choose from various views based on AUD$ table. |
| Periodic management reports of exceptions | This is extremely easy to implement in Oracle. A simple auditing mechanism to audit logons, logoffs, and access to objects, which is triggered when the action is unsuccessful can be useful in identifying a possible attack on the database. In Chapter 8, there is a script that creates this management exception report. In Chapter 8, you will also find a script to generate exception reports on the database server errors, some of which may indicate fraudulent activity. |
| Periodic management reports of all access | Please se the above entry; it's along the same lines. |
| Internal periodic audit of audit trails | In Chapter 8, we have provided several scripts to produce reports that can be studied and analyzed to indicate potentially fraudulent and malicious activity. The reports can be examined periodically to ensure compliance. |

| HIPAA REQUIREMENTS | ORACLE SOLUTION |
|---|---|
| Policies and procedures in place for Access Monitoring, to detect misuse and violations | Please see the above entries, along the same topic. |
| External/independent audit of audit trails | This is an interesting challenge for Oracle audits. Conventional audit trails are typically written to a table called AUD$. However, since the table is subject to manipulation by the DBA, the actions of a malicious DBA would violate the integrity of the table. To address this problem, Oracle allows the audit records to be written to Operating System files. This is accomplished by setting the initialization parameter *audit_dest* to OS, instead of DB or TRUE. Doing this causes the audit trails to be written to small files at the operating system level. If the auditor can secure them, the integrity of the files can be maintained. |

## Physical Security and Disaster Recovery

| HIPAA REQUIREMENTS | ORACLE SOLUTION |
|---|---|
| Secure computer room | It is good practice to have adequate physical security. You can read all about physical security in Chapter 4. |
| Secure access to displays and printers | Specifically this calls for limited access to consoles and line printers. However, in today's technology, limiting printer access may not provide a huge security barrier. However, limiting access to consoles helps stop unauthorized activities such as abnormal shutdowns, etc. The section on Physical Security in Chapter 4 discusses this. |

| HIPAA REQUIREMENTS | ORACLE SOLUTION |
|---|---|
| Network security, no external network access | This calls for putting a firewall around all important access points. Sometimes there should be two different firewalls – one around the entire company network and one around the important servers such as database servers, etc. |
| Secure destruction of printouts, floppies, etc. | This is a procedural issue. As a general rule all media with HIPAA defined sensitive information should be destroyed – electronically or physically by shredding. |
| Secure destruction of obsolete equipment | Procedural issue, again. |
| Burglar alarm monitored by Police | Part of procedures. |
| Secure backup, storage and retrieval | The backup tapes should be secured as diligently as the original database. Anyone who has access to the backups can recreate the database and obtain sensitive data. |
| Multiple backup storage sites | This is a part of the disaster recovery solution – sending the datafile and archived log backups to multiple locations, in the event of a problem with one site. Another solution is to build a set of standby databases in a geographically different location and use them in the disaster recovery strategy. |
| Disaster recovery plan in place | This is a procedural issue. The organization should have a written, well-understood disaster recovery plan in place. The plan should be reviewed periodically and dry runs should be made from time to time to validate the activities laid out in the plan. |
| Disaster recovery plan periodically tested | Please see above point. |

| HIPAA REQUIREMENTS | ORACLE SOLUTION |
|---|---|
| Emergency data access assured in case of disaster | Provision of a Standby Database will ensure the access to all data in the event of a disaster. |
| Data content integrity assured | This calls for application design. Some applications may not be designed to handle exceptions such as power failures very well. This review will help find these out and ensure their validity. |
| Operations recoverability | When an exception condition is cleared, the applications should be able to restart from the point of failure. |
| Non-disruption of critical functions | In the case of exception conditions the issue is whether the critical functions are affected. If the critical functions are too critical to be unavailable, then you might consider a standby database solution. |

## Protection of Remote Access Points and Protection of External Electronic Communications

| HIPAA REQUIREMENTS | ORACLE SOLUTION |
|---|---|
| Firewall for Internet access | Firewalls protect the internal resources of the company from outside access. For a detailed description of the necessity and design of firewalls, see Chapter 4 and Chapter 7. |
| Encrypted Virtual Network for Internet users | This calls for data transmission to be encrypted. Oracle Advanced Networking Option, described in Chapter 7, describes the functionality. |
| Healthcare data available to external network | Procedural issue. |
| Strong encryption required for Internet and Extranet users | Oracle Advanced Networking Option, as shown in Chapter 7, describes encryption between the client and server in Oracle*Networks. |
| Authentication and Digital signatures required for Internet and Extranet users | Authentication is described in detail in Chapter 4. In addition, Oracle Advanced Networking Option Add-Ons, such as LDAP authentication, Public Key Infrastructure, etc., provide a better and more secure authentication. |
| Dial-in protections (e.g. Caller-ID, callback, encryption) | This is described in the section for Individual Authentication of Users earlier in this chapter. |
| Mobile access (laptop/hand-held) physical protection and data encryption | Procedural issues. |
| Healthcare data over Infrared or Radio links encrypted and authenticated | Using encryption will address this issue. |

| HIPAA REQUIREMENTS | ORACLE SOLUTION |
|---|---|
| Control IP addresses, prevent IP spoofing | ValidNode Checking, as described in Chapter 7, provides a mechanism that allows connections only from certain nodes. The more sophisticated Connection Manager, also described in Chapter 7, does the same thing, but with more flexibility. |
| Periodic verification/ maintenance of security measures | This is a procedural issue. The security plan must be periodically reviewed and analyzed for errors and omissions. |
| Policies and procedures in place for protection of remote / external access | Procedural issues. |

## Software Discipline

| HIPAA REQUIREMENTS | ORACLE SOLUTION |
|---|---|
| Virus checking all files | This is probably not so relevant in Oracle data files. However, since the virus can affect the contents of some files and the sources of the data are those files, virus checking of those input files is necessary to ensure integrity. |
| Virus checking electronic mail | Outside the domain of Oracle. |
| Control or restrict user software | This is very important in the Oracle database context. Operating system access control to Oracle related files is critical to maintaining a secured system. In Chapter 4, under the section Operating System Security, we have discussed exactly what steps are necessary to produce a secured system. |
| Control PC software loading | Procedural Issues, outside the realm of the Oracle software or the database. |

| HIPAA REQUIREMENTS | ORACLE SOLUTION |
|---|---|
| Network software periodic census | Procedural Issues, outside the realm of the Oracle software or the database. |
| Version control / Change control in use | In addition to recording version changes, we can also capture the changes to database source code using DDL triggers, as described in Chapter 9.<br><br>Source code should be wrapped, which is a form of encryption that cannot be decrypted. This helps protect the source code from prying eyes, and prevents manipulation. The section on Securing the Code in Chapter 6 describes this. |

## Monitoring of Integrity of Data

| HIPAA REQUIREMENTS | ORACLE SOLUTION |
|---|---|
| Document integrity checking system | The Oracle database takes care of the data integrity if foreign keys, constraints, etc. are properly defined. However, this does not protect the database from being populated with bogus data if the source system is compromised. A periodic review of the entire infrastructure will help reveal flaws. |
| Digital signatures applied to documents | Procedural Issues, outside the realm of the Oracle software or the database. |
| Monitor integrity of backup media | This means testing the backups several times to ensure the integrity. If RMAN is used to backup an Oracle database, there is a facility called Trial Recovery, which can be called to ensure the validity of the backup. |

| HIPAA REQUIREMENTS | ORACLE SOLUTION |
| --- | --- |
| Encrypt/sign database contents | Encryption, especially selective encryption of sensitive content, is quite helpful in enforcing the HIPAA guidelines for Protected Health Information. Chapter 6 is devoted to the discussion and explanation of the Obfuscation Toolkit, which is the Oracle supplied API for encryption.<br><br>The database source code, such as stored procedures, should be wrapped, which is a sort of encryption that cannot be decrypted. This helps protect the source code from prying eyes, and prevents manipulation. This is described in Chapter 6, under the section, Securing the Code. |
| Checksum or signature protection of critical files | Checksum is a method of calculating a value before some action such as transmission, calculating the value once again at the destination, and then comparing the two values. If they are the same, the data integrity is said to be intact; otherwise the integrity is questionable.<br><br>Oracle provides checksums for datafiles using the initialization parameter *db_block_checksum*. In addition, the checksum routine provided by Oracle in the Obfuscation Toolkit, MD5, is also useful in calculating checksums and is discussed in Chapter 6. |

## Conclusion

This chapter was designed to cross-reference the HIPAA requirements with the relevant Oracle technologies to implement those requirements. This can serve as a model to build a HIPAA compliant security system. In the next chapter, we will explore some of the exciting new features related to security in Oracle 11g and Oracle 12c.

# Oracle user access control

CHAPTER

## All about passwords

The use of passwords to validate access rights dates back to Roman times, and thousands of years ago Roman soldiers memorized spoken passwords to gain access to camps. I imagine that the Romans probably used Roma Phrases, maybe like these:

- **Sharpei Diem** – *Seize the wrinkled dog*
- **DBA Non Carborundum** – *Don't let the DBA wear you down*
- **Quantum materiae materietur marmota monax si marmota monax materiam possit materiari?** - *How much wood would a woodchuck chuck if a woodchuck could chuck wood?*
- **Domino vobiscum** – *The pizza guy is here*
- **Fac ut gaudeam** - *Make my day*

Anyway, as our access requirements became more sophisticated over the next two millenniums, the age-old problem of using passwords has caused its own data security crisis. Managing database security has always been a daunting challenge and there are two age-old problems with traditional password-based access:

**Too Many Passwords** – Single sign-on tools such as IBM's Resource Access Control Facility (RACF) and Oracle single sign-on (SSO) have been quite expensive to manage. Single sign-on tools only work for specific types of applications (i.e. web pages, Oracle sign-on), and comprehensive single sign-on tools have failed miserably.

**Cryptic passwords** - Because individual applications desire to make their users change passwords frequently and to use non-obvious passwords (including numbers, at least 7 characters long), end-users everywhere are being forced to write-down their many passwords.
With end-users bypassing the security by keeping lists of passwords, Oracle database security managers are challenged to find alternate ways to positively identify end-users and control their access to confidential database information.

# Who Goes There?

The positive identification of an end-user is the most critical component of any biometrics application and there have been several areas where external identification technology has been explored:

**Iris Recognition** – The human iris is as distinctive as a fingerprint. The cameras are expensive, but the technology is being effectively-used by US border control.

**Fingerprint recognition** – This is the most cost-effective and widely-used positive recognition technology today with units available for under $40.

**Facial Recognition** – Used only by governments today, high-speed computers are used to identify individual faces from different perspectives.
The default values for Oracle password security is very weak and special measures must be taken to strengthen Oracle password security. We can use these password security mechanisms with biometric security to impeove Oracle password security.

## Oracle Security Catalog Script

You can get an idea about scripting Oracle password security profiles by examining Oracle's *utlpwdmg.sql* script located in $ORACLE_HOME/rdbms/admin/*utlpwdmg.sql*. The script notes:

```
Rem utlpwdmg.sql
. . .
Rem utlpwdmg.sql - script for Default Password Resource Limits
. . .
-- This script sets the default password resource parameters
-- This script needs to be run to enable the password features.
-- However the default resource parameters can be changed based
-- on the need.
-- A default password complexity function is also provided.
-- This function makes the minimum complexity checks like
-- the minimum length of the password, password not same as the
-- username, etc. The user may enhance this function according to
-- the need.
-- This function must be created in SYS schema.
-- connect sys/ as sysdba before running the script
```

## Oracle password profile security syntax

Oracle password security is implemented via Oracle "profiles" which are assigned to users. Here is the Oracle security profile syntax:

```
ALTER PROFILE profile_name LIMIT pw_limit(s) range
```

```
where:

pw_limit = PASSWORD_LIFE_TIME
PASSWORD_GRACE_TIME
PASSWORD_REUSE_TIME
PASSWORD_REUSE_MAX
FAILED_LOGIN_ATTEMPTS
PASSWORD_LOCK_TIME

range = UNLIMITED | DEFAULT | expression
```

We start by creating security "profiles" in Oracle and then alter the user to belong to the profile group. Here is psuedocode for creating a profile:

```
all_users
limit
PASSWORD_LIFE_TIME 365
PASSWORD_GRACE_TIME 10
PASSWORD_REUSE_TIME UNLIMITED
PASSWORD_REUSE_MAX 0
FAILED_LOGIN_ATTEMPTS 3
PASSWORD_LOCK_TIME UNLIMITED;
```

We see the following "alter profile" parameters, which are invoked as;

```
finance_user
set
```

## Oracle password security profile parameters

Here are the password security parameters:

**failed_login_attempts** - This is the number of failed login attempts before locking the Oracle user account. The default is three failed attempts.

**password_grace_time** - This is the grace period after the password_life_time limit is exceeded.

**password_life_time** - This is how long an existing password is valid. The default here forces a password change every 60 days.

**password_lock_time** – This specifies how long to lock the account after the failed login attempts is met. Most DBA's set this value to UNLIMITED.

**password_reuse_max** – This is the number of times that you may reuse a password and is intended to prevent repeating password cycles (north, south, east, west).

**password_reuse_time** – This parameter specifies a time limit before a previous password can be re-entered. To allow unlimited use of previously used passwords, set *password_reuse_time* to UNLIMITED.

**password_verify_function** - This allows you to specify the name of a custom password verification function.

## Oracle Password Security with Biometrics

When using biometrics such as facial recognition to enforce the identity of an Oracle user we acknowledge that failed login attempts will be very rare because the user/password combination will be fed by the security software and the end-user will never know the actual value of their username or their Oracle password. Hence:

- The Oracle passwords can be very strong (8 characters, with numbers).
- Password changes will be cumbersome because the biometric software must be changed.
- Account lockdown must be harsh because there will never be a username with an invalid password coming from the biometrics (facial recognition, fingerprint reader).

Hence we want user profile that force a very strong password, keep the password for a long time, and complain loudly of there is a username is disabled for failed password attempts:

```
create profile
all_biometric_users
limit
PASSWORD_LIFE_TIME UNLIMITED,
PASSWORD_GRACE_TIME 0,
PASSWORD_REUSE_TIME UNLIMITED,
PASSWORD_REUSE_MAX 0,
FAILED_LOGIN_ATTEMPTS 3,
PASSWORD_LOCK_TIME UNLIMITED;
```

Hence we want user profile that force a very strong password, keep the password for a long time, and complain loudly of there is a username is disabled for failed password attempts:

```
   all_biometric_users
limit
PASSWORD_LIFE_TIME UNLIMITED,
PASSWORD_GRACE_TIME 0,
PASSWORD_REUSE_TIME UNLIMITED,
PASSWORD_REUSE_MAX 0,
FAILED_LOGIN_ATTEMPTS 3,
```

## *Oracle 11g New Features Tips*

Case sensitive passwords improve the security for the database greatly and it is strongly recommended to use them because this feature makes it much more difficult for a potential hacker to break into the system. There is number of additional rules that apply to **secure passwords** which make the hackers? life more difficult. A secure password is always a **complex password** and Oracle strongly recommends the use of secure passwords.

**A complex password contains**:

- At least 10 characters
- A mixture of letters and numbers
- Mixed case letters (11g!)
- Symbols (11g!)
- Little or no relation to an actual word

Oracle recommends customers to enforce checks and response actions for failed logins, password complexity, password expiration and password reuse.

Password complexity can be implemented through profiles.

The script for password management implementation utlpwdmg.sql has been modified in 11g. It can be used to create a new function to verify password complexity rules. This function is an enhanced version of the verify_function from per 11g versions.

The default settings in the verify_function_11g for password complexity are:

- minimum length of 8 characters

- the password must not be the reverse username
- the password must not be the username with a numeric suffix of 1-100
- the password must not be oracle with a numeric suffix of 1-100
- the password must not be the database's name
- the password must not be the database's name with a numeric suffix of 1-100
- the password must contain at least one digit and one character
- a new password must differ at least in 3 positions from the old password
- the password must not be a string from a predefine list (this list has also been adjusted in the 11g function)

The defaults for the default profile have also been modified in the script utlpwdmg.sql.

Some limits are automatically set if you create an 11g database using DBCA:

```
RESOURCE_NAME LIMIT
-------------------------------- ------------------------------
FAILED_LOGIN_ATTEMPTS             10
PASSWORD_LIFE_TIME               180
PASSWORD_REUSE_TIME              UNLIMITED
PASSWORD_REUSE_MAX               UNLIMITED
PASSWORD_VERIFY_FUNCTION         NULL
PASSWORD_LOCK_TIME               1
PASSWORD_GRACE_TIME              7
```

Password complexity check is not enabled by default!

You must create the verify function and alter the default profile manually to enable it.

# Password checking tool

Oracle has a password checker function called *$ORACLE_HOME/rdbms/admin/utlpwdmg.sql*, which needs to be run manually. The *utlpwdmg.sql* script has a *password_verify_password* function that ensures that the password length is at least 4 characters, but you can modify it manually.
To enable password length checking inside the *password_verify_function*, alter the user profile as follows:

```
PASSWORD_LIFE_TIME 60
```

```
PASSWORD_GRACE_TIME 10
PASSWORD_REUSE_TIME 1800
PASSWORD_REUSE_MAX UNLIMITED
FAILED_LOGIN_ATTEMPTS 3
PASSWORD_LOCK_TIME 1/1440
```

In addition to forcing a minimum password length, the *utlpwdmg.sql* script forces password aging, it will lock the user after three failed password attempts and check for password reuse.

For more details on managing a password length, see MOSC document 114930.1 and 207959.1.

## Verifying password length within Oracle Applications

Within Oracle Applications (Oracle Financials, eBusiness Suite), you are not manipulating Oracle database user ID's. In Oracle apps, you can adjust the user profile option "*Signon Password Length*" for setting the minimum length of an Oracle apps password.

## How to find accounts with default passwords in 11g

Oracle 11g comes with a great number of automatically created user accounts. The following table lists all default accounts of Oracle 11g Enterprise Edition:

| User_name | Account_Status |
|---|---|
| ANONYMOUS | EXPIRED&LOCKED |
| APEX_PUBLIC_USER | EXPIRED&LOCKED |
| CTXSYS | EXPIRED&LOCKED |
| DBSNMP | EXPIRED&LOCKED |
| DIP | OPEN |
| DMSYS | EXPIRED&LOCKED |
| EXFSYS | EXPIRED&LOCKED |
| FLOWS_3000 | EXPIRED&LOCKED |
| FLOWS_FILES | EXPIRED&LOCKED |
| HR | EXPIRED&LOCKED |
| LBACSYS | EXPIRED&LOCKED |
| MDDATA | EXPIRED&LOCKED |
| MDSYS | EXPIRED&LOCKED |
| MGMT_VIEW | OPEN |

| ODM | EXPIRED&LOCKED |
|---|---|
| ODM_MTR | EXPIRED&LOCKED |
| OE | EXPIRED&LOCKED |
| OLAPSYS | EXPIRED&LOCKED |
| ORACLE_OCM | EXPIRED&LOCKED |
| ORDPLUGINS | EXPIRED&LOCKED |
| ORDSYS | EXPIRED&LOCKED |
| OUTLN | EXPIRED&LOCKED |
| OWBSY | EXPIRED&LOCKED |
| PM | EXPIRED&LOCKED |
| PUBLIC | EXPIRED&LOCKED |
| QS | EXPIRED&LOCKED |
| QS_ADM | EXPIRED&LOCKED |
| QS_CS | EXPIRED&LOCKED |
| QS_ES | EXPIRED&LOCKED |
| QS_OS | EXPIRED&LOCKED |
| QS_WS | EXPIRED&LOCKED |
| RMAN | EXPIRED&LOCKED |
| SCOTT | EXPIRED&LOCKED |
| SH | EXPIRED&LOCKED |
| SI_INFORMTN_SCHEMA | EXPIRED&LOCKED |
| SPATIAL_CSW_ADMIN_USR | EXPIRED&LOCKED |
| SPATIAL_WFS_ADMIN_USR | EXPIRED&LOCKED |
| SYS | OPEN |
| SYSMAN | OPEN |
| SYSTEM | OPEN |
| TSMSYS | EXPIRED&LOCKED |
| WK_TEST | EXPIRED&LOCKED |
| WKPROXY | EXPIRED&LOCKED |
| WKSYS | EXPIRED&LOCKED |
| WMSYS | EXPIRED&LOCKED |
| XDB | EXPIRED&LOCKED |

Default passwords are a serious threat and it is strongly recommended to change the passwords for all automatically created accounts right away after database creation. In previous releases it was necessary to use home grown code to find out which accounts still use the default password. The data dictionary of an 11g database can be queried for user accounts which are still using the initial default password.

The view dba_users_with_defpwd shows the DBA all accounts for which the password is still the default and thus should be changed immediately:

```
   *
from
```

```
USERNAME
------------------------------
DIP
OUTLN
EXFSYS
XDB
WMSYS
```

# Index

## E



## F



## G

## H



## I



## J



## K



## L



## M

## Q



## R



## S

## T



## U



## V

## W

# About Arup Nanda

Arup Nanda has been an Oracle DBA since the Spring of 1993. One very special characteristic of his career has been his focus – in the whole ten years, he has been solely an Oracle DBA. Over the period, he has encountered all aspects of database administration – performance tuning, backup and recovery planning, and advanced features like Replication, Standby Database, and Parallel Server.

He has worked as a senior DBA in several large corporations like Blue Cross Blue Shield, IBM, Lucent Technologies, Priceline, Oxford Health Plans, Cigna Healthcare and IntelliClaim. His involvement in developing and managing databases in the healthcare sector has provided him with the unique understanding of security and privacy requirements, particularly HIPAA. This book derives most of its content from his real life experiences.

Arup is a frequent speaker at several Oracle related conferences such as Oracle World, IOUG Live, Oratechs, AOTC, and many user groups around the country. He has written several articles for reputed journals including Oracle Magazine, Select (the journal of International Oracle User Group), DBAZine.com, Oracle Scene (of United Kingdom Oracle User Group), SQLUpdate (of Rocky Mountain User Group), TechJournal (of New York Oracle User Group). He is a regular columnist in TechJournal (the DBA Corner) and is a member of the Editorial Board for Select. He is the Executive Director of the Connecticut Oracle User Group. He is also an active member of a few custom programs in the Oracle beta program.

Acknowledging his outstanding achievements in the application of Oracle database technology and his contributions to the Oracle user community, Oracle honored him with the coveted DBA of the Year Award in 2003.

Arup is the founder of Proligence (www.proligence.com), a new York area based company providing highly specialized Oracle solutions such as planning, design and execution of disaster recovery, security (including HIPAA, Sarbanes-Oxley, Gramm-Leach-Bliey, CSIP, and many others), performance tuning, among others. He lives in Norwalk, CT with his wife Anindita. As of the printing of this book, the Nandas were awaiting for the arrival of their first child.

Need more
horsepower?
Call the Oracle Experts.
Expert Oracle Support
• Remote DBA Services
• Remote Oracle Health Checks
• Oracle Tuning
• RAC & Grid Support
On-Site Oracle Training
• Oracle RAC and Grid Training
• Oracle Tuning Expert Secrets
• Customized Oracle Training
• Follow-up Mentoring
Slow Oracle
Performance?
Help!
BC is a leading provider of Remote
Oracle Database Healthchecks
BURLESON
Consulting
BC
BURLESON
800.766.1884
www.dba-oracle.com

www.ingramcontent.com/pod-product-compliance
Lightning Source LLC
Chambersburg PA
CBHW060949210326
41598CB00031B/4767

* 9 7 8 0 9 9 1 6 3 8 6 9 7 *